Individualism and Inequality

To Will.

Simply the Best!

Ralph.

For Natasha, Adam and Owen in New England

Individualism and Inequality

The Future of Work and Politics

Ralph Fevre

Professor of Social Research, School of Social Sciences, Cardiff University, UK

Cheltenham, UK • Northampton, MA, USA

Published by
Edward Elgar Publishing Limited
The Lypiatts
15 Lansdown Road
Cheltenham
Glos GL50 2JA
UK

Edward Elgar Publishing, Inc.
William Pratt House
9 Dewey Court
Northampton
Massachusetts 01060
USA

Paperback edition 2017

A catalogue record for this book
is available from the British Library

Library of Congress Control Number: 2016935794

This book is available electronically in the Elgaronline
Social and Political Science subject collection
DOI 10.4337/ 9781784716516

ISBN 978 1 78471 650 9 (cased)
ISBN 978 1 78471 651 6 (eBook)
ISBN 978 1 78471 652 3 (paperback)

Typeset by Columns Design XML Ltd, Reading
Printed and bound by CPI Group (UK) Ltd, Croydon, CR0 4YY

Contents

Figures

The Modern Messiah

The cover illustration makes use of a cartoon satirising Oscar Wilde's 1882 American lecture tour and published in the San Francisco periodical *The Wasp*. Wilde makes an appearance in Chapter 10 and, like other Britons discussed in this book – including Adam Smith, Thomas Paine, Robert Owen and Herbert Spencer – his ideas were influential on both sides of the Atlantic. The way that these thinkers' ideas were *transformed* in the USA is of special interest to the story of individualism since, once they had been transformed, the ideas helped to shape American history. They were then re-exported to the UK and other European countries and, in this way, an American culture of individualism spread across the globe.

In a curious way, G.F. Keller's cartoon of Oscar Wilde, titled the 'Modern Messiah', exemplified the American transformation of British ideas about individualism. The kernel of truth in the portrayal of Wilde as Christ entering San Francisco on a donkey is that all Wilde had to offer to Americans was a system of beliefs. The credulous Americans pictured in the cartoon had been bowled over, or pretended to be bowled over, by what *The Wasp* considered an arrogant, affected and pretentious attempt to make aesthetics the focus of personal and public life. Wilde's tour took place a decade before he published his manifesto for romantic individualism – 'The Soul of Man under Socialism' (see Chapter 10) – but in The Modern Messiah we already have a satirical representation of the artistic potential of every individual. Every American – from children to portly businessmen to *The Wasp*'s customary objects of hate, i.e. members of the San Francisco Chinese community – is sporting the sunflower which Wilde chose to symbolize his attempt to elevate human sensibility.

The most scornful element of the cartoon is perhaps Keller's insinuation – with the addition of a dollar sign to the sunflower Wilde is holding – that the great artist is himself motivated by the common-sense end of making money out of the credulous Americans. In a curious way, this trope anticipates the way that, in the next century, American capitalism was able to turn the romantic individualism of Wilde and others to its own ends. It is worth noting that the sunflowers in Keller's cartoon double as advertisements for the cigars sold by the proprietor of

The Wasp and that Keller himself began as an illustrator of cigar boxes. Later chapters of this book explain how our enthusiasm to be artists in, and of, our own lives has been transformed into one of the key resources of neoliberalism. The book argues that the future of work and politics – and particularly future trends in inequality – will be strongly influenced by the fate of this culture of individualism.

Acknowledgements

The time to write this book was provided by Cardiff University in the form of a research leave fellowship. Later chapters report on research projects funded by the Economic and Social Research Council and the UK's Department for Business, Innovation and Skills. All of the colleagues who worked with me on these projects helped me to develop my thinking, but I am particularly indebted to Amanda Robinson and Theo Nichols. Indeed, it was from a conversation with Theo that the first idea for the book emerged. Current colleagues at Cardiff who have obliged me to think about the ideas in the book include Finn Bowring and Deborah Foster. I also owe a debt to all of my students at Cardiff (past and present) for letting me try out some of these ideas on them, and to Claire Crawford, Natasha Fevre and Adam Wood who have helped me to think about the similarities and differences between the USA and the UK.

1. Neoliberalism takes over

Inequality was rising up the political agenda of many affluent countries before the financial crisis of 2008. Five years later, most of these countries were returning economic data which showed the worst of the recession was over.[1] With growth and prosperity slowly returning, inequality was a pressing issue once more, described by Barak Obama in this way:

> Since 1979, when I graduated from high school, our productivity is up by more than 90 percent, but the income of the typical family has increased by less than eight percent. Since 1979, our economy has more than doubled in size, but most of that growth has flowed to a fortunate few ... The top 10 percent no longer takes in one-third of our income – it now takes half. Whereas in the past, the average CEO made about 20 to 30 times the income of the average worker, today's CEO now makes 273 times more. And meanwhile, a family in the top 1 percent has a net worth 288 times higher than the typical family, which is a record for this country. (Obama 2013: n.p.)

The president emphasized that these trends were worse in the USA but had nevertheless affected almost all the rich countries of the world.

The largest study of inequality so far undertaken suggested that the more equal world Obama remembered in the 1970s was something of an anomaly (Piketty 2014). Most incomes did not come from investing in capital but incomes from capital tended to grow much more quickly than incomes from wages or state benefits. Capitalism naturally concentrated the ownership of capital (which generated further wealth) in fewer and fewer hands. Even if capital was destroyed by wars and depressions, states had to take extraordinary measures in order to avoid concentrations of income and wealth. From the 1970s, most rich countries ceased to take effective counter-measures and inequality returned to historic levels and then kept on growing. Further impetus was given to the growth of inequality because, over this same period, more powerful employees (like the CEOs mentioned by Obama) got away with paying themselves larger incomes which, in turn, gave them access to capital.

Why should country after country have apparently lost the will to control the concentration of wealth and prevent higher-earners taking home ever-higher incomes? President Obama blamed the kind of politics that had taken hold in the United States since the 1970s, for example the unpopularity of taxation for the rich, and of public-spending which was of most benefit to the poor. He also identified the loss of power amongst lower-earners with the weakening of trade unions, and equated the bulging portfolios of the CEOs and other high-earners with the loss of community. At the end of the twentieth century, the decline in community had actually been a bigger concern in the USA than rising inequality. There was over-whelming evidence that people were much less likely to take part in collective endeavours in their neighbourhoods, cities and workplaces (e.g. Putnam 2004). Declining membership of civil society associations might be related to the growing gap between rich and poor (Skocpol 2004; Wuthnow 2004), but the link between inequality and declining collectivism is easiest to demonstrate using data on trade union membership.[2]

As Obama pointed out, the USA was far from the only country to have seen steeply rising inequality. The United Kingdom consistently appeared, along with the USA, amongst the four or five rich countries with the most extreme inequality (OECD 2014). Trade union membership in the UK topped out at 13 million in the late 1970s and then fell apace in the 1980s. From the mid-1990s, it settled down at under 8 million (Figure 1.1). People were more likely to be in a union if they were older but membership declined for all ages after 1999 (Figure 1.2).

Several reasons were offered to explain this decline. The legal status of trade unions was weakened by successive Conservative governments and strategic industrial disputes engineered by employers, often with government connivance (Bagguley 2013; Fevre 1989). Other possible causes included structural changes in employment and, although this is highly unlikely,[3] changes in the gender mix of various occupations (Rosenfeld 2014; Willman et al. 2007).

Whatever the reasons behind it, the trend in UK union membership confirmed that inequality increased as collectivism declined from the 1980s. There were straightforward reasons to think these trends were connected. For example, in the UK in the 1960s and 1970s the main purpose of trade unions seemed to be to use any evidence of widening pay inequality to leverage pay claims and therefore ratchet up wages so that their members kept pace with the richest employees. This ratchet acted as a natural adjustment to any sign of increased inequality and, at a time of high inflation, it also meant most employees thought of union membership as a necessity. If collectivism declined from the end of the 1970s, and depressed union membership, the weakening of catch-up pay claims would provide at least one clear reason to expect inequality to grow.

Sources: Department for Business, Innovation and Skills (2015a: 20), drawing on Department for Employment (1892–1973) and Certification Office (1974–2012).

Figure 1.1   *UK trade union membership since 1892 (thousands of members)*

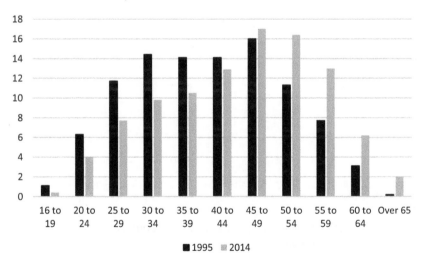

Source: Department for Business, Innovation and Skills (2015b: table A103) drawing on the Labour Force survey.

Figure 1.2   *Age of trade union members, 1995 and 2014 (percentages)*

Similar changes may well have occurred elsewhere because the proportion of employees in trade unions fell across all the richer countries from
1999 (Figure 1.3). This international proof of weakened collectivism was
a good fit with generally increasing inequality (Streeck 2014). On the
other hand, countries with similar experiences of rising inequality still
had very different trade union densities. Of course, there could be other
contributory causes, but if declining collectivism was the major contribu-
tor to rising inequality we might have expected to see UK union density,
for example, well below the OECD average instead of well above it. If it
was the absence of collectivism that placed the UK with the USA
amongst the most unequal rich countries, we would be hard put to
explain why 25 per cent of UK employees remained in trade unions
whereas only 11 per cent of US employees did so. Perhaps there was
something else that these societies had in common that would serve as an
explanation for their common inequality?

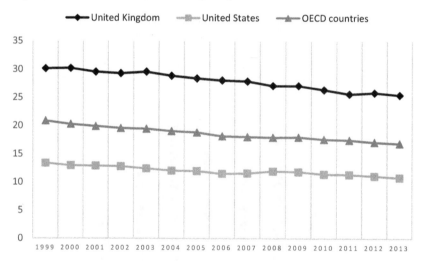

Source: Data extracted 18 December 2015 from https://stats.oecd.org/Index.aspx?DataSet
Code=UN_DEN#.

*Figure 1.3 OECD trade union density, selected countries 1999–2013
          (percentages)*

President Obama was taking a risk by making inequality the focus of his
second term of office but he would have been taking a far greater risk if
he had blamed it on individualism – the idea that society ought to give
each of its members the chance to make of themselves what they will. In
a society which values individualism, the way that people's lives turn out

is not determined by the accidents of their birth. What work they do, who they will marry (if they marry at all), which if any God they worship and how they will spend their leisure is not pre-determined by society's expectations of them. On the other hand, people are expected to know their own minds, and be able to make plans, and take decisions, which help them to achieve personal objectives.[4] There is no requirement for these objectives to be different from other people's goals however. Individualism and conformity are not enemies and individualism need not imply individuality. It requires only that people follow their dreams even if those dreams are the same as everyone else's.

Approval of the idea that individuals must be given every chance to make their own lives was so fundamental to Americans' self-image, so much a part of the political consensus, that to blame it for inequality would have immediately lost Obama most of the potential support he wished to build for action against inequality. All the same, it would have been easy to make a connection between individualism and inequality since a society which gave individuals their heads might find that some used their freedom to increase their incomes and wealth while others failed (Spicker 2013). Individualism would also explain the unpopularity of taxation for the rich because high taxes could be seen as a limitation on individual freedom. Over the long term, a society which was committed to individualism would become more and more unequal.

Another politician, this time from the UK, explained some of this in the week before the president's remarks quoted at the start of this chapter. The Mayor of London's metaphor for a society shaped by people who realized they were in charge of their own fates was a cereal box which was being vigorously shaken by an invisible hand:

> The harder you shake the pack, the easier it will be for some cornflakes to get to the top. And for one reason or another – boardroom greed or, as I am assured, the natural and God-given talent of boardroom inhabitants – the income gap between the top cornflakes and the bottom cornflakes is getting wider than ever. (Johnson, 2013: n.p.)

Since the UK and the USA were consistently seen as the most individualistic of countries (Hofstede 2001; Macfarlane 1978; Tocqueville [1840]2003), this might explain why they both had so much inequality; but surely less collectivism and more individualism are different sides of the same coin (Dorling 2011; Gans 1988; Gilbert 2013)?

On this view, when more and more of us realize that what we do for ourselves can have much more effect on our health, wealth and happiness than any joint ventures, we increasingly shape the world so that those efforts pay off. In this way, increased individualism affects the climate for public policy. It makes us less favourable towards progressive taxation, collective agreements over jobs and pay, public spending and oversight over high-earners' pay rises. As we saw at the beginning of this chapter, this amounts to releasing the brakes on capitalism's tendency to increase inequality. In sum, if we strive harder on our own behalf, and those efforts are more likely to pay off, there will be less collectivism and more inequality.

In this case, individualism cannot explain why inequality levels in the USA and the UK were so similar even though they had such different levels of unionization. If the UK had more people in trade unions, it must, therefore, have had less individualism. This forces us to consider whether there are different types of individualism and whether the inverse relationship between collectivism and individualism is as straightforward as is usually assumed (Lukes 1973). This book argues that the UK was for some time more committed to collectivism (including unions and high taxes) than the USA, but was nevertheless also committed to individualism (also see Spicker 2013). The USA was the laboratory for the development of a strain of individualism which was more hostile to collectivism, and the nature of individualism in the UK eventually changed under the influence of this American strain.

The Mayor of London's remarks were made as part of the annual Margaret Thatcher lecture, commemorating the British Prime Minister most closely associated with the conversion of Britons to a more American individualism. They were persuaded to vote for her Conservative party in sufficient numbers to provide her with the mandate to wrestle with Britain's collectivist institutions. They did not see a need for trade unions in their own workplaces and saw wresting power from the trade unions as good reason for voting for the Conservatives (see Chapter 11). Other reasons for voting Conservative included disquiet over high levels of taxation and public spending, particularly on welfare (Clery et al. 2013; Gilbert 2013).

The fact that the UK retains a higher rate of unionization than many other countries suggests that American individualism has not yet fully replaced the older, British individualism. The same might also apply to the differences in the health of civil society in the two countries, which suggest that other types of collectivism have also been more persistent in the UK (Grenier and Wright 2006; Hall 1999, 2002). All of this tells us that, without the conversion of enough British voters to American individualism, progress would have been much more difficult, perhaps impossible, for the neoliberal bandwagon which Thatcher helped to get on the road.[5] The older British individualism not only found the rampant inequality that accompanied neoliberalism morally repugnant but also played a key role in shifting power and resources from capital to labour over many decades (Streeck 2014). The political defeat signalled by the election of the first Thatcher government helped capital to win back the lost power and treasure and, as it did so, inequality increased.

Despite all of this apparent concentration on the USA and the UK, this book also has something to say about the future of work and politics in other countries. This claim rests on the knowledge that all politics, and all possible ways of organizing work, will have to reckon with one type of individualism or another for the foreseeable future. There seems to be little doubt that many other countries will follow the USA and the UK in completing the transition to the kind of individualism which is wholly compatible with neoliberalism and burgeoning inequality (Streeck 2014). Understanding more about the way in which American and British individualism first diverged, and then converged, will help us to think sensibly about the future of European countries with long histories of social solidarity and former communist countries able to claim none of the individualistic heritage of the USA and the UK (Dardot and Laval 2014; Harvey 2005). In the last two countries, the issue is simple enough for anyone unhappy with inequality: how do they get off the neoliberal train? For Americans and Britons, it would be helpful to understand why they got on the train in the first place and what keeps most people in their seats, even though they may feel the train is no longer headed for a place they want to go to.

MORAL INDIVIDUALISM

Several chapters of this book will be spent explaining the divergence between American and British individualisms in the nineteenth century, but there was an earlier time in which many people in both countries were galvanized by the ideas of individualism propounded by one man, Thomas Paine. Paine, who migrated from Britain to America, was an important actor in the process which extended individualism from elites to the mass of the population or, at least, the male population. This process had in fact begun three centuries before with the Protestant Reformation and continued with the rising prosperity which was necessary to explain the need for, and attraction of, individualism (Hofstede 2001; Inglehart and Welzel 2005; Norris and Inglehart 2009). Elites could get richer without any increase in the majority's appetite for individualism but, with more general prosperity in prospect, men and women could begin to dream of autonomy and self-development, not just for themselves but for all (Spicker 2013). At the end of the eighteenth century, the fault lines between a new mass individualism, which assumed future prosperity for all, and an older elite individualism were visible in their different views of self-interest and charitable giving.

Edmund Burke – once Paine's friend and subsequently his greatest opponent – spoke for the elite individualism which was anchored in a religion holding out against the wilder repercussions of the Reformation. Burke was an Anglican with Catholic leanings and his individualism was centred on the human quality of self-interest supported by religious belief: it was God who had placed self-interest in human hearts (Tawney 1926). The example of charitable giving helps to explain the contrast between this elite individualism and the mass individualism of Paine, in which religious belief was of little account. In eighteenth-century Britain, following God's plan meant, for the most part, pursing self-interest and thereby promoting general prosperity. It was rare when something more than self-interest was required of the British elites and these were occasions for philanthropy. In 1774 Edmund Burke explained that charity was a Christian duty, on a level with settling our debts (though more enjoyable), but we had some choice in regard to when and how we met those obligations. This element of choice definitely added to our satisfaction but it was doing our duty that was the main source of our enjoyment because this earned us 'divine favour'. In other words, philanthropy was mostly self-interest with a small admixture of choice (Burke [1774]1999).

Paine's view of our duties to our fellows was very different. If individualism was for everyone, this required equality of opportunity and that, in turn, meant collective action. His commitment to mass individualism arose from a moral conviction that extending individualism beyond the elites would make for a better world, and not simply a richer one. In *The Rights of Man* ([1792]2014), Paine saw God as the source of both the equality of men and of their equal natural rights 'which appertain to man in right of his existence' (Paine [1792]2014: 198). God was also the source of our duty to treat our neighbours as we expect them to treat us. But, at least so far as political principles were concerned, Paine took the Deist view that God set the world in motion, with natural rights as part of the mechanism, and then sat on his hands.

From this point, Paine thought it was up to men, and sometimes women (Botting 2014), to make those rights a reality. This had been the point of not only the French and American Revolutions of the eighteenth century but also the (British) Glorious Revolution of the seventeenth. Political change was required to enact all the natural rights: 'intellectual rights, or rights of the mind, and also all those rights of acting as an individual for his own comfort and happiness, which are not injurious to the natural rights of others' (Paine [1792]2014: 198). From Paine we can look forward to the extension of democracy in the nineteenth and twentieth centuries, including women's suffrage, the abolition of the slave trade and slavery itself, the civil rights movement and anti-discrimination legislation. All of these struggles were intended to enact natural rights for those who had not yet had the opportunity to determine their own fates (Lukes 1973; Spicker 2013).

The contrast with Burke's self-interested philanthropy is obvious. In Burke's view, God had not left us to our own devices and guided us to carry on with both our self-interest and our occasional charitable giving to curry divine favour. Paine thought that the moral condition of a nation would be measured by its progress in enacting natural rights but he argued that this process required that individuals must also become more moral. In contrast to most eighteenth-century women and men, Paine thought there were many unfortunates who lacked the moral training which would show them how to act to advance their own health, wealth and happiness, while at the same time respecting the rights of others. Even if their natural rights were enacted, these people could not help themselves and would remain both wretched and poor:

> Why is it that scarcely any are executed but the poor? The fact is a proof, among other things, of a wretchedness in their condition. Bred up without morals, and cast upon the world without a prospect, they are the exposed sacrifice of vice and legal barbarity ... It is to my advantage that I have served an apprenticeship to life. I know the value of moral instruction, and I have seen the danger of the contrary. (Paine [1792]2014: 316)

Paine thought that government should spend the money it currently wasted on supporting the poor (and on 'legal barbarity') on a comprehensive scheme to provide general moral education. He also recommended several other innovations, including rudimentary welfare benefits and pensions which anticipated the welfare state, in the cause of putting everyone in the position where they would be able to make sensible efforts to advance their own health, wealth and happiness.

For Paine, enacting the principle of equal natural rights meant getting rid of priests as well as despots, and all established religion (including Burke's) got in the way of the new morality that was so desperately needed by nations and individuals. All religions eventually lose 'their native mildness, and become morose and intolerant' (Paine [1792]2014: 214) and must make way for individualism which was the perfect substitute for religion as a source of the morality of nations and individuals. If the pious sought their principles and policies in the interpretation of God's will, the principles and policies of individualism originated in the interpretation and enactment of natural rights. Of course, these natural rights still required men and women to *believe* in something, just as they might once have believed that the will of God was enshrined in the principles of religion. What was required now, however, was not a belief in supernatural intentions but a belief that every individual shared a common humanity which compelled others to recognize those natural rights. In this respect, humanity had replaced God as the first cause of the belief system from which morality could be developed (Fevre 2000a).

A century later, the French sociologist Emile Durkheim reached the conclusion that the replacement of conventional religion by a religion of individualism had become general (Cladis 1992a, 1992b). It is worth quoting him at some length because his words convey how much of religion's mystique carries over into individualism. In an essay defending the campaigning role of intellectuals like himself in the Dreyfus case, Durkheim explained why any person could expect their natural rights to be treated as sacred by their fellows:

> If he has the right to this religious respect, it is because he has in him something of humanity. It is humanity that is sacred and worthy of respect. And this is not his exclusive possession. It is distributed among all his fellows, and in consequence he cannot take it as a goal for his conduct without being obliged to go beyond himself and turn towards others. The cult of which he is at once both object and follower does not address itself to the particular being that constitutes himself and carries his name, but to the human person, wherever it is to be found, and in whatever form it is incarnated. Impersonal and anonymous, such an end soars far above all particular consciences and can thus serve as a rallying-point for them ... In short, individualism thus understood is the glorification not of the self, but of the individual in general. Its motive force is not egoism but sympathy for all that is human, a wider pity for all sufferings, for all human miseries, a more ardent desire to combat and alleviate them, a greater thirst for justice. Is this not the way to achieve a community of all men of good will? (Durkheim [1898]1969: 23–4)

The relationship between the religious mystique of this individualism and the moral obligation that it placed on its followers to extend its benefits to all humanity will be explored in later chapters. For the moment, we need only to recognize that the individualism of *The Rights of Man* underpinned the reforming social movements of the nineteenth century, including those which most eloquently demonstrated the idea of a social conscience and the importance of emotion to the popularity and success of these ventures in collectivism (Flam and King 2005; Goodwin et al. 2001; Nussbaum 2013).

This is not to argue, however, that all of these necessary conditions for the development of this individualism originated in the nineteenth century and we have to remember that not everyone saw moral individualism as an alternative to religion. I noted the significance of the Reformation a little earlier, and it was through Protestantism (but not Burke's Anglo-Catholicism) that individualism reformed Christianity. In the nineteenth century, evangelical Protestantism produced its own version of moral individualism for the masses but the 'sacralization' of the person – on which the elaboration of human rights has depended – has a very long history. Within this history, Christian thinkers and their secular opponents argued over the meaning of common Judeo-Christian traditions (Joas 2013; Siedentop 2014).

As the nineteenth century advanced, the general loss of religious belief meant that the social movements which pursued equality were increasingly dependent on Paine's kind of moral individualism rather than on its religious counterpart. We will call it *sentimental* individualism. Durkheim often referred to moral feelings as sentiments, and for the author of this book 'sentimental morality' is always derived from beliefs about the qualities of human beings rather than religious beliefs (Fevre 2000a). As we have seen, Paine's sentimental individualism entailed moral convictions. He believed that it was making our own moral decisions that made us autonomous moral beings. Since we live in a time when self-interest is thought to be best served by limitless choice, it is perhaps hard to grasp the connection being made between morality and choice in sentimental individualism.

One way of grasping the connection is to remember that in pre-modern times people had no choice but to fulfil the roles they had been assigned to. They did their duty as king or farmer or miller and this was how they acted morally. When morality is no longer defined by roles, we are speaking of moral individualism in which the choices we make are not defined by roles and yet allow others to judge how moral we are (MacIntyre 1966). This was why Paine contended that moral education was needed to make sure people were equipped to make their choices in a moral way.[6] Simply giving them choices and trusting to self-interest were the cause of vice and degradation and their subsequent punishment.

By the mid-nineteenth century, God had entirely disappeared from John Stuart Mill's statement of sentimental individualism in *On Liberty*:

> We followed not God's plan but our own framing the plan of our life to suit our own character; of doing as we like, subject to such consequences as may

follow: without impediment from our fellow-creatures, so long as what we do does not harm them, even though they should think our conduct foolish, perverse, or wrong. (Mill [1859]2015: 612)

In other words, we must not take away their capacity to be autonomous moral beings. Choice had been directly substituted for self-interest as the source of our morality. It was a very different thing to go in for philanthropy when 'framing the plan of our life to suit our own character' as opposed to ascertaining we have God's favour (Spicker 2013). Mill's book on *Utilitarianism* (1863) explored some of the implications of the change, including the idea that, with the progress of civilization, our plans would be dominated by the idea of serving others. The ability to show ourselves moral by choice would lead us to make the most determinedly altruistic choices. There was a real danger that our social consciences would be over-developed but, in any event, the story of civilization entailed self-interest diminishing, then vanishing, in society's rear-view mirror (Thilly 1923).[7]

All of this suggests we should not be surprised that individualism and collectivism, indeed individualism and socialism, could comfortably co-exist for much of the nineteenth and twentieth centuries (Cladis 1992a, 1992b; Gagnier 2010; Lukes 1969, 1973; Spicker 2013; Thilly 1923). Arguably the most important twentieth-century product of senti-mental individualism was feminism, and the women's movement offered a paradigm for the co-determination of social change by individualism and collectivism right up to the 1970s. Yet self-interest reappeared once more in the secular individualism of nineteenth-century liberalism and, eventually, neoliberalism. We know that when it did so the significance of choice in individualism was radically revised. While many were still able to see philanthropy as a moral choice, many more were preoccupied by the idea that choice was their highway to the satisfaction of whatever wishes and desires they might have. If self-interest was back in charge, where was the reward in philanthropy if there was no God who could show his favour to the philanthropist?

If we are going to explain why neoliberal individualism is responsible for generating and justifying inequality, we must understand why moral individualism apparently fell so far out of favour. Ultimately, this means understanding why people ceased to believe that every individual pos-sessed qualities that required everyone else to recognize their natural rights. During the twentieth century, this *belief* in human qualities was gradually replaced by *knowledge* of human qualities, which stimulated the growth of the neoliberal incarnation of individualism. Chief amongst this knowledge was the certainty that all humans were motivated by self-interest.

Some commentators on individualism have argued that the recognition of the self-interest of the individual was present at its inception.[8] It might be easy for us to take the same view, influenced as we are by the neoliberal version of individualism. This is why it has been necessary to explore the way in which the knowledge of self-interest was kept at arm's length in moral individualism, but we must also spend a little time exploring neoliberal individualism itself. This will also provide an opportunity to explore those writers who argued that the transfer of allegiance from moral to neoliberal individualism made almost all of us worse off because it entailed a Faustian bargain which was hidden from us until long after the deal was sealed.

NEOLIBERAL INDIVIDUALISM

Understanding that neoliberal individualism justifies inequality is straightforward. Since it is founded on the knowledge that everyone who lives in neoliberal society is free to determine their fate, economic success or failure is the responsibility of individuals alone (Boltanski and Chiapello [1999]2005; Dardot and Laval 2014; Honneth 2012). Unlike the societies which Tom Paine was taking to task, all neoliberal societies incorporate the knowledge that the best has been done to ensure (for example, through universal public education and anti-discrimination legislation) that every one of these individuals is in a position to benefit from this freedom (Brown 2015). The poor and indigent can no longer be excused by their lack of moral education in the way that Paine had argued. If their morality is in question, this is the fault of the earlier insistence of the state (in line with Paine's original plan) on providing welfare which made them unfit to take advantage of the myriad opportunities for self-determination provided for them (Somers and Block 2005). Less state interference in their lives will ensure that they fully appreciate the opportunities they have and the responsibility they bear. The proper welfare policies to facilitate individualism are those which make sure work is always more of an attractive alternative than state hand-outs (Dardot and Laval 2014; Spicker 2013). So, inequality is justified, but a wider point applies well beyond those in the bottom 10 per cent of income distribution.

Critics of neoliberalism argue that, for most people in neoliberal societies, individualism now condemns them to less and less freedom, even as common knowledge declares it self-evident that their fates are in their own hands (Boltanski and Chiapello [1999]2005). Most of the writing which argues this point draws on European social theory and social and political philosophy (Bowring 2015). In particular, it draws on French philosopher Michel Foucault (Brown 2015; Dardot and Laval 2014) and German Critical Theory.[9] Yet, it is the recent history of Britain that provides a disproportionate share of the examples given to explain the idea that neoliberal individualism delivers less freedom than it promises. It is often implied that Britain pioneered many of its key features, including the extension of neoliberal individualism to the public sector with 'new public management' (Streeck 2014). The emphasis on the British experience arose from the way European theorists could see in it the starkest, and earliest, example of a society jumping the European tracks to join the USA in a dash towards a neoliberal future. There was also the fascination with the personality of Margaret Thatcher, sometimes portrayed as the author of neoliberal individualism and responsible for the 'clearest formulation of neoliberal rationality'.[10]

In all of this writing, neoliberal individualism is portrayed as making impossible demands on people that diminish their wellbeing and even make them ill. By agreeing that neoliberal rationality describes how the world works, and making its knowledge our own, we commit to much more than keeping our résumés up to date (Rose 1999). Whereas in the early nineteenth century individualism was just a matter of self-determination, later in that century some elite members began to explore the additional opportunities that the advent of Romanticism had created for self-*realization*.[11] By the (later) 1960s and 1970s, such opportunities had become more general and people could apparently use their freedoms not only to act as autonomous human beings determining their own futures but to express themselves and, through experimentation, discover wishes and desires that they might use their autonomy to pursue (cf. Bowring 2015).

This development was most obvious in the sphere of consumption (Streeck 2014), but self-realization was also insinuated in the process by which people determined their own fates by selling their services on the market. The presentation of wishes and desires became an indispensable part of the marketing of individuals who began to act as *entrepreneurs* on their own behalf, focusing all their capacities and emotional resources on getting a job or succeeding at work. The self that the nineteenth-century Romantics were seeking turned out to have identical interests to employers. The innovation of self-government through entrepreneurship can be traced back to the 1940s but, once fully developed, it meant that all employees who were free to govern themselves must be ready to take advantage of any new opportunities they had to make more from exchanging their services. At the same time, their motivations had to match whatever the opportunity (whether a new project or an entirely new job) might require. They must be prepared to embrace enthusiastically every change in their work and market position as the product of their own choices. In this way, their own wishes and preferences were revealed as identical with those who authored the changes, usually their employers.

Managers could not escape the Faustian bargain of neoliberal individualism, indeed they might put more of themselves at stake, but the services they provided to their employer supplied the technology required to enforce the bargain. This might be most obvious in the writings of Peter Drucker, the American management writer (born in Austria) who gave us the term 'management by objectives', or in the British experience of new public management which Drucker influenced, but numerous empirical studies showed the techniques management used to force people to behave like entrepreneurs (Fevre 2003). This meant discontinuing any remaining collective objectives or rewards and making all objectives and rewards effective at the level of individual employees. The employment relation was entirely reduced to that between the employer and the individual, with quantitative data apparently underpinning robust and objective knowledge of the individual's contribution.

The supposedly objective judgement of individual employees was meant to derive in some way from assessment of the degree to which the needs of the client or customer had been met rather than against criteria derived from the organization's hierarchy or procedures. In this way, every employee, not simply those with managerial responsibilities, was placed under direct market pressure. All of these techniques were geared to ensuring that employees were continually reminded that they were in competition with each other (Streeck 2014). One aspect of the Faustian bargain is revealed: an individual's autonomy at work could only be used to put them in a position where they were required to use greater and greater self-control. In typical Foucauldian fashion, the managerial technology meant individuals only did well if they submitted to disciplining themselves and learning to live with the increasing demands they were obliged to heap on their own heads (Brown 2015; cf. Bowring 2015).

There is a large English-language empirical literature on these management innovations (see Chapter 9), but the theoretical literature on neoliberal individualism draws mainly on the French management and work literature (Coutrot 1998; Le Goff 1999, 2003). Similarly, although there is a great deal of American and British empirical sociology on the way workers suffer from the demand to counterfeit authenticity, the theorists all made use of the work of French sociologist Ehrenberg (2009)

on the rise of depression (as measured both by presentations of symptoms and the consumption of medication). Ehrenberg ascribed this
phenomenon to employees' permanent state of anxiety about their
performance, not simply their fear of losing their jobs but an existential
insecurity about themselves and their capacities which floated free from
any specific fear of loss on income. They were in fact made ill by their
experience of the gap between the promise and the reality of neoliberal
individualism.

While not always as specific as self-blame, the gap was filled with a
type of introspection that ushered employees onto a slide into depression.
Indeed, depression might begin when individuals were told to make the
plan of their lives out of the resources they found inside themselves
(Ehrenberg 2009). Self-realization now appeared to be a curse which
insisted on constant self-examination which damaged people. Later in the
book, we will explore the idea that those who were most at risk of this
damage were those employees who had not yet abandoned the idea that
their choices made them autonomous *moral* individuals. They therefore
retained an expectation of recognition whereas their organizations had no
memory of their mutual history and cared only for the entrepreneurial
employee and the demands of the project in hand.

Though writers of social theory disagreed on how much was intended
and how much was a sort of happy accident (for capitalism that is), for
all of them neoliberal individualism represented a way of getting more
out of employees. For some, the benefits for capital lay in the delayering
of management, the refinement of flexibility and the facilitation of
'network capitalism' that self-governing neoliberal individuals offered.
We should not, however, under-estimate the more straightforward benefits of work intensification (see Chapter 14). These benefits depended on
reducing employees' commitment to trade unions and collective bargaining and on a straightforward shift in the balance of power between
capital and labour (Perelman 2005; Streeck 2014). Getting employees to
abandon collectivism meant persuading them of something that was far
from straightforward: that a new, American kind of individualism was in
their interests and that neoliberal capitalism was the guarantor of that
individualism.

The journey from the individualism of the early nineteenth century to
its neoliberal version involved transforming the capitalist enterprise's
supreme indifference to the self-determination (and still more, the
self-realization) of its employees to such a degree that the enterprise,
along with the market, would seem to be individualism's natural home.
Employees had to be persuaded that the success of enterprises depended
on the thoroughness of their adherence to the principles of individualism.

They had to believe, in the hackneyed phrase of their managers, that this was a 'win-win situation' in which it was the individualism that really was in their employees' interests that would best serve capitalism. So successful was this approach that 4 out of 5 employees became convinced that they were treated as individuals in their workplaces (see Chapter 10). In fact, neoliberalism portrayed the enterprise and the market as the only legitimate arena for individualism to flourish. All of this persuasion required a heroic effort from 'administrative elites, management experts, economists, pliant journalists and political leaders ... in virtually every country' (Dardot and Laval 2014: 229), but also 'human resources departments, recruitment agencies and training experts'. Responsibility even extended into academics and 'well-intentioned reformers, who believed that a secure, flourishing worker was a more motivated, and therefore more efficient, worker' (Dardot and Laval 2014: 286).

PROSPECT

This rarely, if ever, features in the writing we have been discussing, but the success of a mission to persuade employees that the individualism they crave could only be found in the market and the workplace goes some way towards explaining why so many employees of relatively modest means showed their support for neoliberal politics at the ballot box. This success is not a sufficient explanation for burgeoning inequality, however. The opening chapters of this book show how sentimental individualism did much to stimulate reform in the nineteenth century because the status quo was so far from that in which people could put any trust in their own actions to prosper (Meyer 1987: 250). When so many had so little control over their own fates, this kind of individualism was utopian and, *for that reason*, it moved millions to activism and to demands for reform. Yet, when utopia failed to arrive for decade after decade, the conditions needed for popular support for sentimental individualism began to dissolve. The evident disenchantment with sentimental individualism came to the fore long after the structural changes that it demanded had been completed. For example, the complaints of too much trade union power, or a burgeoning culture of poverty, became a popular chorus only at the point that changes in social policy, education, economic policy and employment relations appeared to have failed (Streeck 2014). By this I mean that they had not levelled the playing field for individualism in the way Tom Paine had anticipated when he planned to put an end to 'wretchedness' (Somers and Block 2005).

The dissolution of the elements that had succoured sentimental individualism involved not only disappointment and disillusion with failure but also the concrete achievements that individualism wrought in the architecture of the richest nations. Neoliberal societies did more than simply incorporate the knowledge that the best had been done to ensure (for example, with universal public education and anti-discrimination legislation) that every individual was now in a position to benefit from the freedom to determine their own fate. For example, individuals' access to universal education and their acquaintance with modern employment relations systems made them open to the idea that everyone, including their employers, could benefit from a self-interested individualism. In other words, the concrete achievements of sentimental individualism helped to put in place the necessary conditions for the reappearance of an individualism that could be equated with self-interest.

Almost all of the writers referenced in the previous section saw the triumph of neoliberal individualism as neither a conspiracy nor a reflection of the logic of capital. It was not the result of a well-worked plan but was tentative, contingent and gradual. At times, developments in very different spheres (sociological, philosophical and economic, for example) came together in an uncoordinated way that might be described, after Max Weber, as 'an elective affinity' (Honneth, 2012). I share this reluctance to read co-ordination and strategy into history. I prefer to see neoliberal individualism as the consequence of the failure of promised utopia to arrive and changes within capitalism and individualism which produced an apparent symbiosis in neoliberal individualism.

If history and contingency are inescapable, I ought to be very reluctant to make predictions but, nevertheless, this book can tell us something important about the future of work and politics. As Marx might have said, neoliberalism contains the seeds of its own transformation, and this is especially true of work. Later chapters suggest that the experience of employment provides a daily test of the fidelity of neoliberal individualism which it frequently fails. At the end of the book, I consider the possibility that awareness of this failure might re-establish sentimental individualism in a way that re-activates the perceived need for collective action and reinvigorates the politics of inequality. Inviting people to think of themselves as individuals while at work turned out to be a trap for employees in the medium term but perhaps, in the longer term, the invitation might rebound on capitalism? Making employees think they can make a difference at work is presently the key to their self-control, but what if they refused to give up on the promise they thought they had been made? If people refuse to abandon the hope that they are individuals, rather than undifferentiated labour power, individualism might once again offer a utopian ideal which cannot condone inequality and stimulates criticism and reform (Spicker 2013).

NOTES

1. For example, the OECD reported G20 GDP growth was up by 0.1% in the third quarter of 2013: www.oecd.org/std/leading-indicators/CLI_Eng_Dec13.pdf
2. Although a more comprehensive demonstration would also involve the data on strike action which show the virtual disappearance of strikes in many countries after 1989 (Streeck 2014).
3. Especially since the majority of UK union members are now women (Department of Business, Innovation and Skills 2015).
4. I make frequent reference to 'neoinstitutionalist' sociology in the chapters that follow, particularly in discussions of the USA. The ontological status of individuals must always be problematic for sociologists but these writers recognize individualism as one of the most potent forces of modernity, for example: 'the individual is an institutional myth evolving out of the rationalized theories of economic, political and cultural action ... Modern "individuals" give expression to the institutionalized description of the individual as having authorized political rights, efficacy and competence; they consider themselves effective choosers of their occupations' (Meyer et al. 1987: 21; also see Scott and Meyer 1994a, 1994b).
5. Accounts of neoliberalism identified the Thatcherite revolution in the UK, along with the parallel changes introduced under Ronald Reagan in the USA, as the inspiration for the advent of similar policies, and politics, across the developed world.
6. Spicker (2013) distinguishes 'ethical individualism' which requires moral behaviour of individuals from 'moral individualism' in which people are to be treated as separate from one another. Given how important the cultivation of character was to the development of moral individualism – and especially its sentimental variant – I find this distinction difficult to sustain in practice.
7. Dardot and Laval (2014) argued that Mill followed Tocqueville in finding a solution to the problem of the isolated individual's lack of power in their combination into associations (also see Stivers 2003).
8. According to Dumont, Adam Smith was responsible for 'the elevation of the individual subject, of man as "self-loving", labouring-and-exchanging, who through his toil, his interest, and his gain works for the common good, for the wealth of nations' (Dumont 1977: 97). Thus, the rise of economics and the rise of individualism were two sides of the same coin. Beteille criticized Dumont for conflating many different interpretations of individualism (Beteille 1983, 1986). As we will see, it is perfectly possible to have an individualism that has an affinity with equality (a connection made since Tocqueville) and a different kind of individualism which equates with the achievement and legitimacy of unequal rewards.
9. In the following discussion, I draw particularly on Boltanski and Chiapello ([1999]2005), Dardot and Laval (2014) and Honneth (2012) but I might also have used Bourdieu (1998).
10. Dardot and Laval (2014) find that the clearest expression of neoliberal rationality is Margaret Thatcher's interview with the *Sunday Times* (www.margaretthatcher.org/document/104475), in which she regretted 30 years of growing collectivism which had meant people had forgotten about the person. It was in order to reinstate the 'personal society' that she was pursuing her economic policies.
11. Self-realization had already been conceptualized as self-actualization in the 1970s (see Chapter 10) and I will use the terms interchangeably.

2. Anti-slavery and the secret of human rights

The literature produced by historians, political philosophers, literary scholars, public policy researchers, anthropologists, sociologists and economists identifies many different types of individualism. They are sometimes differentiated by intellectual ancestry (their 'genealogies'), or according to the countries, or academic disciplines, most closely associated with them (Lukes 1973). Some writers distinguish good and bad individualisms or, as Friedrich Hayek (1948), Austrian economist and philosopher, preferred, 'true' and 'false' individualisms. British sociologist Stephen Lukes (1973) teased apart the ideas of nineteenth-century individualism to find the combination of ideas that launched movements for social and political reform, including anti-slavery and other human rights campaigns. In his analysis, this combination was separated from the ideas that were developed in classical liberalism which included the right to property and to make a living as one chose, free-thinking, self-help, minimal government and taxation, and free trade (also see Spicker 2013).

According to the historian Gregory Claeys, Tom Paine 'insisted on an idea of the equality of rights and mutual respect which was stunningly radical in his own time, but is now central to modern civility' and his message remained relevant around the world wherever human rights were denied (Claeys 1989: 16). Paine's writings on individualism included elements of *both* types of individualism identified by Lukes, however. For example, he thought the market provided the best illustration of why people required minimal government since self-interest ensured they took care of each other's rights when they were left alone. Wherever they occurred, democratic revolutions could take the market as a model for how people should be governed and ought to favour minimal government and low taxation.

When he wrote about what he saw happening in commercial society, particularly in America, Paine was cataloguing knowledge. He knew that the market facilitated individualism and did not have to believe in it, as he did in the dignity of all human persons, because he could see the evidence everywhere in his adopted home. So, when Paine supported classical liberal ideas, he was drawing public policy out of what he already knew to be effective. When he insisted on the right of individuals to property and to make a living as they chose, and that the market should be left to its own devices, with minimal government and minimal taxation, Paine was drawing on cognition.

The distinction between sentiment and cognition was used in my earlier work to describe the different epistemologies used to make sense of the world within Western culture (Fevre 2000a). Sentiment uses belief or intuition and cognition relies initially – in 'common sense' ways of understanding – on the evidence of our five senses (as described by Hobbes and Hume, for example). For example, we cannot know that we or anyone else has feelings or, in the language of the nineteenth century, sentiments. Our five senses confirm for us that we and they will sense things but the way people feel, in their hearts or minds, is always a matter of belief.

Since the Enlightenment, and certainly by the time of Paine and the development of the ideas of classical liberalism, cognition had developed more sophisticated variants. In addition to their own personal experience, people could draw on the systematic summaries of human knowledge of a great many people and things they had never seen. They could, for example, use the knowledge made available in statistics which summarized the aggregate experience of huge numbers of individuals they had never met. Yet, the basic principle of cognition remained the same: evidence was required for any convictions people might hold about individualism. For example, if it appeared that one society provided better conditions for individualism than another because it had a freer market and less government, it was possible to recommend that form of government to the populations of other countries.

The recommendations of cognitive individualism were not always so radical. For example, if personal experience showed that the poor were feckless and untrustworthy, it might well be the personal characteristics of individuals that led some to comfortable prosperity and others to poverty and crime. The twentieth-century equivalent of this cognitive individualism was just as conservative.[1] For example, observed differences in the performance of individuals in schools and labour markets were taken as evidence of differences in their capacities and talents.

Tom Paine was relying on cognitive individualism when he argued for smaller government but not when he argued for universal education or a proto-welfare state. He was not satisfied with the evidence of his own, or anyone else's, eyes. He believed that the characters of the poor were formed by their poverty and that all individuals were capable of acquiring the same characters if they were given the chance. It was his belief in the qualities of all human beings that drove him to put aside the evidence which was meat and drink to cognitive individualism. It gave him a vision of individualism that was better than the one he saw in operation, even in the USA, and the source of this vision was not cognitive individualism but moral individualism.

Respect for individuals was especially important to Paine (Claeys 1989: 91) and Lukes understood that this was the cornerstone of the type of individualism that launched reforms and human rights campaigns:

> [T]he principle of respect for persons, as 'ends in themselves', in virtue of their inherent dignity as individuals, is at the basis of the ideal of human dignity ... It amounts to the contention that all persons are deserving of respect, and should be treated accordingly ... this principle is strongly egalitarian, since it asserts that respect is *equally* due to all persons – in virtue of their being persons, that is of some characteristic or set of characteristics which they have in common – and ... respecting them involves doing all one can to maintain and increase their freedom (and to discriminate between them in this regard is to fail to show them equal respect). (Lukes 1973: 125–6, emphasis in the original)

The language ('principle', 'ideal', 'contention') used in this passage indicates that respect and dignity have their roots in belief systems rather than knowledge systems.

In the previous chapter, I argued that Paine's moral convictions arose from sentimental beliefs about humanity rather than the religious beliefs that could be an alternative source of moral individualism. As we saw in Chapter 1, there is an argument that respect for human dignity has religious roots: the conviction that people should be treated as sacred arises from the belief that they are God's creations (Elliott 2007; Mathias 2013). It is sometimes suggested that the Enlightenment's insistence on the primacy of reason over religious belief obscured the religious origins of the idea and presented a more secular version of the universal respect due to people. In the case of Paine's writings, the best hope of finding evidence that the religious roots of equal human dignity were being obscured by reason is his discourse on 'natural rights'.

In what follows, I will suggest that what was actually going on when Paine wrote about natural rights was not an appeal to reason to take forward the lesson already provided by religion. Instead, Paine was introducing an alternative belief system to a world that was hostile to Deists like himself. As Paine was later to find out from the reception that greeted his anti-Christian arguments in *The Age of Reason*, this hostility could easily prevent people listening to what he had to tell them. Far from reason camouflaging the religious roots of human dignity, the primacy of natural rights in Paine's writings could be seen as a way of using religion to cover up the secular roots of a new, sentimental individualism which was to provide a more powerful motivation for human-rights campaigns than religion ever could.

The idea of natural rights which all human beings are born with was introduced in Chapter 1. In common with others (both Christians and Deists), Paine identified the state of nature with the Creation and '[t]he divine origin of rights and of the idea of natural liberty was thus central to Paine's account' (Claeys 1989: 73).[2] Indeed, the very fact that we were capable of appreciating the idea of natural rights was due to God making sure our minds had this capability. The appreciation of natural rights was not confined to an educated minority and so natural rights really were universal. After *The Rights of Man*, '[m]ankind could now be understood as belonging to one universal fraternal community where all possessed equal rights and duties which upheld the fundamental dignity (a word of immense importance to Paine) of each' (Claeys 1989: 91).

In Chapter 1, I suggested that Paine's Deism meant that he could not rely on God to help men reinstate their natural rights and this was why he had no option but to incite people to pursue equal rights themselves. As Claeys notes, the radicals who followed Paine took him at his word: '[r]ights were now widely construed in an anthropological sense, as inhering in each individual regardless of rank' (Claeys 1989: 123) and

> the new radicalism gave less stress to the historical existence of a state of nature than the intrinsic possession of rights by all. John Thelwall, for example, defined "man in his natural state" to mean "simply as an individual, stripped of all the relations of Society, independent of its Compacts and uninfluenced by its reciprocations". Rights hence were defined according to human nature, by wants and their satisfaction, and faculties and their capacity for improvement. (Claeys 1989: 124)

This points towards another important distinction made in my earlier work (Fevre 2000a): the idea that beliefs about human beings are in a different category to beliefs about all other things depends on valuing a distinction between human and non-human things. As humans thinking about human nature we have inside information, but as humans thinking about flowers and sea-horses we are outsiders.

We now have an ontological distinction to add to the earlier epistemological one and it gives us four potential arenas of sense-making: human belief (sentiment), non-human belief (religion), human knowledge (cognition) and non-human knowledge (science). These can be represented in the form of a simple matrix (adapted from Fevre 2000a: 141), as seen in Figure 2.1.

Ontology		
	Human	**Not human**
Belief	**Sentiment**	**Religion**
Knowledge	**Cognition**	**Science**

(Epistemology — left axis label)

Figure 2.1   Four ways of making sense in Western culture

The distinction between these four categories of sense-making pre-dates Christianity and the elaboration of new ideas in each of the four arenas had taken place many times before the new ideas of the late eighteenth and nineteenth centuries appeared. The cognitive individualism of that time was an example amongst many of new sense-making in human knowledge. There were, for example, the ideas of the emerging social sciences, which assumed (in common with Kant) that knowledge about people was not the same as knowledge of the natural world. At the same time, there was invention in the arena of human belief, particularly in the ideas that animated sentimental individualism. This process of sense-making and innovation was separate, both logically and empirically, from both cognitive *and* religious individualism and Paine would make an important contribution to it. Paine's writings were a significant part of a process of reinvention and reinvigoration of sentimental sense-making that spanned the eighteenth and nineteenth centuries. This process was as important in the long history of this arena of sense-making as the Enlightenment was to cognition or as early Christianity was to religion. I am not suggesting that Tom Paine furnished its first inspiration, however. Just as Paine contributed to cognitive sense-making with his development of cognitive individualism, so earlier thinkers of the Enlightenment had accomplished sentimental sense-making alongside their major contributions to cognition. Yet, Paine had a big part to play in popularizing the ideas of the wave of sentimental sense-making beyond the salons of the elite. This was particularly the case in Paine's popularizing of the key idea of equal respect for human dignity.

In my earlier book, I suggested neither new sense-making, nor the social movements to which it gave life, could be successful unless it filled a gap in people's understanding of the world: it must solve or at least clarify problems, explain and justify inchoate feelings, and so on. When they read Paine, people saw their own resentments articulated because Paine had the 'ability to seize the gist of a particular moment, and to give voice to the inchoate but deeply felt longings of the many. No political tract has ever been published which was more successful in this regard over a similar period of time than *The Rights of Man*' (Claeys 1989: 113).[3] When they heard that their wants and satisfactions were just as important as any aristocrat's, and that one honest man was worth all the crowned ruffians, people outside the elites were able to make a connection between their inchoate longings and the newly-minted sense-making. I argue that we cannot understand this by reference only to cognitive or religious individualism and that we must not be deceived into thinking Paine was laundering religious into sentimental individualism simply because he mentioned natural rights. Neither Paine nor the people who were inspired by his ideas required that religion first sacralize persons, and it was a secular belief in human dignity that was the source of the moral outrage that fuelled much nineteenth-century reform as well as the human rights movements. I will support my contention about the fundamental importance of sentimental individualism by analysing the history of the first of these movements.

Paine campaigned against legal approval of slavery in America throughout his life (Claeys 1989). One of his first pieces of writing on arriving in America was an anti-slavery essay, published in 1775, in which the influence of Quakerism was evident, just as it was in the writings of the English abolitionists. In the following year, Paine tried unsuccessfully to have an anti-slavery clause inserted in the Declaration of Independence and was probably instrumental in the Pennsylvania anti-slavery act of 1780. In London in 1791, he produced another anti-slavery tract and a decade later, and back in America, he tried to dissuade Congress from retaining slavery in (newly-acquired) Louisiana and to persuade Jefferson to admit the entry of slaves fleeing San Domingo.

In Paine's cognitive individualism, he argued from the evidence he knew that the system of government in the USA was better for individualism. When he thought about slavery, he argued for change in that system of government and lost friends in the process. In doing so, he ignored those who pointed out the conservative lessons that cognitive individualism could draw from slavery, for example that the evidence available in the Southern states showed that slaves were fit only for slavery. It was not cognitive but moral individualism that elicited Paine's anti-slavery initiatives. The history of the campaign against the slave trade, and slavery itself, will help us to analyse the individualism at the heart of human rights and determine if the sentimental-individualist argument can be logically and empirically separated from religious individualism.

THE FIRST SOCIAL MOVEMENT

The anti-slavery movement was 'the most important human rights movement of the nineteenth century' (Joas 2013: 86) and an example of the way moral individualism revolutionized attitudes towards inequality and human rights in a way we now find difficult to comprehend. Slavery seems so profoundly abhorrent to us that it is hard to understand the size of the effort required to remove it. At the end of the eighteenth century, slavery remained entrenched in the most advanced economies and an anti-slavery movement was unthinkable. Yet, the world's largest slave-trading nation resolved to abandon slave trading in 1807 after two decades of anti-slavery campaigning. Adam Hochschild (2005: 5), an American writer on human rights, explained that while slave rebellions were common, anti-slavery was 'something never seen before: it was the first time a large number of people became outraged, and stayed outraged for many years, over someone *else's* right. And most startling of all, the rights of people of another color, on another continent' (Hochschild 2005: 5). Not only did thousands who had nothing to gain from ending slavery petition Parliament, but these thousands included workers of modest means who knew their own prospects and wages would be harmed by ending the trade.

Hochschild (2005) suggested that the secret of the first human rights movement was the way imaginative public relations could tap into natural empathy: to show why we need sentimental individualism to explain anti-slavery, we must consider the limitations of such accounts. Hochschild pointed to the movement's ability to put the facts before the wider British public, a public which could make a connection between these facts and their own situation. This meant moral outrage was very effectively mobilized and propagated widely across the population, the greater part of which remained un-enfranchised. This was all the more remarkable because anti-slavery began with very little support and little apparent chance of success. Most intellectuals did not condone slavery but none seemed to believe there was any possibility of ending it soon. Beyond the intellectuals, the trade in slaves seemed remote from most people's lives and, moreover, most of those people had no experience of political action, including voting.[4]

Hochschild's view aligned with the accounts of the abolitionists since they too believed that the success of the anti-slavery movement came from laying out the facts of how the slaves were treated, drawing on an early form of investigative journalism. The secret of anti-slavery was simply to make people see the horror hidden in plain view and '[t]he abolitionists placed their hope not in sacred texts, but in human empathy'. Hochschild recognized that all 12 founders of the movement 'were deeply religious' but insisted 'they also shared a newer kind of faith. They believed that because human beings had a capacity to care about the suffering of others, exposing the truth would move people to action' (Hochschild 2005: 366). That the slave trade was attacked so effectively in Britain, and with so little warning, was explained by the historical fact that a movement of this kind with its public relations expertise happened to begin there. No other explanation was required except that the British public found it easy to see parallels between their own situation and that of the slaves because they were also deprived of human rights.

Thirty years after the abolition of its trade in slaves, Britain freed its (800,000) slaves. There had been a brief manumission in France and none of the other European nations with slave colonies (Spain, Portugal, Sweden, Denmark and Holland) had entertained abolition. Hochschild noted that the absence of a popular anti-slavery movement in the last three of these was noteworthy since they 'were relatively enlightened societies with far higher literacy rates than Britain, and the last two shared the compact geography that had made it so easy for new ideas to spread there' (Hochschild 2005: 222). Again, he thought the difference might lie in Britons' empathy because of personal fear and close knowledge of the enslavement of their fellows, particularly in the naval press gang. Despite insisting that mass support for anti-slavery entailed the sacrifice of immediate self-interest, extending to loss of trade or livelihood, he was now arguing that (largely anticipated) self-interest made the un-enfranchised support anti-slavery.

According to Hochschild, if leaders like Wilberforce (but not Clarkson) were horrified at the idea of moving on from slavery to other human rights, the rank and file were not. The leaders' strategy was to incite parliamentary pity for the slaves rather than to invoke human rights or argue for equality, but the successful mobilization of broad support could not help but spread the idea of human rights (including the vote) amongst supporters at all levels of society. At this point, *The Rights of Man* provided a strong bridge between anti-slavery and the bourgeoning radical movement which also copied the strategies which had proved successful against slavery. These were 'a media campaign, cheap pamphlets, mass meetings, petitions to Parliament', and by the 1820s and 1830s the movement for reform was generating sufficient energy for it to breathe new life back into the struggle against slavery (Hochschild 2005: 334).

Hochschild argued that Britons' concern for their own human rights helped to reinvigorate their concern for the slaves, though by his own account this process more often worked in the other direction. Thus, 'agitators for domestic reform of all sorts drew on the antislavery movement as a tactical model and on slavery itself as a powerful metaphor' (Hochschild 2005: 352).[5] Hochschild mentioned petitions against working conditions in the factory system and for laws on minimum wages, but it was the fight against child labour that was the immediate beneficiary of the successful struggle against slavery. The use of the testimony of sailors and ships' doctors by the abolitionists prefigured the use of such evidence in the various commissions on child labour and the parliamentary hearings which set a precedent for much later social reform.

In fact, the seminal nature of anti-slavery for human rights was not only a matter of tactics and metaphor. Anti-slavery could change people's views of the world and the most important change occurred with the dissemination of the beliefs and moral convictions of sentimental individualism. The struggle against slavery gave campaigners their convictions about individualism and when these were conveyed to the public a mass movement developed. Hochschild argued that this movement had resulted from the apparent empathy with the slaves displayed by Britons who were also deprived of human rights. If, instead, we recognize that it was anti-slavery that gave them their individualist convictions, the apparent anomaly of Britons caring so much for the plight of the slaves long before they agitated for themselves is explained. We can also make more sense of Hochschild's position that, while this care was rooted in an awareness of their own, similar, situation, those Britons who supported anti-slavery were ready to make their own plight worse by lending that support. We see, instead, that it was through the beliefs acquired in the course of anti-slavery that Britons were able to recognize those similarities with the situation of the slaves.

Hans Joas, the philosopher, agreed that a well-organized, mass social movement was a big part of the story of anti-slavery,[6] and the articulation of suffering and injustice was vital to the movement (Joas 2013: 92). He was also unconvinced by the argument from empathy, arguing that people had to be motivated to use their capacity for empathy and this motivation depended on individualist beliefs. Unfortunately for the clarity of this exposition, he refused to use the label individualism, preferring to refer to 'the sacralization of the person', a more fundamental process than empathy which 'motivates us to show empathy; empathy alone does not engender the sacralization of the person, of all persons' (Joas 2013: 61).

For Joas, 'individualism' was irredeemably tarnished with self-interest, including the egoism Durkheim feared, and its contemporary associations with neoliberalism risked obscuring what he considered to be the secret of human rights. Joas therefore chose 'person' instead of 'individual'

> in order to ensure that the intended belief in the irreducible dignity of every human being is not immediately mistaken for the unscrupulous, egocentric self-sacralization of the individual and thus the narcissistic inability to break away from self-referentiality. The concept of the person has the additional advantage that unlike that of the individual it cannot be understood as contrasting with society (or community). Instead it implies the inevitable sociality of the individual and the specific type of social life of which the personhood of every individual is constitutive. (Joas 2013: 51)

I cannot follow Joas in dispensing with the label because the tainting of individualism is in large part what this book is about and the confusion over what individualism might be will help us to understand our past, present and future. For the moment, however, we are discussing sacralization because it is on this idea that Joas staked his claim that it was in religious belief that the concern for human rights was anchored.

Joas argued that the sacralization of the person spread more widely and swiftly in Britain and America and could help to explain why anti-slavery was so closely associated with Britain. Britons shared with the Swedes, Danes and Dutch a Protestant heritage, European Enlightenment and, at a later stage in the history of anti-slavery, the ideas of *The Rights of Man*, but Britons were imbued with the sacralization of the person at an earlier stage. As in Hochschild's account, there was no need for us to ask why this should be so since history was explanation enough. If we understood how Britain adopted sacralization so thoroughly and quickly, we understood the contingencies that led to the success of anti-slavery and the waves of social movements that followed.[7] In other words, the contingency of sacralization explained Britain's pre-eminence in the struggle for human rights rather than Britain's peculiarity explaining sacralization.

Lukes (1973: 126) believed that the principle of equal respect for all 'has been at the heart of the ideal of equality from early Christianity to the present day' and Joas ascribed the origins of sacralization to Christianity. The crucial role in anti-slavery was played by the 'originally

Christian impulse toward moral decentering' (Joas 2013: 63), which meant taking moral responsibility for humanity and not just your own family or what concerned your self-interest. It made Christians declare slavery a sin, count abolitionism as living the kind of moral life their religion required, and vow to evangelize the slaves. There were two basic elements from Christianity at work in this impulse. First, there was the immortal soul which gave every human being, including slaves, a sacred core which the rest of God's creation lacked. In time, Joas explained, the soul was secularized as the self – again, a universal characteristic but one which was less easily separated from the body. Second, there was the idea that life is a gift that entails obligations towards other human beings 'which limit our right to self-determination' (Joas 2013: 7):

> So to conceive of life itself as a gift is one of the most effective ways of protecting it from instrumentalization ... [It] entails the ideas of universal human dignity and inalienable human rights ... it allows believers to dedicate themselves to the dignity of all people and to take the risky step of participating in creative processes that depend on such belief. (Joas 2013: 170)

Joas saw these core Christian elements of the sacredness of the person as antecedent to the Enlightenment and the Reformation, as well as the French and American Revolutions. Nevertheless, these events helped to lodge the idea in the hearts and minds of ordinary people. The Enlightenment, as well as the Reformation, was a religious reform movement which could not help but increase individualism, as individuals were required to take more responsibility for their relationship with God. If we wished to weigh how influential these events were at diffusing the idea of the sacredness of the person, we ought to recognize that the French Revolution rarely considered the whole of humanity as worthy of respect in the same way that American Protestantism did.

Developments we might think to be doing service to individualism in place of Christianity were, for Joas, simply doing the job of taking Christian ideas into hearts and minds. The contribution from the Enlightenment or the eighteenth century revolutions to human rights always occurred in conjunction with those Christian ideas. Here, Joas took his lead from earlier thinkers (principally Jellinek and Troeltsch) who claimed that a non-Christian idea of natural rights was never capable of delivering human rights on its own.[8] Joas followed Troeltsch to argue that natural rights reinforced rather than replaced the Christian notion of sacredness, for example in the thought and practice of American Protestants who emphasized personal sin and redemption, making it possible for many more people to become politically active than the simple message of the Enlightenment could.

What Hochschild put down to brilliant organization, empathy and some prescience of self-interest, Joas saw as dependent on the sacralization of the person. Moreover, Joas did not see anti-slavery as a prototype for the interest-led movements that succeeded it, going so far as to argue that more academic study of the anti-slavery movement had revealed it to be more like the 'new' social movements of the late twentieth century in which people whose material wants had (now) been satisfied were moved by issues of principle rather than their own interests. To this I wish to add that, contra both Hochschild and Joas, we should not think of anti-slavery as the only nineteenth-century movement that was driven by moral individualism rather than self-interest.

The campaign against child labour in the factory system, already mentioned by Hochschild as benefitting from anti-slavery, was not driven by the children who laboured or their families. The vast majority of the supporters were not beneficiaries, moreover the provision of the facts was not simply a matter of letting them speak to people's innate empathy. There was very often an explicit appeal to the sacredness of the person, as in the hands of romantic poet Robert Southey (1807) alluding to soul and gift in an account of child labour in a Manchester cotton factory. The novels of Dickens and Kingsley and others could produce further examples but the added interest of Southey is that he wrote *Letters from England* in 1808 or 1807, at the same time as the abolition of the slave trade. Thus, moral individualism prompted concern for human rights beyond the slave trade, even before the organizational success of anti-slavery could be reproduced in order, once more, to elicit public empathy.

TWO MORAL INDIVIDUALISMS

When he talked about an affinity between natural law and Christian belief, Joas explained that sacralization could migrate and attach itself to new things – not to God but the person – but that nothing was lost of the religious source: 'religious or cultural traditions may therefore discover new areas of common ground without abandoning their unique perspectives' (Joas 2013: 7). In fact, Joas seemed to be deeply distrustful of any idea that a belief other than religious belief could motivate the empathy that human rights required.[9]

To sum up, Joas thought that religious individualism was secularized – by which he meant given a rational gloss – in two ways. The first was the admission of natural rights. We have already seen that this could well be a non-Christian's disguise for beliefs about shared human potential which were a long way from the conservatism of cognitive and religious individualism. The second was the translation of the soul into the self. This is certainly an example of rationalization but it did not feature in the sentimental individualism of Paine or anti-slavery. The soul is a step on the road to sentimental individualism in that it represents a belief about human beings, albeit one that is inextricably tied up with the other religious beliefs. In sentimental individualism proper, there were beliefs which were neither rationalized nor religious. For example, underpinning the belief in the equal dignity of human beings was a more fundamental belief in universal human feelings. The universality of this belief was certainly new and yet it had nothing to do with either the soul or the rationalized self.

Imagine individualism as a tidal wave washing over a whole culture as prosperity became more widespread, having different effects, at different times, in different elements of that culture. Although the wave did not break over some parts of the culture for another 400 years, individualism impacted on religion from the Reformation onwards (Ramirez 1999). Beginning first with Protestantism, individualism made believers responsible for their own relationship with God and for the fate of their souls (Mathias 2013). From this point, it mattered that Christians had a soul and that life was a gift and that Christians had duties towards others: small wonder that good works, including evangelizing, were high on the agenda of individuals. As we learned in Chapter 1, following the duties of your given role was no longer enough since you, the individual, had become accountable. For Joas, this much is all we need to explain the motivations of the leading anti-slavery campaigners, including Tom Paine who was so influenced by his Quaker background. On the other hand, Hochschild's argument that leaders' motives were not the same as those of the rank and file is persuasive and it applies as much to subsequent movements, for example those against child labour, as to anti-slavery.

The people who made anti-slavery a mass movement were drawn from the same section of the population that so admired Paine. Claeys points out that Paine's unparalleled influence was felt in a society in which Christianity legitimized rather than challenged inequality: 'the natural, God-given inequality of men and property was repeatedly taught from pulpit and hustings and probably not hitherto widely doubted anywhere' (Claeys 1989: 125). When we look for a British mass movement in which the rank and file were all of one mind with Christian evangelical leaders like Wilberforce or Shaftesbury, we should look instead to the voluntary sector in the second half of the nineteenth century. At the zenith of the golden age of Christian evangelism and voluntary work, many more women were working in the British voluntary sector than in the cotton industry. They were, however, generally far more prosperous activists than their counterparts in the anti-slavery movement (Wolf 2013). The leading historian of this immense voluntary effort, Frank Prochaska, argued strongly that it was the fruit of Christian individualism: a belief that Christian duty required that believers work together to put the less fortunate individuals in society in a position to live the same moral life that their benefactors were attempting to live (Prochaska 2006). Here, then, was a mass movement which appealed to deeply-felt longings and helped a particular kind of person to make sense of their lives.

Religion did provide much of the motivation for the leaders of British human rights campaigns from anti-slavery to child labour to unilateral nuclear disarmament, but this does not explain why these campaigns became broad social movements. Hochschild was right that the foot-soldiers were crucial to the success of anti-slavery and it was not always religion that made them feel morally bound to campaign for other human beings on another continent. In *The Rights of Man*, Paine explained that nature had given all of us a 'love of society' which acted throughout our lives (Claeys 1989: 76). We could not be happy without the company of others, yet this did not guarantee universal empathy. His proto-welfare state proposals would save '[t]he hearts of the humane ... [being] shocked by ragged and hungry children, and persons of seventy and eighty years of age, begging for bread', but not everyone was humane. The rich and privileged of Britain (and Turkey and Russia) were condemned by their ignorance of the fate of their fellow human beings to be inhumane, to 'speak and feel for yourselves alone' (Paine [1792]2014: 341). From this, it is obvious that Paine thought the belief in the feelings of others, even those far beneath us on the social scale, required a kind of evangelism in their own right. There were far too many inhumane people who did not take the feelings of other human beings seriously and it was the job of campaigners like himself to proselytize the belief in those feelings.

It is the effect of the tidal wave of individualism on this sentimental way of making sense that constitutes the secret of human rights. The result of its impact is that we do not 'feel for yourselves alone': we think of ourselves as feeling individuals and assume others must also feel and so extend our feelings to cover their experience. The motivation for the empathy discussed by Hochschild and Joas need not derive from the religious duty entailed by a belief in God but from the duty to uphold the dignity of others which is entailed in a belief that other humans feel as we do. The creation of this obligation is possible because our sense-making includes a further, non-religious, route for elaborating moral principles in a way that is not possible within cognition.

The effect of individualism on sentimental sense-making was not evident until the nineteenth century. In earlier centuries, this form of sense-making usually assumed that human feelings were not universal and this led to the elaboration of moralities which allowed different duties for elites, for example duties deriving from the noble sensibilities they alone possessed. There was no duty to respect the dignity of slaves or women in ancient Greece any more than there was to respect the dignity of commoners in feudal Europe. The arrival of individualism meant it was now possible to believe in the nobility of all human beings. This was synonymous with creating a new first cause for sense-making and universal human sentiment could now sit alongside God and human nature (and nature itself). It worked in just the same way as Joas described for religious belief: 'it allows believers to dedicate themselves to the dignity of all people and to take the risky step of participating in creative processes that depend on such belief' (Joas 2013: 170). The new first cause spawned a morality that consisted not in following religious precept but in behaving in a way that took account of the feelings of others, most often expressed as respecting human dignity.

In the dissemination of this morality of sentimental individualism, sentimental language played a key role. Joas is quite right to point to the importance of 'subjective self-evidence and affective intensity' (2013: 2–3) to the genealogy of human rights since sentimental individualism created social movements by moving people's feelings. This was attested to by the prose of Southey, Dickens, Kingsley and many others, which we often recognize as characteristic of the 'sentimental turn' of the nineteenth century. Again, Joas (2013: 60) is heading in the right direction when he mentions Lyn Hunt's theory that the expansion of empathy was fuelled by the development of art.

CONCLUSION

We must not forget that, as well as religious and sentimental individualism, the period in history discussed in this chapter also featured the development of the ideas of cognitive individualism which will play an increasingly important part in the story this book has to tell. Despite the earlier remarks about the incompatibility of Tom Paine's anti-slavery and cognitive individualism, cognition played a role in human rights, albeit a subsidiary one. The discourse of human rights had to be translated into the language of cognitive individualism in order to produce human rights instruments. For sociologists who find the sacralization idea useful, these instruments were a 'rational-legal means of protecting and empowering the "sacred" in modern society' and they only began to proliferate in relatively recent times (Elliott 2007: 352–5).

In later chapters, we will see how cognitive individualism eventually prepared the ground for neoliberalism and the virtual eclipse of both moral individualisms (religious and sentimental). At the same time, the potential for new social movements was steadily eroded because of the conservative potential of cognitive individualism discussed earlier. For example, once human rights instruments were in place they were treated as part of the knowledge base from which cognitive individualism was drawn. Thus, people might be thought to behave as they did because they had particular rights; they might, for example, abuse those rights and want special treatment, placing their self-interest over the interests of others. Arguments like this began to appear in the second half of the nineteenth century, for example in the writings of Herbert Spencer (see Chapters 6 and 7) but, up to this point, seeing how cognition was subservient to both types of moral individualism helps us overcome some contradictions in the literature on anti-slavery.

Adam Hochschild gave us an example of an account of human-rights campaigns which paid little or no attention to the generation of new moral principles. Attention was concentrated on how campaigners went about persuading others that something was wrong and reforms were needed. Why campaigners bothered, and others listened, was of secondary importance, however this neglect created contradictions in the account of history being offered. The only way to resolve them was to find out where moral individualism originated and why it had such wide appeal. The solution offered by Joas was convincing in neither respect. His conception of moral individualism could not chime with the deeply-felt inchoate longings of so many ordinary people, but sentimental individualism – with its new ideas of equal respect for human dignity – certainly could. We must not confuse this sentimental individualism with the product of Enlightenment rationality. Cognition only came into play when moral individualism had to be put into practice with rational-legal instruments. This was how sentimental individualism was prepared for translation into cognitive individualism, and not how religious individualism was rationalized.

NOTES

1. Spicker (2013) refers to this as 'substantive individualism'.
2. Although Claeys (1989: 197) saw a shift in Paine's later work, particularly in Agrarian Justice which was part of a transition to a more secular natural law theory.

3. 'During his life, his writings were read by more men and women than any other political author in history' (Claeys, 1989: 1), the success of *The Rights of Man* was 'unparalleled in the history of the printed word' (Claeys 1989: 111) and for a time it seemed as if 'a single book might revolutionize an entire society' (Claeys, 1989: 115).
4. In 1790 only 5% of the population of England and Wales could vote (Claeys 1989: 7).
5. For example, see Richard Oastler's 1830 and 1831 letters to the press, 'Yorkshire Slavery' and 'Slavery in Yorkshire' in Ward (1970: 76–9).
6. Joas (2013: 63, 91) also approved of American historian, Thomas Haskell, who argued that the growth of international capitalism also gave people the opportunity and the duty to do something about their moral concerns.
7. 'The historical codification of human rights was, of course, generally affected by the opportunistic and strategic considerations of social actors, by constellations of power, and by structures of opportunity' (Joas 2013: 25).
8. In his debate with Durkheim, Joas (2013: 53–4, 64) seems not to have taken into account the possibility that Durkheim had in mind a non-religious category of belief. Whereas he insisted that Durkheim was thinking of a religion of human rights, I argue that Durkheim's definition of religion included the sentimental sense-making I have described here.
9. In part, this stemmed from an idea Joas adapted from James about religious faith being an appreciation of reality that did not involve believing in particular propositions (Joas 2013: 55, 170, 177).

3. Adam Smith and American individualism

Can the USA and the UK really be treated as equally important to anti-slavery and other examples of human rights campaigns in the way Hans Joas suggests? Chapter 2 certainly suggested that human rights did not owe as much to American Protestantism as he contended. This chapter discusses the idea that the combination of ideas drawn from religious, sentimental and cognitive individualism – their relative import-ance and the degree to which one strand influences the other – are of primary importance in the trajectories of polities, societies and econ-omies. The USA was not wholly lacking in sentimental individualism but the mixture of individualist ideas that developed there did not have the same explosive effect documented in British anti-slavery, for example.

INDIVIDUALISM DIVIDED

Lukes (1973) was hardly being controversial when – writing a few years before neoliberalism began its take-over – he sharply distinguished the individualisms of the USA and the UK. In nineteenth-century Britain, the ideas which underpinned equality and freedom – respect for human dignity, autonomy, privacy and self-development – were stronger.[1] In the USA, the dominant strand of individualism was associated with classical liberalism and its emphasis on the right to property and to make a living as one chooses, free-thinking, self-help, minimal government and tax-ation, and free trade. What caused this difference was that, in the USA, cognition filled the gaps in understanding (and law and policy) that sentimental individualism occupied more fully in the UK. The best evidence of this divided individualism was the way in which the UK abolished both the trade in slaves and slavery itself, some decades before the USA.

This suggestion is more controversial than Lukes's analysis of indi-vidualism: Joas (2013), for one, argued that American Protestantism played a key role in the genealogy of human rights. Yet, we know the leaders of anti-slavery were inspired by evangelical and Quaker ideas (and in Paine's case, Deism) and this is not quite the American religious influence Joas had in mind. In fact, far from American Protestantism inspiring anti-slavery across the Atlantic, we might conclude that it was only the success of sentimental individualism in the UK that, decades later, crossed the Atlantic to give the USA the impetus it needed to finally catch up with British progress on human rights. Hochschild (2005) was well aware that the British influence was decisive, however we know from the previous chapter how little he thought the success of British anti-slavery had to do with sentimental individualism.

He thought the reasons were more straightforward, for example the UK had the good fortune to have given birth to the first radical social movement with the requisite organization, investigative techniques and public relations acumen. The UK was also further away from the places where slaves were put to work and did not have to worry about secession and civil war. The USA, on the other hand, had no first-hand experience of the press gang and felt much *less* impact from the slave rebellions in the Caribbean. There are other minor factors in Hochschild's explanations for the tardiness of American abolition but some of the major reasons are contradictory. Thus, Hochschild celebrated the way the UK gave up slave trading, even though it was more important to British prosperity than any other nation on earth. When it came to slavery in the USA, his argument was reversed: Americans could not give up slavery because they had so much more at stake than the UK.

Americans did finally abolish slavery, of course, but this was not accomplished in the relatively painless way it was in the UK. Even after all the blood had been shed, slavery took a very long time to die – think only of the dismissal and non-enforcement of Section 2 of the Fourteenth Amendment to the Constitution. To determine whether the extreme and protracted pain the USA endured followed from the fact that sentimental individualism had so little hold in the USA, we need to discuss another example. We need a human rights case where the ad hoc reasons given by Hochschild for American tardiness were less likely to apply. This case has already featured in a supporting role in the previous chapter in the discussion of the legacy of anti-slavery: the abolition of child labour in the UK and the USA.

As with slavery, progress on child labour was more gradual in America than in the UK, even though British progress seemed unbearably slow to many. The 1833 Factory Act, which coincided with the emancipation of slaves in the British Empire, made it illegal for textile factories to employ children under 9 years of age. More laws limiting child labour in factories followed and the last of these, in 1867, made it illegal for factories and workshops to employ children under 8, while those aged

8–13 had to receive at least 10 hours of education a week. These laws could be evaded, however: inspectors could be deceived about children's ages and factory owners did not always feel bound to put aside the 10 hours. Fines for breaches were not large and for employers, and even the families of the children concerned, the risk of a fine might be worth taking given the foregone profits, or income, if children did not work (Nardinelli 1980).

Despite the legislation, Charles Booth reported 58,900 boys and 82,600 girls under 15 employed in textiles and dyeing in 1881. Numbers of children in mining remained stubbornly high: there were 30,400 boys under 15 still employed and 500 girls under 15 (Tuttle 2001). Compulsory education was recommended as a solution to child labour by the 1876 Royal Commission on the Factory Acts and the 1880 Education Act made school attendance compulsory between the ages of five and ten. The 1891 Assisted Education Act provided state funding so schools would no longer charge fees. All the same, by the early 1890s 18 per cent of 5–10 year olds were not attending, with loss of income being seen as a major reason for truancy. Many children also worked outside school hours, perhaps 300,000 in 1901 (Read 1994). On the other hand, when the British compulsory school-leaving age was raised to 14 in 1918, there remained at least a million 10 to 15 year olds (8.5 per cent of the cohort) at work across the Atlantic in the USA.

According to Hindman (2002), the historian of child labour, the abolition of slavery should be considered the first child labour reform in the USA. Further reform did not take place for several decades, while the amount of visible child labour in factories and mines (as opposed to farms) increased with later (than the UK) American industrialization. The count of 1 million 10 to 14-year-old child labourers in the 1920 census would have been even higher if it had included all the children under 10 who were working, the children in (mostly seasonal) agriculture (the census was taken in January), other seasonal work, industrial homework and vacation work. Moreover, after the 1920 census 'child labor increased as a result of the withdrawal of the last federal child labor law – all industrial statistics show an increase' (Hindman 2002: 75). Opposition to child labour legislation came from proponents of the rights of individual states as well as laissez-faire capitalism.

The American equivalent to the nineteenth-century British crusade against child labour was concentrated in the short-lived Progressive era. Moreover, Hindman (2002) suggested that eventual reform was a less effective deterrent than the Depression which made adult labour available at whatever rate employers were willing to pay. Employers were also under pressure to improve productivity because of minimum-wage regulation and limitations on hours. Historians and economists have argued about the extent to which child labour legislation in any country has trumped economics, but it is not obvious why economics would explain the demise of child labour in the UK while it remained so robust in the USA. The weakness of sentimental individualism in the USA helps to explain not only why American legislation appeared at such a late hour, but also why (as with slavery) attempts to restrict child labour were flouted more often in the USA than the UK.

The familiar photographs Lewis Hine took of American child labourers played a similar role to the techniques the abolitionists had used to lay the facts of slavery before the public, but American equivalents to the sentimental case against slavery made by Southey, Dickens, Kingsley and others were in short supply. According to Hindman, the 'Declaration of Dependence by the Children of America in Mines and Factories and Workshops Assembled', did not appear until 1913 or perhaps a little earlier and Hindman concluded:

> While it expressed sentiments that had been gradually emerging and coalescing since the post-Civil War industrialization boom, it could not have been written at the time of the Civil War (at least not in the United States) and certainly could not have been written in the eighteenth century – it simply would have made no sense. The child labor problem was not understood, from our colonial period through the Civil War, in the same way that McKelway and early twentieth-century reformers understood it. (Hindman 2002: 45)

Until the National Child Labor Committee came into being in 1904, it was organized labour that made all the running in the American campaign, using arguments that Tom Paine had helped to hone at the end of the eighteenth century. From the earliest days, it was argued that more equal educational opportunities for all future voters were essential to the health of democracy and in 1829 the Workingmen's Party of New York wanted 'a system that shall unite under the same roof the children of the poor man and the rich, the widow's charge and the orphan, where the road to distinction shall be superior industry, virtue and acquirement' (Hindman 2002: 49).

Hindman was determined to exonerate the trade unions from the charge of protectionism, but opponents could easily turn union support of child welfare into a handicap for the campaign because it could be presented as market interference. For this reason, the trade unions kept in the background and allowed the lead to be taken by 'federations of women's clubs, church organizations, and, when they were established, state child labor committees' (Hindman 2002: 50). In order to understand why it was essential that the movement against child labour should avoid visible contamination with collective responses to inequality such as trade unions, we need to grasp how American cognitive individualism understood the only source of prosperity as the division of labour.

Thus far, this chapter has shown how the weakness of sentimental sense-making explained the American failure to make progress on human rights but this weakness did not create a vacuum in US society. The space that sentimental individualism might have occupied was filled by a system of ideas also developed in the UK (Grampp 1965; McCoy 1980; McNamara 1998). These ideas provided the foundations for American cognitive individualism, including the idea that the division of labour was the source of all prosperity. The different ways of earning a living which it created brought unequal rewards and the market was the only way in which people could be assigned to these different roles without diminishing overall prosperity. Inequality was the price that had to be paid for prosperity. There was no possibility of ameliorating inequality with collective interference because this would prevent the market operating efficiently and would therefore damage prosperity. Before they became the 'economic realities' of American cognitive individualism, these ideas were first articulated by Adam Smith, but this was not the only, or even the first, theory this Scottish philosopher and political economist developed.

Anglo-American differences in the trajectory of campaigns against anti-slavery and child labour can be traced to differences in the mixture of religious, sentimental and cognitive individualism in the two countries. It would, however, be a mistake to assume that this difference always meant the USA was slow to act. Over the next three chapters, I will show that the USA was actually much quicker than the UK to put in place the kind of schooling that we now expect of a modern country. In the field of education, the way that sentimental individualism exploded in the UK proved something of a handicap. Partly because of its success and vehemence, indeed its virulent potential to build powerful social movements, British elites were galvanized into opposing anything that looked like universal education which might benefit the working class. The relative weakness of sentimental individualism made American individualism a much less combustible mixture and this helped to bring in earlier education reforms, sometimes a full century before the UK. For all that he was a Scot, the works of Adam Smith offer the best insight into this American individualism, but by this I do not mean the popular neoliberal version of Adam Smith that reduces his thought to nostrums and clichés. Such wilful misreading of Smith has been going on long enough – for example, Smith was 'bitterly opposed to slavery' yet, with judicious abridgement, the defenders of slavery claimed his later theories supported their arguments (Fleischacker 2013: 493; also see Sen 2013). Smith however provides the best account of the way sentimental and cognitive individualism fitted together in the USA – or shall we say the North and East of the USA – for the greater part of the nineteenth century before America's late industrialization began to take effect.

THE THEORY OF MORAL SENTIMENTS

One scholar has called Smith's *The Theory of Moral Sentiments* (*TMS*) ([1759]1976) 'the fundamental text for Smith's analysis of the experience of the modern individual; the book where Smith lays out his "theory of the subject" under capitalism' (Harkin 2013: 514). It is Smith's views on the utility of self-interest that are most frequently used, and abused, by later generations. In *TMS* Smith acknowledged the influence of self-interest on human behaviour and he was not at all convinced that self-interest was identical with morality or even with rising prosperity. Indeed, he was consistently sceptical that chasing riches (or fame) could make us happy and moralized about the small minds of those with an attachment to comfort (Fricke 2013; Hanley 2013; Tegos 2013). Along with regretting our abiding admiration for the rich and famous (who were themselves increasingly prone to egoism), Smith bemoaned the way people admired and respected authority and loved to dominate each other (Kelly 2013). He believed the most dangerous risk of intemperance came from thirsting after esteem and that our self-interest was better served by being content with our lot (Hanley 2013). Smith did not follow the stoics in saying happiness was maintaining tranquillity, no matter how much suffering we endured, but he did think that being comfortable ought to be enough and it was how we reacted to inequality that made us miserable. While we should put an end to grinding poverty, exaggerating 'the difference that more goods or a higher social status makes to one's happiness is, for Smith, a great moral mistake and the source of much unhappiness' (Fleischacker 2013: 493).

In *TMS* Smith moralized about two flawed character types which later featured in nineteenth-century fiction, most notably in Charles Dickens' great works of sentimental individualist propaganda. Smith would have recognized James Harthouse in *Hard Times* whose indolence and cynicism left him only enough energy to pursue his own pleasure; and he sketched the character of the protagonist of *The Christmas Carol* a century before Dickens brought to life Ebenezer Scrooge, a man so concerned to escape poverty that his worldly cares eclipse any opportunity for happiness. Smith's moral was that we have to keep our self-interest in check for our own piece of mind (Hanley 2013).

While Smith believed that inequality would be more bearable if people did not allow it to disturb their own equanimity, he subscribed to a 'moral egalitarianism' which informed his abolitionism and his long-standing concern with justice (Fleischacker 2013: 486; Griswold 1998). He argued that moral behaviour depends on believing other people have feelings, or *sentiments*, and believing that the sentiments of each individual are of equal value.[2] This summary of the starting point of *TMS* would be equally useful in an encyclopaedia entry for sentimental individualism. Before we explore the implications of this theory for equality, we need to be convinced that it was belief, rather than knowledge, that lay at the core of the theory.

For Smith, any moral theory had first to recognize that we have no way of knowing the minds of others in order to determine the nature and validity of their feelings. To explain how this obstacle could be overcome by human belief, Smith invented an impartial spectator to show how we made the journey into the minds of others through acts of faith. Like us, the imaginary observer only has access to the outward show of feelings made by other individuals. This may be a poor guide to what those individuals actually feel but the impartial spectator also has access to knowledge that no real person can possess. Since they are not a real individual with their own prejudices, preconceptions and peculiar view of the world, the impartial observer is able to judge what sentiments would be *appropriate in any situation* (Fleischacker 2013: 487). They can then judge not only that a child labourer is quite right to feel miserable but that a happy slave is merely making the best of an awful situation or that the complaints of a university don who claims to have too much work should not be taken seriously.

Now of course these are not judgements that we would shrink from but we do not make them with the knowledge of the impartial observer about what sentiments really are appropriate in any situation. We make our human judgements by *believing* the slave is being stoical and *believing* the don is whingeing. The device of the impartial observer teaches us that morality depends on our belief in the reality of other people's feelings but it also teaches us that this belief is fundamentally egalitarian. When we seek to walk in the shoes of others, we cannot vary our beliefs about their feelings according to our prejudices and preconceptions about the differences between one individual and another. We cannot, for example, say that the feelings of the slave are less civilized, or refined, and that this is why s/he is better able to bear indignity and pain. Nor can we say the finer feelings of university professors make their complaints both understandable and just.

Smith's theory does not allow us to vary our beliefs according to the individual we are judging because we have, at all times, to do our best to judge people as the impartial spectator would and the impartial spectator is imagined in such a way that they cannot make such distinctions between individuals. If our moral behaviour depends, as Smith says it does, on our behaving like the impartial spectator, then it depends on our treating all individuals as capable of the same feelings (Fleischacker 2013). Given the centrality of belief in feelings, this is certainly a sentimental philosophy but what makes it sentimental *individualism*?

In answering this question, we can also see how individualism is integral to Smith's 'moral egalitarianism'. Why would entering into other people's minds be the foundation of our morality if there was not a prior commitment to the reality of these individuals (Fleischacker 2013)? Why would we even care to walk in another's shoes unless we were committed to the equal worth of each individual as an individual? It is nothing they have done that makes them of equal worth, nothing they have suffered, but only their status as another individual. It is this that makes them the object of our concern and, again, it cannot help but be a fundamentally egalitarian concern.

This point comes through loud and clear in the secondary scholarship on *TMS*. Even if we are only thinking about the small morality of propriety – what people like us do – this is done by reference to a community of individuals in which each has equal standing (Fleischacker 2013; Hanley 2013). Adam Smith scholars point to the way in which he shows us how behaving morally means realizing that we are no better than anyone else: 'We learn "the real littleness of ourselves" when we occupy the moral standpoint, Smith says, and he uses similar language over and over to assert that our greatest moral mistakes come when we try to assert superiority over other people' (Fleischacker 2013: 488). Smith also explains how sentimental individualism produces our sense of injustice when any individual (including ourselves) is disrespected. We feel the resentment that fuels the sense of injustice because

> even where the material harm done is slight, an act of injustice suggests that the victim is somehow less worthy than the agent, and thereby constitutes an important symbolic harm. The anger that boils out of the passage indeed captures wonderfully how we feel when another person seems to imagine that we 'may be sacrificed at any time, to his conveniency or his humour'. (Fleischacker 2013: 488)

Of course, Smith's sentimental individualism did not depend on all individuals having identical capacities or being similarly good persons. This is already recognized in the necessity to judge the stoical slave and the lazy academic, but what did the morality of his sentimental individualism imply for policy, say on the distribution of wealth? According to Fleischacker, 'it is difficult to see how great inequalities in goods can be justified if human equality is our basic norm' and Smith's views anticipated 'a more radical socio-economic egalitarianism' (Fleischacker 2013: 489, 498). In Smith's day, 'most people held that poor people should be *kept poor*' and the implications of Smith's thought for both civil and political equality, and socio-economic inequality, had to wait for society to catch up (2013: 499). Fleischacker turned to *The Wealth of Nations* (*WN*) to find evidence that Smith saw the potential for government to take the side of those with the least power, including slaves and workers in dispute with their employers. His fears that this potential might not be fulfilled were certainly borne out by the history described in the previous chapter.

THE WEALTH OF NATIONS

It was not from *TMS* that American cognitive individualism developed the awareness of economic realities that helped to delay abolition (and foment civil war) and preserve child labour in the USA until well into the last century. Knowledge of these realities certainly owed a lot to the writings of Adam Smith but their source was his treatise on political economy, *WN*, published in 1776, 15 years before *The Rights of Man*. It was from this work that people learned that collective attempts to challenge market realities were doomed to fail and perhaps backfire, as unintended consequences took their toll. It was, however, the *combination* of sentimental and cognitive individualism laid out in *TMS* and *WN* that John Dewey would recognize in a golden age of American individualism (see Chapter 8). Looking back from the onset of the Great Depression, Dewey had no doubt that this was an 'economic individualism', even the 'rugged individualism' of American myth, but it was nevertheless profoundly moral in a way that its successor was not. In later chapters, we will find that the change Dewey lamented was in part the consequence of American cognitive individualism leaving behind some of the ideas of *WN*, as well as the moral philosophy of *TMS*. Both forms of abridgement were necessary to prepare the ground for neoliberalism.[3]

Over time, the popularity of the idea that inequality was the unavoidable consequence of economic realities made the USA more receptive to the idea that there were variations in human nature that meant some people were better suited to the best jobs in the division of labour than others. This prepared the ground for the ideas of another British thinker, Herbert Spencer, discussed in Chapters 6 and 7, where it is explained how American individualism learned to combine the idea of talent winning out through individual competition with the notion that nothing could be done to prevent those with privileges using them to get ahead. This may seem a contradictory combination but American cognitive individualism proved itself well able to accommodate the tension between these two ideas. There was, however, no such tension in *WN* because it featured 'a running argument' that the division of labour neither reflected nor utilized natural differences in talent (Fleischacker 2013: 490).

In part, this argument stemmed from Smith's view that such differences were small but what Smith knew about the way people were assigned to places in the division of labour also suggested that differences in talent played little or no part in making people unequal. He introduced the division of labour without seeing the need to mention differences in capabilities to explain it and when, later in *WN*, he referred to these differences it was to explain that they were caused by the differences in training people had in preparation for taking up their role in the division of labour (Fleischacker 2013). Smith wrote that what appeared to be natural differences in talent arose from 'habit, custom and education' (Smith [1776]2005: 20–21) and, in any case, these differences in capabilities had little to do with inequality which was mainly the result of the interplay of the division of labour, self-interest and luck.[4]

Neoliberalism urged governments to prioritize education and training as a panacea for economic success since the division of labour was constantly changing, requiring not only different skills to the ones provided by basic education but skills that were higher and more complex. Once again, this is in stark contradiction to the arguments of *WN*. Smith held that the division of labour was the main reason for inequality but he did not talk about increasing demands for many and varied skills (Smith [1776]2005: 638–9). He thought that in the more advanced societies, like his own, very little skill, knowledge and judgement were required in people's work, which usually consisted of one or two operations with very predictable outcomes. Other societies would soon follow suit because, as they became more complex, societies always tended to create more and more different tasks in which workers had to exercise fewer and fewer skills. This specialization and simplification might be the result of mechanization but, with or without new machines, all the varied skills needed to keep body and soul together were distributed into these separate, undemanding jobs (Aspromourgos 2013). Most work was, or soon would be, concentrated in these, with a smaller number of tradesmen and professionals still able to exercise specialist skills.

Smith would have thought the neoliberal creed which demands individuals and governments recognize the need for continual re-skilling, in order to meet the changing demands of the division of labour, entirely unhelpful, and not only if it involved public expense. In his own day, he had a ready example in apprenticeships of the futility of equipping people with supernumerary skills. Requiring apprenticeships for entry to a trade limited the supply of labour and therefore kept wages higher but exaggerated the quantity of real investment in skills which the training represented. Since the vast mass of jobs did 'not require extraordinary dexterity and skill', the existing pattern of training was no proof that so much training was required and that such skill was difficult to acquire (Smith [1776]2005: 88). Most apprenticeships were far too long and should be replaced with practice and training on the job, with transparent incentives to encourage workers to learn their trades. The result would be that the masters would lose the apprentices' free labour and face more competition. The journeymen would also have new competition but general prosperity would increase ([1776]2005: 107).

In Smith's view, it was impossible to flout the division of labour in the way that apprenticeships did without reducing prosperity overall. What he had to say about women furnishes a particularly stark example of the brutal implications of this economic realism. Women from sufficiently prosperous families (ones that did not require their earnings) should prepare themselves for the only role in the division of labour they could fill.[5] Their goal was a good marriage and appropriate preparation involved improving their beauty and making sure they acquired the virtues of reserve, modesty, chastity and economy that would make them well-behaved mistresses of a family (Smith [1776]2005: 636–7). Women might be capable of anything of which men were capable, but what was the point in them acquiring further capacities when they had no place in the division of labour in which to exercise them?

Like women, children from poorer families would never get the chance to demonstrate their equal potential. Parents had the division of labour, sexual and otherwise, in mind when they prepared their children for the world. Once children were 6 or 8 years old, the society of Smith's time started to prepare children differently for the place in the division of labour suited to their station, and now the differences (though greatly exaggerated by many commentators) started to appear – but as a consequence of the division of labour rather than as its cause (Aspromourgos 2013; Smith [1776]2005: 20). Smith said that parents who could afford to prepare their children for the better-paid places in the division of labour did so from this age. It might look as if the children's different talents were winning through, but it was actually distinction and difference being manufactured because the division of labour encouraged it. Privilege started here: it not only looked as if some children were more talented than others, but the children of the less well-off seemed to be capable of only the most simple tasks.

A veil was thrown over the reproduction of privilege because those who could afford to pay for it got the education and training which then gave them access to the jobs with the most specialist skills. Smith therefore thought inequality resulted from people investing in its perpetuation because it was in their self-interest. For everyone else, self-interest entailed accepting the simple jobs in which their potential would remain undeveloped and their labours poorly rewarded. What made the minority so different was that they had enough spare resources to be able to invest in developing the potential of their offspring, but self-interest meant that in order for this to pay off they had to get access to the better-paying jobs. Smith compared people to expensive machinery.[6] Time and effort spent in education was like building a machine with an expectation of 'at least the ordinary profits of an equally valuable capital' 'in a reasonable time'. Of course, such calculations were unnecessary for most people since they could not hope to access 'any of those employments which require extraordinary dexterity and skill' (Smith [1776]2005: 88).

If the appearance of inequality in people's skills and talents merely reflected differences in the amount of money parents had to invest in their offspring, could the veil be torn away by providing education at public expense? As an egalitarian, Smith would be obliged to consider this possibility but he did not think it would succeed because allowing people to access education and training at no (financial) cost to themselves would mean many more people would acquire the necessary skills and the supply of those skills would exceed the demand. The premium that once paid for the private investment in education and training would no longer be paid and wages would drop through the floor. Those who were trying to pass on privilege would then look elsewhere for a way to invest in their offspring. In Smith's society, there was ample proof of this in every parish since most training of the clergy was done at public expense. Individuals were only investing time, and not money, in training for the clergy so people flocked to the occupation. In consequence, many were less well paid than such time in, and effort on, training would imply. If they had been educated at their own expense, there would have been less competition and the rewards to investment would have followed. If doctors and lawyers were educated at public expense, the lower barrier to entry would soon reduce wages in those occupations as well and soon only those who were educated that way would enter these occupations (Smith [1776]2005: 113–14).

Smith thought that putting in your own time was not enough to get access to the best opportunities the division of labour had to offer. Moreover, spending your own money was the only way you could guarantee that the education or training that was provided was any good. Not only did public education flood the market with too many qualified people, but it also took away the link between spending money on education and deriving an income from education. Wherever this link was weakened, education would be bound to make a very bad job of preparing people for employment. Smith's primary example here was the education of gentlemen in which their parents paid for them to go to public school or university rather than paying a teacher directly to deliver a particular capability. This meant that the people who taught their sons had no incentive to deliver the education and training needed to realize their potential. Rivalry and competition between people who depended on doing well to get paid showed in the care and precision with which they carried out their work. It would be better if self-interest and duty were aligned. If people were paid to do something whether they delivered it or not, they did not deliver it; or, if they were forced to, they did it badly (Smith [1776]2005: 620–22).

Smith contended that when there was no public education you got the best teaching: fencing or dancing schools for young men were his examples. There was public education for the three Rs but it was more commonly done by private schools so he claimed that was why there was so little illiteracy or innumeracy (Smith [1776]2005: 625). Once more, it was a different story for women from well-off families since there was no public education for them and therefore 'nothing useless, absurd, or fantastical, in the common course of their education' ([1776]2005: 636–7). A woman's fortune was in her private education but that education would be wasted if it taught her to think for herself or seek autonomy. In this section, we have seen a little more of the reasoning that lay behind the economic reality that American cognitive individualism inscribed in stone: the market would have its revenge on any misguided attempt to pursue equality. If sentimental individualism prompted recourse to a collective solution like public education, it was sure to backfire on those it aimed to help, but how did Smith plot an escape from these brutal economic realities?

UTILITY AND VIRTUE

Smith thought that some inequality was inescapable as long as the goal was prosperity but he did not think inequality was morally justified and he was far from averse to sacrificing prosperity for moral ends (Aspromourgos 2013). Yet, is it not true that the best-known passage of *WN* claims that we owe our prosperity to people's self-interest and there is more morality in that self-interest than any amount of state interference or do-gooding (especially the kind that requires taxation)? A brief exegesis of that passage will solve the conundrum.

When he claimed it was 'not from the benevolence of the butcher, the brewer, or the baker that we expect our dinner, but from their regard to their own interest', Smith was explaining how the division of labour first arose (Smith [1776]2005: 19; also see Sen 2013). He was seeking to dissuade us that the development of the division of labour was planned and, instead, that it happened because of the human preference for exchange which was a good way of getting what we wanted, and certainly more reliable than begging favours. Our wants grew as society developed and we very soon reached a point at which subsisting and accumulating could only be managed by exchanging what we could produce ourselves for what we could not, and so the division of labour expanded.

The famous passage showed why the division of labour increased but, as we know from the previous section of this chapter, the advance of the division of labour meant that there was increasing inequality between the mass of routine jobs and the surviving trades and professions. In this sense, then, inequality was an unavoidable product of rising prosperity, however at the point in history Smith occupied, self-interested behaviour was exacerbating inequality. These stimuli to inequality had nothing to do with advancing the division of labour and often served to retard it. This was happening, for example, when self-interest drove masters and apprentices to try to hang on to the training required by an older division of labour, when the Catholic hierarchy was rewarded with both riches and prestige and when rich fathers bought their sons jobs in the professions.

Some of this could successfully be addressed with public policy and some of it could not, but no fair reading of Smith would allow us to conclude he thought that inequality was morally justified (Heath 2013). However, moral issues did not simply arise from injustice in the way inequality was achieved. Inequality of any kind – including the inequality which necessarily followed the advance of the division of labour – had moral consequences. The danger to our happiness came not only from thirsting after riches, and admiring people for their wealth or fame, but also from becoming blind to the lives of others (Rasmussen 2013).

An extreme division of labour was a threat to our capacity to believe in the feelings of others. Massive inequality would make it more and more difficult to imagine what it was like to walk in other people's shoes. The impartial spectator would become nothing more than an empty thought experiment since no actual person could ever hope to judge the feelings of someone at the other end of the division of labour. An extreme division of labour thus made it more feasible to vary our beliefs about other people's feelings according to our prejudices and preconceptions about the differences between one individual and another. Since their lives were so different to our own, we could easily believe the feelings of the poor and destitute were less developed and that they were somehow better equipped to endure privation than we would be. Not only would we be less inclined to feel compassion, we might not even treat them with common courtesy, they may become less than fully human and the quality of our interactions with others impoverished, and we may be amiable and sociable only with those of our own station (Boyd 2013). In sum, an extreme division of labour was a danger to the equality of individuals which Smith placed at the core of his moral theory.

Commercial society could put such 'irregularities' in people's moral sentiments to good ends, for instance thinking riches would make us happy increased our productivity and admiring the rich kept social order (Campbell 2013). It would, however, be a mistake to think that Smith argued that unbridled self-interest was necessary to maximize utility or even thought that utility was always paramount (Hanley 2013). In the decades after *WN* was published, cognitive individualism was able to reach quite different conclusions because it could draw on a theory which insisted that knowledge of self-interest and utility was all that was required to make moral decisions. Jeremy Bentham's *An Introduction to the Principles of Morals and Legislation* appeared in 1789, 13 years after *WN*, and set out some of the principles that would eventually be used to bowdlerize Smith.[7] If cognitive individualism incorporated Bentham and the political philosophy of utilitarianism, it could argue that the satisfaction of self-interest (usually described as maximizing happiness) was the only source of morality. Satisfying self-interest was usually achieved by maximizing prosperity so, if that entailed inequality, this was not only inescapable but it was moral too.

Smith certainly did make utilitarian calculations, indeed on several occasions in *WN* he referred to utility to decide whether equality might be increased at the same time as prosperity. Thus, it was bad for general prosperity when people raised entry barriers for a trade (for tradesmen or employers), prevented the free movement of labour or got away with as little (or as bad) work as they could. These and similar acts of unwelcome self-interest happened all the time. Just as Bentham might have done, Smith was prepared to frustrate them for the sake of the general good. In this case, Smith argued that the principal way to frustrate self-interest was to get rid of policies which provided protection for this kind of behaviour and increase exposure to the market. His prescription differed from the laissez-faire idea that all regulation should be removed in order to give free rein to self-interest, and Smith actually proposed the regulation of incomes where inequality was clearly tractable and could be addressed without damaging prosperity.

An example of tractable inequality could be found in the Catholic hierarchy. Smith considered one of the causes of inequality in pecuniary reward could be found in 'the nature of the employments themselves', including 'the agreeableness or disagreeableness of the employments themselves' (Smith [1776]2005: 87). This was why the 'honourable professions' were underpaid: in them, the promise of honour (even if not always fulfilled) recompensed for the meagre pay. Smith argued that the promise of esteem was sufficient motivation to join the clergy without the aid of the huge pay differentials for the higher-ranking clergy dished out by the Catholic hierarchy. The proof of this was the healthy recruitment of clergy to Protestant churches which had no such extravagant differentials ([1776]2005: 113–14). In this case, Smith was arguing for self-interest to be brought to heel in the cause of prosperity but doing so would also have the effect of increasing equality.

The policy conclusion he drew from this analysis applies beyond his example of the clergy being trained at public expense. Not only does it contradict the doctrine of laissez-faire but it has direct relevance to contemporary justifications for the vast gulf between the pay of CEOs and their employees, including the neoliberal assumption that handsomely-rewarded CEOs are also the most deserving of honour and esteem (Streeck 2014). But, for all that Smith did not advocate giving the greatest freedom to self-interest, all of these examples rely on calculations of utility. In the case of apprenticeships, utilitarians would follow Smith's lead so long as the happiness of the majority who benefitted from their ending (including the public who got cheaper goods and the workers and employers who could now enter the trade) outweighed the happiness of the disappointed apprentices (who would eventually have entered a lucrative trade) and their employers (who were no longer subsidized with cheap labour). The same situation obtained in the case of inequality in the clerical hierarchy. Utilitarians would weigh the self-interest of those who got the higher pay (and those who might get it) against the self-interest of the public. In these cases, the public policy prescriptions of both Smith and Bentham entailed greater equality.

One difference between Smith and Bentham lay in the status given to empirical evidence in their arguments. For Bentham, there was little point in bothering with such evidence since it could be assumed that the self-interest of individuals usually aligned. This might not be the case in respect of religious beliefs – where the happiness of one sect might be bought at the cost of the happiness of another – but the economy was a different case. Smith thought that self-interest in the economy was as likely to be out of alignment as it was in religion. In particular, he found the interest of minorities with a little leverage and some resources very frequently ran counter to the interests of the majority. Because of their methodological individualism, Bentham and the utilitarians assumed that economy could never be a zero-sum game: some individuals benefitted from increased prosperity and others were unaffected or all gained. Examples of individuals satisfying their self-interest at the cost of negating the self-interests of others were all too common in the pages of *WN*, however.

Smith was well aware that the unregulated operation of self-interest tended to produce inequality, but the greatest difference between Smith and Bentham was that Smith did not conclude that the result of the utilitarian calculus would always be the most moral outcome. Let us consider another example of calculating the effect of increasing equality on prosperity but one where Smith seems to have been clear that inequality could not be reduced without diminishing prosperity. Prosperity would not be affected if the sons of the poor could simply swap places with the sons whose rich fathers had (effectively) bought them places in the professions. Yet, the only circumstance in which Smith could see this substitution actually taking place was if training in the professions was subsidized with public money. The resulting increase in labour supply would force down wages, bringing about an overall loss in prosperity when the cost of the training was weighed against equality. In this case, the utilitarian calculus was that not only were the rich worse off, but the poor were no better off and the public was worse off. Yet, what Smith found merely intractable, utilitarianism would also judge to be the most moral outcome. The touchstone for utilitarian public policy was the morality of that policy as judged by the calculation of the satisfaction of individual interests. There was therefore no cause for regret that inequality could not be addressed, no hint that society could be ordered better than that which lingered after the calculation. The way the rich used their power and resources to pass on privilege to their children maximized utility and therefore could not be improved on.

Smith would have disagreed with the idea that his work provided a moral justification for inequality because he did not think that morality consisted in the satisfaction of self-interest, though was he prepared to put morality (e.g. equality) before utility (e.g. prosperity)? To answer this question, we need to think a little more carefully about the relationship between morality and self-interest. Bentham declared that everyone was self-interested and that the motivations of rich and poor were therefore morally equivalent. This idea of equivalence is usually considered an egalitarian move by Bentham, but it prevented him from following Smith in moralizing about the rich who identified their self-interest with the reproduction of privilege. For Bentham, their behaviour would be moral as long as overall utility was maximized. For example, it would only cease to be a moral guide to public policy if the happiness of the fathers was outweighed by the unhappiness of the sons dragooned into the professions, added to that of the unfortunate clients who had to deal with professionals who had no love of their work, and of the more worthy candidates who should have got their positions.

Bentham declared that the only way to judge if the outcome of people's behaviour was moral was to weigh up the total satisfaction achieved by these self-interested individuals. Unfulfilled self-interest was acceptable if total satisfaction was maximized, but the underlying reason why such a calculation was moral was that people could not help being motivated by self-interest. No matter how they chose to delude each other, all human beings were actually motivated by the avoidance of pain and the maximization of pleasure. Bentham insisted that these were facts rather than beliefs and, moreover, they were incontrovertible. We have already seen that Smith, on the other hand, held to some of the beliefs that Bentham would not entertain. In particular, Smith believed in the existence of human virtues and, under certain circumstances, he thought prosperity should be sacrificed to protect or enhance them.

A belief in virtues was all of a piece with the centrality of beliefs about human feelings to Smith's sentimental individualism. The summary of Smith's view of virtue provided by Fricke (2013) identifies two types: the gentle virtues were employed by those who were not too blind to observe the lives of others, while greater virtues governed our impulses and desires. In *TMS* propriety and prudence could be satisfied by ordinary standards and might begin and end with the accumulation of private property, but benevolence could lead us to deny the part of our human nature that desired this property (Hanley 2013). Acquiring these virtues was a lifelong task, and most of us would fall foul of distractions, such as our persistent admiration for the rich and famous, and make do as observers with a received sense of propriety. Making do with 'common rules of morality' and the 'established rules of behaviour' or 'of duty' would suffice and almost everyone would pick up these rules in the course of normal socialization (and moral education) and behave with 'tolerable decency' (Fricke 2013: 195 – the quotations are from *TMS*).

Smith's most rare and perfect virtues involved not only seeing through the empty promise of prosperity but sacrificing personal for public interest (Fricke 2013). In normal cases, however, propriety still came before utility: 'although we might well seek after pleasure and hope to avoid pain, the utility of our action in Smith's terms is irrelevant to our initial moral judgement' (Kelly 2013: 203). For example, when Smith said it was 'the interest of every man to live as much at his ease as he can', he believed many did not choose to maximize their ease because they were virtuous (Smith [1776]2005: 622). Virtue was an end in itself and Smith was a virtue ethicist, defining 'the virtues of the flourishing character and that are most likely to lead to happiness' (Hanley 2013: 222).

Smith saw virtue as an end in itself for individuals which also had utility for society: commercial society required virtues like prudence, integrity, industry, courage, justice and beneficence to function (Hanley 2013). For example in Smith's view, morals were necessary for markets to work properly (Paganelli 2013). If the rich and powerful were corrupt, markets might be impaired or even destroyed. Markets which made people more prosperous might be good for morality because prosperity was better than poverty for moral behaviour;[8] and market institutions enhanced freedom which further enabled morality and impartial judgement. Markets were, however, bad in that they promoted 'wars, interest groups, ignorance and irresponsibility' (Paganelli 2013: 334). In *TMS* Smith described an innate desire for approbation from two sources: moral behaviour and the display of wealth. We were willing to trade off one for the other so the availability of wealth could corrupt morality. Thus, in mercantilism, merchants and manufacturers garnered monopolies, made legislation answer to their special interests and perverted justice. This degenerate form of commercial society caused not only inequality but also mass starvation and the destruction of whole societies (Paganelli 2013).

CONCLUSION

Just as markets could be both good and bad for morality, so morality need not also have utility for society. While people liked praise, they liked deserved praise even more, and being praiseworthy but not caring whether we are recognized was prized above all. Propriety could involve magnanimity, nobility and heroism but concern for earning praise could lead to indifference to others, and a balance between selfishness and benevolence was good for society as well as our own happiness (Hanley 2013). In sum, virtue was independent of utility for individuals and society, and any synergy between them was perhaps best understood in terms of the unintended consequences which figure so prominently in Smith's accounts (Berry 2013; also see Aspromourgos 2013; Tegos 2013). Virtue might sometimes be in our self-interest and sometimes not,[9] sometimes good for prosperity and sometimes good for equality. The question of whether Adam Smith always identified self-interest and virtue is not simply of importance to debates within moral philosophy. When, at the end of the nineteenth century, Americans no longer said, with Smith, that inequality was simply inescapable, but decided it was also moral, the effects on their society were immense.

NOTES

1. Spicker (2013) is right to insist that autonomy is more than the absence of constraint. For example, it entails positive freedoms which give people the rights and capacities to determine their own fates (see Chapter 7). For this reason autonomy is often inextricable from self-development.
2. In contrast to some nineteenth-century campaigners, Smith considered love the least of these feelings (Harkin 2013).
3. I am not implying here that the founding fathers of neoliberalism, such as Friedman or Hayek, were responsible for the misrepresentation of Adam Smith (see Smith 2013).
4. According to Smith ([1776]2005: 116–17), inequalities in income came about because of policy (for example, the Poor Laws) and because of five types of differences in the work people did: whether the work was agreeable, easy or cheap; difficult to learn; secure; required high trust; and offered much prospect of doing well ([1776]2005: 87).
5. Harkin (2013: 503–4) thought Smith was well aware that working-class women had to be employed, yet portrayed an idealized bourgeois family in *WN*.
6. Smith said the fixed capital of society included 'the acquired and useful abilities of all'. They might be costly to acquire but the outlay would be repaid by higher productivity of the individuals and the society in which they dwelt (Smith [1776]2005: 227). Two hundred years later, the two ideas in this statement would be popularized by Theodore Schultz and Gary Becker as 'human capital theory', one of the key concepts of neoliberalism.
7. Craig Smith (2013: 551) allowed for some people putting Smith in the same tradition as Bentham and Spencer, with many, including Hayek, disagreeing. Sen (2013) recalled how Bentham took Smith to task for seeing faults in the market.
8. A view Smith shared with Engels (Bowring and Fevre 2014).
9. Assuming we are not distracted by what Lukes called, with reference to Hobbes and Hume, 'a piece of conceptual legislation prescribing that all ostensible acts of altruism or benevolence are to be redescribed as really self-interested' (Lukes 1973: 99).

4. Inequality, welfare and the cultivation of character

In the last chapter, I suggested that the relative weakness of sentimental individualism in the USA helped to bring earlier educational expansion there. In this chapter and the next, we explore American and British versions of sentimental individualism in some detail. This chapter concentrates on the UK but it begins with the educational proposals made by Adam Smith in *The Wealth of Nations* since they were to prove influential in both countries.

Smith was not content to leave the development of modern society in the hands of the market because the way the division of labour was tending left so much individual potential unrealized. Since the division of labour was sovereign, there was no point in developing this potential for economic reasons since, no matter how well educated people were, they could not do jobs that did not exist. Nevertheless, Smith was concerned about individuals' lack of opportunity for self-development precisely because the division of labour was demanding less and less skill and knowledge. So implacable was the division of labour that an 'essential part of the character of human nature' was 'mutilated and deformed' and he believed something must be done to counter-act the 'gross ignorance and stupidity' it created amongst the mass of the population (Smith [1776]2005: 642).

Smith scholars see the negative effect of the division of labour on dignity as an area in which Smith had a great deal in common with Rousseau and, for some of these scholars, Smith's ideas also provided the foundation for Marx's version of character analysis (Rasmussen 2013). This was not simply a matter of a common opinion of the way the division of labour brutalized character but consisted in the underlying idea that it was the experience of day-to-day living, especially making a living, which determined character (Pack 2013). In this view, Marx and Smith were both materialists who saw morality as determined by time and place, for example by whatever the society in question counted as propriety.

While all of this may be true, it does not negate the argument made in the previous chapter that Smith was committed to sentimental individualism in which moral sensibilities could arise only from believing that other human beings shared our feelings and imagining how others might be feeling as they endured suffering or privation. Smith's sentimental individualism meant attaching moral value to self-development and making this a focus of public policy. Where self-development and autonomy were noticeably absent from Smith's economic realism, he argued for the moral importance of self-development in certain circumstances. These circumstances included an advanced division of labour which did not need most of its population to acquire skills beyond the few acquired through practice doing the one or two simple tasks most people did to make their living. The simplicity of the tasks people performed was as much a problem as the lack of variety: they were not given problems to solve and had no opportunity to put their understanding to the test or think creatively.

As we might expect from the analysis at the end of the previous chapter, Smith ([1776]2005) thought the moral good of self-development might coincide with utilitarian benefits for society as a whole. Where the division of labour was extensive, education was extremely good for society but not worth the while of most individuals to invest in because they would not recoup their costs, still less make a profit. Smith concluded that more public education was needed in more advanced societies because so little skill, knowledge and judgement was required in people's ordinary work that some way must be found to correct the dullness and ignorance this produced (Smith [1776]2005: 638; Tegos 2013). This is more or less the opposite of the neoliberal argument in which education is required to make people a better fit for the advanced division of labour.

Exactly why was education so good for society? What were the great advantages to society that were lost if people were condemned to dullness and ignorance? Smith thought that without education there would be no rational conversation, finer feelings, good judgement in private life, deliberation over public matters or capacity for national defence, and health and wellbeing would be diminished (Smith [1776]2005: 638–9). As we will see, the civic republicanism in this argument anticipated Paine, but the more remarkable feature (at least in contrast with neoliberalism) was that it made no allusion to productivity. Smith's proposal was not public education per se but intervention in early childhood education through a mixture of subsidy, incentive and sanction which influenced Paine[1] and Robert Owen, as did the general principles underpinning Smith's education proposals. According to Fleischacker, the importance which Smith attached to early education in the development of character was further proof of his egalitarian convictions. Just as real differences in talent between children were small, so virtue did not depend on a sophisticated education but on the formative experiences of early education and the influence of an upright family (Fleischacker 2013).

Smith proposed universal, basic education in the three Rs before people were condemned to the mind-numbing effects of the division of labour. Most teachers' pay was to be provided by the state but parents would make a contribution. It was necessary that parents pay something towards their children's education if only to make sure they would let the teachers know if they were neglecting their duty. The market was an indispensable tool but how could parents be incentivized to pay for what was still not worth their while? The answer was not to be found in markets but in policy: a school-leaving certificate would be the entry requirement for most jobs, or at least the better ones (Smith [1776]2005: 640, 649–50). Smith's proposal for a school-leaving certificate was not at all intended to increase productivity in the jobs to which it gave access. It was what would later be labelled as credentialism: the point was not that people would be able to do their jobs any better but that qualifications were being required for access to jobs (see Chapter 8). He was simply using employment as an incentive to make parents do what was needed so all could gain from the wider benefits of self-development.

INEQUALITY AND WELFARE

Tom Paine's proposals on public education in *The Rights of Man* included six months education per annum in the three Rs for every child up to age 14, at which point they could be apprenticed. Instead of paying from their own pockets, parents would be given public money which must be spent on their children's education. In contrast to Smith's proposal, this was a conscious element of welfare provision which accorded with Paine's other proposals, for example on pensions (see below). As we know from earlier chapters, Paine agreed with Smith that economic development was creating new problems for society, but where Smith wanted education to ameliorate the mind-numbing effects of the extension of the division of labour, Paine saw education as a remedy for increasing inequality. He believed education improved abilities and hence reduced the numbers of the poor, for example even being apprenticed was not enough to guarantee social mobility if general education was lacking. The most talented were stuck in manual work instead of 'getting forward the whole of his life from the want of a little common education when a boy' (Paine [1792]2014: 338).

We will return to the trajectory that British sentimental individualism gave to education policy in the next section, but this section describes the way that it propelled debate in the UK towards consideration of an active state, indeed a state which could address inequality, for example by redistributing wealth (Spicker 2013). Yet, as with education policy, at the beginning of this process any differences with Adam Smith were more a matter of nuance than we might imagine. According to Fleischacker (2013), there is a good argument that Smith's concern for the poor made him an intellectual progenitor of the welfare state. Evidence for this conclusion might be found in Smith's proposals to abolish primogeniture and entail (which preserved wealth that had not been earned over the generations), on liberalizing access to trade and free movement of labour and on tax reform. Smith even suggested on occasion that progressive taxation would ensure '"the indolence and vanity of the rich" can contribute to the well-being of the poor' (Fleischacker 2013: 494). None of this earned Smith the opprobrium that Tom Paine encountered, however.

Popular support for Paine was adversely affected by his attack on Christianity but it was the challenge to the idea that commerce necessarily entailed inequality that elites found most distasteful and dangerous.[2] The attacks on Paine for his commercial apostasy began with *Common Sense* (published in 1776, the same year as *The Wealth of Nations*), which argued that American Independence need not have disastrous effects on prosperity as its opponents declared. The book 'advocated commercial liberty, but none the less assumed a vision of commercial society which even now (much less in 1792) implied far less inequality than did Adam Smith's *The Wealth of Nations*' (Claeys 1989: 46). According to Claeys, Paine's argument depended on the voluntary sacrifice of self-interest by large numbers of people (remember, Smith thought that only the very few were capable of this kind of virtue).

While there was no doubt that political virtue and commerce were fundamentally in conflict, Paine thought self-interest, including economic self-interest, could nevertheless provide the basis for a republican polity along with virtue. The circle was to be squared by people choosing to sacrifice their self-interest in the cause of 'collective economic good' (something Paine himself did with his famous distaste for treating his own books as opportunities for commercial gain). From the late 1770s and 1780s, Paine's insistence on the restraint of self-interest by public virtue showed he had not 'slid far down that slippery path from republican civic virtue towards "free enterpriser" followed by many in late eighteenth-century America' (Claeys 1989: 59).

By 1791–2, Paine had come to the conclusion that his ideal of minimal government was only appropriate in new countries like the USA where there had yet been no opportunity for inequality to burgeon. According to Claeys, he had reached this conclusion by the time he wrote the second part of *The Rights of Man*. Established countries like the UK needed a reduced and fairer burden of taxation and collective responses to inequality.[3] In *Agrarian Justice*, published in 1795, Paine went on to claim that increased prosperity had increased poverty. He also argued that perpetual property rights were an alien imposition on the world that God had set in motion and that 'the accumulation of personal property is, in many instances, the effect of paying too little for the labor that produced it; the consequence of which is that the working hand perishes in old age, and the employer abounds in affluence' (cited by Claeys 1989: 202–3).

Thus, Paine thought equality could be achieved without sacrificing prosperity and, as his thoughts matured, he concluded that it was the constitution of society that dictated inequality should increase along with prosperity. An alternative form of society would have to rely on morality (to temper self-interest) and collective responses and, despite his preference for as little government as possible, Paine thought the state would have to impose remedies for inequality. Chapter 1 explained that he believed the money presently wasted on the poor rates should provide welfare benefits and pensions. Along with his proposals on education and property taxes, this was a programme designed to put every member of society in a position where they could advance their own health, wealth and happiness. At present, there was little hope of escape from burgeoning poverty and degradation, and escape attempts were generally punished with imprisonment or the death sentence.

Without the reforms Paine proposed, individualism was only viable for the well-heeled and fortunate. It was not available to the soldiers who were thrown on the scrapheap when their service ended[4] or to the likes of respectable shopkeepers who fell on hard times. These individuals deserved not grace and favour but a right to support,[5] and so might all of us if we found ourselves aged or infirm and unable to subsist by our own efforts. Paine also proposed making work and lodging available to help the young men and boys trying to make their fortune in London. These proposals relied on the same assumption, one of great significance for British individualism: no matter how hard you try, following your own self-interest might not be enough to save you from poverty. Individualism therefore warranted collectivism to bring about greater equality.

This meant a much bigger government role than Paine had previously implied but the proposals were to be funded by progressive taxation on inheritances and redistributing the tax revenues which were presently lavished on the elite. Not only were his proposals intended to address the problem of growing poverty while abolishing the poor rates, they also removed restrictions on wage bargaining, gave some public-sector workers pay rises and introduced a tax on profits of holders of stock in the national debt. Claeys claimed that, in 1792, this redistribution of wealth and reassertion of people's rights was on a significantly greater scale than anything Smith had in mind:

> Government now had a positive function which 'society' could not perform, which was to alleviate the chief vice of society, the failure of the system of exchange to support the population at all times ... [Paine] transformed a soft or imperfect right (or one which could not be compelled) to charity into a hard right to justice enforceable by government. This vision we today identify not with 'negative liberty', but with the welfare state and social democracy, where a regulated economic liberty supposedly predominates, and government substantially mitigates poverty as well as providing some employment for the poor beyond what the market allocates. (Claeys 1989: 99–100)

It was the way Paine developed an analysis of the roots of inequality that made his ideas so powerful in the cause of egalitarian individualism.

In 1795, Paine was still arguing that inequality was inescapable to the extent that some people worked harder than others, some had superior talents, some were better managers of the resources they had, some were very frugal and some were simply lucky, but in *Agrarian Justice* Paine went further. The poor had claims on improvements made on landed property (taxing the rich was fair because they had monopolized the opportunity to grow wealthy when they appropriated the land) and Paine saw low wages and exploitation at the root of poverty along with burdensome taxation (Claeys 1989: 196–7). For Claeys, all of this was necessary preparation for the ideas of the radicals and the followers of Robert Owen from the 1820s onwards.

Once more we find Paine bridging different ideas, in this case millenarian ideas about land nationalization and economic and moral arguments for goods in common made by the Owenite socialists. For the socialists, Paine's early emphasis on excessive taxation as the main cause of poverty was misguided. The real cause was low wages which also led to overproduction and underemployment. If goods were exchanged according to their labour value, periodic crises would be avoided, poverty and inequality would be remedied and labour would be fairly rewarded. There would be no profits and the rich would no longer monopolize wealth as they did in the competitive society which now obtained (Claeys 1989: 206).

The Owenites proposed that socialism be pursued outside that competitive system in communities self-sufficient in agriculture and manufactured goods where property would be communal but, Claeys argued, Owenism also increased expectations of the state beyond those which Paine had expressed. Epecially after the failure of Chartism in the mid-nineteenth century, it was the Owenite diagnosis of the roots of inequality in competition that persuaded radicals that they could expect the state to do something about the social and environmental problems of industrial capitalism, especially increasing inequality. Indeed, there was already some proof that the state could do this since it had carried through some factory reform and showed that it was not completely indifferent to the conditions of the working class and not 'too deeply corrupted' to be a part of the solution to inequality (Claeys 1989: 215).

THE CULTIVATION OF CHARACTER

We will see in the next chapter how, in keeping with the ideas of Adam Smith, Americans made schooling in virtue one of the most potent ideas of mid-nineteenth-century American individualism. It was particularly important in the development of American education because it served as a binding idea between the disparate parts of American individualism. It built bridges not only between the sentimental and cognitive individualism we encountered in Adam Smith's works in Chapter 3 but also with American (Protestant) religious individualism. (Although Joas may have made too much of the significance of American religious individualism in anti-slavery, the same cannot be said for American education.) In the UK, early signs of the same binding effect to ideas about the cultivation of character eventually gave way to disharmony as British sentimental individualism developed the more collectivist solutions already encountered in the discussion of welfare in the previous section.

Earlier in the chapter, it was noted, in passing, that both Smith and Paine thought public education was necessary to better equip the populace for public affairs and the defence of the nation. Smith thought the division of labour deprived people of the knowledge and interest demanded of citizens and the appetite for risk shown by soldiers (Smith [1776]2005: 638–9; Tegos 2013). Education could remedy these deficiencies and, at the same time, deter the population from rebellious ideas. Paine thought this guarantee of social order was all the more urgent in a democracy.[6] Partly inspired by republican ideals, he wanted a more virtuous electorate, for example *The Rights of Man* declared that education was needed to curtail the profligacy of youth (Claeys 1989). The concern for civic virtue also appeared in the works of abolitionists, for example Wilberforce's speech introducing the first parliamentary bill to abolish the slave trade on 18 April 1791, a month after *The Rights of Man* was published.

Wilberforce made similar arguments to Paine but in regard to slaves: as long as people had morality, individualism required only self-government; but welfare and education were required where the people lacked the moral or physical resources for individualism. The best illustration of this was the remark he made in *favour* of the retention of slavery (but not the trade in slaves) until civic education had taken place. For the previous two years, Wilberforce had told the House of Commons that the enslaved population did not yet have the moral character it needed to be free. This could only be provided by education and, to his deep regret, Wilberforce had to tell the House this was not happening: 'It was not merely that they were worked under the whip like cattle; but no attempts were ever made to instruct them in the principles of religion and morality' (Wilberforce 1791: 199). He continued:

> The Negroes were creatures like ourselves: they had the same feelings, and even stronger affections than our own; but their minds were uninformed, and their moral characters were altogether debased. Men, in this state, were almost incapacitated for the reception of civil rights. In order to become fit for the enjoyment of these, they must, in some measure, be restored to that level from which they had been so unjustly and cruelly degraded. To give them a power of appealing to the laws, would be to awaken in them a sense of the dignity of their nature ... a sudden communication of the consciousness of civil rights ... would be dangerous to impart, till you should release them from such humiliating and ignominious distinctions, as, with consciousness, they would never endure. You must first conduct them to the situation in question, having first prepared them for it, and not bring the situation to them. To be under the protection of the law, was, in fact, to be a free man; and, to unite slavery and freedom in one condition, was a vain attempt; they were, in fact, incompatible, and could never coalesce. (Wilberforce 1791: 216)

Like Paine and Smith, Wilberforce saw moral education as a guarantee of social order. He pointed out that Jamaican slave rebellions were begun by Africans who were enslaved while they were aware of the civil rights they had enjoyed before enslavement and could not endure their treatment in the West Indies (Wilberforce 1791).

It is usually assumed that Wilberforce was motivated by evangelical religion and, as we saw in Chapter 2, for the evangelicals, moral reform of all kinds was intended to save individual souls rather than advance freedom and equality.[7] Yet here was Wilberforce arguing from the first cause of sentimental individualism – universal human feelings – that, because of the depredations of slavery, slaves needed to be educated so that their dignity could be respected and their autonomy secured. This marriage of sentimental and religious individualism was present in much of the activities of the nineteenth-century moral entrepreneurs. From our present vantage point, it might be hard to understand that attempts to shape character which were aimed at gambling (and particularly the state lottery), intemperance and sexual incontinence necessarily entailed the valuation of human dignity. However, it is easier to grasp the connection that is being made with sentimental individualism in respect of the nineteenth-century concern for the physical and sexual abuse of women and children.

If it is conceded that intervening in character formation was intended to nurture the dignity of the victims, it is worth considering that nineteenth-century reformers saw temperance as one of the surest ways of reducing abuse. It may be that the unsympathetic portrayal of Victorian moralizers as hypocrites and killjoys owes a great deal to the propaganda of cognitive individualism. Indeed, the echoes of these battles can still be heard today wherever commercial interests dictate the relaxation of gambling laws, restrictions on the sale of alcohol or laws concerning sexual conduct. In the nineteenth century, the conjunction of religious and sentimental individualism made concern for morality a powerful stimulus to reform.

Wilberforce, the evangelical, and Oastler, the scion of the Church of England, said they wanted to save souls, but they identified slavery and the factory system as the obstacles in the way of Protestant individualism. Sinful behaviour was the manner in which these institutions put souls at risk but it was not the underlying cause. In this, they were little different from the supposed Deist, Adam Smith, who blamed the division of labour for moral failures, or Karl Marx who blamed them on capitalism.[8] Of course, these views were opposed by many, for example Oastler and Marx saw child labour turning parents into slavers, and the defenders of the factory system saw individuals freely deciding how to support their families and making rational decisions to maximize prosperity. In the USA, these arguments continued into the twentieth century.[9]

The promotion of parental love as a primary virtue did not consist only in moralizing against temperance and incontinence but also in cultivating love and care for others. This was clearly the aim of the evangelicals, particularly those who took part in the voluntary effort to support mothers. Thus, Prochaska (2006) described how volunteers cultivated their own feelings of love, compassion and service and incited the same feelings in those less fortunate than themselves. But this was also the aim of the Deist, Robert Owen, who thought that all children should be taught that they must do everything they could to make each other happy. In *A New View of Society*, first published in 1813, Owen declared that in an enlightened society every individual would understand that making each other happy was 'the essence of self-interest, or the true cause of self-happiness' (Owen [1813]1817: 115; also see Claeys 1986). This was also something Owen shared with Adam Smith. In *The Theory of Moral Sentiments*, Smith argued that mutual kindness was inscribed in human nature and happiness would elude us unless we followed this impulse: 'Beneficence is thus the virtue that enables its possessor to achieve both "the purposes of his being" as well as to promote social utility through kindness' (Hanley 2013: 228).

For Owen, the task of nurturing this virtue was not one for the thousands of volunteers who peopled Prochaska's (2006) history of Christian social service but for the state. Robert Owen's essays constituted a significant advance on the arguments made by Smith and Paine for the state's assumption of a collective responsibility to form and sustain individual moral character. With this development, the strains in the temporary marriage between religious and sentimental individualisms became more evident.

Long before he developed his ideas about utopian communities, Owen had trusted in the ability of governments to cure the moral ills of society by reforms which encouraged the cultivation of character. When he was himself a manager and employer, Owen chose to badger members of the elite (including European monarchs) rather than strive to build a social movement (Donnachie 2000: 146–53). His essays contained some moral censure of sexual behaviour outside marriage and strong drink,[10] but their goal was to correct the common assumption that 'each individual man forms his own character, and that therefore he is accountable for all his sentiments and habits, and consequently merits reward for some and punishment for others' (Owen [1813]1817: 90). Owen thought it was unjust that people should be punished and rewarded for things that were beyond their control but he was also wary of the effect of sanctions and inducements on character formation.[11] For example, he was opposed to the appearance of carrots and sticks in the classroom because he disapproved of attempts to encourage self-interested choices about education (O'Hagan 2011).[12] Attempts to instil virtuous behaviour which relied on such self-interested choices would backfire. Indeed, relying on self-interest and reinforcing it by teaching people to be selfish (Owen [1813]1817),[13] as was now the norm, was disastrous. Unfortunately for the clarity of this exposition, Owen called this disaster the 'individualist system'.

When Owen and the Owenites attacked 'individualism', they were doing something similar to Hans Joas (see Chapter 2): labelling the cognitive individualism which overwhelmed morality. Joas used the idea of 'sacralization of the person' to refer to the alternative but the Owenites eventually settled on 'socialism'. British socialism was one of the movements sparked by sentimental individualism in the nineteenth century, but the term 'socialism' had originally been used as a way of describing the voluntary sacrifice of self-interest which Paine, amongst others, proposed. Claeys (1986) explained that the opposition between 'individualism' (meaning anarchy or egoism) and the social (as in 'social economy' and 'social science' as well as socialism) was acquired from France where Comte and the Saint Simonians were equally scathing of the idea that people made their own character. Owen also derided the idea that there could be no harmony between individual interests and hence no collective solutions which did not harm them and he proposed a universal system for the cultivation of character (Claeys 1986; O'Hagan 2011).

Since character was a blank slate on which good or ill could be inscribed,[14] the character of the poorest was presently

> formed without proper guidance or direction, and, in many cases, under circumstances which directly impel them to a course of extreme vice and misery; thus rendering them the worst and most dangerous subjects in the empire; while the far greater part of the remainder of the community are educated upon the most mistaken principles of human nature. (Owen [1813]1817: 16)

Owen believed, even more strongly than Smith, that it was possible to teach any young person[15] 'any language, sentiments, belief, or any bodily habits and manners, not contrary to human nature' (cited by Owen [1813]1817: 20). They were now learning to behave most irrationally in that their happiness was reduced in proportion to their selfish behaviour. This was particularly evident for the poorest, who turned to idleness, crime and vice because that seemed to be what self-interest dictated, but actually the opposite was true.

Owen wished to persuade the governing elite that they were foolish to think that the inequalities in rewards and punishments that existed throughout society reflected essential differences in human nature. There were some differences between infants, but everyone was equipped with the same desire for happiness and 'the germs of his natural inclinations, and the faculties by which he acquires knowledge' (Owen [1813]1817: 111). No two individuals were the same in these respects that produced different talents, tastes and preferences, even when their characters were formed in similar environments. Owen did not believe, however, that these inclinations, likings or even talents had any influence over people's station in society because the nature they were born with was still 'without exception universally plastic':

> No one, it may be supposed, can now be so defective in knowledge as to imagine it is a different human nature, which by its own powers forms itself into a child of ignorance, of poverty, and of habits leading to crime and to punishment; or into a votary of fashion, claiming distinction from its folly and inconsistency; or, to fancy, that it is some undefined, blind, unconscious process of human nature itself, distinct from instruction, that forms the sentiments and habits of the man of commerce, of agriculture, the law, the church, the army, the navy, or of the private and illegal depredator on society. (Owen [1813]1817: 146)

Once they had grasped the difference between social inequality and the tiny differences that existed between individuals of any species, the governing elites would realize that 'by judicious training the infants of any one class in the world may be readily formed into men of any other class, even to believe and declare that conduct to be right and virtuous, and to die in its defence, which their parents had been taught to believe and say was wrong and vicious' (Owen [1813]1817: 147).

Owen was not suggesting that children should be set on the road to self-development so they could decide for themselves what role they might fill. Their character would be formed by training in various good habits which would prevent them from becoming dishonest and they would be rationally educated and directed to do useful work. Throughout the British Empire, government would provide the useful direction of labour along with the training and honest jobs which people would prefer to the dishonest occupations that did them no good. Training would be appropriate to the role that those who provided the direction had in mind: workers must be taught the facts that could serve them in whatever place in the division of labour they were to occupy.

There was no agency other than government that could enact this plan. It would not appeal to business which was obsessed with short-term personal gain and most of Owen's concrete proposals concerned legislative reform, including repealing the Poor Laws which encouraged lazy, stupid and drunken spendthrifts, and putting in their place a national plan for training and educating the poor and uneducated which would cultivate intelligent, virtuous and industrious workers. There were, however, obvious benefits to be reaped from this cultivation by their employers. Owen ([1813]1817) was proposing extensive state involvement in the planning and co-ordination of education, training and the labour market, but he argued that this would give the employers more productive workers. Smith may have thought that particular virtues were valuable to commercial society but Owen claimed specific increases in productivity for employers who cultivated their employees' characters. In return, the employers would provide decent wages, education and pensions, even housing and affordable goods for their employees to buy. Good character would boost productivity and profits and in return capitalism would reform itself so that the welfare burden borne by the state would shrink.

Owen thought he had proved what we might call the business case for his proposal with his pilot for the national plan: his experiments at his New Lanark mills from 1799. In his evidence before the Select Committee on the State of Children Employed in Manufactories in 1816, Owen described how the children of New Lanark learned more than the three Rs (plus sewing for the girls) because the morality and dispositions of the children were so important. Proof of the improvement of their moral habits was that children were no longer punished and children preferred school to playing by themselves. Moreover, because their employer made them so comfortable, they accepted much lower wages there than they might reasonably expect elsewhere.

It would, however, be a mistake to see this as 'an essentially utilitarian approach to practical learning, embedded in the vocational needs of a manufacturing community' (O'Hagan 2011: 77). The emphasis on self-development in the New Lanark institutions was still there in 1841 when Owen wrote about Self Supporting Home Colonies, listing

> the subjects, skills and – most importantly – *dispositions* that should inform the schooling of the young in an ideal society ... Even the stress on 'knowledge of some one useful manufacture, trade or occupation' is highlighted for its contribution to self-fulfilment as well as to employability, undertaken by the pupil 'for the improvement of his mental and physical powers'. Technical mastery is carefully subordinate in Owen's thought to what he here terms 'knowledge of himself and of human nature, to form him into a rational being, and render him charitable, kind and benevolent to his fellow creatures'. (O'Hagan 2011: 77, emphasis in the original)

This sounds like a manifesto for collective action in pursuit of the goals of sentimental individualism. Did Owen's certainty that good morality equated to organizational efficiency (O'Hagan 2011) serve to undermine those goals? There was little individual autonomy in the direction of labour that Owen envisaged and there were limits on the freedom and equality that could be achieved inside the capitalist model. Owen grew more aware of these limitations as the years passed and the New Lanark model for all capitalist reform was replaced by utopian communities which were designed to do without capitalism altogether (Donnachie 2000).

CONCLUSION

Adam Smith proposed extending education as a means to cultivate virtues which suffered from the depredations of the division of labour. Tom Paine's proposals took Smith's argument from sentimental individualism much further. Equal respect for human dignity required that all members of society should have access to pre-conditions for dignity and autonomy. Paine proposed collective solutions in education and welfare which would put these conditions in place. These ideas would be enormously influential in the history of the UK but were marginalized within sentimental individualism in the USA. Their implications for controls over capitalism, positive liberty and socialist thought soon became important elements of the Atlantic divide between the two countries (Spicker 2013). For a short time, there appeared to be an affinity between sentimental and religious individualism in the UK, at least in respect of the need to cultivate character. The alliance between the two moral individualisms would turn out to be much more important in the USA, however, and particularly so in the case of educational expansion. In the UK, sentimental individualism eventually took a very different direction to religious individualism in respect of both welfare and education. This parting of the ways between the two moral individualisms is important because it helps to explain differences in British and American public policy. It also helps to explain why the USA later served as a nursery for neoliberal politics.

NOTES

1. Claeys (1989) thought that Paine was in accord with Smith in many respects but insisted that Paine came to some of the same conclusions independently.
2. Not just the American elite since, in Britain, the new style of conservative Whiggism which grew out of the reaction to the French Revolution used Smith to justify the inequality that accompanied British commercial success. It argued that, while relative deprivation might increase, absolute poverty would have been much worse if Britain had fallen under the spell of Revolution and egalitarianism. Claeys (1989: 155–7) considered this 'the central argument against Paine'.
3. Bear in mind that, for Paine, the problem with existing taxation was that it redistributed wealth from the poor to the rich.
4. This problem continued into the present century; see, for example, White (2012).

5. Paine put a right to subsistence in place of the right to charity and it was 'a step of immense importance in the history of ideas of public welfare' (Claeys 1989: 205).
6. He also argued that the extension of civil rights would strengthen government's legitimacy amongst the poor and put an end to riots and disorder.
7. In 1836, Richard Oastler, the abolitionist and reformer, told the Archbishop of York that '[t]he factory question is indeed, My Lord, a soul question: it is souls against pounds, shillings and pence' (Driver 1946: 306).
8. Compare Smith ([1776]2005: 638–9) and see Chapter 15, section 3 of Marx ([1867]1990).
9. Hindman included an example of one of Lewis Hine's famous photographs being used to make this point in the American campaign against child labour. This was in the twentieth century, not the nineteenth, but the National Association of Manufacturers was still happy to defend the charge that the factory system was damaging the family (Hindman 2002: 55).
10. In later life, Owen became an advocate of the reform of marriage and divorce, sympathetic to birth control and, perhaps, tolerant of sex outside marriage (Donnachie 2000). See Owen's Fourth Essay on reducing the number of licences for selling strong liquor and also on discontinuing the state lottery (also a target for some abolitionists – Hochschild 2005).
11. As proposed by Bentham (Donnachie 2000).
12. Compare to the discussion on payments to encourage children to read in Standish (2009) and Sandel (2012).
13. Compare to Smith's remarks in *The Theory of Moral Sentiments* on children learning to moderate their selfish impulses and act in accordance with propriety in their community (Fricke 2013).
14. An idea Owen shared with Locke, Rousseau and James Mill as well as Paine and William Godwin (Green, 1990).
15. 'Before they have acquired strength and experience to judge of or resist the impression of those notions or opinions, which, on investigation, appear contradictions to facts existing around them, and which are therefore false' (Owen [1813]1817: 144).

5. American ideology: millennium and utopia

In Adam Smith's view, cognitive individualism provided all the rationale that was required for private education. People pursued it because there was evidence to suggest that this pursuit would bring a satisfactory return on their investment.[1] It was sentimental individualism that necessitated public education. Until the last decade of the nineteenth century, the American approach to public education was much closer to the approach proposed by Adam Smith and, at least in part, modelled on the existing system of public education in his native Scotland (Meyer et al. 1979). Yet, how can the rationale for American public education have been provided by sentimental individualism, when we have already seen how little headway sentimental individualism made in American debates about slavery and child labour? To a degree, the answer to this question is the point made in Chapter 2 about historical contingencies.

It would be thoroughly ahistorical to argue that nineteenth-century America was intrinsically incapable of basing policy on sentimental individualism. The slow progress of abolitionism in the USA was a result of real historical processes but this chapter will show that there were other historical processes which made it possible to expand public education to achieve sentimental individualist ends. These contingencies were also implicated in the causes of the Civil War (Higham 1974), which finally brought an end to slavery, but they did not extend to the limitation of child labour. Indeed, action against child labour was the spectre that stalked public education campaigns in America for much of the nineteenth century.[2] Those who campaigned for public education were forced to take great pains to make sure that their opponents could not argue that their real target was child labour since this would have caused possibly fatal damage to their cause. Even the suggestion that public education was having an *unintended* effect on the availability of child labour would be damaging. Historical contingency determined that there were definite limits to the reach of sentimental individualism in public policy in one other, crucial respect. The extension of public education in America was as egalitarian as any policy underpinned by sentimental individualism, yet it made very few inroads in those parts of America in which the economy had been based on slavery.[3]

We will shortly see that the remarkable contingencies that allowed public education to spread across the North and the West included the development of a social movement that was, in some ways, similar to the British abolitionist movement. Both movements drew strength from arguments forged in religious and sentimental individualism, could not be explained by self-interest[4] and drew on support from across the classes. Neither Britain nor any other European country generated such a powerful social movement which campaigned for public education and all of these countries paid the price by falling further and further behind the USA in the provision of public education.[5] Education then became a powerful exception to the more usual story of American tardiness in adopting improvements in public provision, most obviously in the form of the welfare state, pioneered in Europe (Green 1990; Skocpol 1992).

THE COMMON SCHOOLS MOVEMENT

The USA expanded public education for white children further and faster than any European country, including Prussia which kept pace with the US provision of primary education for a while (Rubinson 1986).[6] This process began in the Jeffersonian period, a few years before the publication of *The Rights of Man* and many years before full adult (white) male suffrage. The federal Congress granted new state resources to support public education (Skocpol 1992) but this was the limit of any federal government influence on the growth of public education. America was not to follow Scotland (in the seventeenth century) and Prussia (in 1826) where a school had been mandated by government for every parish.[7] Literacy rates (92–95 per cent) for American men born early in the nineteenth century were high (Green 1990; Meyer et al. 1979), and the USA was arguably the world's most heavily schooled society (Skocpol 1992),[8] but neither of these facts were the fruits of a public, or even national, education system.

In the first half of the nineteenth century, there were plenty of schools in places like Massachusetts. A substantial majority of whites aged 5 to 19 were enrolled in schools in the Northeastern concentrations of the population by the 1830s (Green 1990; Meyer et al. 1979). These were a mixture of public, private, religious and charity schools but even these labels sometimes failed to indicate what funds the different types of schools relied on (Rubinson 1986).[9] More to the point, these schools provided the kind of education which Smith had thought did not require state intervention. From the 1840s, however, the pressure of a new social movement began to build a public education system that was founded on common primary schools and would eventually add common secondary schools. It was to be complemented by a diverse mix of colleges and universities with unusually high participation in higher education (Skocpol 1992).

The common primary schools were the first step in the development of an education system that enrolled individuals in the same schools, and offered them the same teaching, regardless of their class origins. Whatever they claimed to be the case (Rubinson 1986), the capitalist class did not drive this process, but nor did the working class, although workers and trade unions did support the movement for common schooling in the middle of the century (Green 1990; Katznelson and Weir 1985). Just as important as the cross-class origins of the social movement was the fact that this was very largely a rural movement that occurred well in advance of significant industrialization in most of the country:

> Across the country outside the South, many communities, including the villages and small towns of rural America, built free public schools and sent children to them for at least part of the year. To spread schools across the land, networks of ministers, lawyers, teachers, and other educational promoters worked with whatever local allies they could find in each place, endeavouring (not always successfully) to standardize patterns of schooling across localities. (Skocpol 1992: 89)

A big part of the reason why this happened in the USA was the way political individualism had developed there, particularly its expression in the extension of the vote to adult white males with some restrictions by 1820 and the dropping of most property or tax-paying restrictions on the franchise by 1850 (Green 1990):[10]

> Democratic voting rights and the sense of belonging in the national polity encouraged all citizens to demand more and more access to schooling for their children. And the elected officials who dominated the policy usually supported the creation of all varieties of educational institutions and the broadening of access to them, because schools were widely popular in American democracy. (Skocpol 1992: 92)

But it was not just the extension of adult male suffrage that explained the spread of public education in the USA. Historians, and historically-minded sociologists, have argued that the *absence* of a strong state, or even of a religious establishment, was a crucial ingredient. Public education looked like a right to ordinary Americans, not just because it looked like something they could use their newly-won votes to win, and to lay claim to as the right of citizens in a democracy, but because no strong state was imposing schools on them. This was in marked contrast to Prussia where the state's view of educational development as equivalent to military power left no room for individualist reasons for expanding education (Green 1990). Public education was not identified in American minds with the (perhaps untrustworthy) motives of the upper classes or bureaucrats or with the dictates of an established clerical hierarchy (Skocpol 1992).

The social movement which blended sentimental and religious individualism, rural roots and cross-class activism in the expansion of public education in America could be found in the Common Schools Movement (1830–1860) which aimed to bring uniformity and integration through licensing and regulation of what was taught and who did it and where.[11] It succeeded in most of the country (including the West but not the South), bringing mass enrolment in a national system where anyone might have a good idea of what was going on in any school. This was done by making available public funding which made public provision the norm against which the religious (especially Catholic) and private schools were forced to measure themselves. The Common Schools Movement was able to persuade politicians to vie for votes by offering funding and voters (especially Protestants) responded favourably. As suggested earlier, the Movement was not aided by federal government or even constituent states (there were few resources and little authority available for education in the states) but it created the political authority it needed in state legislatures. Where the British abolitionists organized mass meetings and petitions amongst the un-enfranchised that led to parliamentary debates, the Common Schools Movement persuaded politicians to appeal to voters and use their state legislature to fulfil their electoral pledges.

The religious element in the Common Schools Movement is hard to miss. Spreading out from New England, the Movement was firmly identified as Protestant, not least by Catholics who resented interference with their parochial schools (Meyer et al. 1979). Indeed, it was a product of a Protestant religious revival (Higham 1974) and, since the time of Martin Luther, small Protestant societies (including Scotland) had made much of the education of the individual. In America, Puritanism had featured in the conception of the nation from colonization onwards. Like the revival from which it drew strength, the Common Schools Movement was explicitly Millenarian (Meyer et al. 1979). Public education was not simply being used to save individual souls but to make it easier for men and women to conform to God's will here on earth. The Common Schools were to be the mechanism by which Americans would create a polity which was a heaven on earth compared to the intolerant, discriminatory and decadent societies of Europe (Green 1990).

Common schooling for all would help America to redeem the sins of mankind (Higham 1974) but the Common Schools Movement was not oriented towards universal human rights and some school promotion was prompted by the economic, political and even religious interests of the moral entrepreneurs as well as the aim of enlarging the nation (Meyer et al. 1979: 601).[12] Millenarianism was not the only type of nation-building that impelled the Common Schools Movement, however (Green 1990). It was coupled with republicanism[13] which required that every citizen learn that the great society would not be built without their participation: '[s]aved individuals, freed from the chains of sin and tradition and ignorance and aristocracy, were the carriers of political authority and meaning and responsibility' (Meyer et al. 1979: 599). Citizenship must be active, and at times selfless, for example when discharging a civic duty; and this obviously recalled the proposals made by Smith and Paine for public education to improve the condition of the polity. For example, the early leaders of the Common Schools Movement such as Horace Mann wanted the schools to teach citizens the great value of holding on to civic republicanism and not ceding 'political authority and meaning and responsibility' to political parties and their partisan manoeuvrings (Skocpol 1992: 90).

The collaboration between republicanism and millenarian Protestantism was sealed by a mutual agreement that it was America's destiny to make a reality of the dreams of humanity (Green 1990; Higham 1974). Women were not excluded from this destiny since they too could undergo education in citizenship and an interest in female education was a driver for the expansion of rural schools in the North. Although women were encouraged to continue their self-development into their adult lives, the virtues they should nurture were specifically feminine virtues and by far the most important fruit of this education was the contribution mothers made to nation-building by shaping the character of their children (Green 1990). Both men and women were to be taught the virtues appropriate to a polity 'located in individuals and in the exchange relations of a free society' (Meyer et al. 1979: 599). This aim also recalled the sentimental individualism of Paine, and particularly Smith.

The ideology of the Common Schools Movement incorporated the attitudes appropriate to the agrarian, freeholder capitalism on which most of the Americans who sent their children to these schools were reliant. We already know that public education expanded before the great industrialization of the USA and that the greatest impact of public education in the nineteenth century was in rural America. In the middle of that century, most Americans were small entrepreneurs and many of them were farmers – even in 1900, 42 per cent of the population were still living on farms – and they were dependent (mostly directly) on selling agricultural products overseas (Meyer et al. 1979). In keeping with Smith's original proposals, the rural common schools were not charged with giving children the skills they needed to work in the agricultural economy. Nor were they charged with ensuring the acquiescence of labour – as envisaged in Owen's *A New View of Society* ([1813]1817) – or with demonstrating that failing to trust in big business was irrational. Instead, capitalist activity could be promoted as the sphere in which every (male) child would exercise self-determination as part of an ongoing project of nation-building (Green 1990). As the historian Higham pointed out, the 'animating idea' of the American ideology produced by the collaboration of American nationalism and American Protestantism was 'a belief in the equal rights of individuals in the interest of maximum personal autonomy'. For all that it was through capitalism that every individual could determine their fate, in this formula equality was just as important as self-determination (Higham 1974: 16).[14]

It was through capitalism that individuals would see their hard work and their virtues rewarded. Some of these virtues were the same as those promoted by Owen (and many Victorians), including respect for the property of others, thrift and clean living.[15] The common schools were certainly not charged with making farmers, and the entrepreneurs who relied on the agrarian economy, into unprincipled egotists (Higham 1974). Such an economy necessarily entailed a great deal of co-operation, mutual aid and reciprocity, not simply in terms of sharing labour but also ideas. The character that suited agrarian capitalism was, to a very large degree, the same character that was required by republicanism. In both cases, individuals had to be capable of putting others' interests before their own. As I have already suggested, there was no use for this sentimental individualism in the South where the plantation economy had no space for freeholders and even freed slaves had very limited access to the vote, even more limited after Reconstruction (Foner 1989; Green 1990). Religious individualism offered a way out of poverty and slavery in the next life but this was not nearly enough to give purchase for the Common Schools Movement in the South. Protestantism had just as strong a grip on the South, but the labourers on the plantations were excluded from any millennium the Common Schools Movement might be trying to build (Meyer et al. 1979).

There was similar long-distance, large-scale production in the South but this was not a moral economy of individuals who all had a stake in agrarian capitalism. Neither the slaves nor the great majority of those in

the caste society that followed had such a stake (Meyer et al. 1979: 600).
There were far fewer capitalists and they had already paid for their
children's education and were not interested in other Southerners'
aspirations to individualism. Where Wilberforce had argued that education must precede the arrival of civil rights, the plantation economy had
no use for civil rights and so no use for public education. Wilberforce
had warned of slave rebellions of course, and the control of labour on the
plantations was a perennial problem. Since those who supplied the labour
would never own farms or small businesses, there was little point in
raising their expectations and making them even more intractable. The
result was substantially lower enrolment in Southern schools with fewer
school days (and lower education expenditure) and it stayed this way for
decades (Meyer et al. 1979).

In contrast to the South, the political, economic and social orders of
the rural settlements of the North and the West took a great deal of work
to sustain them, and the Common Schools were put in place to do much
of the heavy lifting (Meyer et al. 1979). Converting to individualism
people who had once relied on the certainties of European tradition (and
what Higham called 'primordial' unity) in communities in which their
families had been embedded for generations was no easy matter.[16] It did
not make it easier that these generations had probably been ruled by a
strong European state and were accustomed to apathy and even to
assuming their souls were someone else's concern (Green 1990). The
huge task of building a new 'moral polity' had to be accomplished with
moral authority alone (Meyer et al. 1979: 601; also see Green 1990).
Sentimental individualism contributed, along with religious individualism, to both the moral authority and the moral polity that it produced.
Common Schools were indispensable to this process and they were built
by a movement that drew on moral authority in very much the same way
as the abolitionism described in Chapter 2.

Some of the historical contingencies which explain the apparent
anomaly of sentimental individualism driving public education in the
mid-nineteenth-century USA have now been explained. This was a
largely pre-industrial society but one in which the working class already
had the vote and there was no strong state. This allowed a cross-class
social movement that was driven by religious and sentimental individualism as much as it was by the drive to exercise political self-
determination (Green 1990). In Europe, the lack of early enfranchisement
meant that when industrialization arrived working-class parties would
develop in order to win the vote. The arrival of working-class parties
ruled out the broad, classless appeal that public education had in the
USA.

In England, for example, the ruling classes resisted the extension of education to the working class at the same time as they resisted their other demands for the vote, trade union rights and the chance to escape their station in the emerging industrial division of labour (Rubinson 1986).[17] The lack of opportunity for a broad movement to extend public education also confirmed that when it finally arrived in European countries it would take a much more stratified form than it had in the USA. There, the Common Schools had offered the same curriculum to all-comers but in Europe schools were heavily stratified with separate education for working-class and middle-class children. This stratification was bolstered whenever public funds were used in the schools (Katznelson and Weir 1985; Rubinson 1986). In the USA, history chose to neutralize the negative effects that class could exert on education but in Europe these effects were magnified, producing inflexible stratification and limited enrolments from the working class (Rubinson 1986).[18]

I have already noted that ensuring the acquiescence of labour was largely unnecessary in mid-nineteenth-century America but in industrializing Europe this was a prime goal of the limited enrolments and stratified systems. In time, the demands of industrial capitalism forced a retreat from universal access to the same curriculum in the USA, but, until that point, public education was a bulwark against the threat of industrialization to the political and economic status quo:

> [E]arly capitalist industrialization created a potential for disorder that was managed by the creation of public schools as one way to protect the political regime and the economic order. The participatory federalism of the American political system helped spur the creation of public education by local elites in coalition with working-class voters. Citizenship, schooling, republicanism, and civic virtue went hand in hand. (Katznelson and Weir 1985: 24)

In England and parts of continental Europe public education had still hardly begun.

England and Wales in the middle of the nineteenth century had levels of school enrolment that lagged behind the slave states, never mind the North. Forty years later, a quarter of English and Welsh children were not enrolled, whereas the German states had almost universal enrolment half a century before (Green 1990: 13–15). Green explains the particular tardiness of England as a result of the earlier solution to the problem of nation-building there without the help of public schools. In consequence, England and Wales were 50 years behind France (let alone Prussia) in many respects. It was impossible to speak of a full public system of education before 1870 and most of the country was untouched by compulsory education for at least another decade. Elementary education was not provided without charge until 1891 and it was another decade before the state created secondary schools and began to consolidate the educational bureaucracy. When public grammar schools were created in 1902, this was exactly a century after the French state had introduced the *lycée* (Green 1990).

NEW HARMONY

For much of the nineteenth century, the English and Welsh working class could access only charity schools or factory schools whose mission was to perpetuate the class system. For much of his career, Robert Owen, enlightened promoter of factory education, did not acknowledge that the division of labour itself might play some part in the demoralization of the working class which he deplored. He believed that, despite all the evidence, the most demoralized could become the most worthwhile individuals, but his vision for education offered none of the promises of self-determination made in the American Common Schools.[19] Instead, Owen agreed with the complaints other employers made about their lazy, dishonest and unruly employees and argued that education would teach the rational frame of mind that would allow these employees to acquire kind and benevolent characters. This would make them not only govern-able but also self-governing because they would understand the identity of their best interests and those of their employer. Far from agreeing with Smith about education serving as an antidote to the debilitating effects of the division of labour, Owen argued that public education could shape character to make the working class a better fit for the new industrial division of labour. His mechanism to ensure best fit was of the extreme kind Spencer would later identify with military society.[20] The state would educate people and then direct them to the places they had been made fit for.

  We will see in Chapter 8 that something like this pattern was adopted in the stratified European education systems of the first half of the twentieth century, but Owen himself eventually abandoned his proposals for factory education when his certainty that the cultivation of character would benefit capitalist employers by increasing productivity and profit-ability disappeared. He became convinced that capitalism was so incor-rigibly committed to distributing rewards unfairly that no amount of reform would allow the cultivation of character to its full potential. This must be pursued outside capitalism in utopian communities. His utopian conceptions of the role of education recall some of the Millenarian ambitions of the school reformers in the USA and, indeed, Owen's most serious attempt to construct his utopia took place in Indiana.

From his days as a mill manager in Lancashire, Owen had been convinced that it was possible for an enlightened employer to shape the attitudes of his employees in a way that was helpful for productivity. His marriage to Caroline, the daughter of Scottish businessman David Dale, in 1799, gave him the opportunity to put his ideas properly to the test. Dale had built the New Lanark cotton mill a decade earlier and on marriage Owen gained ownership (with his partners), and control, over the mill and the community Dale had established to house its workers. While New Lanark was a commercial success under his control, Owen's ambitions for his experiment expanded beyond the horizons of his partners. In 1813 he arranged to have their shares bought by investors who he felt would also be interested in the social improvements he had in mind, and not simply in the rate of return on their capital. The new investors were Jeremy Bentham and William Allen, a prominent Quaker abolitionist.[21]

Owen trumpeted his success in garnering interest and financial support for the idea of an experimental working community in *A New View of Society* in 1813. Four years later, he proposed an extension of the idea to solve the unemployment exacerbated by the slump in demand at the end of the Napoleonic Wars (Owen, [1813]1817). Self-supporting communities of up to 1500 members would combine living accommodation with co-operative agriculture and manufacturing. They would replace all existing arrangements for supporting the poor and could be built by individuals or any level of government from parishes up to the national government itself. When combined with the ideas about character development propounded in *A New View*, Owen's enthusiasm for 'home colonies' set him on the road to a vision of utopian communities in which the competitive and (cognitive) individualist society would be left behind.

It took another 12 years before there was an attempt to found a home colony in Britain and shortly afterwards Owen gave up control of New Lanark and bought an existing German Lutheran settlement in Harmonie, Indiana, with a view to trying out his ideas of co-operative self-sufficiency in the USA. The community, renamed New Harmony, was to be Owen's first step towards a society of communal living and communal property. Neither the British nor the American experiment lasted beyond two years but when Owen returned to Britain it was as a proponent of socialism and secularism rather than as a successful capitalist owner-manager. He did not abandon his advocacy of utopian communities, but proposed additional innovations which would ease the transition from capitalist to socialist society. There was the establishment, from 1832, of two 'equitable labour exchanges' in which 'labour notes' allowed the exchange of labour for goods but not for capital. Again, the experiment was short-lived but, in a speech at the London exchange, Owen set out some of the key principles of his utopian socialism.

In the speech, Owen engaged to 'denounce the Old System of the World, and announce the Commencement of the New'. Labour notes were presented as an alternative to 'the present degrading and demoralizing mode of distributing wealth by the ordinary method in practice, of buying cheap and selling dear', but what was required was a new division of labour and an entirely new social system to go with it (Owen 1833: 196). His thinking about this new social system suggested that Owen was grappling, for the first time, with the implications of his social thought for personal freedom.

Prosperity for all remained the foundation of Owen's social designs but now his idea was that the huge increases in productivity he foresaw should be channelled to the good of all rather than to improving capitalists' profits. Owen had always argued that astonishing increases in productivity could be brought about by organizing labour more rationally but his practical suggestions had often amounted to what we would now call the techniques of human resource management. At this later stage in his life, Owen was more interested in the rational organization of society as a whole and in running production, distribution and exchange on scientific principles. This would create so much wealth that nobody would feel poor and both the envy, and admiration, of wealth would disappear. Once this was achieved, people could concentrate on making each other happy rather than on competing with each other:

> [W]e renounce the principle of individual competition in the production and distribution of wealth, as being, in its most immediate and remote consequences, not only the most demoralizing principle on which man can now act and govern his affairs, but as being, also the greatest obstacle, in practice, to the beneficial production and distribution of wealth, to the formation of a superior individual and national character, and the well-ordering and good government of the people. (Owen 1833: 197)

But how were production and distribution to be organized in Owen's alternative society?

Without mentioning him by name, Owen recalled the irresistible, yet degrading and demoralizing, trend in the division of labour described by Adam Smith. It had been brought about by an increase in population density, but forcing people to undertake ever more simple tasks had resulted in 'the destruction of their health, their mental faculties, and all the higher enjoyments of a rational existence' (Owen 1833: 200). By using the science of society, a way could be found to divide labour which would be neither degrading nor demoralizing but also extraordinarily productive. The ultimate source of this well of productivity was co-operation in education, production, distribution and government (Owen 1833: 201). The key was to bring people together in workplaces and communities in such a way that they would be helping each other rather than competing with and hurting each other. This would not only enhance prosperity and happiness but also individual freedom. The rational organization of production and distribution would permit

> the highest degree of individual freedom and happiness that human nature, in its present state of knowledge, is capable of enjoying. Thus will man, as a member of an association formed purposely for his benefit, experience the utmost share of individual freedom that is compatible with the still higher privileges of a social state of existence. (Owen 1833: 201)

Freedom was now equally as important an objective as happiness, whereas this certainly had not been the case in *A New View* where freedom did not rate a single mention. In his speech, just as in *A New View*, Owen still saw happiness deriving from voluntary co-operation so personal freedom had its limits.[22] In utopian society, people would get together with the specific aim of making each other happy and individual freedom must always be circumscribed by this social existence. Put simply, preferring competition to co-operation with others would put everyone's happiness at risk. In effect, Owen was agreeing with Southey's criticism (see Chapter 9): the individual freedom he had enjoyed as a capitalist owner-manager might have been bought at the cost of the freedom (and happiness) of others, particularly his own employees. Certainly, the pursuit of individual freedom without care to preserve co-operation would prove self-defeating, but Owen was now clear that this co-operation would make space for a great deal more personal freedom than was presently available within capitalism. It is this strand of sentimental individualism which later writers such as Grant Allen and Oscar Wilde drew on when they elaborated on the notion of socialist individualism (see Chapter 10).

In order to make space for people to join together in ensuring each other's happiness and freedom, Owen proposed getting rid of all the places in which people presently congregated because all of them had been 'accidental' creations rather than conscious and rational attempts to co-operate. This meant abandoning institutions (such as companies, universities, prisons and workhouses), as well as all existing settlements, because they prevented people from being as prosperous, happy and rational as it was within their power to be (Owen 1833). The division of labour had been created in the same accidental way, but for any detail about the way production and distribution would be organized we need to turn to a lecture Owen gave five years later in Manchester on 'the natural and rational classification of society' (Owen 1837).

The rational and natural basis that Owen found for assigning places in the division of labour was age. Age-appropriate tasks would replace the artificial differences of class and social position which had emerged along with prisons and other institutions when we lacked the science which could tell us how to create a happier and more prosperous society (Owen 1837). One of the great attractions of classification by age would be that it would create much more freedom for the individual than a division of labour based on class could ever offer. Owen was adamant that the reason the division of labour which Adam Smith had described was inimical to equality was precisely because it limited the freedom of the individual, particularly their autonomy. Thus, some were given a subordinate class or station and must do what others told them to do. They were not free to do whatever work they were capable of and they lacked autonomy in the work to which they were assigned. So far had Owen's ideas developed that this autonomy was now a key condition of equality.

Owen told his audience that the old, irrational and artificial division of labour denied people a natural right to autonomy which ought to be enjoyed equally by all. Owen expressed this right in terms of positive freedom (the freedom to do interesting, enjoyable and fulfilling things) and negative freedom (freedom from others telling you to do things you would rather not do). Co-operation involved some limitations on autonomy but 'equal rights' meant '[N]o man has a right to require another man to do for him, what he will not do for that man'. In this way, as much autonomy could be enjoyed as was compatible with equality. It was only if some people appeared to want more autonomy than they were prepared to grant others that some sort of limitation on individual freedom would be necessary. Whereas the division of labour in capitalism had been completely inimical to the right to autonomy, the new, age-based division of labour would preserve equal rights to autonomy in perpetuity (Owen 1837). The division of labour was to be designed to meet the varying needs of different members of society, including their different wishes and capacities for autonomy. Each age would have activities which it could do, would want to do and would benefit from doing; and individual freedom and opportunities for self-development were essential elements of each stage.

The division of labour was to be humanity's faithful servant instead of its implacable master. There would be no drudgery[23] and, instead of the orders and coercion of the factory system, there would be direction and instruction along the lines of the Lancasterian system for schools in which much teaching was delivered by older children and teenagers. The division of labour under conscious and rational control would necessarily be more productive (and less wasteful) and this productivity would be further boosted by technological progress, for example making up for children's want of strength with 'the superior, mechanical and chemical power which will be contrived and arranged' (Owen 1837: 207). Moreover, a division of labour under conscious control would make the class system obsolete: by the age of 20, the members of utopian society would be 'equal in their education and condition, and no artificial distinction, or any distinction but that of age, will ever be known among them' (Owen 1837: 209).

CONCLUSION

In the first part of this chapter, we saw how, in close partnership with nationalism and religious individualism, sentimental individualism played its part in American educational reforms. It did not generate new human rights as the anti-slavery movement had in Britain. Indeed, neither the reforms, nor the social movement that inspired them, had any impact on the slave states. Nevertheless, the social movement and the schools that developed from it were intended to transform morality in a similar way to the anti-slavery campaigns. This morality was partly republican – citizens had a duty to participate as individuals if their democratic polity was not to degenerate – however the morality the public schools nurtured was also intended to integrate communities and keep them prosperous. While there was none of the admiration of riches against which Smith warned, the schools promoted the 'lesser virtues' which were appropriate to agrarian capitalism.

In the second half of the chapter, we saw how sentimental individualism played its part in very different developments within European societies using the example of the evolution of the ideas of Robert Owen. His ideas were formed by his experience of one of the least egalitarian, democratic and well-educated of those societies. Over time, Owen came to the conclusion that fundamental change was required, not only to market capitalism (which Owen had first seen as part of the solution to demoralization) but also to the division of labour itself. In the American case, sentimental individualism endorsed the existing division of labour but in Europe it wished to transform it. With or without the label of alienation, the idea that the existing division of labour was deeply antithetical to sentimental individualism would play an important part in the development of socialism and Marxism.

NOTES

1. Albeit that their perception was sometimes distorted by an over-estimation of their chances of success.
2. Andy Green (1990) argued that, in mid-century, reliance on child labour got in the way of extending education in England, whereas there was less child labour in the USA and those who opposed universal education could not cite its loss as a reason for their opposition. Green seemed to have forgotten that industrialization took place at a later date in the USA. In mid-century, most US child labour was in agriculture, and particularly on family farms, so there were naturally few counterparts to the English manufacturers' power over politics and public opinion. Once rapid American industrialization was occurring, the threat to child labour was an important reason for capitalist resistance to the expansion of education (Rubinson 1986). So persuasive were these arguments that American educational reformers were very reluctant to be seen attacking child labour. It was a way of losing support not gathering it, as in England, and Green may have therefore been misled into assuming that child labour was less of an obstacle to reform.
3. On the exclusion of slaves and Native Americans, see Green (1990). For them, the American system would remain highly stratified and underpinned by racist beliefs (see Chapter 15).
4. Certainly not economic self-interest but Green (1990: 193) cited Kaestle, declaring educational reform also served 'individual goals of enlightenment, morality and personal development'.
5. Within Europe, Britain was generally much slower to expand education and training than both Germany and France (Green 1990).
6. Although note that the inception of public education – with schools financed and controlled by the state with an educational bureaucracy – occurred first in Prussia, France, Holland and Switzerland (Green 1990).
7. The Prussian regulations of that year introduced compulsory education for 7–14 year olds, set up an elementary school in every parish and mandated that teachers be trained. In the following decade, Prussia had universal compulsory education up to age 14 in a co-ordinated national system of state elementary and secondary schools (which also provided education for the elite from age 15). With this co-ordination came rigid state control over the curriculum. France did not get compulsory, free, universal elementary education until 1882 (Green 1990).
8. Green (1990) suggested that this may not have been true until the advent of high schools in the 1860s.
9. Although note that, as in Britain, charity schools tended to cater for the poor, while it was mostly the middle classes who sent their children to private schools.
10. Most European countries did not reach these milestones until the following century (Rubinson 1986).
11. This account of the Movement relies on Rubinson (1986). Green (1990) was keen to emphasize that 1830 was no watershed in that schools were still involved in the same basic task of nation-building.
12. These interests included middle-class concerns with demoralization in the cities (Green 1990).
13. Meyer et al. 1979: 599. Higham describes near 'complete convergence' between the two ideologies in which millenarianism acquired a 'secular character' and Protestant religious leaders 'identified the Kingdom of God with the American Republic'. Protestant ideology

thereby 'supplemented' American nationalism which drew on 'the Enlightenment and the tradition of classical humanism'. As a result, the two ideologies 'forged the strongest bonds that united the American people during the nineteenth century' (Higham 1974: 14–15).

14. Higham noted the 'corollary' between these individualisms but he also saw a contradiction within the American ideology since 'its basic task of building solidarity was not compatible with the competitive, acquisitive values the ideology also legitimized' (Higham 1974: 17).

15. American educational reformers were similarly worried by urban demoralization. With family life and routes into traditional occupations decaying, they saw schools as a means of producing civil and industrious workers from the urban poor. For Horace Mann, the main point of the schools was 'the formation of a lovely and virtuous character by the habitual practice of cleanliness, delicacy, refinement, good temper, gentleness, justice and truth' (in Green 1990: 62–3).

16. See Chapter 4 on how Paine and Owen made more of this motive for public education than Smith. For example, members of the religious communities in New Lanark which gave Owen considerable trouble – some of whom spoke a different language – had things in common with some immigrant communities in the USA (Green 1990).

17. Green (1990) confirmed that the American working class carried much less of a threat.

18. Green (1990) pointed out that even in the USA *secondary* schools had very limited working-class participation in the mid-nineteenth century.

19. In this Owen was no different to other middle-class radicals (Green 1990).

20. See Chapters 6 and 7 on Spencer and note that this was just the point Spencer made when he drew parallels between the direction of labour under socialism or communism and in military society.

21. Who also had an interest in 'home colonies' and the Lancasterian education system which had much in common with the system of educational supervision described in *A New View*, as well as the arrangements for industrial training and supervision Owen later proposed for utopian communities.

22. Compare to J.S. Mill who thought the wish to serve society might become a secular religion which would reduce individual freedom and individuality (see Chapter 1).

23. 'There will be no occupation requisite to be performed by one which will not be equally performed by all, and by all, far more willingly than any of the general affairs of life are now performed, by any class, from the sovereign to the pauper' (Owen 1837: 204).

6.   Classes and evolution

The relationship between individualism and inequality can only be successfully theorized with knowledge of the historical circumstances within which sentimental, religious and cognitive individualisms developed. Without this grasp of history and contingency, we would not be able to understand why sentimental individualism in the UK, but not in the USA, was closely related with nineteenth-century anti-slavery. Nor would we understand why American, but not British, sentimental individualism was associated with educational expansion and reform. We now move on to extend our grasp of the relationships between individualism and inequality from anti-slavery and education to the division of labour.

Adam Smith believed that we tamper with the division of labour at the cost of damaging prosperity and that, on its own, the division of labour produced little of the inequality he saw in eighteenth-century British society. Smith thought it was the way that people understood and shaped their relationship to the division of labour that was the cause of inequality. *WN* included a powerful critique of the cognitive individualism which used the differences in the talents and efforts of individuals to explain inequality. He also pointed out that cognitive individualism's assumptions about the freedoms that individuals enjoyed were deeply flawed.

Modern misrepresentation of Smith might easily lead us to believe he wrote nothing about the class system of his time, or saw it as a type of social structure that would be swept away by the operation of free markets and replaced by healthy individual competition. In fact, Smith was an astute observer of the British class system and knew very well that it continued to prosper even as the influence of markets increased. He did not think that the division of labour was responsible for its persistence, however. For example, the division of labour was not responsible for the widespread perception that the working class were good for nothing but menial tasks, for which they deserved little respect, whereas skilled workers and professionals had characteristics which deserved better pay and higher status.

Much of this is already implicit in Smith's contention that most of the tasks required by the increasing division of labour were (ever more) undemanding and in his repeated assertion that much education and training had little do with what was actually required in work. His scepticism about the claims to particular necessary skills extended beyond the skilled trades and he had a fairly jaundiced view of the level of skill required in almost all professions, including those of university professors. Moreover, rather like Owen, he did not think there was anything but minimal differences between people's abilities, even when it came to the most extravagant talents such as those possessed by opera singers and dancers (Smith [1776]2005: 93).

ADAM SMITH AND THE BRITISH CLASS SYSTEM

Smith did not think class was produced by the division of labour but he knew other people were all too ready to believe it was. He thought their credulity arose from some very common human failings which made them blind to the actual requirements of the division of labour and the way these were fulfilled. The tenets of cognitive individualism convinced people that inequality in the class system was a consequence of the way competition between individuals aligned the requirements of the division of labour with differences in the talents and aptitudes of individual human beings. For Smith, these tenets were rooted in almost universal characteristics of human nature which led people to misapprehend their world in a systematic way and to find evidence to support their mistaken assumptions at every turn. They concluded that people were rewarded with riches and esteem because they were talented, or tried hard. They imagined that there was nothing stopping any individual accessing these same riches and esteem if they had the necessary talents and put in the required effort. They concluded that failure was the result of the laziness, ineptitude or mediocrity of the individuals concerned.

Smith thought that the characteristics of human nature which led people to find evidence that supported the tenets of cognitive individualism everywhere they looked, amounted to deeply-regrettable human failings akin to the vanities described by religion (particularly Protestant Christianity). Chapter 3 mentioned that Smith regretted our abiding admiration for the rich and famous and the egotism this seemed to fuel amongst the rich and famous themselves. His regret was partly explained by his conviction that such admiration led to individual unhappiness, but he went on to make admiration of worldly success the foundation for a theory which explained why people consent to an unequal social system.

From our present vantage point, we can see that, in contrast to feudal inequality, the class system required popular acquiescence and often enthusiastic approval. Smith's theory made an important contribution to understanding this new, ideological basis for inequality in a society which had been transformed by individualism.

In a few pages of *WN*, Smith ([1776]2005: 87–96) elaborated on what he understood to be an insight into human nature into the kernel of a critique of the British class system which still has validity today. Their susceptibility to admiration and egotism meant people who enjoyed riches and success always considered that they deserved them. They would not have been able to think this if they had believed their success was the result of circumstances outside their control. Their propensity to admire success therefore predisposed them to think they had succeeded because they had won a free and fair competition between individuals in which their peculiar qualities, and perhaps virtues, had proved to be superior. In this way, cognitive individualism explained away inequalities, such as those which featured in the class system, but at the same time it rendered invisible the real sources of inequality.

Chapter 3 described the way in which Smith identified a major cause of inequality in the willingness of parents to buy their sons access to better-paying jobs by investing in education and training. The tasks the jobs entailed did not really require this investment but expensive education and training erected a barrier which kept out poorer competitors and therefore kept up wage levels. The inequality produced by these higher wages was not caused by differences in talent. If anything, the reverse was true: differences were being manufactured to create inequality which would benefit the few who could make their children appear to be particularly talented or knowledgeable. Chapter 3 also explained that this was the point at which the losers in the class system were identified as capable only of the regular jobs created in huge numbers in the modern division of labour. These jobs required no, or very little, skill and were therefore open to competition to all which resulted in constant downward pressure on wage rates. Since they had no money to invest in the transmission of privilege to their children, the poor were forced into these lower-paying jobs in each successive generation, making it seem as if they were fitted for nothing better.

According to Smith, a certain level of investment in education and training got your name into the draw which determined who rose to the top of the (lucrative) professions, but what happened after that was down to luck. People were no more likely to recognize this than they were to recognize the role of the conscious and deliberate transmission of privilege in the creation of class differences. They were loath to believe that luck played such a defining role because they were committed to admiring riches and success, including, where possible, their own riches and success. By ignoring their good fortune, they were able to make it seem plausible that getting to the top of a profession was the result of competition between individuals in the same way that (so they also believed) initial access to professions was determined by competition between individuals. Cognitive individualism was blind to the role of luck in determining success: those who did not rise to the top of the professions had only themselves to blame, just as did all those who could never have entered the professions because of their lack of education.

If there were large swathes of society which never succeeded in individual competition, this demonstrated how inadequate these individuals were. Thus, the absence of working-class professionals demonstrated that members of that class were only capable of menial jobs. What was more, the free and fair competition between individuals had recognized the virtues of the upper classes and this amply confirmed they deserved all the admiration, indeed the deference, of others. While this sounds very British, there was also the paradoxical truth that people's beliefs about class were founded in the idea that the labour market was a free and fair arena for competition between individuals regardless of their class origins. This is easily recognizable as a fundamental assumption in the American Dream, however we have learned that this idea was not coined by Adam Smith but treated by him as a social phenomenon which required explanation and criticism.

Already, in the eighteenth century, Smith could see that the idea of a classless competition in which individuals competed with each other helped to produce a society mired in class and, at the same time, allowed people to accept, even welcome, the inequality and subordination that this entailed. For example, people were blind to the mechanisms that ensured the working class were kept in their place and privilege was passed on from one generation to the next. Far from seeing the working class as disadvantaged by their lack of access to the education required by the professions, people were convinced that such education would be wasted on the working class who would never (for the most part) be fit for anything but menial work.

Smith's views on the role of cognitive individualism in the creation of the class system must come as a surprise to anyone who believes that Smith taught that competition between individuals was a part of the market alchemy which distributed resources (including people) to their most productive uses. Of course, he thought competition helped to increase prosperity and was better for most people than rent-seeking behaviour (like that of the guilds or the Catholic Bishops – see Chapter

3). Policy should not support the kind of artificial barriers which prevented labour moving to satisfy demand and reduce prices (of labour and the goods it made) because this would damage prosperity. But it was no part of Smith's theory that the market increased prosperity by sorting individuals into the roles where they would be of most use by hosting a competition between them.

According to Smith, the market moved relatively undifferentiated labour power around the economy, rather than assigning variously talented individuals to their appropriate places in the division of labour. Labour power was only relatively undifferentiated because there were some undeniable differences between the various trades and professions. A lawyer might make a poor cooper but the point was that one lawyer or cooper was not that different to the next one and any minor individual differences that might exist would not explain the different patterns of employment or remuneration. Compared to these insignificant individual differences, the class system was a major influence on inequality.

For example, many people might have, or be capable of acquiring, the skills of entertainers but snobbery about making a living in this way reduced the supply of people who were willing to do it. Opera singers were well paid because so few people who possessed their talents were prepared to endure the loss of honour that followed when they displayed them in public in order to make a living (Smith [1776]2005: 92). It was the class system that made it look as if these were rare skills when in reality they were much more common. The silver lining was that the work that was shunned by the majority offered a route to riches for some individuals. People who were otherwise condemned to relative poverty had found a gap in the armour of the class system, which was created by the rejection of such ways of earning a living by those who would not sacrifice honour for riches.

This is not to say that the poor would always sacrifice honour for money. The human desire for esteem extended from impecunious philosophers to penurious sailors. There were more members of both occupations than we might expect from their poor rewards and, at least for the sailors, the considerable hardships and dangers involved. The attraction was not pecuniary but the chance of honour, glory or recognition. In fact, this pattern was a common product of the class system, extending to the more lucrative professions like the law. People were so keen to chase esteem that the numbers of well-paid and esteemed lawyers were far outnumbered by those who had abandoned the law or clung on even though they had failed to make a living at it.

In the twentieth century, something very similar happened to entertainers and sports stars when they became more generally esteemed than earlier cohorts of these occupations had been. Now NBA basketball stars and professional soccer players were frequently held up as examples that proved the truth of the basic assumptions of cognitive individualism. It was said that their astronomical pay reflected the eagerness of the public to appreciate individuals with such rare talents. Smith would not have been surprised at this transformation since he did not think that snobbery about acting, singing and dancing for a living would necessarily endure forever. Yet, he said that if 'public opinion or prejudice ever alter with regard to such occupations, their pecuniary recompence would quickly diminish', since then there would be much more competition for these jobs (Smith [1776]2005: 93).

In contrast to the eighteenth century, we may now esteem entertainers, however, at first sight, Smith's prediction that their rewards would diminish because of massively increased competition appears to have been confounded. This impression is only supported by estimating the net worth of those at the very top of their professions, however. Once we take into account the many thousands of aspiring, and subsequently disappointed, pop stars, models, sports and film stars, we begin to get an idea of the average returns to these occupations. When the top of these occupations began to attract high esteem as well as high pay, they attracted thousands more hopefuls than could possibly earn a living wage. The current situation is analogous to the one which Smith believed was occupied by the lawyers of his day.

For every successful lawyer, there were 20 failed students of law or impecunious lawyers. These proportions are wild underestimates for the equivalent ratios of failed Hollywood actors, NBA stars and professional soccer players, but the effect on average rewards is in the same direction. In Smith's day, there were fewer poor entertainers because the profession was disreputable and so they were all rewarded well. When basketball and soccer became as honourable as practicing law, even people with the most prodigious talents failed to make a living this way. Yet, thousands were prepared to take the risk because, as Smith said of eighteenth-century young men, their 'natural confidence' in their own capabilities combined with the glamour of the prize to seduce them. Thus, both participants and observers in these competitions continued to validate the assumptions of cognitive individualism. Even though the prejudices of the class system appear to have been revolutionized, it remained the case that inequality was explained and excused by putting down to individual competition what was in reality the result of strategies to perpetuate privilege or good fortune.

The top lawyers of Smith's time were well paid, despite the carnage amongst the competition, and Smith theorized that this was more likely to happen the more access to these top spots was dependent on luck. He saw one of the causes of big differences in pay between one profession and another as 'the probability or improbability of success in them' (Smith [1776]2005: 87). The more entry to, and subsequent success in, a job resembled a lottery, the more money that the lucky minority who succeeded would get paid. Each entrant to the lottery backed themselves to win and, just as in any ordinary lottery, they did so not in the face of any rational calculation of their chances, but in 'the natural confidence which every man has, more or less, not only in his own abilities, but in his own good fortune' ([1776]2005: 9). In order to entice many more to buy a ticket than could possibly win the lottery, the prize had to be big, but that might mean simply sufficient hopes of honour to risk your life on ([1776]2005: 91–2).[1] For young volunteers at the start of a new war, their 'romantic hopes make the whole price of their blood. Their pay is less than that of common labourers, and, in actual service, their fatigues are much greater' ([1776]2005: 94).

Smith thought it was perfectly understandable that the people who won such games of chance would rather see them as games of skill in which their superior talents had been rewarded. They were only too ready to believe that succeeding in this kind of lottery 'is the most decisive mark of what is called genius, or superior talents' ([1776]2005: 92). This was what people thought of Smith's leading eighteenth-century lawyers, and it is also what they think of stars in a variety of high-revenue sports and of extravagantly-rewarded CEOs (Streeck 2014). It is one of the favourite saws of neoliberalism that CEOs are as well paid as sports stars because of their rare talents, but Smith would undoubtedly refer us back to the lottery in order to explain their astronomical rewards. He might also compare CEOs (or hedge-fund managers) to the Catholic Bishops of his day, who managed to maximize their monetary rewards and their public esteem through rent-taking because their place in the hierarchy kept their numbers small and guaranteed exclusivity. Rather than recognizing their luck, they congratulated themselves on their superior talents and expected admiration and deference from others.

As already remarked, it takes little imagination to see Smith's analysis and criticism as equally applicable to the notion of the American Dream as it was to the eighteenth-century British class system. For example, Smith's point that people have the sort of irrational faith in their own chances of success that we are used to seeing amongst inveterate gamblers is routinely evidenced by US polling data, which show that, in spite of their knowledge of the odds against them, people nevertheless expect to succeed. They also accept personal responsibility for their (more or less inevitable) failure.

Even after the onset of the Great Recession, 2011 Pew polling reported that 68 per cent believed that they were in control of their economic situation and the same proportion said they had achieved or would achieve the American Dream (Pew Trust 2011). Evidence that this optimism held despite seemingly more clear-eyed knowledge of inequality in American society was provided by the same poll, and a host of other polls which showed majorities thinking that the American Dream no longer held true for everyone (e.g. Blake 2014).

It is a testament to the power of cognitive individualism that such apparently contradictory views can be held simultaneously. The key is the 'presumptuous hope of success' documented by Adam Smith, together with retained faith in competition between individuals as the determinant of this success. This faith, so evident in public opinion polls, has also been shared by America's prominent public intellectuals. For example, the notion that the astronomical pay of basketball players was a good example of the way American society rewards exceptional individuals who give the public what they want, was common to American philosophers apparently as far apart as Robert Nozick and Ronald Dworkin (Freeman 2010; also see Spicker 2013). Despite being the more liberal of the two, Dworkin shared the assumption of cognitive individualism that people should be held responsible for their choices. Samuel Freeman echoed Adam Smith when he concluded from a survey of Dworkin's thinking that 'the concepts of personal responsibility and holding people responsible for their choices do not justify using markets and market contingencies as a benchmark for determining permissible inequalities and just distributions of income and wealth' (Freeman 2010: 947).

The American claim to be a class-free society took hold at the end of the nineteenth century. The earlier American ideology that had animated the Common Schools Movement was replaced by an economic individualism which made John Dewey despair. In Chapter 7, we will see how industrialization helped to bring about a change in the character of cognitive individualism which made it much more influential than religious or sentimental individualism. This new, more influential cognitive individualism was able to usurp the moral power of sentimental and religious individualisms in a much more effective way than straight-forward utilitarianism ever had. This was not simply the result of industrialization, urbanization and immigration, however. It also relied on a diffusion of the ideas of another British thinker, Herbert Spencer.

PARADISE POSTPONED

Like Paine and Owen, Spencer was extraordinarily important in his
time: 'the world philosopher of the late-nineteenth century ... He was
especially idolized in the United States, where he had many more
followers than Darwin or Marx' (Francis 2007: 8). In Britain, he had a
louder voice in liberalism than J.S. Mill and by some distance he was the
leading English philosopher of his time. Across the world, there were
many who thought him the greatest thinker in history but, rather like
Owen, Spencer was prone to change his convictions (Francis 2007;
Taylor 1992). This makes for plenty of room for debate about what he
actually said and the two main secondary sources I use in this discussion
did not even agree on whether Spencer was a theorist of individualism.
For Francis, the biographer, he only (latterly) had a 'tincture of individualism', but for Taylor, the historian, writing about Spencer's influence on
other political thinkers of the time, he was the leading light of nineteenth-
century individualism. Taylor saw *The Man versus the State* (*MVS*)
(Spencer [1884]1960) as '[t]he chief document of Individualism' and
'Spencer was simply the leading philosophical spokesman for a significant and influential late nineteenth-century political ideology', namely
individualism (Taylor 1992: 4).

MVS, published in 1884, argued that the British Liberals and Tories
were in the process of swapping sides. The Tories used to be the party
clinging on to legislation that advantaged their wealthy, landowning
constituency but now it seemed the Liberals (amongst whom Spencer
counted himself) were following suit. Spencer did not mean by this that
the Liberals were amassing laws to protect the interests of the industrial
bourgeoisie. The problem was, rather, that the Liberals were building up
legislative protection for the working class. For the most part, the
legislation he had in mind was exactly what the sentimental individualism of reformers like Paine and Owen had demanded: laws on education
and welfare and laws which curbed market excesses through regulation.
According to Spencer, liberalism should not be about passing laws to
make it possible for all individuals to enjoy the freedoms presently only
enjoyed by the privileged and wealthy. Its only purpose was to dispense
with legislation and it did not matter whether this was the Corn Laws that
had protected the landed interest or later factory reform which protected
the working class. In this light, Spencer and his allies were the true
liberals arguing for a return to core principles and their opponents within
the party, 'the radicals', were traitors to the cause.

Taylor (1992) suggests that Spencer's argument was convenient for the industrial bourgeoisie who had already joined the elites that were powerful enough to have laws made in their interests. Unless Spencer seriously proposed scrapping their legislation, he was encouraging them to kick over the gaming table just at the point the dice might turn against them. When Spencer wrote about scrapping laws in *MVS*, the vast majority of examples he gave were not the protections enjoyed by the bourgeoisie but the laws extending some small protections to the working class. We can readily understand the radicals' argument in favour of extending the liberties of modern industrial democracy down through society, but Spencer and his allies – who Taylor called the individualists – thought that it had always been the state that stood in the way of liberty. This was as true at the end of the eighteenth century as it had been a century earlier when Paine had targeted the laws that favoured monarchs and aristocrats.

Spencer thought the only legitimate sphere for state action was the pursuit of equity and justice (see below), but when they aspired to improve society in any other respect law-makers were blindly wielding clumsy and dangerous weapons. They were not clever enough to understand the effects of the policies they made because those effects took a long time to appear and the most important of them were often unintended, perhaps the opposite of what the legislators meant to happen (Taylor 1992). There was also a natural process of amelioration going on all the time which was much better left alone, especially by legislators. Spencer believed that evolution was changing how human beings thought. Experience was turning them away from warlike and competitive modes of thought and behaviour and – eventually, but not yet – into beings who could co-operate with and care for each other. For Taylor (1992), it was this natural, evolutionary process of social amelioration which helped Spencer out of the bind of trying to portray himself as a liberal when arguing for the status quo. For Francis (2007), it was the importance of this process to Spencer that should make us wary of describing him as an individualist.

When Spencer saw our evolutionary journey taking us from a past in which all life was cheap to a future in which we would be capable of treating other people as individuals like ourselves, he was describing a change in the beliefs human beings had about each other. Spencer insisted that it was our beliefs that underpinned our perceptions and our rules for behaviour and his expectations for evolution could be summarized as the hope that, through experience, humanity as a whole would become converted to sentimental individualism. In other words, it was because there were not enough sentimental individualists around at the end of the nineteenth century that any attempt to legislate in accordance with sentimental individualism would be doomed to fail.

Of course, we have already seen that Robert Owen also recognized that sentimental individualism was in short supply but he thought the problem could be solved by sustained efforts to grow the right kind of characters. For Spencer, sentimental individualism was a nice idea but absurdly ahead of its time, and therefore doing more harm than good. This proved to be one of the most powerful notions that Spencer bequeathed to American cognitive individualism, but there was more to Spencer's American legacy than the intellectual ballast for the dismissal of 'bleeding-heart' liberalism. Spencer also provided intellectual under-pinning for the idea of the classless society and the American Dream.

American usage of 'liberal' and 'conservative' refer, respectively, to a government's liberality and stinginess with taxpayers' money. Describing how, in 1887, Bruce Smith defined the new uses of 'liberal' and 'conservative', which were to become so familiar in US politics in the twentieth century, Taylor (1992: 263) ascribed Bruce Smith's approbation of conservatism to Spencer's individualist ideas. Committing to Spencer's theories meant arguing against big government while defending the status quo and this sounds like an introduction to the internal tensions of conservative politics in the USA. It was, however, bleeding chunks of Spencer's theories that crossed the Atlantic rather than the full, some-times confused and contradictory, corpus. Indeed, one large organ of Spencer's body of theory was altogether left behind: his evolutionary utopianism. Americans largely ignored the fact that Spencer was talking about a process of evolution that had replaced God and in which our wills and desires were of no account and democracy was an irrelevant side-show. As a result, they confused his utopian hopes with a description of them and their American democracy.

Spencer's theory of progressive improvement through epochs was perhaps like Hegel's theory but entirely without God: blood-thirsty militarism was followed by industrialism and then some kind of utopia. There is disagreement on how we should characterize this utopia, with Taylor referring to 'dreams of a distant anarchistic Utopia' and Francis describing Spencer as a 'utopian individualist'. Earlier, it was suggested that it might even be better to conceive of it as a sentimental individualist utopia in which human character had been transformed. In contrast to Owen's utopian dreams, this was the result of evolution rather than human contrivance. Whereas for Owen character formation was all about rational, scientific intervention for the good of all, Spencer had evolution firmly in charge.

Spencer was one of those opponents Owen found most hateful: those who thought there was no help for the poor because their character could not be redeemed by human intervention. Just like them, Spencer thought the poor may as well die and this would be better for everyone because they could not be helped. Our minds were not blank slates and the development of character could not be rushed. To transform degenerate human beings into the benevolent and altruistic denizens of an anarchist utopia would take many generations (Taylor 1992).[2] Later in his life, Spencer gave up his earlier belief that civilization brought superiority, recognizing that those who were civilized were often more virtuous (for example, honest and gentle) than those who forced civilization upon them. Evolution was now seen not as a linear process of perfecting human nature but as a correction to the damage wrought by competitive militarism in which life was cheap on the simple morality that had survived throughout the previous generations (Francis 2007). It might be best to think of these qualities as instincts improved by use. They were used amongst indigenous people and then, later on, in industrial society where they appeared to be very similar to the virtues admired by Smith and Paine: the altruistic sentiments, self-help, prudence, responsibility, love of justice, of property and liberty (Taylor 1992).

To bring about the industrial society Spencer could see all around him, humanity had gradually given up the dog-eat-dog attitudes of militarism because those who did best now were adapted to do well in industry rather than in military conflict and intimidation. Since co-operation and peaceful interaction were the keys to success in industrial society (Francis 2007), Spencer's vision of the future shared some of the co-operative features of Owen's utopia. The individual benevolence which people had to practice if character was ever to be transformed would be developed in collectives. Spencer thought they would be voluntary but such associations for mutual assistance, mutuality and co-operation were essential for the nurturing of benevolence and sym- pathy and other more elevated capacities. Long before the promised utopia, there would be opportunities for voluntary action in industrial society, including for charitable ends, as the state withdrew (Taylor 1992). Americans were inclined to take this as validation of their own, existing society.

There are themes in Spencer's work that we have repeatedly encoun- tered in the discussion of both cognitive and sentimental individualism. For example, as in Smith and the early works of Paine, the development of commerce and the division of labour made people capable of, and anxious for, self-government. Spencer acknowledged that the old military (monarchical) societies required government, for example when the population had to be forced to provide products or labour to the armed elites that ruled them. In industrial society, people were spontaneously co-operating because the division of labour meant this was necessary. People knew they were mutually interdependent and did not need coercing any longer.

In military societies, status determined subordination: serfs or peasants had to give up goods or labour to nobles and monarchs. In commercial society (Paine) or industrial society (Spencer), status could be replaced by contract. If society hung on to status too long, it could not make a timely transition to contract and this hindered the development of a more complex division of labour. Spencer taught that, as long as the state backed up contracts with the law, it could leave any other task of government to industrial organization. This would allow people to evolve ethically and shed their martial attitudes.

Not only would people no longer think life was cheap but they would start to develop many of the virtues that Smith and Paine talked about, including the commitment to freedom and justice, to respect the claims of others and their rights to property, and a stronger desire for independence would replace the duty of obedience. Spencer's 'law of equal freedom' often served as a sort of shorthand for the ethical condition that Spencer thought evolution was bringing about. We have already encountered this 'law' under other guises, for example Durkheim's moral individualism: it simply means I get as much liberty as I can conducive to just as much liberty for everyone else (Taylor 1992).

When we encountered this idea, it was as a morality built on the core belief of human equality within sentimental individualism. Spencer was not persuaded that people were equal but he confidently predicted that they would come to believe that they were. Rather than being based on his own belief in equality, his law of equal freedom derived from his science: evolution was equipping people with the characteristics that would make them want to apply the law of equal treatment to all their actions. If allowed to do this – i.e. the state did not get in the way with its disastrous law-making – then utility, and particularly happiness, would be maximized. In fact, an all-persuasive law of equal freedom would be a good sign that utopia had been achieved (Taylor 1992). Indeed, in *Social Statics* (1865) Spencer seemed to promise a state of evolution in which we should all be so highly evolved that we would need no government at all. When this is compared to Bentham's stipulation that utility maximization might require limitless state intervention, we can see again why it was the legacy of Spencer (and not Bentham) that played a crucial role in the development of American cognitive individualism (Taylor 1992).

It is important to understand why Spencer thought that character would change over time through experience. Competitive, selfish and aggressive traits would die out because they would no longer be worth inheriting: rather than ensuring survival and worldly gain, they might land you on the gallows. As industrial society developed, the desirable moral characteristics – including respecting the rights of others, self-reliance and prudence – proved to be so helpful to one generation that they were passed on to the next and subsequent generations. Spencer thought that 'socialistic' legislation would interfere with this process because it would prevent the right characteristics being as helpful as they ought to be. Without that legislation, people who did not acquire the right characteristics would fail to thrive, as would those who inherited their characteristics, thus these characteristics would disappear because such traits were a poor fit with the society developing around them (Taylor 1992).

It might help to point out that Spencer had two different conceptions of the 'survival of the fittest', a phrase he is usually said to have coined.[3] In military society, it really did entail the elimination, or at least the ruthless exploitation, of the weak by the strong. In an unmistakeable example of use inheritance, war-like characteristics ensured survival. Spencer hoped we had seen the last of militarist society and in industrial society strength was irrelevant. The fittest were simply those best adapted to a society in which the less martial and more virtuous characteristics helped people to prosper. Unlike their predecessors in industrial society, those who survived and prospered would, quite understandably, want to help those who were unfit. They should however forbear because 'true beneficence will be so restrained as to avoid fostering the inferior at the expense of the superior' and so

> [i]f left to operate in all its sternness, the principle of the survival of the fittest, which, ethically considered, we have seen to imply that each individual shall be left to experience the effects of his own nature and consequent conduct, would quickly clear away the degraded. (Spencer 1893, cited in Taylor 1992: 88)

Survival of the fittest did not require those who survived to grind down and eliminate the poor but simply to avert their gaze while those afflicted with the wrong sort of character failed to reproduce and disappeared from the face of the earth.

Housing and education can be used as examples to help us understand the policy implications of this programme of eugenics. According to Spencer, there was no point in improving the housing or education of the poor in the hope of changing their character because their character had been shaped by generations of deprivation. The next generation would still inherit their parents' characteristics and what was needed was for the lessons of experience to pass to succeeding generations in the shape of altered nerve fibres. Environment shaped character but only through the race, not the individual in one or two generations, so it was pointless giving the poor education or decent houses because they lacked the character needed to appreciate the new conditions. Setting out to reform character by education, for example, was a were of time, as was amply evidenced by the fruitless efforts of the Christian church to do just that (Taylor 1992). What was required instead were 'sentiments responding to the requirements of the social state – emotive faculties that find their gratification in the duties devolving to us' (Spencer 1864, cited in Francis 2007: 119).

This acquisition of sentiments would be postponed if social reform removed or perverted the link between behaviour and consequences. Of course, homilies against misplaced benevolence had currency from biblical times, but here Spencer brought scientific legitimation to the idea that state intervention prevented character from developing. These 'demoralizing effects of government' were exemplified by the welfare provided by the Poor Law which Spencer called 'a kind of social opium eating', in which 'extravagance has been made habitual by shielding [the poor] from the sharp penalties extravagance brings' (Spencer, cited in Taylor 1992: 125). Similarly, Spencer thought the old-age pensions mooted from the 1890s would increase improvidence and decrease self-control. Like Edmund Burke (see Chapter 1), he also argued that such state intervention deprived private individuals of the opportunity to exercise beneficence. The suffering caused by removing a safety net such as the Poor Law would be worth it because its replacement by voluntary help would encourage self-help and altruistic sentiments at the same time (Taylor 1992).

HERBERT SPENCER AND AMERICAN INDIVIDUALISM

The policy implications that Spencer drew from his analysis could be detached from their scientific legitimation. Once we take away the underlying theory of evolution and use inheritance, we are left with some familiar arguments against welfare benefits. So, mistaken ideas like the Poor Law prevented the inheritance of useful characteristics from happening by encouraging improvidence and enabling the improvident to 'multiply', but opposition to the Poor Law did not require a belief in use inheritance (Spencer [1884]1960: 34). Nor was a commitment to evolution required in order to believe that relieving poor children encouraged the production of fatherless children as a kind of meal ticket. This sort of criticism of British welfare legislation had been commonplace since at least as far back as Burke (and people made the same criticisms of Owen's proposals for 'home colonies' for paupers) and could be held to without having the slightest notion of evolution changing character. This removed any obstacle to the policy objections of Spencer's theory crossing the Atlantic: American cognitive individualism could be reinforced by Spencer's ideas without going to the inconvenience of acquiring a belief in evolution.

If American cognitive individualism chose to ignore the idea of use inheritance and the theory of evolution, it was at liberty to misread Spencer: as condoning economic competition as a means for moral improvement. This entails the very mechanism Spencer argued had passed into history with military society. According to Spencer, the strong were no longer the cause of the weak failing to prosper; indeed, though this would put a spanner in the works of evolution, they would be much more likely to want to help those who were failing to thrive. It was because Spencer did not see struggle for survival as the key to progress in modernity that Francis (1992) declared Spencer no individualist. If individualism was taken to mean individual competition, Francis could argue that Spencer thought we had reached a point where people were no longer improved by individualism. Indeed, competition might now threaten progress and prevent the state from developing in the way it should. By the same token, since Spencer was exported to the USA shorn of any reference to human evolution, American cognitive individualism was free to interpret Spencer as the great advocate of economic competition as a mechanism for the moral improvement of humanity.

For Spencer, any interference in evolution, for example laws which might give the working class limited protection against exploitation and the worst living and working conditions, was bound to backfire. Evolutionary theory showed the folly of designing policy from a belief in the equality of human beings. Rather than raising people to the level at which they could benefit from individualism, such well-meaning policies would multiply the poor and prolong their misery. Truly compassionate government let evolution winnow out those who were not well adapted to living with capitalism. In fact, all government intervention impeded the moral progress that was the key to evolution and was best served by leaving people free to make their own choices and enjoy, or endure, the consequences. This in turn required Spencer's 'law of equal freedom' under which 'every man may claim the fullest liberty to exercise his faculties compatible with the possession of like liberty by every other man' (Spencer 1865: 94).

Spencer's ideas changed and reinvigorated American cognitive individualism in a way that allowed the USA to leave behind the combination of cognitive, sentimental and religious individualism which Higham called the 'American ideology'. Readers of *MVS* were instructed to observe the 'unparalleled progress of the United States, which is peopled by self-made men, and the recent descendants of self-made men'. This was in stark contrast to stagnation on the continent of Europe where self-made men were scarce (Spencer [1884]1960: 169). These feelings of admiration were mutual. America was an ideal environment for the synthesis between Spencer's ideas and American individualism, which sowed the seeds for the twentieth-century popularity of neoliberalism amongst voters.

This was acknowledged by Albert Jay Knock, an important figure in early (mid-twentieth-century) neoliberalism, who influenced Murray Rothbard and Ayn Rand, amongst others. Knock wrote the introduction to the 1940 Caxton edition of Spencer's *MVS* and in it he represented himself as one of the last few intellectuals clinging to Spencer's truths in a global sea of 'Statism'. Knock said that the recent (1932–39) history of the USA, for example progressive taxation, replicated the British slide into Statism (1860–1884) that Spencer had railed against. The battle to enshrine Spencer's principles in Britain had been lost but Knock believed it was not too late for American individualism to hear Spencer's call to arms. Knock is sometimes described along with Hayek, Von Mises and Milton Friedman as a libertarian conservative but his reverence for *MVS* suggests why the term 'neoliberal' eventually stuck. It contains Spencer's most trenchant defence of his claim to represent the liberal tradition and his certainty that it was the radicals and the Liberal Party that had deserted the tradition. The idea of a revived or resurgent liberalism which preserved the tradition pervades the essays in *MVS* and if we had to wait until 1938 for the term to be coined, Spencer had already explained why this particular neologism was most apt.

The world's 'greatest living philosopher' confirmed everything Americans hoped was true about their country, even if they were not actually convinced of its divine inspiration and destiny. For example, Spencer said there were scientific reasons the American Constitution should have prioritized negative freedom and why Americans were right to be circumspect about changing it. Moreover, Spencer's theories provided scientific reasons for thinking that the USA was more of a utopia than any other country on earth. Many Americans believed that the wish to found a utopia on American shores had animated American history from the original settlement through the Revolutionary War to the present day. However, for Americans who did not believe in God's investment in their nation, the need for further validation was pressing. In Spencer's theory of history, society evolved 'from a custom-bound, hierarchical society based on relations of status and subordination to the open, free, progressive society of classical liberalism with its voluntarily assumed social relations' (Taylor 1992: 167). Most Americans thought themselves citizens of that open, free and progressive society and already in the sort of social equilibrium Spencer described in *First Principles* (1867).

In many of its citizens' estimation, America was already infinitely closer to a utopia of individual freedom and fully developed morality than were the countries of Europe with their bloated, undemocratic governments. Spencer's predictions about the pace of change in human society seemed overly pessimistic. It had taken barely a couple of hundred years to get the USA to its current state, so evolution could simply be omitted from his theories. There need be no slow progress towards a distant utopia via further extension of personal liberties and the shrinking of the state. American enthusiasts thought the point was to defend the liberties they already had and they agreed with Spencer that any hint of socialism would put progress in reverse and return society to the various degrees of un-freedom associated with militarism (Spencer [1884]1960; Taylor 1992). The warnings Spencer gave in *MVS* about socialism's inability to resist militarism and the unimaginable horrors of communism would help Americans gird their loins to defend their utopia for generations to come. They were, after all, holding the hopes of the human race in their hands (Francis 2007).

A less self-confident America might have lacked the temerity to put itself in place of Spencer's utopia and ignore the contribution of evolutionary theory to his ideas. In fact, the altruistic values of Spencer's anarchistic utopia had little in common with those of American individualism. His speech at a banquet in his honour in New York in 1882 made it plain that the USA had a long way to go before it could claim to possess the values of a truly advanced nation. The most obvious proof of this was the American obsession with work. With the transition from military to industrial society, work had replaced fighting but this was far from the end of the story. Once nature had been tamed, the work ethos would lose its grip and humanity would discover that 'life is not for work, but work is for life' (cited in Francis 2007: 105).

Spencer declared 'the average conduct, under the pressure and excitement of social life as at present carried on, is in sundry respects repulsive' (Spencer [1884]1960: 57) and his idea of fully evolved human beings over-lapped with Robert Owen's. He shared Owen's expectation that less and less work would be required of people in the future but in Spencer's case this expectation was underpinned by evolutionary theory. Even laying aside the centrality of the work ethos, there was probably little of American individualism that appealed to him. For example, he had no sympathy with a utilitarian moral philosophy and he thought it bizarre to admire selfishness when so much aesthetic pleasure resulted from caring for the feelings of others. The evolution of human beings required increasing self-restraint which unnecessarily restricted opportunities for pleasure, particularly sensual pleasures (Francis 2007).

Omitting evolution also allowed American individualism to finesse the fact that Spencer's anarchistic utopia was meant to supersede capitalist society (Francis 2007), but substituting capitalism for the forces of evolution made little practical difference to the policy implications which American individualism could glean from Spencer's writing. Knowledge of Lamarckian use inheritance and the increasing complexity of all organisms, including human institutions, produced infallible scientific predictions of human behaviour, and ought to guide all of our policies and political activities, but it suggested that laissez-faire was the best policy (Taylor 1992). This was obviously true for the economy and for social policy, although less obvious in respect of justice and equity (see below). The same policy conclusions could also be reached without the science. According to Spencer ([1884]1960), human beings were inherently unpredictable and, because there was no telling what the effects of a particular policy would be on their behaviour, it was better to leave well alone. Laissez-faire was therefore the only safe recipe for all public policies, including those which affected the workings of the economy. Spencer was not above claiming at the same time that laissez-faire was good for prosperity, but cognition (as opposed to science) suggested that the main problem with interfering was that we could not tell the effect of policies on people's characters.

The scientific injunction to laissez-faire may have simply reinforced policies which Spencer could have arrived at on the basis of cognition alone, but it brought a degree of confidence in the process of policy analysis that cognition (with its emphasis on the unpredictability of policy intervention) could not justify. Science had no such doubts: it told us what certainly would happen if we interfered with use inheritance and increasing organic complexity and the severity of these consequences meant that there really was no alternative to laissez-faire. This confidence was transferred to American individualism, even though it omitted Spencer's evolutionary theory.

A halo of certainty, as captured in the maxim There Is No Alternative (or TINA), was to become one of the hallmarks of twentieth-century neoliberalism (Streeck 2014), but it was derived from the same intellectual error that was implicated in some of the most horrific events of that century. As I explained in *The Demoralization of Western Culture*, totalitarian systems in Nazi Germany and the Soviet Union drew on science to inform politics. It was the Nazi certainty that the party served as the instrument of evolution, and the Soviet certainty that the party served as an instrument of a science of human progress, that led in both cases to immorality of the most extreme kind imaginable (Fevre 2000a). It is just as well that American individualism neither needed, nor had room for, Spencer's evolutionary theory but the certainties it took from the traces of evolutionary theory in Spencer's rhetoric were dangerous enough.

In my earlier work, I argued that to make human feelings of no account was a characteristic of totalitarianism of all kinds. This was what happened when science was used to push aside sentimental sense-making in the twentieth century and this is precisely what Spencer was doing when he argued that, as moved as he was by the suffering of the poor, there was no alternative to letting evolution take its course (Francis 2007). American individualism took the same stance but with capitalism acting as evolution's amanuensis. In the process, it laid the foundations of a neoliberalism that was a far cry from nineteenth-century laissez-faire. According to Andrew Ure (1835), for example, the people who imagined feelings were hurt were themselves deluded as when, for example, they imagined that children did not enjoy as well as profit from their labour in the factories.[4] Similarly, the ideologues of the Manchester School saw capitalism as productive of the best of all possible worlds.[5] None of these apologists and enthusiasts for capitalism believed, with Spencer, that the only possible road to human progress entailed untold human misery.

CONCLUSION

Adam Smith was dismissive of the idea that market forces, rather than luck and the class system, were responsible for inequality, but Herbert Spencer trusted in them to do the work of evolution. He was convinced that intervention in markets would obstruct the human evolution which would eventually produce a society ordered by the principles of sentimental individualism. However, the only means to this earthly paradise was to allow cognitive individualism free rein since it was self-interest that would lead to the adaptation to market forces (through use inheritance) that was necessary to develop human beings fit to live there. Unlike Smith, Spencer thought the market cultivated virtue and many Americans could recognize this, and other convictions, in their own ideology. Spencer's philosophy seemed to them to suggest that America represented the future of all human societies and any attempt at an alternative route to the summit was bound to end in disaster. This dogma endorsed the atrophy of compassion and a much crueller American individualism was now in the making.

NOTES

1. Some abolitionists went on to campaign against the state lottery.
2. And 'a future state of human perfection ... could be achieved only over the course of many generations and as a consequence of the misery of the idle, the improvident, and the destitute' (Taylor 1992: 130).
3. Used in *MVS* (Spencer [1884]1960: 110, 138) but also in *The Principles of Biology* (Spencer 1864).
4. Andrew Ure, *The Philosophy of Manufactures* (1835), p. 299.
5. The Manchester School included prominent abolitionists and promoted the universal benefits of free trade. For example, the working class as well as the manufacturers were supposed to benefit from the repeal of the Corn Laws.

7. Sowing the seeds of neoliberalism

Chapter 5 described the combination of religious, sentimental and cognitive individualism – deriving from a curious mixture of millenarian Protestantism, American nationalism and civic republicanism – which Higham called the American ideology. Overhauling the American ideology to fit the ideas of Spencer would mean promoting cognitive over sentimental and religious individualisms. It would require celebrating inequality rather than civic virtue and shrinking the state rather than deliberative democracy. Cognitive individualism would be left to do its benign work and, as long as those with soft hearts did not intervene, the obvious evidence of individual success and failure would accomplish the necessary evolutionary changes (Taylor 1992). More extreme inequality, with extravagant success and harrowing failure, would get them made more quickly. This chapter explains in more detail how Spencer's theories anticipated the next phase in American individualism, particularly in respect of his views on negative freedom, capitalism, the division of labour, social stratification and the state.

NEGATIVE FREEDOM AND THE AMERICAN CONSTITUTION

Spencer thought the only thing that really mattered in politics was whether there was interference in the private lives of citizens. If individuals were not protected against political intrusion, the process of evolution might be disrupted. Spencer did not think that democracy was any more likely to prevent such interference than a monarchy. His only preference was for government that would improve justice and equity and there was no reason why a democracy could guarantee this (Francis 2007). Representation and legitimacy were neither here nor there; Spencer eschewed the language of individual rights and, in later life, recanted his old belief in the vote as a natural right. Character would have to change before the suffrage could be extended because then citizens would better appreciate justice and respect other people's property (Taylor 1992).

As we will see in later chapters, democracy may have outlived its usefulness to neoliberalism (Brown 2015; Streeck 2014), but what did those raised on the American ideology make of Spencer's indifference to democracy and individual rights? Spencer disapproved of American pork-barrel politics and expressed indifference to the American Constitution, as he did to other constitutional arrangements (Spencer [1884]1960). He did not think they could change anything for the better and he was not interested in safeguarding individuals' rights through them (Francis 2007). Nevertheless, Americans were able to see his insistence that politics be kept out of their lives as entirely in keeping with the negative freedom which was the essence of their democracy.

Spencer's views endorsed an interpretation of the Constitution as the guarantee of negative freedom and helped Americans to leave behind, for practical purposes, the egalitarianism of the American ideology. Spencer's theories supported Americans who wished to argue that negative freedom was the only condition that need apply equally to all. Robber barons and simple farmers needed to be equal only in that they were equal beneficiaries of the Constitutional guarantee and this was exactly as Spencer prescribed. In the essay on 'The New Toryism', in the early pages of *MVS*, Spencer ([1884]1960) made it clear that, while the compulsion of the individual was the root of all evil, there was nothing of interest about any particular free choice an individual might exercise. It did not matter to Spencer if welfare varied wildly between individuals and this should not be a consideration when people were contemplating how they should be governed (Francis 2007).

Spencer's theories validated a new American individualism in which the poor had no practical options to exercise the freedom they had been equally guaranteed by the Constitution but must pretend otherwise. They must assume the wishes and feelings of citizens who are grateful that their futures are in their own hands. This double-think had particular relevance in a society distinguished by slavery followed by racial persecution and segregation. While Spencer opposed slavery, consider the implication of his theory for Reconstruction when freedom was, apparently, safely preserved in the Constitution and the welfare of individuals was their own concern. Where was the rationale for reforming those institutions that existed to perpetuate racial domination? Action would only be justified if the Constitution itself was flouted. Spencer's theory helps us to understand why America's doctrine of privileging negative freedom justified the omission of actions through which abolition may have had a more noticeable material effect on the lives of ex-slaves.

The Americans who found Spencer's theories appealing were not only comfortably middle-class but overwhelmingly white (Francis 2007; Taylor 1992). Just as Spencer confirmed Americans' good opinion of themselves, and approved of their reverence for their political institutions, so his theories confirmed the rectitude of their attitude to people of colour. This point is infrequently made not simply because of Spencer's well-known opposition to imperialism, but because racial attitudes are so often left out of discussions of American individualism. Consider, however, how closely Spencer's views describe widely-held attitudes towards people of colour in the USA from Reconstruction to the present day (Foner 1989; Francis 2007). While they could be made literate and numerate, there was no point in educating the masses because their political stupidity would persist. They could not acquire civic virtues and were only capable of understanding the world from their own, narrow point of view. In *The Man versus the State*, Spencer painted the poor as morally-degenerate, welfare cheats living off the labour of others. This view validated a transition from the nationalism of the American ideology to the racism of a new American cognitive individualism.

Spencer's insistence on negative freedom not only validated inequality but also reinforced Americans' reverence for their Constitution as the guarantee of that freedom. By treating their Constitution as sacrosanct, Americans would make sure it was not chopped and changed to fit in with the wishes and desires of those who shouted the loudest or mustered the most votes. The effect was exactly what Spencer required when he insisted that political institutions could not be changed more quickly than evolution changed the character of the citizens. He thought that there was no point in changing institutions to maximize utility, as a Benthamite might propose, if character was unaltered (Taylor 1992). Ultimately, it was evolution, through the modification of character, which would bring about contentment rather than any calculus of individual utility (Francis 2007).

According to Spencer, tampering with any political institution for the material benefit or increased happiness of a particular generation meant destroying a precious, organic growth. Change could only be contemplated if a way could be found to consider the happiness of a population over a much longer period. Even then, the causes of happiness were far too heterogeneous to make a basis for policy, and founding politics on the claim to be able to increase happiness took politics into the spiritual world (Francis 2007). Spencer's view that political institutions were organic rather than manufactured reinforced the prohibition against interference with negative freedom in pursuit of utility, for example

material comforts. Small changes could be tried, and rejected if ineffective, but the essence was unhurried, incremental increases in institutional
complexity (Taylor 1992), as exemplified, for example, in amendments to
the Constitution and the work of the Supreme Court.

Spencer thought the best defence against the slippery slope which led
to socialism and communism was to shrink the state as fast as democracy
was extended (Taylor 1992). Most Americans came to share his opinion
that some sort of defence was needed and that no amount of democracy
would make it acceptable for the state to curtail negative freedom
(Francis 2007). At the very least, they pointed to the checks and balances
afforded by the Constitution, but there was an element of the new
American individualism that was prepared to lean much further in the
direction of Spencer's anarchist utopia. This libertarian strand did not
think democracy any better than militarism – it was all un-freedom
because that was always what the state engineered[1] – and its influence
would be evident within neoliberalism.

INDUSTRIAL CAPITALISM AND THE DIVISION OF LABOUR

The American ideology was strongly identified with agrarian capitalism
but in the UK Spencer had seen the rapid industrialization and urbanization that the USA would undergo as the American ideology was
transformed. His ideas about the cognitive individualism appropriate to
industrial capitalism were already wildly popular in the USA before the
transformation took place there. Spencer's theory required him to
embrace industrial capitalism no matter what the cost: for some, the
losses would be catastrophic but these did not matter since the alternative
was an irresistible slide backwards into almost universal slavery. For
Spencer, evolutionary gains in character could only be preserved by the
forward motion that industrial capitalism facilitated.

He was not averse to drawing on sociological or economic evidence
which bolstered his side of the argument. For example, when he was
describing some of the catastrophic losses that industrial capitalism
would cause to humanity, Spencer sometimes chose to claim that this
was, nevertheless, contributory to the greatest happiness of the greatest
number. On other occasions, for example in *MVS*, Spencer declared that
'the great majority' suffered and their sufferings were more than our
sympathy could bear. He also saw people behaving abominably, for
example cheating each other through adulterating goods. Inequality was
extreme and 'at variance with that ideal of human relations on which the

sympathetic imagination likes to dwell'. All the same, Spencer continued, we must not forget how much we benefitted from capitalism through its technological advances and the availability of cheaper goods (Spencer [1884]1960: 57).

The material advantages of capitalism would be grist to the mill of American cognitive individualism, but what made the contribution of Spencer so decisive was evident as this passage of *MVS* continued. Spencer described 'the major evil' in capitalism as the way managers took an unfair share of the product of workers' labour. Spencer went on to sow the seeds from which neoliberalism would eventually grow when he argued that this was preferable to the evils entailed in any other system (Spencer [1884]1960: 58). For Spencer, capitalism was doing the work of evolution and stopping this happening would be much the greatest evil of all. As we have noted already, this was a qualitatively different argument to that made by the great majority of nineteenth-century enthusiasts for capitalism.

Unlike the proponents of laissez-faire and the utilitarians, Spencer put the economy in charge of the future of humanity by treating it as if it were an amanuensis for evolution and, as Taylor (1992) puts it, a natural process. Francis (2007) was right to distance Spencer from laissez-faire and from the idea that capitalist freedom was the acme of human development, but wrong to conclude that this meant Spencer had no contribution to make to neoliberalism. Neoliberalism differed from laissez-faire precisely in its certainty that there was no alternative to capitalism. For laissez-faire, capitalism was the system most capable of satisfying human needs and desires, but for neoliberalism it was a matter of life or death for humanity. Neoliberalism also took from Spencer the implications for *positive* freedom of his idea that evolutionary gains in character require people to fit into the environment. For now, this meant that people must be good consumers and producers. Spencer hoped it would not last, but he recognized that the obsession with 'living to work' at the heart of American individualism was a product of capitalist society.

The specification of positive freedoms for consumers or producers was anathema for both American cognitive individualism and, subsequently, neoliberalism. This is evident from their common opposition to, for example, the specification of good choices (for example, in health care) that should be available to all, including the poor. Neoliberalism involved capitalism shaping our wishes and feelings as consumers and producers while insisting that there was no alternative (Brown 2015; Fevre 2000a). In policy debates suffused with neoliberalism, positive freedom and choices outside a market framework were what politicians came to call the 'live rail'. Tom Paine's recommendations for policies that would put the poor in the same position to make the choices others could make as a result of the triumph of individualism were now the hallmark of the 'greater evil': socialism.

We will return to the fear of socialism which united Spencer and the next phase of American individualism, but here it is worth noting that his view of the way people had to fit in as producers entailed a second principle beyond the evolution of character. For Spencer, evolution was synonymous with growing complexity throughout the universe. This process was neither Social Darwinism nor Lamarckian use inheritance but involved organisms becoming more complex, not because of the need to adapt to the environment but 'because homogenous structures are inherently unstable' (Taylor 1992: 139). Like Adam Smith, Spencer noted the specialization entailed in increasing complexity but Spencer's template was the specialized functions of the body. When he wrote of specialization increasing 'efficiency', it was not Smith's efficient markets he had in mind but the organic analogy: 'each aids all and all aid each with increasing efficiency; and the total activity we call life, individual or national, augments' (Spencer 1898, cited in Taylor 1992: 140).

This was an argument for all of society's 'organs', including the state, sticking to their core functions, but it was also a theory of the division of labour which was not at all like Smith's. In *WN*, the division of labour boosted prosperity by making more things affordable to all, while making most work deadening to the mind and soul. In Spencer's theory, the division of labour was driven by more monolithic forces than human desires and needs. Society, like any organism, would become more and more complex, creating different functions and different structures to perform them. There were compensations for increasing functional and structural differentiation and Francis (2007) listed them as three negative freedoms – freedom from superstition, poverty and violence – but these compensations were not the reason why differentiation and specialization occurred.

For Spencer, the differentiation and specialization which accompanied the increasing division of labour undoubtedly meant a loss of individual self-determination and the new American individualism recognized the division of labour as just such an irresistible force. Spencer was sure that the organism that individuals were a part of gave them a job to do, just like any other cell, and individuals were only valuable as long as they performed their assigned functions (Francis 2007). While this flatly contradicted sentimental individualism and its belief in the value of each human being, it was much more attuned to the American individualism which began to appear at the end of the nineteenth century. Sentimental individualism might wish (as in the works of Robert Owen) to reconstruct the division of labour to create the conditions for human flourishing, but cognitive individualism took the division of labour as its fundamental reality. Individual adaptation might not be the point of the increasing division of labour according to evolution theory, but adapting to the division of labour was what Americans did if they wished to survive and prosper.

As well as promoting realism about conforming to the division of labour, Spencer's legacy also contained a distant promise of individuality. Spencer's theory brushed aside Adam Smith's prediction of a soul-deadening division of labour with which neoliberalism would have found it hard to win hearts and minds. Far from reducing everyone to packages of undifferentiated labour power, the increasing complexity of the universe meant that people must be increasingly differentiated in order to fill increasingly specialist roles. While we must change and adapt, or perish, the increasing complexity of the division of labour held out the prospect of an opportunity to develop and express our individuality as we made our contribution to the organism (Francis 2007). Individuality did not, however, imply free choice because the place in which we could best make our contribution would be chosen for us by the market when it assessed our individual capabilities.

The *promise* of individuality at some unspecified point in the future was one of the neoliberal seeds carried by American individualism. Without an alternative to Smith's gloomy view of the division of labour, neoliberalism would have had a very hard job persuading us that the future to which there was no alternative had its compensations. In Chapter 3, I explained how Smith's prediction of the ever-increasing simplification of the division of labour was a very bad fit with the high hopes of neoliberalism. Far from finding the main source of neoliberalism's authority in Adam Smith, we ought to consider Spencer the main source of neoliberalism's authority for *contradicting* Adam Smith. Moreover, Spencer's theory easily accommodated the further complexity that would produce a social organism on a global scale. Indeed, some neoliberal explanations of globalization (for example, networks, 'head and body nations') originated in the lexicon of concepts inspired by the organic analogy. Spencer expected competition and selection between industrial societies with those which were farthest along the road to heterogeneity winning out and 'replacing' the laggards (Taylor 1992: 180). This threat of Social Darwinism at the societal level became a familiar part of the armoury which neoliberalism employed to encourage adaptation to the changing needs of the division of labour.

SOCIAL STRATIFICATION AND THE CLASSLESS SOCIETY

In Spencer's theory, the organic trend to differentiation and complexity that drove the division of labour was accompanied by selection according to individual characteristics which contributed in turn to Lamarckian use inheritance. This is the source of much misinterpretation of Spencer's contribution to neoliberalism. A particular bugbear has been the notion that Spencer bequeathed the notion that capitalism was simply the less bloody version of the trial of strength endured in military society. In this version of his theory, the characteristics of the strongest were still passed on to succeeding generations but strength was measured in success in economic competition rather than in fighting and killing people. In the second half of this book, I will show that, if this was an accurate description of neoliberalism, it would be impossible to imagine how neoliberal ideology could have taken over the liberal democracies. Is it, however, an accurate description of the ideas of Herbert Spencer which were available for the transformation of the American ideology into a new American cognitive individualism?

When Spencer referred to 'merit', he was sometimes referring to whether a human being deserved to survive and reproduce. In earlier phases of evolution, they did not deserve to do this if they could not compete for food and shelter and escape enemies. Merit in capitalism was still as much to do with evolution as it had been in military society but the species' 'fitness for its mode of life' was no longer determined in the same ways (Spencer [1884]1960: 105–7). In capitalist society, survival had become a matter of making a living, usually through an occupation. Rather than having to wrest food and shelter from others, people deserved to survive if they could hold down a job. That people might compete with each other to get hired for these jobs was of little importance to Spencer. Instead, he chose to emphasize the spontaneous co-operation of the division of labour (as opposed to the compulsory co-operation insisted on by governments). His view of the evolutionary function of capitalism told him that it was how people fitted into the more specialized places in the division of labour that was important. Specialization was the product of complexity and differentiation that increasing co-operation had made possible (Taylor 1992).

Where Adam Smith had punctured the vanity of people who imagined it was their talent or hard work that had got them into a lucrative job, Spencer thought their self-aggrandizement was fully justified because they deserved the jobs and rewards that went with them. Smith thought they got those jobs by jockeying for position and seeking every advantage, fair and foul. They were die-hard competitors who observed no rules and certainly not the law of equal freedom. Spencer did not think people fought each other for jobs in this way. The division of labour chose between them according to their talents, therefore this was selection not competition and the criterion for selection was efficiency. This did not extend to state employment because state employees were not selected for their efficiency any more than they were incentivized for it. Selection for efficiency only occurred in capitalist enterprises (Spencer [1884]1960: 138).[2] Where Smith would have taken any incumbent's claim to deserve their place because of their efficiency with a pinch of salt, Spencer was convinced that the characteristics with the highest merit were those with the greatest impact on efficiency.

Since Spencer entertained none of Smith's cynicism about the justifications which people put about to explain their privileges, he did not think it was necessary to measure efficiency directly. We should instead take it on trust that the more efficient workers would be in the highest demand and would therefore be the best paid. We could therefore impute differences in their efficiency from differences in their rewards (Taylor 1992). The rewarding of superior characteristics was necessary to evolution through use inheritance but we were not rewarded for beating our fellows. Rather, they rewarded us because we were providing them with something they valued. Again, co-operation trumped competition in setting the right conditions for evolution under capitalism.

Spencer defined three conditions which were necessary for superior characteristics to be rewarded. These were the liberty (constrained only by the law of equal freedom) to serve others as well as one could, the rewards (enforced by contracts) given according to the relative worth of one's services to others, and the peace to be able to use those rewards to satisfy one's wants and raise children who would also possess the worthy characteristics. If these conditions were satisfied, there would be social progress because the most worthy individuals would be more likely to prosper and reproduce than those who were less worthy. The key product of the three conditions was that the difficulties any individual would face in thriving and, crucially, raising children, would diminish according to the rewards they received (to reflect the worth of their services in the labour market which in turn reflected their superior characteristics) (Spencer [1884]1960: 107). State regulation or interference with any of the three conditions jeopardized this key evolutionary process (Taylor 1992).

For Spencer ([1884]1960), it was the importance of these conditions to evolution that made it worth maintaining the individual rights they depended on.[3] Far from lumbering American cognitive individualism (and eventually neoliberalism) with a dogma about the necessity of dog-eat-dog competition, Spencer bequeathed the idea that the rights cherished by Americans were vital to the allocation of jobs, and associated rewards, according to merit. These conditions established what would much later become known as a 'meritocracy' which was, in turn, vital to social progress. In other words, the neoliberal idea of individuality growing as the division of labour became more complex did not depend on Social Darwinism. Instead, it took from Spencer only ideas which would increase its attractions, and plausibility, for the citizens of democracies.

So long as they were working in the private sector, Spencer's theory was a great fillip for anyone who was doing well in capitalist society and might worry about growing inequality. It would be especially reassuring for those who no longer believed their success was a sign of God's favour. However, reassurance did not depend on absorbing Spencer's ideas about evolution. All one had to know was that inequality was a reflection of differences in the demand for various characteristics which themselves reflected differences in the value of those characteristics to other people. While there was no need to believe you were prospering because you were right where evolution wanted you, there was every reason to expect that your children would be able to hold this position because they too would be able to demonstrate merit. All that was required was hard work and education (not, as Smith would have it, the reproduction of privilege through investment in your children).

It was small wonder that, in Britain, Spencer's ideas were most popular amongst the rising Victorian middle classes, including the professions (Taylor 1992). Spencer 'provided the politically confident bourgeoisie a classless vision of the future' and this judgement was even more apposite in the USA (Francis 2007: 249). After all, that classless vision is still more often known as the American Dream. The new American individualism inherited from the American ideology a view of America as a relatively level playing field for individual endeavours – certainly much more level than anything the Europeans could offer. Americans understood that their country already satisfied the conditions which Spencer had stipulated for a meritocracy: liberty within the law of equal freedom, rewards proportional to the value of the services provided and the peace to enjoy the fruits of one's labours.

Spencer was unconcerned by the possibility that people would use their rewards to act in the way Adam Smith described, making sure that their children got good jobs because their parents could afford to pay for their education and training. This was simply one way in which parents might pass on to the next generation the characteristics that had given them access to good jobs. Some of Spencer's contemporaries thought that the inheritance of privilege undermined the conditions he said meritocracy required. The evolutionary theorist Alfred Russell Wallace argued that, without a level playing field provided by education, it was impossible to know that the characteristics best fitted to the society were being rewarded (Taylor 1992). Spencer did not think education could produce equality. The working class were less sensitive because they laboured mechanically and education could not make up for their deficient psychological traits (Francis 2007). The level playing field did not require state interference in education but, in the final section, we discuss the roles Spencer did assign to state supervision.

THE STATE AND THE RULE OF LAW

H.M. Hyndman (1884) pointed out that Spencer failed to recognize that, like the state, businesses relied on bureaucracies and were just as much concerned with coercing individuals and limiting their freedom (cited in Taylor 1992: 183). This criticism would have made no impact on Spencer since it was perfectly clear to him that business bureaucracies were determining the fate of individuals – and a good thing too since this was necessary to capitalism's role in evolution. The case of the state was entirely different because the danger was that it would obstruct evolution rather than facilitating it by straying far beyond the function it provided for the organism and pretending to 'know each man's needs better than he knows them himself' and to 'possess superhuman power and intelligence' (Spencer [1884]1960: 127). Society was far too complex for the state to be able to pull policy levers and affect behaviour in the way it desired. There would inevitably be unintended consequences beyond the areas that had the state's attention.

Businesses had no wish to shape behaviour in this way, but, because they were fulfilling their functions as parts of the organism under the control of the market, they could not help but spontaneously produce order. Taylor (1992) pointed out how this anticipated neoliberalism and Hayek's admiration for the way the activities of millions of individuals were spontaneously co-ordinated by the market. For Spencer, the efficiency of the private sector was a sure sign that it was doing the good work of evolution, but these arguments could inspire a new generation of American individualists who had no interest in his evolutionary theories. Thus, Spencer claimed that the state was massively less efficient than private enterprise, even when discharging its proper duties of justice and defence, yet the current doctrine was to '[s]light the good and faithful servant, and promote the unprofitable one from one talent to ten' (Spencer [1884]1960: 126). The state's inefficiency was even more obvious when it stepped outside its proper limits, but in all cases of state employment the employer failed to do what capitalist enterprises could not help but do: act as the instrument of evolution.

Spencer's proof of this was, again, state inefficiency, which he described in the terms Adam Smith had reserved for his attacks on the universities. Corruption and laziness flourished where there was no 'such antiseptic as free competition' (Spencer [1884]1960: 141). State employment encouraged patronage and all kinds of veniality in recruitment and, just as in *The Wealth of Nations*, the antidote was to have the decisions (especially hiring and firing) made by people who would personally lose by inefficiency. When applied to the state in the last quarter of the twentieth century, this argument provided the rationale for what became known as New Public Management (see Chapter 11).[4] Of course, Spencer's central recommendation was to shrink the state but here there were more vested interests to battle. Creating government jobs gave the middle classes an interest in the growth of the public sector.

Which other of Spencer's policy prescriptions could be taken up by the new American individualism and passed on to neoliberalism? Spencer's economic arguments were of the type made familiar by Margaret Thatcher when she appealed to the good sense of the British housewife who knew how to manage her household budget. So, when the state grew, it sucked resources from the private sector because the state did not make wealth but depended on the wealth that industry, commerce and distribution provided. Any kind of state subsidy – for example, to wages or housing costs – would mean taking resources from the employers who created jobs and wealth. This was all of a piece with Spencer's acceptance of the idea of a Wages Fund and the inevitable reduction in jobs which happened when wages were increased. It is therefore hardly surprising that Spencer ([1884]1960) thought (inefficient) nationalized industries would squeeze out the private sector.

Just as a bloated state took resources from the more efficient private sector, so welfare payments transferred resources from the worthy to the indigent. As a result, the worthy would themselves be so reduced in circumstances that they too would become dependent on the state. The state aimed to alleviate the suffering of the least deserving by intensifying the suffering of the most deserving. At the same time, it thwarted the purpose of the evolutionary 'struggle for existence' which was to make sure that the characteristics of the worthy – for example, their diligence – were passed on to their children. As a result of the interference of the state, their children inherited 'artificial evils in addition to the natural evils they have to bear' (Spencer [1884]1960: 113–14).

The imperative to shrink the state also applied to regulation because it gave duties to government which took away from individuals their responsibility for looking out for their own interests (Francis 2007). Spencer argued that people would have arranged for their most important needs and wishes to be met – for example, by voluntary co-operation – long before the state got round to interfering in their lives. It was therefore inevitable that any needs and wishes the state was seeking to satisfy would be the less important ones that people had not thought it worth the effort to pursue. Since resources were limited, it was better that the state leave well alone as its action could not help but mean a more important thing would be left undone. Spencer concluded that rather than the state telling society what it needed, we should let society 'feel what it most needs' (Spencer [1884]1960: 157).

Elsewhere in Spencer's writing, it is easy to find arguments that would not be out of place in later neoliberal agendas, for example the argument that a little state interference – such as free school meals and clothing for indigent London children – inevitably led to a lot. Later campaigns against 'the nanny state' and uncontrolled and obsessive regulation, for example of health and safety, could easily be discerned here (Francis 2007). Some of Spencer's most trenchant arguments were aimed at the regulation of employment, child labour and education. For example, he criticized the compulsion of parents to educate their children and warned of a slippery slope that would lead to free public education. There was scarce a goal of sentimental individualism that Spencer did not deride, including a belated enactment of Adam Smith's proposal in favour of credentialism to child labour in agriculture (Spencer [1884]1960: 13).

Spencer only gave one interview on his visit to the USA in 1882 in which he must have baffled American readers by telling them he was not in favour of laissez-faire where justice and equity were concerned (Francis 2007). Rather than disclosing his hidden egalitarian leanings, what Spencer had in mind was 'the "civil equality" of equality before the law' (Taylor 1992: 33). For example, he considered the epitome of state promotion of justice and equity to be the supervision of the contracts which ensured people were properly rewarded for the services they provided for their fellows. Every argument Spencer made for the shrinking of the state was in some sense about equity. For example, he opposed the regulation of employment for the same reason he favoured land nationalization: because laws which protected narrow class interest – in one case the working class, in the other the aristocracy – were not equitable (Taylor 1992). Every time Spencer argued that evolution must be allowed to do its work, he thought he was also arguing for greater justice, as in the case of the contracts which people must observe to maintain the link between merit and reward.

We know that Spencer ([1884]1960) thought the sentimental individualism that misguidedly anticipated utopia was responsible for a string of calamities in public policy. In *Social Statics*, he described the 'pure evil' that sentimental individualism wrought when it breached equity by severing the connection between actions – for example, indigence – and consequences. This was prohibited by the law of equal freedom and there was nothing just about a policy which 'tends to fill the world with those to whom life will bring most pain, and tends to keep out of it those to whom life will bring most pleasure' (Spencer 1865: 381). The struggle for survival had to go on within the framework of justice represented by the law of equal freedom and the state should act as referee to make sure everyone respected this framework (Taylor 1992).

Spencer saw it as the state's responsibility that citizens would get what their characters and actions deserved so far as this was compatible with treating all citizens in the same way. Given the earlier discussion of negative freedom, it is no surprise that Spencer called the state's role 'negative regulation'. As well as making sure contracts were observed, it entailed the state in administering justice and ensuring national defence (Taylor 1992). The state was needed to 'forbid unfairness; to adjudicate when called on; and to enforce restitution for injuries' (Spencer [1884]1960: 127). Far from condoning a trial of strength, the state should restrain individuals from 'directly or indirectly aggressing on his fellows'. This was 'negatively coercive, not positively coercive' (Spencer [1884]1960: 19).

Although Spencer's interview might have caused some confusion, everything that he said in general terms about equity and justice could readily be absorbed as part of the new American individualism. Indeed, it was in the USA that his prescriptions for this aspect of the state's role were most scrupulously followed. This was not just a matter of making sure that capitalists could rely on the rule of law, particularly on enforcing contracts. Even more important for American individualism was the pursuit by individuals of the ideal of legal redress for breach of contract and restitution which even today makes so many outsiders think the USA a particularly litigious society. Certainly, no other country has tried harder to observe Spencer's injunction that (in theory) everyone has the right to pursue justice. Inequality in ability to pay for this justice was not a problem for Spencer anymore than any other type of privilege.[5] Taylor (1992) concluded that (in practice) all of his principles benefitted the bourgeoisie who could now make a contract with anyone they liked and who faced no impediment of birth or religion as they ascended the social ladder.

Spencer did not think the state should protect trade unions from legal responsibility. Their members were just as self-interested as anyone in industrial society and they must not be allowed to interfere with the freedom of individuals. The passage of *MVS* in which Spencer spelled out the consequences of this principle was pure neoliberalism. Socialism's belief in the altruism of the current working class hardly accorded with their current competitive and individualistic behaviour: 'a pursuit of private interests no less keen than among traders'. Spencer ([1884]1960: 74–5) then elaborated on an argument about the unions trampling on the freedoms of individual workers – including their right to work – that recalled the speeches made by Margaret Thatcher during her assault on the British trade unions in the 1980s.

On the other hand, we learnt earlier in this chapter that Spencer ([1884]1960) was not happy with the general chicanery of industrial society and, while human character remained imperfect, he expected the government to act against it, for example to punish the adulteration of products. He did not want a central bank or banking regulations, but he did want the state to pursue financial wrongdoing rather than wasting time on the petty crimes of the poor (Francis 2007; Taylor 1992). All of this made good sense to American individualism and the US justice system engaged in more vigorous consumer protection, more ready prosecution of frauds[6] and more anti-trust activities than many other capitalist societies. This accorded with the 'respect for the rule of law' which American individualism placed on a par with its insistence on negative freedom for the individual. By claiming to live by Spencer's law of equal freedom, Americans were, once again, seeing themselves as the embodiment of Spencer's utopia because for Spencer ([1884]1960) justice was not solely a characteristic of public policy. It was also the key part of character which must be formed by evolution. Once everyone had acquired the sentiment of justice, people would no longer require protection from each other and the state could shrink to nothing (Francis 2007; Taylor 1992). Not only would they now be evolved enough to make the law of equal freedom their own, but they would be sufficiently jealous of their own self-determination to ignore what government said anyway.

Although he knew its dangers, Spencer ([1884]1960) recognized that private charity would persist, although it had better be directed towards the deserving poor. Relying on private philanthropy rather than state welfare certainly has been more common in the USA than elsewhere. Spencer thought that state charity would atrophy the impulse to private benevolence (Francis 2007)[7] and that there was no point in the state distinguishing the deserving from the undeserving poor because neither met the criteria for state action in pursuit of equity or justice. The only exception would be if there was genuine evidence that the poor were suffering as a result of 'a positive act of oppression'. This was the case, for example, where sympathy for the indigent pushed aside the (just) sympathy for the hard-working families who actually had to pay for it (Spencer [1884]1960: 115). Similar attributions of hypocrisy have long attended attacks on 'bleeding-heart liberalism' – the maudlin sympathy and egalitarianism that is an affront to equity and justice. American individualism could agree with Spencer that such sympathy was responsible for 'a greater total of misery than the extremest selfishness inflicts' (Spencer 1896, cited in Taylor 1992: 87–8).

CONCLUSION

Francis was mistaken when he concluded that Spencer had no influence on the genesis of neoliberalism. We can agree with him that Spencer thought the state should not care about any individual's welfare, or the individual calculus of utility (Francis 2007: 273), and he was obviously correct that Spencer did not think individuals knew best. However, his insistence that there was no room for a doctrine of individualism in Spencer's vision of social change placed the cart before the horse. This chapter has argued that Spencer's theories informed American individualism rather than that individualism informed his theories. Once this relation was put on its feet, rather than its head, the potential for Spencer's ideas to sow the seeds of neoliberalism became obvious but, for these seeds to germinate, it required some changes in American society, for example in education.

NOTES

1. 'To him state regulation always suggested the militarization of social life' (Francis 2007: 310).
2. This passage is very similar to one in *The Bell Curve*, a much later neoliberal text (Herrnstein and Murray 1996: 52).
3. In effect, Taylor (1992) and Francis (2007) agreed that Spencer did not base his individualism on the rights of the individual or utilitarianism but on his evolutionary science.
4. Although Spencer ([1884]1960: 30) had a diatribe *against* paying teachers by results because it encouraged cramming and injured the health of teachers and less able pupils.
5. But Spencer wanted the state to supervise the lawyers and the courts to make sure litigation really did mean justice ([1884]1960: 162–3).

6. Just as US companies are now held criminally responsible for their employees' financial crimes (Fisher et al. 2013: 162).
7. Prochaska (2006) used the same explanation to account for the decline of Christian philanthropy in the UK.

8. Education, individualism and inequality

As the examples of anti-slavery and Common Schools have shown, sentimental individualism was a major stimulus to egalitarian social movements in the UK and the USA. This chapter shows how these social movements lost their impetus and how sentimental individualism was increasingly subordinated to cognitive individualism in public policy. Both processes will be illustrated with a further discussion of education which suggests that different countries followed a model of work and politics pioneered in the USA. This educational convergence made a major contribution towards setting the stage for the arrival of neoliberalism and globalization. The chapter begins by explaining, first, how education in the USA changed with industrialization, urbanization and continued immigration and, second, some international differences in education systems.

THE ATLANTIC DIVIDE IN EDUCATION

While the majority of the English population was urbanized by the middle of the nineteenth century, it took another 50 years before most Americans were not living on farms. When industrial society finally arrived, American public education was transformed into an arena for individual competition but, even before this, the changes that accompanied industrialization and urbanization made the moral enterprise of the Common Schools Movement seem a very distant memory (Green 1990). In the last third of the century, the immigrants who had established ethnic enclaves in American cities began to see education as the other half of their democratic rights along with the vote. This increased the demand for public education, not least because each ethnic group considered it unacceptable for its children to have less education than children from other ethnic groups, but it sometimes threatened the fundamental ethos of the Common Schools Movement including standardization and compulsory attendance (Skocpol 1992).[1]

For example, a consensus for Common Schools gave way to conflict in Chicago and San Francisco, partly because immigration and the new salience of ethnicity divided the working class once they left their places of work every day (Katznelson and Weir 1985). Another contributory factor was the growth of race, ethnic and class segregation in the cities (and then the suburbs) as urbanization proceeded. This destroyed the possibility of real Common Schools and made public education an arena fraught with accusations of unequal treatment. Unequivocal working-class support for compulsory education, partly motivated by the aim of reducing child labour, gave way to ambivalence when education became entangled with religion and community (for example, the status of parochial schools in San Francisco, and the issue of language learning in Chicago). It was left to the professional educators to drive education reforms, bureaucratization and standardization.

The way industrialization and urbanization proceeded in the USA meant that the link between the expansion of public education and the aspirations of sentimental individualism was attenuated. The cognitive individualism represented by the educators, schools and curricula was now free to develop a life of its own and further distance education from the aspirations that had inspired the Common Schools Movement. The professionals and bureaucrats proceeded to make twentieth-century pub-lic education a better fit with the demands of an industrial division of labour. Urban Massachusetts had developed a bureaucratic approach to public education in the middle of the nineteenth century but its general adoption did not occur until the bureaucracies had grown and the economy had become more centralized (Meyer et al. 1979). From this point, competition over educational resources was not only something that occurred between religious or ethnic groups vying for priority for their special interests. There was also increasing competition between individuals and families.

Amongst farming families, the common elementary schools of the middle third of the century offered very little opportunity for competition of this kind since most school-leavers ended up in very similar occupa-tions (Green 1990). There might be competition between neighbouring farmers but there was little opportunity for this to be expressed in the schoolroom. In industrial capitalism, many people worked for large organizations, and specialization and differentiation required that people be graded and assigned to their proper places in the division of labour. The shift from farming to industry, and urbanization, meant that the opportunity to invest in education now seemed to be relevant to an even larger proportion of the population in the USA than in the eighteenth-century Europe described by Adam Smith. Much of the further growth of education in the USA after 1890, lasting well into the twentieth century, could be explained by the increased demand for just such an opportunity, bringing new provision and boosting enrolment in elementary schooling, then secondary schooling and, finally, tertiary provision (Katznelson and Weir 1985; Rubinson 1986).

Smith had explained why investing in the educational capital of a wider range of children would reduce wages, rather than giving more people access to the higher-paying jobs to which education was a gateway. Two centuries later, Boudon, Hirsch and Collins extended the analysis of the way in which the attempt to widen the opportunity to invest in education appeared to be self-defeating (Rubinson 1986). When everyone went through elementary education, there was no pay-off for their parents' investment. This increased the demand for secondary education but when this too became more or less universal, there was increased demand for a further stage of education at which the invest-ment in educational capital might finally reap its return. Fulfilling this promise depended, of course, on some students or families dropping out of the race, but why was it only in America that this desperate drive to use education to give children an advantage over their peers led to such an extravagant expansion of educational provision?

Prussia's progression rates were stagnating at the end of the nineteenth century and in other European countries the growth of schooling was tailing off (Rubinson 1986). Part of the reason for this difference was that European provision remained much more highly stratified than it was in the USA, even as standardization proceeded and secondary schooling spread. For example, the organization of education in England and Wales reflected the rigid class system which offered little to any working-class families wondering if education could bring social mobility, prosperity and social esteem. The working class would have benefitted from universal provision which spread the costs of education, and from an unstratified system which did not invite the upper classes to close off parts of the labour market to them. This would have required an educational system in which anyone could progress through each stage of schooling and access a common curriculum which did not restrict some children to a vocational education (Rubinson 1986). The working classes of Europe did not begin to gain access to a system like this until the last third of the twentieth century. In England and Wales, for example, the grudging moves towards a national elementary system in the 1870 Education Act were an attempt to control the fall-out from the extension of the franchise to part of the urban working class three years before (Green 1990).

Educational expansion was only a capitalist aim where aristocracies or religious elites kept the children of the rising bourgeoisie out of its schools. Once they had the means to invest in their children's education, the bourgeoisie were only interested in restricting access to the education they used, rather than in further expansion. This necessitated the stratification of the system if any working-class children were to be educated at all. It was not in the bourgeoisie's interests to provide the working class with access to what Hirsch described as 'a positional good' which gave prestige or political power or economic advantage. If the working class had to be educated, this would be in mass schooling which gave no access to ruling class values or opportunities (Rubinson 1986).

There were other reasons why educational expansion of the American model was not a capitalist aim. The kind of 'expansionary spiral' which took place in the USA made education very costly in economic as well as social terms. The bourgeoisie would always have an additional financial interest in resisting further expansion of public schooling if it believed it would end up shouldering the burden for expansion through increased taxation. If expansion could not be headed off by political controls, then the answer was, once again, stratifying the system into elite and mass streams (Rubinson 1986). Early exits for the working class would keep down costs, while a general education for the elite would help them to close off access to jobs with the highest status.

So far as the relationship between education and the division of labour was concerned, the default position of the bourgeoisie was not (yet) that education was required to prepare workers for the fast-changing demands of an increasingly complex division of labour. Indeed, they resisted compulsory schooling because it would limit child labour. If education for the working class was unavoidable, they preferred vocational education which would prepare children for working-class and lower-middle-class jobs. This might, in any event, save on the costs of training new recruits. Neoliberal emphases on preparing workers for the unpredictable demands of globalization were entirely absent and the bourgeoisie did their best to keep working-class children from taking instruction in sciences, foreign languages and literature and to restrict their learning to material deemed useful in their future occupations. Academic high schools would only be for the smaller numbers of middle-class children and far less of a burden on bourgeois taxes (Rubinson 1986).

These bourgeois wishes had largely been frustrated in the USA where the majority of students in secondary education learnt from a common curriculum and their progression to jobs or further study was not closed off by centralized decisions about the proportions of each cohort required for each destination. This permitted competition across the cohort and kept on the pressure for the extension of public provision for successive stages of schooling as parents sought ways of helping their offspring to get ahead of the increasingly educated crowd. Cross-class politics in the USA had deprived the American elites of the ability to restrict this costly expansion but it was different in Europe. When the majority of students throughout Europe were finally able to access secondary schooling, it was for vocational education rather than the general education enjoyed by their American counterparts.

In European countries, there was a usually a selection point at the end of comprehensive elementary schooling between the ages of 10 and 12 at which better-performing students (almost all of whom had middle-class parents) were allowed to access general secondary education. Only so many were allowed through as would find middle-class jobs waiting for them. Those who were rejected at the end of elementary schooling were sent to vocational education to prepare them for manual or technical occupations. There was little overlap between the curricula of the vocational and general secondary schools, and if there was increased investment in education it was in parallel systems which gave access to completely different parts of the division of labour (Rubinson 1986).

American employers had not been able to enforce vocational education in the USA but in Europe, where education so clearly remained a class issue, employers made an ally of their states and enforced vocationalism on the professional educators. These European states could enact central-ized bureaucratic programmes that would have been impossible in the USA because the state was weak (Rubinson 1986). This weakness could be measured by the manner in which individual states in the USA – with their puny bureaucracies – simply gave post-hoc approval to what was already the reality when they made schooling compulsory. This also meant that there was very often a negative correlation between the level of enrolment and how much was spent on education in a state (Meyer et al. 1979).

As well as the differences in state organization, Europe and America differed in the degree to which the ruling classes had been able to cement their power by building their own political parties. We saw in Chapter 5 that early access to the vote for white adult males in the USA meant that the political clout the ruling class needed to be able to limit and stratify education against the interests of the working class (with support from professional educators and middle-class reformers) did not exist. The result was that the extension of public education to the secondary level reflected 'the egalitarian and individualistic values of the country' (Rubinson 1986: 538; also see Green 1990). In Europe, it had however been possible for the upper classes to organize their own class-based parties and capture the big European state bureaucracies.

As a result, the European working classes were less likely to take a positive view of education, and particularly of educational expansion. Why make your children stay on later in school when it would make no difference to the job they finally got and yet be financially burdensome? In these circumstances, the most likely reason for working-class support for education would be a religious one (Rubinson 1986). For most of the twentieth century, the majority of Britons (for example) had no opportunity to invest in education because they simply did not have access to the kind of education that would lead to a middle-class job. Since education was of such limited use to them, it is small wonder that successive generations of British working-class parents resisted every proposal to raise the age at which compulsory education ended (Fevre et al. 1999). These were not the conditions conducive to an American-style expansion of public education but, over the (much) longer term, they were productive of growing political opposition to the stratification of education. When Britain finally embraced secondary schools with comprehensive entry, it was the end of a campaign that had begun with (the later) Owen and the Owenites but took more than a century to achieve its goal. Throughout this campaign, there was strong resistance from the employers Owen had originally seen as major beneficiaries of wider schooling.

European conditions were much more conducive to fostering class identity. Indeed, the term 'class system' conjures up the European pattern in which people work, live and receive their education in separate locations. Once competitive education was in place in the USA, it further reduced the chances of a strong working class developing, which might give birth to its own political party.[2] If your children could only succeed by pushing ahead of your neighbours' children, the opportunity to make common cause with your neighbours was reduced (Rubinson 1986). In this case, fostering individualism really did affect the conditions for collectivism (Green 1997). We therefore reach a paradoxical conclusion. In the USA, the capitalist class did not have the power to resist the expansion of education and the arrival of mass, comprehensive schooling. This had the unintended effect of limiting the degree to which people made common cause as members of the working class. In Europe, the relationships were reversed: because the capitalist class got their way, the class formation they would have been anxious to avoid proceeded apace. How could the members of the European working classes not make common cause, given the way that they were treated as second-class citizens in the schools (Rubinson 1986)?

The resistance of European ruling classes to educational expansion, and particularly to comprehensive secondary schools, delayed by decades the arrival of anything that might look like a classless society, but this kind of society was a necessary condition for the arrival of neoliberalism and its version of individualism. The European conditions which were so conducive to class formation eventually allowed, after many decades, a British socialist government to deliver the comprehensive education which had helped to prevent the American working class from developing its own socialist party. The final section in this chapter will show that this meant that, in effect, it was the working class that eventually delivered a necessary condition for neoliberalism in Europe. They did this in the teeth of opposition from many of those who would later benefit from it.

FROM THE AMERICAN IDEOLOGY TO TECHNICAL UNITY

Alongside the differences in class formation in Europe and America, there were important differences in the combinations of religious, sentimental and cognitive individualisms that held sway, but these combinations of ideas were not static. The American ideology had not simply required the cultivation of respect for property, freedom of speech or the civic virtues needed to temper self-interest, since self-interest itself had to be educated. Far from encouraging materialism or neoliberal enthusiasm for debt (Streeck 2014), gambling and other short-cuts to riches, the purpose of the cultivation of character was to encourage prudence, restraint and moral economy (Meyer et al. 1979). For John Dewey, the American philosopher, social critic and educational theorist, the most valuable fruits of the cultivation of character were Americans' independence and individuality. With greater hindsight still, Michael Sandel (1998) admired its communitarian effects, underpinning not just a participatory democracy but morality in action in politics and public policy.

   John Higham (1974), the historian, described the transformation of the nation-building ideology that had established Common Schools as a transition from the American ideology to 'technical unity'. His emphasis was, of course, on the ideological glue that held the USA together under threat from both divisive and centrifugal forces rather than changes in component factors such as the nature of individualism (Green 1990). Nevertheless, Higham also noted the significance of the ideas of Herbert Spencer in the transformation. Higham thought Spencer one of the two most influential philosophers in US history after the Civil War, sharing a mission to convey how social organization must respond to the needs of technology, specialization and co-operation. In particular, the evolutionary characteristics Spencer thought should evolve were the same as those post-war American education attempted to instil (Higham 1974).

Higham explained that Spencer's doctrine that spontaneous co-operation arose from specialization and differentiation meant that order – as represented by educational bureaucracy, for example – was created out of technical necessity in the place of ideology. As long as people knew that their occupations were interdependent, there was no need for the old ideological glue. It was not only that, since the early days of the manufacturing division of labour, interdependent occupations were a daily fact of life. People also came to ascribe value to this interdependence, for example by thinking of themselves as parts of a complex machine (Higham 1974). In the terms of the theory developed in earlier chapters, these were the values of cognitive individualism, derived from knowledge of the realities of industrial capitalism rather than the dreams of the American ideology which hoped to perfect humanity. Accordingly, these values began to replace the morality that sentimental individualism had inspired.

Higham (1974) argued that America had a particular affinity for technical unity which societies like the UK could not share. Not only could Americans think of themselves as cogs in the machine; they also liked and appreciated all kinds of technologies which extended human control, from machinery to social statistics. From the middle of the nineteenth century, the embrace of technical unity entailed a retreat from idealism, 'a despiritualization of life', the 'loss of heroic affirmation' in art and novels, a declining emphasis on teaching morality in textbooks between 1840 and 1880, and in principles (rather than techniques) in self-help books at the end of the century. In other words, cognition and cognitive rules replaced sentiment and moral principles (Higham 1974: 23).

In place of a focus on the cultivation of moral character, American education would now cultivate Spencerian habits of mind and follow his doctrine that fitting people into the division of labour required the recognition of differences in abilities. Urban schools would strictly grade children by age and ability and at all levels of education there would be a greater emphasis on evidence and the relation between cause and effect including the increasing use of statistics (Higham 1974). A little later, the development of the comprehensive high school in the USA (1890–1920) was accompanied by increasing professionalization, bureaucratization, testing and standardization, Taylorism and modern management techniques (see Chapter 9).

Some Americans fought a rear-guard action to reverse the subordin-ation of sentimental to cognitive individualism. Their failure led John Dewey, amongst others, to the same conclusions Owen had eventually reached: the aims of sentimental individualism could not be achieved while the future shape and direction of the division of labour was in capitalist hands. When he reached this conclusion, he was reflecting on the attempts to rededicate America to the old sentimental individualism in a new age of industry and technology which were the hallmarks of the Progressive era which spanned the period 1898–1918. These were the years in which it became clear that Adam Smith's view that change in the division of labour was a one-way street – in which minds were numbed by ever-more simplified and repetitive work – would have to be revised. Complex organizations were apparently demanding employees with specialist knowledge, but this was to be incorporated into a revived American ideology with all the old romantic fervour of an earlier sentimental individualism. The Progressive movement was out to evan-gelize and to rededicate the country to 'freedom, equality, and heroism'. Bureaucracies and their associated technologies were now to be captured and directed to democratic and egalitarian aims suited to the machine age (Higham 1974).

Although he did not use the term (preferring 'participatory' freedom), Higham saw positive freedom as an essential ingredient of the Progres-sive era. Socialists also played a part in generating this new vision of American destiny and, like the socialists, the intellectual leaders of the Progressive era thought that individualism necessarily entailed partici-pation in important decisions (for example, about the division of labour) rather than laws to protect individuals from interference. There could be neither freedom nor equality without the opportunity to determine how society was ordered. Since science was so democratic, it provided a template for the way citizens could be given equal opportunities to determine both the common good and their own fates (Higham 1974).

This vision soon failed because people no longer believed that there was an 'inner affinity' between the democratic ideals and scientific and technical methods since the latter seemed to have taken over.[3] Once again, sentimental individualism was overwhelmed by cognitive individu-alism. The diminishing chances of bringing Americans together for a revival of the American ideology were evident from a stunning expansion of the number of articles published in American magazines on applied science, while articles on religion, philosophy and pure science declined (Higham 1974). Social theory as well as history confirms that this cultural shift did not only affect individualism. As I argued in my earlier book, the side-lining of attempts to reinvigorate morality was part of a more general shift away from belief in favour of knowledge and particularly technology and applied science (Fevre 2000a).

Higham was writing in the 1970s but John Dewey (1929/30) reached his conclusions about this cultural shift half a century earlier. He argued that the Progressive era had always been bound to fail because it was an attempt to turn back the clock to an older idea of sentimental individualism which could not be revived.[4] It was not only the intellectuals of the Progressive era who were misled into imagining that sentimental individualism persisted. In the 1920s, most Americans still imagined they lived in an older world in which the sentimental individualism that flourished with agrarian capitalism found air to breathe.[5] Beliefs which Dewey summed up as 'an idealism [which] is probably the loudest and most frequently professed philosophy the world has ever heard' (Dewey 1929/30: 47) had yet to catch up with rapid industrialization. A particular effect of this lag was that Americans had lost sight of the fact that they might actually need to act to make equality happen. The belief in equality remained the 'genuinely spiritual element' of our 'essential Americanism', but it had only intermittent importance in politics and, while it had built the public schools, it did not determine what they were for or how children were taught (Dewey 1929/30: 49).[6]

Dewey thought the farmers might still hold on to the morality of sentimental individualism[7] but

> [t]he spiritual factor of our tradition, equal opportunity and free association and intercommunication, is obscured and crowded out. Instead of the development of individualities which it prophetically set forth, there is a perversion of the whole idea of individualism to conform to the practices of a pecuniary culture. It has become the source and justification of inequalities and oppressions. Hence our compromises, and the conflicts in which aims and standards are confused beyond recognition. (Dewey 1929/30: 49)

What Dewey wanted instead was to find a way to reinstate 'the distinctive moral element in the American version of individualism' in a society dominated by large corporations and associations. The key was, once again, positive freedom and every individual's participation in shaping culture and society without which the ideals of freedom and equality were empty rhetoric (Dewey 1929/30: 57).

The corporations were the natural homes of the new competitive 'economic individualism' that Americans actually lived by in the twentieth century. This was Dewey's term for American cognitive individualism in a world of competitive education and burgeoning corporations. It was a far cry from the cognitive individualism of the American ideology but he thought it was also quite different from the world envisaged by

Herbert Spencer, in which people were 'automatically assigned' to work commensurate to their abilities and their rewards varied according to 'capacity and enterprise'. It was no longer possible to believe that individual energy would be directed to the good of all (Dewey 1929/30: 78). The corporation had no concern for the good of all and this 'undoes the individual' (Dewey 1929/30: 70). The antidote was to take equal opportunity seriously.

Dewey's attention to the significance of the large corporation led him to argue that the imperative to buy was now as essential to individualism as thrift had been in the previous century. Capital no longer needed Americans' savings; it needed their spending, fuelled by higher wages (rather than debt, as in neoliberalism). Flourishing consumption was accompanied by rampantly increasing inequality which could not be resisted because that would be 'an aspersion to our rugged individualism and an attempt to stir up class feeling' (Dewey 1929/30: 93).[8] According to Dewey, the schools could not do their work properly while they were dominated by the 'money motif',[9] and education did not produce individuality but immaturity. Americans had technical knowledge but their education was narrow and they knew little of the social problems of their time. When graduates got out into the world, their only objective was to enter business and make money (Dewey 1929/30: 102–3). Dewey thought it still possible for the education system to develop values, just as it had done over the years when introducing immigrants to American individualism and democracy, but it must be made fit for an industrial society dominated by those large corporations.

Dewey's solution was that the corporations should be directed by the state to serve the scientific and technical genius of the new society instead of being parasitic on it. Just as Robert Owen had finally concluded, Dewey came to realize that the division of labour must henceforward be regarded as a means to social utility rather than as an end in itself. Control over the division of labour was necessary to banish insecurity, alienation from labour and the products of our labour, and inequality. Freedom would be greater with social planning than it would be if people's fates were determined by decisions based only on profitability. Control over the division of labour was the most essential positive freedom for the new individualism, according to Dewey. It was necessary for those who produced to have an 'imaginative, intellectual, emotional' share in saying who did what and how they did it. Dewey's vision of sentimental individualism would make sure that workers' hearts and minds were engaged in production. They would take part in planning, not simply carry out orders, and work for a purpose rather than simply to earn an income. Sentimental individualism required that their minds not be 'warped, frustrated, unnourished by their activities – the ultimate source of all constant nurture of the spirit' (Dewey 1929/30: 104). Once the division of labour was under co-operative control, Dewey, like the older Owen, thought human potential would be released, for example through ample opportunities for self-development. Dewey was also insistent on the need to exercise emotion as well as thought in the workplace.

In the next chapter, we will see how Dewey's prayers were apparently answered by the corporations themselves, for example satisfying his wishes by mandating emotional labour, and by engineering employee engagement in which men and women were meant to find an emotional satisfaction and release that was missing in their private lives (Fevre 2003). Just like Robert Owen in the previous century, an advocate of co-operative control unwittingly spelt out the ideas that corporations would use to defuse sentimental individualism as a source of critique and opposition. As sociologist Georg Simmel (1972) might have argued, the intention to liberate sentimental individualism led to an institutional response which frustrated that intention (Honneth 2004).[10] Jurgen Habermas (1987) made a similar point when he referred to the use of the rationalized means of politics and economy to achieve goals generated beyond them (also see Gorz 1989). In the process of making those goals achievable by such rationalized means, the goals were subverted and absorbed. This problem could only be addressed with the 'communicative action' which social movements could enact (Habermas 1987). In the terms of the theory explained in my earlier book, this rationalization produced guidelines to action which substituted for moral principles and encouraged category mistakes in which people sought sentimental meaning in the wrong places (Bauman 1993; Fevre 2000a).

UK EDUCATION 1944–1976

Some of Dewey's ideas had been anticipated in Britain, decades earlier, by Matthew Arnold, Oscar Wilde and William Morris (Gagnier 2010), but it was many years before British education was affected by an egalitarian ideology that owed much to socialism but perhaps more to feelings of national solidarity which had grown during World War II. The provision of free, state education up to age 15 was achieved by a wartime Coalition government with some Labour Party ministers, but had little impact on educational stratification and provided a constant source of stimulus to post-war class conflict. This was not the aim of the politician most closely associated with the 1944 Education Act, the moderate

Conservative R.A. Butler. The 1943 White Paper, *Educational Recon-struction*, which he had put before Parliament, had identified problems in the stratification of the education system as well as in the paucity of overall provision (Board of Education 1943). It noted that 9 out of 10 British children were leaving school at 14 and this was obviously too early for 'the conditions of modern life'.[11] What is more, the majority of those aged 11–14 were finishing their education in the same crowded elementary school where they began it. While most British children were not receiving a secondary education worth the name, the minority who did were not always selected on their ability. Well-off parents could circumvent their child's failure of a selection test at 11 years old by paying fees equivalent to about a third of the real cost to 'buy a place in the secondary school'. Up to three-quarters of secondary school places could be bought in this way, which was 'against the canon that the nature of a child's education should be determined by his capacity and promise and not by the financial circumstances of his parent'.

The decisive impetus to address these problems came from Britain's wartime experience, and especially from the decreased salience of class during the war. As Butler later commented, it was the public's 'intense desire for greater social equality' that made the White Paper popular. Because of wartime feelings of solidarity and the extensive, but egalitar-ian, wartime regulations, people wanted a 'more closely-knit society' (Butler 1945). Nevertheless, the White Paper was adamant that the additional schooling must vary according to pupil needs and capabilities. After the age of 11, equality of opportunity and diversity were of equal importance but the different kinds of secondary schools the White Paper proposed would all have the same status. The 1944 Act certainly avoided sending all children to the same kind of secondary school but neither the Act nor its subsequent implementation lived up to Butler's original vision.

The Act formalized the split between primary (5–11 years old) and secondary (11–15 years old) education that already existed in many local authorities and made all schooling maintained by local authorities free. Although it only referred to 'secondary schools', the Act created three different kinds of state secondary schools: grammar schools, secondary modern schools and technical schools.[12] The school leaving age was not actually raised to 15 until 1948. It took the next 20 years to double the number of children and teachers in maintained schools and it was only in 1972 that the school leaving age was raised to 16. Perhaps most disappointing to Butler, selection at 11 (by means of an intelligence test) was retained. He had seen the one-off test as inappropriate for assessing

a child's ability and wanted selection based on school records supplemented by intelligence tests if needed. The White Paper had also argued
strongly against the inflexibility of an early make-or-break selection
point, proposing that the child's trajectory be kept under review up to
age 13.

Many girls and working-class boys now entered secondary education
for the first time but the secondary modern schools that most of them
went to (80 per cent of each cohort) were poorly-resourced and often
failed to provide better educational opportunities than were available in
the system they replaced. For the vast majority who failed the '11 plus',
there were no second chances. Once they were in a secondary modern,
they followed a different curriculum which made it very hard indeed to
catch up with their peers in a grammar school, even if they should
somehow be able to demonstrate they had the aptitude. In fact, very few
grammar schools were prepared to give them that chance. The curriculum
followed in the secondary moderns shielded pupils from the rigours of
academic preparation for external exams and prepared them for unskilled
or semi-skilled work or labour in the home. This was not the parity of
esteem imagined in the White Paper and nor did Butler get his way in
respect of the proposed technical schools. Few opened and the UK never
established the full tripartite system in place in Germany.

Over time, evidence began to appear which suggested that it was social
class, rather than intelligence, that was distributing pupils between
secondary modern and grammar schools. Some adjustments were made
to the secondary moderns, usually in response to pressure from parents
and pupils and a realization within them that school status and morale
depended on making an attempt (albeit vain) to ape the grammar schools.
There was a gradual increase in secondary modern pupils entering
external O level examinations after 1951 (Chitty 1989). Nevertheless, it
was still the case in 1963 that the number of former secondary modern
pupils sitting A levels, the higher tier of school examination, was 318 and
none went on to university. These changes were insufficient to insulate
the secondary moderns from the changes going on in wider society. The
ongoing evolution of the industrial and occupational structure interacted
with class politics to push the UK towards another reassessment of the
shape and purpose of its education system.

The number of jobs in traditional working-class occupations dwindled
while the labour requirements of clerical, technical and professional jobs,
particularly in the service sector, increased (Chitty 1989). The demands
of the latter could not be satisfied by school-leavers with a handful of
CSEs (the qualification tier below O levels) and there were more and
more disaffected parents with children in the secondary modern system

who did not accept that their children should be denied access to those jobs by virtue of failing a test at age 11. Many of these parents were themselves middle class, or had middle-class connections (Jackson and Marsden 1962), and the numbers of their children in the secondary modern grew as part of the baby-boom generation between 1957 and 1970. Grammar school places were not increased quickly enough and the points required at 11 plus for grammar school entry were increased. Children were now being streamed into the secondary modern schools where their older siblings would have entered the grammar schools.

The idea of British comprehensive schools had been tried before the war, and there had been more local experiments in the 1950s, but the Labour government that came to power in 1964 conceived them as one of the key elements in the reform of the British education system in which the only limitation on a person's achievements would be her/his aspirations and abilities. Neither class nor, increasingly, gender would enter into the way the schools treated their charges. In 1965, the Labour government issued a circular implementing the Comprehensive System (although it took 20 years for most secondary moderns to disappear), however Labour's intentions had been signalled two years earlier in one of the most influential British speeches of the post-war era, given by Harold Wilson, who would become Prime Minster, while he was in opposition.

The speech Wilson gave to the Labour Party's Annual Conference in 1963 was aimed at shifting the party's electoral strategy away from a reliance on traditional working-class votes that were now dwindling away with occupational and industrial change, towards the increasingly better-off voters in skilled manual and lower-middle-class occupations. If they desired nothing else, these voters wanted to see the end of an education system which might deny their children access to the education enjoyed by the quarter of each cohort who passed the 11 plus (Fielding 2008). Wilson's first speech as leader was certainly shaped by an analysis of the effect of occupational change on the political landscape, but it would also be difficult to miss the intellectual influence of John Dewey, and particularly Dewey's attempt to project a progressive vision for a state response to the demands of technical unity.

Wilson (1963) said that Britain's future depended on adapting to change, and the pace of change was now unprecedented. The next 15 years would bring technical change greater than in the last 250 and the only way to respond to this challenge was with socialist planning. Just like Dewey, Wilson thought the private sector would only create just enough automation to make for mass redundancies and would not create any replacement jobs. Like Dewey, he thought that leaving the private sector in charge would mean that technological advances would forever catch the country unawares. Instead of stumbling backwards into a future that was beyond control, the future Labour government would plan technological change and scientific progress to achieve the living standards and opportunities for leisure which might once have been thought utopian. Wilson wanted science to increase productivity and solve the problems of international development and world poverty. To achieve this, science had to be organized by the state with state-sponsored research and development and the state controlling the resulting new industries.

The best way to recognize the reality of the large corporation was to place it in public ownership, but education was also marked down for a key role. First, many more scientists would have to be trained but this would require attitudes at every level of education to be transformed. Britain could no longer afford the 'segregation' from age 11 upwards that denied the chance of education to three-quarters of each cohort in a way that other leading nations did not. Yet, getting rid of segregation was not enough because the problem of insufficient places which had affected entry to the grammar schools had now reached entry to higher education. Wilson (1963) said that at least a quarter of those with the right grades were not getting places, and the problem described by an industrialist as a 'rat race' was getting worse each year. All the while, Britain was falling further behind other countries and Wilson proposed an expansion of higher education which, though modest by later standards, set the political tone for the next half century.[13]

Wilson's 10 per cent target of participation in higher education was not achieved by the end of the decade. It was another 20 years until it approached 20 per cent; and ten further years until a third of each cohort was entering higher education. The USA had already reached this level of enrolment by the early 1990s. By this point, the UK had closed the gap with US enrolment in comprehensive secondary education. There were no secondary moderns left, and grammar schools survived in only a few local authorities. In 1977 the Labour Secretary of State for Education, Shirley Williams, described the UK as having one of the longest periods of compulsory education in the world (Chitty 1989: 98). The USA still had more people in education for longer but the UK was already beginning to exhibit some of the features the American system had displayed for decades, particularly the increased individual competition that had correlated so closely with the expansion of the US system. British sociologists eventually began to develop their own applications of the theories developed in the USA by Hirsch and Collins (Brown 1995, 2000).

The left, and many sociologists, had harboured some hopes that the comprehensive schools would increase social mobility or, at least, take the edge off the British class system by reducing the educational segregation between classes (Chitty 1989). These hopes were fading even before the comprehensive system had been fully adopted. Westergaard and Resler (1975) argued that comprehensive schools simply obscured the class system rather than reforming it. At the same time, the Labour government began to modify its education policy in response to criticism from the right in a way that prepared the UK for its immanent transition to neoliberalism (Chitty 1989). This shift recalled the transition from the American ideology to technical unity described by Higham (1974).

Along with Shirley Williams, the politician who was most closely identified with this shift was James Callaghan, who became prime minister following Wilson's shock resignation in 1976. As Callaghan took over, ever more strident criticisms of state education from the middle classes and the employers were being reported in the press. This co-ordinated attack was perceived as a serious electoral threat. The employers complained that the curriculum was irrelevant to the world of work, and that young people were entering the labour market without the required skills of literacy or numeracy and were totally unprepared for workplace discipline. Teachers were blamed for being satisfied with lower standards of performance and for encouraging pupils to follow their own interests and set their own schedules. An individualism which fostered autonomy and self-development was exactly what British industry did *not* require, particularly since recent changes in the workplace had reduced 'the scope for individual reaction and initiative' (from a discussion paper prepared by two government quangos quoted by Chitty 1989: 61). It was the teachers' job to prepare their charges for the economic realities of adult life, something that the teachers themselves had too little direct knowledge of. While many of them appeared to have no stake in capitalist democracy, the nation had made considerable investment in the expansion of education and it was now necessary to see some dividends from it (Chitty 1989).

In 1976, in a speech at Ruskin College Oxford, Callaghan announced the Labour government's change of direction. From now on, there would be some central control over the curriculum and, whatever the teachers might say, the schools were going to be made to do a better job of preparing pupils for the division of labour. For example, they must shift the emphasis from humanities to science and engineering, and schools must play their part in increasing skill levels. The 1944 Act had been wrong to reject the core curriculum and schools would be more closely monitored and the relations between industry and education would be strengthened (Callaghan 1976).

CONCLUSION

From this point on, UK governments became addicted to frequent educational reforms with a common rationale spelt out in the Ruskin speech. Ideas of the knowledge economy, learning society and lifelong learning were not yet in fashion, but it was already clear that education was there to serve, even anticipate, the division of labour. Indeed, education was to be the key means by which any government could hope to make its population fit for the changing requirements of global capitalism. The socialist vision of technical unity which sounded so like the ideas of John Dewey was on the way out, but corporations had been listening to what Dewey and others had been saying about engaging employees and fulfilling the promises of sentimental individualism in the workplace. The next chapter considers whether the evangelism, romance and heroism that briefly flowered in the Progressive era were now to be found in those corporations.[14]

NOTES

1. Green (1990) pointed out that professionalization was badly needed since there was very little training of teachers in the USA up to this point.
2. As Green (1990) pointed out, there was nothing to fear from the American working class, but perhaps he meant the white working class?
3. And 'technical organization is essentially undemocractic' – it does not recognize equal rights as an organizing principle (Higham 1974: 26).
4. Dewey anticipated the arguments of MacIntyre (1987) and Fevre (2000a) that we are misled into crediting the persistence of the morality of earlier decades by people's readiness to espouse beliefs on which they are not prepared to act.
5. Dewey referred to 'a fusion of individual capitalism, of natural rights, and of morals founded in strictly individual traits and values, under the influence of Protestantism' (1929/30: 78). Its twentieth-century legacy included an education system more successful in proselytising literal interpretations of the bible than scientific knowledge.
6. The importance of this spiritual element to Dewey should not be under-emphasized. He identified its roots in medieval religion rather than the Reformation and thought the industrial revolution gave individualism a 'secular and worldly turn' (1929/30: 77).
7. The same applied to the workers who refused to press home their advantage in industrial conflicts (Dewey 1929/30).
8. There is an obvious parallel with resistance to President Obama's attempts to focus on inequality (see Chapter 1).
9. A familiar refrain in British sociology of education in the 1980s and 1990s.
10. Bowring (2015) points out that Simmel also charted the emptiness of the negative freedoms described in the previous chapter.
11. An increase over the 1938 figure of 8 out of 10 caused by special wartime measures.

12. For which the mandate was provided by section 8.1 of the Act.
13. In 1938, less than 1% had made it to university in the UK and overall participation in higher education still stood at 3.4% in 1950.
14. As described in the novels of Ayn Rand. In the following chapters, it will become clear that Rand was more a cheerleader than a prophet.

9. An introduction to people management

We saw in the previous chapter that the influence of individualism on American education was increasingly centred on preparation for work, including the acquisition of attitudes and orientations to the division of labour. As the requirements of the division of labour changed, so an elaborate system evolved for shaping the future workforce. This system extended beyond the school gate: developments in workplaces and labour markets embedded individualism in practices and institutions (Scott and Meyer 1994a). The term *people management* best describes those practices and institutions. It encompasses the rise of personnel and human resource managers but also includes the legal framework under which workplaces and labour markets operate.

The next two chapters take the history of people management up to the point at which we left the history of (British) education in 1976. In that year, an American management book declared businesses knew 'that freedom for self-development is the finest value in life' and that 'a basic principle of personnel management concerns the "sacredness" of individual personality' (cited in Anthony 1977: 161). We must understand how people management reached this point and, in doing so, we meet a new theme: the systematic exaggeration of the capacity of cognitive individualism to make the hopes of sentimental individualism a reality. This exaggeration arose from the category mistake in which cognition was presented as a perfect substitute for belief.

Once sentimental beliefs were interpreted as human aspirations, they could be translated into cognitive sense-making. Aspirations for equality, or respect or autonomy for all individuals, were seen as goals to be achieved by educational reform, or the reform of labour markets or workplaces. Once those aspirations were demonstrated to be unachievable, the beliefs that had originally inspired them were portrayed as well-meant but hopeless idealism. This dismissal was the inevitable consequence of the original category mistake in which cognition took on the job of making the world a better fit for our beliefs but, on finding this an impossible task, judged those beliefs wanting. Scepticism about the whole enterprise of sentimental sense-making was increased and cognition expanded further. In this way, sentimental beliefs eventually suffered the same marginalization as religious beliefs and in both cases morality was weakened as a result. In consequence, people experienced the confusion and loss of direction described by Dewey and other writers on demoralization (see Chapter 8).

In my earlier work, I described the way in which groups and institutions created substitutes for lost and weakened moral codes (Fevre 2000a, 2003).[1] These substitutes were always 'ersatz moralities' since they were not founded on religious or sentimental beliefs but on more deliberate and strategic attempts to manufacture lost moral elements that had been found to be important to social order. To the extent that cognitive individualism replaced sentimental individualism, it was responsible for demoralization, but, at the same time, cognition claimed to provide its own (ersatz) moralities in place of those that sentiment and religion could no longer provide. In earlier chapters, we noted that the social changes which occurred when individualism gave people new liberties worried elites. They preferred people to be educated, trained and managed to take advantage of their access to individualism in a way that did not trespass on the freedoms the elites already enjoyed. This same process involved cognitive individualism progressively marginalizing the beliefs that underpinned sentimental individualism and simultaneously manufacturing ersatz morality.

The neoinstitutionalist writers referenced several times in previous chapters described organizational responses to the expansion of the individual, for example managing the autonomy that came with individualism, but we also need to notice that organizations responded by replacing sentiment with cognition. For example, Scott and Meyer (1994a: 211) noted that '[t]he rationalization of the individual creates organizational work', and they referred to a vast increase in the complex properties of individuals that came with individualism. Organizations certainly had to deal with 'these rather forward and much differentiated people' (Scott and Meyer 1994a: 209), but the forwardness and differentiation that organizations had to cope with were readily translatable into the terms of cognitive individualism, for example psychology (Frank and McEneaney 1999; Frank et al. 1995). It is no wonder, then, that those individuals had the characteristics that would fit into the organizations that employed them.

Putting all this together required management, and particularly specialists in dealing with human resources (Scott and Meyer 1994a). If they could demonstrate that they were advancing cognitive individualism, the proponents of people management could access resources, influence and authority. In order to do so, they competed with each other and so were further tempted to exaggerate the extent to which they could advance cognitive individualism. Public opinion was swayed by the inflated claims to be able to put the hopes of social movements into practice. It rewarded the proponents of the new orthodoxy with power and resources and they continued to turn sentimental hopes into the knowledge appropriate to a world that dealt in knowledge rather than beliefs. Category mistakes multiplied as cognitive individualism was built up to be a complete and perfect substitute for sentimental individualism. The social movements inspired by sentimental individualism lost impetus as the desiderata of cognition, like efficiency (see below), steadily eclipsed any of the considerations that might be derived directly from beliefs (Fevre 2000a, 2003).

TAMING CHARACTER

We learnt in Chapter 5 that owner-manager Robert Owen was preoccupied with the immoral behaviour of the working class. I claimed that his determination to reform their characters in the interests of efficiency as well as morality would later resurface (O'Hagan 2011; also see Anthony 1977). His worries about 'a "ferocity of character" among the labouring classes' created by the Industrial Revolution were shared by his fellow nineteenth-century entrepreneurs, but they rarely agreed with Owen that it was the employers' job to mould the 'the sentiments and manners' of their employees and thereby increase efficiency, and here lay the origins of his long-delayed contribution to neoliberalism (O'Hagan 2011: 80).

A New View of Society described how, before Owen got to work on their characters, the workers of New Lanark thought the changes he made in the mills were intended to intensify work and increase his profits. Like so many of his contemporaries, he said his workers were only united by conflict with their employers. So, Owen told his fellow employers to

> turn your thoughts more frequently from your inanimate to your living machines; you will discover that the latter may be easily trained and directed to procure a large increase of pecuniary gain, while you may also derive from them high and substantial gratification. (Owen [1813]1817: 73)

Owen claimed that the improvements to the 'living machinery' at New Lanark had already given in excess of a 50 per cent return on his investment and much more was to come. The romantic poet Robert

Southey, who toured New Lanark in 1819, compared Owen's factory to a plantation where his workers were

> as much under his absolute management as so many Negro slaves. His humour, his vanity, his kindliness of nature (all these have their share) lead him to make these human machines as he calls them (and too literally he believes them to be) as happy as he can, and to make a display of their happiness. (Southey 1819)

Such was the genesis of modern training and development but, from the beginning, this was not conceived as a task for employers alone.

Owen tried repeatedly to get the state involved, if only because the employers had proved themselves too short-sighted to act on their own behalf (see Chapter 5). It was not uncommon for employers to see education as the solution to a ferocity of character, for example in 1835 Andrew Ure articulated a common view that the only way to cultivate character amongst the working class was through religious education (Ure 1835). Nor was it unusual for employers to request the state's assistance in providing the right kind of workers. For example, also in 1835, Edwin Chadwick, the Poor Law Commissioner, received a request from a northern manufacturer keen to fill the Northern mills with workers of good character, not 'refuse population and insubordinate sturdy paupers ... Hard working men, or widows with families, who preferred gaining an honest living to a workhouse'. This was claimed to be the only way to head off stronger unions, more drunkenness and still higher wages (Greg 1835). Without low wages and high food prices to discipline labour, the factories needed the government to provide education. The northern working class were sufficiently literate and numerate but their education had not equipped them with the necessary morality, attitudes and orientations to work.

Owen's innovation was to insist on a rational, rather than religious, education and the involvement of employers like himself in the delivery of that education alongside the state. Decades later, Owen's emphasis on rationality still featured in the lexicon of people management, as did the old concern with 'irrational' limitations on output and workers making common cause with other workers. But the ferocity of character had been recast by psychologists as attitude problems or dysfunctional emotions, while complaints of immorality had disappeared from the language of employers. Such complaints had already become scarce by Frederick Taylor's heyday. Taylor talked not of employees' vices but of the way managers could maximize their employees' initiative. Similarly, the first theorists of human resources conceived of the problems Owen had described in a way Spencer might have recognized: as maladjustment to an industrial society.

In the two centuries after Owen published *A New View of Society*, managers took on the job of turning beliefs into reality, however it was not their reputation for efficacy and competence which suffered but the value of sentimental beliefs (Fevre 2003, 2013; Fevre et al. 2011). Developing the knowledge and techniques required in order to treat people as individuals was a central theme of the story of how managers came to power. It was an essential component of managerial legitimacy, management education and management consultancy (Anthony 1977) and a cornerstone of the professionalization of management, a process which paralleled the rise of education professions described in earlier chapters. Professionalization would have been impossible if managers had not been able to avail themselves of the political opportunity offered to them to become the bearers of cognitive individualism in the workplace. At the same time, different types of managers were not above competing with each other for power and resources, and this competition helped to shape the way they delivered on their promise to embed cognitive individualism in the workplace and the labour market (Fevre et al. 2011).

The creation of a class of managers pursuing power and resources, and of factions of managers who competed with each other, is an illustration of the way in which real, messy historical processes lead to cognitive over-reach and category mistakes (Fevre 2000a). From Owen onwards, managers claimed they could solve the leading problems of civilization, including many of those addressed by social movements in the nineteenth and twentieth centuries. There were two key features in their rise to power: the notion that cognitive individualism could deliver ever-increasing efficiency and the idea that managers were capable of knowing everything about human behaviour (Fevre 2003; Scott and Meyer 1994a). Both features contributed mightily to undermining sentimental individualism but they were, at first, simply the essential elements of the managerial bid for power and legitimacy.

Managers' claims to omniscience and control over efficiency were evident when they made their bid for a central role in the extension of individualism to everyone. Their pitch was that the more individualism there was in the labour market and the workplace, the more efficiency would be delivered. Since improving efficiency was the reason employers had taken them on, they were the best-placed members of society to deliver individualism, so why would society need social movements or politicians to extend individualism? Managers did not win the day by presenting their task as an easy one but, rather, by persuading others that their specialized knowledge allowed them to succeed where others could not. For example, the job of determining individual capabilities and fitting them to work might be daunting but their knowledge of human behaviour uniquely qualified them for this role (Fevre 2003).

The claim to be able to perform this pivotal function determined the characteristics of management (Fevre 2003). Managers needed control over assigning places in the division of labour and employees' experiences of the workplace in order to fulfil their function, and these needs defined the management jobs that were created. A noticeable consequence of the managers' success in carving out their niche was that many simply took it as axiomatic that employers would go out of business if they did not treat their employees as individuals, and developed policies and procedures designed to persuade employees that individualism would prosper under their care.

Over the decades, it was accepted that the efficiency of capitalist labour markets, and the productivity of capitalist workplaces, depended on giving free rein to individualism. The association with capitalist efficiency eventually gave individualism a place in the public mind far removed from the concerns of the abolitionists: not only overwhelmingly cognitive (hard-headed, practical, not too sensitive about feelings) but also made in the image of the kind of economic rationality that apparently needed it so much. This explained, for example, the frequent assumption that individualism and competition were constant companions. After the managers got to work, demonstrating that free rein was given to individualism was the very epitome of rationality itself, and this is why so many (like Hans Joas in Chapter 2) have seen the very idea of individualism as hopelessly contaminated and no longer capable of describing a set of beliefs.

Another important consequence of the managers' efforts was widespread acceptance that all sorts of inequalities, not just in incomes, were the unavoidable corollary of increased efficiency and the prosperity it brought. Managers made a direct contribution to this inequality when they acquired higher salaries and (eventually) attractive stock options. In order to appear to deserve these benefits, they were under continuous pressure to demonstrate that they were increasing efficiency through the application of specialized knowledge. Opposition to this bid for a greater share of resources might have come from social scientists, but they were usually all too ready to believe the managers' explanation that they were increasing the size of the cake by improving efficiency and thus spreading prosperity to their employees.

CONTRACTS AND TRAINING

Cognitive individualism in the labour market and the workplace pre-supposed that individuals could enter into contracts with their employers (see Chapter 6). There was, indeed, little space for recognizing individual capacity and potential, let alone developing autonomy, when people were being made to work simply because they were in a subordinate group of slaves or provided corvée labour. For Spencer (and Durkheim and Weber), a legally enforceable contract was the only way to make sure that people got their just desserts. We saw in Chapter 7 that the link between merit and reward was extremely important to industrial society and, ultimately, to the progress of both justice and evolution. Society therefore had to change so that there was no longer any limit on who could make a contract with whom. The state and the judiciary would take on a supervisory role to make sure those contracts were observed.

It was also pointed out in Chapter 7 that, in the nineteenth century, freedom of contract was more of a benefit for the upwardly mobile bourgeoisie than anyone else. If the working class did make contracts with the employer directly, they were on very uneven terms, but, as subsequent scholarship has shown, many members of the working class either did not make contracts or did not make them freely. For much of the nineteenth century, and some of the twentieth, working-class people (adults as well as children) laboured as unfree labour of one kind or another (Fevre 1984, 1990, 1992). What is more, the contracts that governed free labourers were often not made with their employers at all but with subcontractors both inside and outside the factory. In sub-contracting, the employer could delegate every aspect of the managers' function in the division of labour to someone else, such as the head of a family working in the domestic system, or a foreman supplying and supervising labour within the factory system. These managerial substi-tutes might prefer force and the threat of violence to the methods more appropriate to workers who made a contract with their employer. They certainly had none of the managers' incentives to claim that efficiency depended on their development of a unique capacity to treat employees as individuals.

Managers could more plausibly lay claim to their unique ability to increase individualism alongside efficiency when both they and the employees were contracted by the same employer. Yet, even when contracts became the most common means of putting people to work in capitalism, many individuals remained excluded. For example, European restrictions on women's access to such contracts were many and various.[2]

Even if everyone gained access to individual, legally-binding contracts, this did not, of course, put an end to the long and tortuous tale of individualism and inequality. If we no longer assume an over-riding efficiency imperative within capitalism,[3] we make space for more political forces. As part of their commitment to people management, liberal politicians and policymakers and lawyers were heavily in favour of individual contracts of employment (Scott and Meyer 1994a). Thanks to them, the managerial class would be in a position to base their legitimacy on their role as gatekeepers to employment and authorities in the workplace. Both aspects of their role were essential to the claim to advance individualism along with efficiency and both depended on contracts.

It has sometimes been suggested that, while they did not actually increase efficiency, managers were able to increase exploitation by making people work longer for the same or less money (Fevre 2003), but we need to bear in mind the two-edged nature of contracts of employment. Managers needed contracts to give them a role, but contracts also gave power to employees who could, for example, now leave their employer for the one down the street who paid a little more. They could also combine to force their employers to agree more favourable contractual terms (Anthony 1977). Neoinstitutionalist writers saw this as part of individualism's challenge for the managers (Scott and Meyer 1994a). The individual employment contract was simply the most obvious example of the challenge that reliance on cognitive individualism for legitimation of their status had created.

Monahan, Meyer and Scott (1994) were able to show how, in the USA, training grew with personnel systems in a series of stages. Their first was a period of proto-individualism – such as that described by Adam Smith – with free contracts but undifferentiated labour power for which the market was the normal mechanism which determined who got a job. An individual had to be in the right place at the right time to strike a mutually acceptable bargain to do whatever the buyer of their services needed (Fevre 2003). There was little stability and endemic conflict between employers and employees and the trick was to build an organization that could hold the market forces stable for a while. As American firms grew in size from the 1880s, this task was increasingly delegated to foremen who might choose between workers according to favouritism and/or by asking for bribes (Monahan et al. 1994).

In America, the second stage was prompted by soaring labour turnover and unrest, and by some state intervention in industrial relations and employment rights (Monahan et al. 1994). This was also the period described as 'technical' in the previous chapter. It was characterized by changes in the division of labour from tasks that used undifferentiated labour which the market could provide unaided to more technical and elaborate divisions. There would also be more of the technical control provided, above all, by the assembly line (Fevre 2003), but, even before Fordism, there had been far-reaching changes in approaches to people management, particularly around World War I. Employers put a renewed emphasis on finding disciplined and trainable employees and, in place of the foremen's bribery and favouritism, personnel departments developed (Monahan et al. 1994). Over time, the new personnel managers tried to establish job descriptions and pay structures as well as hiring, training and promoting workers. The blueprint for these changes is often traced back to Frederick Taylor (1919) and his 'scientific management'.

Taylor's central claim was to be able to double or treble output by maximizing the efficiency of every individual. This involved matching tasks to the individual's capabilities with 'training and development' (1919: 12) to perfect their performance. In another of those recurring semantic ironies, Taylor presented scientific management as an antidote to 'individualism', which for him meant leaving each worker to get on with their work free of managerial assistance. He wanted managers to take on their new role of deciding who should do what job and in what way. This did not mean any loss of individuality, originality or opportunity to show initiative but, rather, employees ceding control to managers with whom they would work in harmony. Alongside the well-known stipulations for work study, selection, training and relatively high wages, Taylor wanted an ersatz morality of '[i]ntimate friendly cooperation between the management and the men' (1919: 140). He believed that personal contact would blunt the sharper side of the employment contract, minimizing conflict and reassuring workers that increasing output was not a threat to jobs, as the unions so frequently claimed.

Along with selection, training was key to Taylor's plan to get each employee to use his initiative – 'his best endeavors, his hardest work, all his traditional knowledge, his skill, his ingenuity, and his good-will' – to maximize returns to the employer (1919: 32). He thought that managers of his day were misguided when they offered to pay for this initiative with extra financial incentives which rarely worked because they acknowledged the clout employees had derived from the employment contract. The separation of conception and planning from execution was a better solution but managers would have to take on new roles and responsibilities to achieve this. They must codify the knowledge that had been known only to each worker, study how each task could best be done and 'scientifically' select employees, then train and develop them. In time, these new roles and responsibilities would provide the foundation for the managers' bid for increased power and resources.

Further developments in Monahan, Meyer and Scott's second stage, based on the 'technical model', were associated with the human relations school of management which developed out of the Hawthorne research (named after the plant near Chicago where the research was conducted) between 1924 and 1932 and was closely associated with Elton Mayo. It might have been concerned with 'sentiment and community' but human relations also involved the same expansion of the psychology of the worker. This meant more training, including for managers and supervisors, who would need to internalize the corporate approach and improve their management techniques (Monahan et al. 1994).

The Hawthorne researchers were as frustrated as Owen and Taylor had been by what they saw as the workers' 'irrational' limitation of output to prevent management raising the threshold at which they reached their bonus rate.[4] The source of this irrationality was informal social groups in the workplace which were a desperate attempt to make a community in the factory to make up for the dysfunctional families and demoralized communities outside the factory gates. This emphasis on demoralization recalled Owen's concerns, but Scott and Meyer (1994a) saw it as part of the institutional response to the psychological aspects of the expanded and complex individual who had not had a dysfunctional family or attachment issues before this point in history. Once these issues were identified, managers could assume new responsibilities to deal with them.[5]

The Hawthorne workers' 'irrationality' can be seen as a collective, almost socialistic, response to the employer's attempts to make them conform to cognitive individualism. Their response was more in tune with sentimental individualism, protecting the weakest and refusing to put economic gain above all else. Mayo and his colleagues denied that the Hawthorne workers' behaviour was collective or moral (Fevre 2003). The proper response to it was an even more specialized version of Taylor's 'intimate friendly cooperation' in which individual counselling and covert manipulation of informal groups of workers would become the job of the employer. If workers needed a surrogate family in the factory, the employer should not leave this to chance but create for them a high-functioning alternative to the demoralized world outside the factory gates (Monahan et al. 1994).

The third stage was the 'citizenship model', beginning in the USA during World War II and well established by the 1970s. By now, organizations were dealing with 'a complex person whose motives can be managed and even trained' but also 'organizational citizens' with 'a sovereign capacity to manage their own participation in organizational life' (Monahan et al. 1994: 257). These citizens could benefit from many more types of training and self-development, often in tune with the development of the organization. Just as previous chapters described a limitless faith in the benefits of education, so all sorts of training (for example, time management and dealing with change) now made sense. Employees were increasingly presented with a picture of themselves which was an abstraction. They were no longer hired to do *these* tasks in *this* shop with *these* co-workers but to become one of the 'abstracted citizens' of the organization who just happened to work here or there. As part of the same process, training added new layers of ersatz morality, including an organizational culture which required its citizens to invest in civility (Monahan et al. 1994).

Part of the impulse for the citizenship model was the increased power and legitimacy of trade unions. Personnel departments and their practices continued to develop in response, for example they attempted to increase loyalty and minimize turnover by promising job security and extra benefits, together with internal labour markets (ILMs), which offered more employees the possibility of a career. In part, these developments were shaped by wartime controls and government intervention in employment. Technical training for workers was now joined by human relations training for those who supervised them and courses on self-development and self-management courses, for example courses on career building and problem solving. There was also training on 'health and personal well-being, including safe diets, exercise, mental health, injury prevention, holiday health, stress and nutrition' (Monahan et al. 1994: 262).

Training was increasingly presented as rational and necessitated by changes in American law and the activities of professional bodies (Scott and Meyer 1994b). Indeed, institutional processes increasingly made training in the abstract appear to be a good thing, independent of whatever specific technical requirements the organization had. While training was still seen as less productive of transferable skills than education, it had nevertheless developed a unitary style and legitimation. Employees in different companies might be receiving very similar sorts of training with no mention of their transferability. Moreover, it was increasingly obvious that all types of training were meant to benefit organizations not society. There was no need for auditing or inspection because courses were under the control of professionals (Scott and Meyer 1994b).

The high degree of institutionalization in training meant that there would be minimal technical content linked to the jobs and tasks with organizations copying 'generally valued models, only loosely linked to their specific tasks and purposes'. There was, however, no escaping training because it now seemed to be essential to much of what the organization might wish to do (Scott and Meyer 1994b). By the mid-1970s, the abstract idea of training was an unquestioned virtue and a core principle of the modern American organization. Any organization which did not recognize the importance of investing in training was backward, but the days had long gone when organizations came up with training requirements by analysing their needs and designing provisions to meet them. Instead, they accumulated training packages on the advice of professional bodies and consultants and by mimicking competitors. Nor did they usually bother to evaluate the effect of training on efficiency, making good with the ubiquitous end-of-course feedback from participants. The efficacy of training was a faith commitment (Monahan et al. 1994). In this respect, training simply reflected the position managers had achieved by advertising their mastery of cognitive individualism: their ability to simultaneously increase efficiency and individualism was also taken on trust (Fevre 2003).

That training had become virtuous and non-specific and that all that was required to be progressive was to show that one was offering the latest training packages, regardless of their relationship to organizational needs or efficacy, might be taken as proof that employers were doing their best to respond to sentimental individualism. Monahan et al. (1994) could certainly see the parallel between the sentimental individualist stimulus to mass education for American citizenship and training for American organizational citizenship. The construction of the individual as more layered and complex seemed to be consistent with sentimental individualist beliefs but was also quite in accord with the competent individual who worked in a modern organization. Indeed, Monahan and colleagues concluded that the 'expanded self... is an organizational member, not a private entity' (Monahan et al. 1994: 269).

CONCLUSION

For Monahan et al. (1994), there was no contradiction between organizational rationality and the kind of individualism that was being developed, for example by training which made sure employees imbibed corporate culture and absorbed its values. There might, however, be reason to worry whether the hopes of sentimental individualism were being disappointed and if, rather than expanding it, organizations were limiting individuality. After all, in return for more rights and duties, organizational culture was now requiring employees to submit their wills to its purposes. Many decades of the development of people management led organizations to make a great many promises to their employees about the degree of individualism that was possible in the workplace. We explore more of those promises in the next chapter.

NOTES

1. See particularly Fevre 2003: 171–2, 228–35 and Chapter 3.
2. For legal comparisons between Britain and the continent, see Erickson (2005).
3. What Scott, Meyer and associates (1994) called an explanation of the rationalizers.
4. For more on Hawthorne, see Fevre (2003) and Gillespie (1991).
5. 'Psychology has been given free play in expanding human motives and capacities' (Scott and Meyer 1994a: 213).

10. From 'stupid' to 'self-actualizing' workers

The rise of the individual employment contract meant employers had to hire people, rather than coerce them, or pay others to procure them (while giving jobs to their favourites or those who paid them the biggest bribes). Perhaps the most common way to do this was to let it be known by word of mouth, or advertisement, that workers were needed and then hire the first ones who applied. The employer made no effort to differentiate one worker from another and all that separated the workers who got the jobs from the rest was that they applied when a vacancy was available. This is best described as 'matching' workers who wanted jobs with employers who wanted employees (Fevre 1992). It is usually imagined to occur when labour is plentiful and employers have no need of workers with specialist skills. It might apply, for example, to any discussion of recruitment in *The Wealth of Nations*, where Smith assumed that, as the division of labour increased, there would be less and less need to recruit workers who were skilled. Since it was only experience on the job that made some workers more efficient than others, employers might as well treat labour supply as undifferentiated. They could choose who to take on with a toss of a coin and whoever they hired would be able to pick up almost any job that was on offer in a matter of days (Smith [1776]2005).

Two centuries later, Taylor was largely concerned with the management of exactly the same category of worker: in most of his discussion, he was not talking about 'an educated mechanic, or even an intelligent labourer' (1919: 46). In fact, Taylor's most famous case study of scientific management was of the selection, employment, training and supervision of a supposedly strong but 'stupid' labourer. Nevertheless, Taylor insisted that, far from treating labour as undifferentiated, the scientific manager must take care in deciding who to hire from the 'very ordinary men' who presented themselves to do even the most unskilled labouring (Taylor 1919: 62). His insistence was an example of a manager claiming to be uniquely placed to select the best person for the job; a claim that is the epitome of the assertion that cognitive individualism is synonymous with efficiency (Meyer et al. 1987).

We should bear in mind how rare it would have been for employers to behave in this way early in the twentieth century. In the first place, Taylor proposed that every potential recruit was to be seen as an individual with their own unique abilities and the recruiter must make a point of talking to only one worker at a time when deciding who to hire. As well as interviewing, they must also judge the worker's attitude from their employment history and reputation amongst other workers. In this way, the recruiter would learn of their habits, character and ambitions: for example, were they prudent, hard-working and intent on prosperity? Depending on the job being hired for, there might then follow an appraisal of strength or another apposite characteristic. For example, some 'girls' were particularly adept at spotting defects and rejecting faulty products. Even though they were not necessarily the most intelligent or hard-working, this capacity was sufficient to make them good recruits (Taylor 1919: 90).

SELECTING THE BEST

Selecting some candidates for employment, and rejecting others, became popular as part of the technical model where people were supposedly being hired because of their fitness for particular tasks. Taylor was amongst the first who popularized managers' overblown claims of what they could do for efficiency in order to justify their places, and their incomes. The essence of their claims was the possession of knowledge of the sources of efficiency which would tell them how to design the practices and policies that would make individualism a cognitive reality. It was precisely for this reason that managers made great show of the degree to which selection had replaced discrimination and matching. In earlier work, I argued that it was by no means obvious that selecting according to the technical requirements of the job was any more efficient than hiring the first available worker (Fevre 1992; cf. Fleetwood 2006). Nor was it necessarily more efficient than the favouritism and discrimination that was associated with the foremen delegated to hire and fire. Precisely because they assumed that treating employees as individuals was more efficient, 'rationalizers' like Max Weber would have disagreed, yet it was extremely difficult to find definitive evidence that selection did lead to greater efficiency (Fevre 2003; Scott and Meyer 1994a). Indeed, many employers seemed to have been perfectly satisfied to carry on matching and discriminating, rather than selecting, well into the twentieth century (Fevre 1984, 1992).

This need not mean those employers were simply ignoring the technical model since employers might use matching in an effort to meet the technical values of the workplace (Fevre 1992, 2003). A typical example would be where the technical requirements of the work resulted in a labour shortage, perhaps combined with high labour turnover, which meant selection was not feasible. Employers would resort to putting up a 'help wanted' notice (perhaps not literally) and taking anyone they could get. Matching might give them 'cheap labour' in the normal sense of low pay and dirty or dangerous work, but matching has also been used as a solution to the technical requirements of the workplace where much more highly skilled labour is needed (Fevre 1992, 2003). Thus, the post-war history of the National Health Service in the UK would have been very different if doctors and nurses had not been recruited from less developed countries to make good the service's chronic labour shortages. There was little selection between individuals beyond that implied by checking medical qualifications and registrations and the results of language proficiency tests. Beyond this point, hiring was simply matching: if you came through the hospital door you got the job.

It was not unusual for many of the workers who filled chronic labour shortages in developed countries like the UK to be non-white, even if they were not migrants, and even if the shortages were not in high-skilled jobs. In part, those workers may have been available to provide this cheap labour because they faced discrimination elsewhere in the labour market (Fevre 1984). Just as managers could combine matching with the technical model, so managers might also conclude they could satisfy technical requirements by discrimination; indeed, many of their employees assumed this was the case (Fevre 2003; Fevre et al. 2011).

Rationalists would have us believe discrimination is only ever about trying to favour particular people, and matching is the abdication of any influence over hiring. Both are contrasted with selecting the best worker for the job which is meant to be all about meeting efficiency requirements. But when Taylor wrote about the lazy and unintelligent 'girls' who were good at spotting defects, it probably did not occur to him to mention 'boys' who could do the same thing. In common with most twentieth-century managers and employers, Taylor combined selection with discrimination in order to meet technical needs in what he declared to be the most efficient way (Fevre 1984, 1992). He assumed certain jobs were the province of each gender because of technical requirements for strength, or 'nimble fingers' or a particular kind of intelligence (Fevre 1985). Selection between individuals only took place at the secondary stage after recruitment had been limited to men or women.

The technical model was by no means as pure as we might imagine. Not only was it capable of accommodating discrimination and matching, but selection might happen for other reasons than those arising from the technical requirements of the workplace. In particular, managers might select workers in order to meet organizational or economic as well as technical values.[1] In the former case, a manager might decide to recruit a good sport or corporate citizen who they believed would help to maintain the general atmosphere of the workplace. In the latter case, they might decide to select by picking the worker prepared to work the most hours for the least pay. This was not matching since some effort was made to distinguish individuals: here the distinction was made according to what the recruiter found out about their attitudes towards pay. An accountant might call this hiring for efficiency but it was a far cry from the technical model (Fevre et al. 2011; Meyer and Bromley 2013). It was, nevertheless, a part of what Taylor did when selecting his strong but 'stupid' workman: he made sure of how much the man wanted to earn at the start.

As we will see shortly, it was usually legislation, rather than any obvious epiphany about inefficient hiring practices, that made selection particularly popular amongst managers. We should not, however, infer from that popularity that selection was every recruiter's default hiring practice. Hiring processes are necessarily opaque and we must rely on what the hirers tell us about the way in which they made their decisions (Ashley et al. 2015; Fevre 2003; Fevre et al. 2011; Fleetwood 2006). We have reason to be sceptical of their accounts because they almost always have a vested interest in telling the world that they have selected the best person for the job and therefore maximized efficiency. The consequences of hiring a worker on the toss of a coin may be much less grave than the consequences of broadcasting this method of hiring to others, especially the employer. The success of recruiters depends on portraying what they do as selection, and persuading others that selection equals efficiency, but they have no obvious interest in determining that either proposition is actually true. We ought to dispense with 'the premise that organizational practices are structured by extrasocietal principles of efficiency and attend to how the evolving institutional constructions of individualism and efficiency affect organizational practices' (Dobbin et al. 1994: 299; also see Dobbin and Sutton 1998).

Over the decades, self-interest has led recruiters, and other types of managers, to claim to possess more and more knowledge of the human requirements of the workplace and the characteristics of individual human beings. Let us deal first with the requirements of the workplace which, on closer examination, appear far from obvious. When Taylor insisted on work study, he was making the requirements of the workplace apparent not so much by closer inspection but by (re)constructing them. As he pointed out, this involved a great deal of managerial effort, even for unskilled labouring jobs.

In order for this to be possible in more complex workplaces, Taylorism would require the aid of technological change, and particularly the assembly line. These innovations allowed managers to get in on the ground floor of work design and gave them a high degree of control over what workers would actually do. The technologically-assisted process of constructing workplaces in such a way that managers might be able to understand their human requirements continued for many decades (Taylor and Bain 1999). Managers' struggles to understand their workplaces were also aided by managerial innovations such as management by objectives (see below). There must therefore have been many decades in which managers who were unable to follow Taylor's lead had precious little understanding of what was required, even of semi-skilled workers, in their workplaces. This was not, however, what they told their employers: they claimed not only to understand what was required but how it might be done more efficiently.

If managers had an impossible job working out what needed to be done, they had a worse one working out whether potential recruits had the right qualities to be able to do it. Again, they had placed themselves in a position where, in order to hold on to their jobs (and accumulate wealth and status), they must pretend to know more than was humanly possible (Fevre 2003). In this respect, they were greatly aided from the 1940s, beginning in the USA, by psychologists who had learnt that business endorsement might be one way to build a career (Anthony 1977; Meyer 1987). Innovations like the Myers–Briggs Type Indicator could help managers to translate what they did not know about work require-ments into what they did not know about the people who they might hire. American managers were, however, slow to give up on attempts to devise recruitment tests like the ones Taylor recommended until these finally appeared to fall foul of equal opportunities legislation (Dobbin et al. 1994). Elsewhere, for example in the UK, employers persisted in looking for new recruits who closely resembled their existing workforce. This was another way of avoiding the difficult task of finding out what the work required, and which workers might be best equipped to do it, but it also reproduced existing patterns of inequality, particularly those associ-ated with social class (Fevre 2013).

Neoinstitutionalists convincingly argued that, between 1964 and 1974, US legislation on discrimination, and subsequent court judgements, expanded the coverage of individualism – for example, extending the concept to women, minorities and people with disabilities – forcing organizations into an institutional response (Dobbin et al. 1994). The response that came was a commitment to more formality which would reinforce hiring on ability instead of ascribed features like race or gender. Firms adopted formal procedures for hiring and promoting on merit and, with the support of the law, this become the more or less universal answer to discrimination (Dobbin et al. 1994). Amongst the general increases in formality and rationality in hiring and promotion procedures, employers were particularly keen to point to the virtues of internal labour markets (ILMs) as mechanisms for selecting workers in ways that would maximize efficiency. All employees who were included in ILMs were to be recognized 'as ambitious and achievement-oriented in the process of formalizing and rationalizing promotion decisions' (Dobbin et al. 1994: 272). ILMs had been proposed as a solution to several different challenges to personnel managers such as industrial unionism in the mid-1930s, and wartime controls, but it was not until the 1960s and 1970s that ILMs were seen as channels for cognitive individualism within people management.[2] Through a process of trial and error, organizations were able to align this response with the requirements of the legal framework (Dobbin et al. 1994).

Since discrimination is very hard to observe, even when it is legal, we have no way of knowing if the institutional response to equal opportunities legislation, most often in the form of ILMs, was largely cosmetic. Organizations certainly advertised their vested interest in selection – because they were required to increase efficiency – and made concrete changes to hiring and promotion practices. These were first proposed by personnel managers who

> sold their bosses on formal evaluation and promotion systems with two arguments: these systems thwarted discrimination and, at the same time, rationalized the allocation of human resources. Their rhetoric coupled the ideas of equity and efficiency. (Dobbin et al. 1994: 281)

In 1974, the likes of the *Harvard Business Review* were promoting job descriptions, performance evaluations and salary classification to keep organizations out of the courts: qualifications and pay scales had to be justified on business grounds. Other recommendations included regular performance reviews so that protected groups did not miss out on promotions (and the organization could point to written records as a legal defence). US contract compliance law meant federal contractors had to keep this kind of paper trail anyway.

The articles written for personnel managers described an opportunity in the anti-discrimination legislation to increase the efficiency of their decisions. In fact, the opportunity afforded by American Equal Employment Opportunity law, and its interpretation by the courts, influenced people management for decades to come. In came job descriptions, performance evaluations and reviews and the business case for selection strategies. Out went the employment tests that had been around since Taylor's time, along with those more recent innovations: quota hiring of protected categories of workers (Dobbin et al. 1994).

Cognitive individualism was enshrined in US public policy responses to concerns about equity and then shaped employment practices. Those practices – for instance, ILMs – then fed back into cognitive individualism, for example making everyone appear equally interested in achievement. From now on, being an individual meant being somewhere on a career ladder and even those on the lowest rungs were meant to be as driven by the same ambition to move up the ladder as those at the top. Moreover, employees were now more likely to be able to evaluate their employer's performance in meeting the criteria for cognitive individualism, not simply in terms of the functioning of ILMs but through a variety of innovations, including the responsibility of employers to safeguard workers' integrity with innovations such as policies on sexual harassment. Once it was necessary that 'ambition and self-actualization came to be represented as characteristics of *all individuals*, not just white males' (Dobbin et al. 1994: 276, emphasis in original), American managers adopted sexual harassment policies, employment-at-will clauses to protect employers from employees, and various schemes for making work more interesting and rewarding (see the next section).

The evolution of European employers' selection procedures was influenced just as strongly by institutional developments as in the USA (Dobbin et al. 1994; cf. Fevre 1992). The American example influenced employment practices in other countries both directly and by way of its influence on public policy. For example, US equal opportunities legislation had considerable influence on British laws passed in 1965 and 1968. Further acts in 1974 and 1976 were greatly influenced by the concept of indirect discrimination which had seen off employment tests in the USA (Sooben 1990). In the UK, the idea that an employer could not deploy selection criteria which might favour a protected group without an explicit efficiency justification set the tone for cognitive individualism in the workplace for the next 20 years.[3] Without experimenting to a noticeable degree with employment tests or quotas, employers in many European countries went through exactly the repertoire of changes in selection methods which were portrayed as good for equity and for efficiency. Most obviously, they employed more and more formal recruitment procedures (beginning with written applications) in line with changes in public policy (Fevre 1992, 2003).

NON-ALIENATED LABOUR

The final element of people management that was in place by the mid-1970s was memorably described by Peter Anthony, a British sociologist of work and organizations, as the effort to persuade employees that they were no longer being hired to provide non-alienated labour. Bowring (2015) described the attempt to foster self-realization as a travesty of positive freedoms which could only be achieved by political struggles. In a similar vein, the effort to provide non-alienated labour can be seen as an attempt to have cognitive individualism deliver on the wildest dreams of sentimental individualism, and a category mistake which might have all sorts of unforeseen effects. In his 1977 book, Anthony argued that since all employment was alienating, the audacity of this rebranding was breathtaking. Even the managers who promoted it might have been daunted, except for the fact that they were the only category of employee who had always refused to see their own work as alienating.

Just as they introduced ILMs which promised to give other employees access to careers like them, so managers also went about redesigning, or at least repackaging, the division of labour so that others could access the kind of work they had: work that gave their lives meaning (Anthony 1977). As ever, people management argued that this was necessary for efficiency. Dewey had complained that profit-seeking meant employees were seen as 'hands', and there was no attempt to engage hearts and brains (see Chapter 8), but such sophisticated engagement was now the key to efficiency. This was not simply a matter of the productivity of workers' daily drudge, because the future of enterprise depended on, for example, the innovation and quality improvements which would come from encouraging workers' autonomy and self-development.

There were hints of this aspect of people management earlier on in this chapter in discussions of the neoinstitutionalists' ideas of the expanded (organizational) individual and self-actualization. These writers saw a new idea of individuals and their motivation gaining ground from the mid-1960s:

> The personnel practices that symbolized the employee as motivated by reward and punishment (the drive system), as a self-interested cog in the wheel of production with a limited capacity to learn (Taylorism), as a malleable

political entity (welfare work), or as a member of an oppositional interest group whose actions demanded legal restraint (the industrial relations approach), gave way to practices that represent the individual as self-actualizing, future-orientated and psychologically complex. (Dobbin et al. 1994: 276)

Yet, while the input of psychologists was undoubtedly important to this expression of cognitive individualism, it was not the original inspiration.

Psychologists provided the means – with concepts like motivation and self-actualization, as well as their measurement technologies – for managers to mount their attempt to make romantic hopes of non-alienated labour a reality, but the romance did not originally come from the pages of psychology books. Adam Smith wrote about the romantic hopes of youngsters who joined ships or armies, and even of young men who sought glory in the professions, and we also encountered romanticism in the Progressive era. However, its most cogent expression was in the vision of a socialist society peopled by worker-artists, popularized in Britain at the end of the nineteenth century by Ruskin, Morris and Wilde (Gagnier 2010; Sayre and Löwy 2005). These romantics were committed to sentimental individualism in which people were the priority, rather than cognitive individualism in which people were important because they could increase efficiency,[4] and they thought that non-alienated labour was impossible with a capitalist division of labour. They understood that the achievement of positive freedoms for the individual would entail political struggle (Bowring 2015).

Writing in 1891, Oscar Wilde declared that the only people in any position to take advantage of individualism were those who were *not* employed in capitalist enterprises, either because they had independent means or were lucky enough to be doing something they loved for a living. Wilde's examples of these were poets, philosophers, scientists and 'men of culture'. Self-realization, or self-actualization, was impossible for most people because they worked because of economic need and did work which they did not like. Some of the things Wilde counted as expressions of individualism which were denied to the majority were very similar to those Adam Smith thought the division of labour deprived people of: 'grace of manner, or charm of speech, or civilization, or culture, or refinement in pleasures, or joy of life' (Wilde 1891: 257). But Wilde was much more explicit that this deprivation was the result not of tedium and the undemanding nature of their labour but of the fact that people were not treated like individuals. Each individual was 'merely the infinitesimal atom of a force that, so far from regarding him, crushes him: indeed, prefers him crushed, as in that case he is far more obedient' (Wilde 1891: 257).

Barely 70 years later, the agents of that crushing force were claiming not only to value individuals but to act as if it was only through the fullest expression of individualism in the workplace that capitalism could flourish. Grace, culture and charm were now rebranded as soft skills or emotional intelligence which were vital to efficiency, and the workplace was now claiming to give people their best chance of joy of life, though it might now be called fun. The preparation needed to make artists of wage slaves began in the 1940s and 1950s, for example in the highly popular works of Peter Drucker, often called a humanist precisely because he translated sentimental, and romantic, individualism into the cognition which the workplace needed. He encouraged organizations to think of all their employees as assets, rather than costs. These assets required nurturing if they were to be able to show their true value to the organization and without autonomy, and the opportunity for self-development, they would be unable to demonstrate that they were their employer's key resource. In a word, the more a person could be an individual, the better a worker they would be.

Drucker (1995) laid out the principles which were to inform cognitive individualism but he also promoted concepts like 'outsourcing', new public management and the 'knowledge workers' who were to be so essential to the modern economy. He also advocated for the adoption of new managerial techniques including management by objectives (MBO) in which employees were motivated by individual goals which would, in turn, contribute to the overall objectives of the organization. People would be happier, and function more efficiently, with this level of clarity about their work. Together with generally improved communication, this meant it was easier to measure their contribution and suggest ways to improve it. Again, the model for all employees was how managers themselves were meant to conduct themselves in the workplace.

Anthony listed MBO as one of the characteristics of the new management style (along with, for example, productivity bargaining, performance appraisals and group target setting), which was based on the mistaken idea that what motivated managers would motivate others (Anthony 1977). But he argued that there was a limit to how much the managerial model could be extended to other employees. The new approach required maximum 'psychological participation' but offered workers *less* actual control over what they did and how they did it. After all, people management was not trying to make labour appear less alienating with the same aims as Ruskin, Morris, Wilde or Dewey. The aim was for managers to get more of their own way with their employees than they had when they coerced them, or relied only on financial incentives. Now they had attempted 'to extend their own, much more efficient, moral involvement in the organization' (Anthony 1977: 255).[5] If it worked, this strategy would undermine any other moral attachments that employees might have to trade unions or informal work groups, which stood in the way of improved efficiency, productivity and adaptability.

American initiatives to present labour as non-alienating had coincided with a period of trade union strength and the proliferation of such initiatives in the UK occurred against the background of an impressive upsurge of union power (Streeck 2014). The events of May 1968 in France had been followed by the Upper Clyde workers' sit-in in 1970–71, work-ins at 40 engineering employers and other examples of union resistance to the exercise of managerial rights. British employers had been finding it more difficult to live with strong trade unions than their counterparts in the USA. The industrial relations model that worked in the USA had never worked as well in the UK, so British businesses were indebted to the American psychologists who had turned the hopes of British socialist romantics into knowledge that managers could use to extend cognitive individualism in the workplace (Anthony 1977).

Herzberg, McGregor and Argyris were the psychologists most frequently given credit for the translation of sentimental into cognitive individualism. For example, McGregor had argued that employees achieved their goals by working for the success of the employer. All of the psychologists seemed to be concerned with achieving

> greater efficiency by promoting the development of organizations that are more humane and less irksome to their inhabitants, by sharing control, by allowing for greater participation, by recognizing the reality of conflict, by acknowledging the needs of employees for responsibility and growth. (Anthony 1977: 255)

Although Anthony was very sceptical about any real effects on wellbeing or efficiency, this was a potent combination of ideas which could put the power of social groups at the disposal of the organizations. Almost all opposition to the employer within the workplace would be eliminated and democratic control would be undermined, largely because people would not see who it was who was exercising authority over them.[6]

In the early 1960s, Argyris declared that the ever-greater division of labour would always be problematic because it gave workers no part in planning anything to do with their work, or in working out when it was done well. As a consequence, workers became more and more dependent, unable to think or act for themselves. This was a recipe for conflict and low self-esteem and wellbeing. The latter might be evident in increased trade union power, disorganized opposition (absenteeism, go-slows, sabotage and so on) or extravagant wage demands. Argyris' conclusion that workers would prefer self-actualization to money would be even more welcome to British managers than American ones (Anthony 1977).

In the 1960s, psychologists had argued that conflict could be traced back to managerial errors and, once it had its own house in order, an organization could begin to persuade employees that conflict was irrational and not in their interests. In the UK, managers would later be able to tell their employees that, far from it being in their interests to engage in guerrilla warfare with their employer, they should find in their managers their only source of sanity, as long as they were willing to take a 'positive' attitude to work.[7] Making their mental health dependent on the employees' willingness to take work as seriously as their managers was a bold move. If it worked, the employees would have internalized control and organizations could proceed to dismantle their bureaucracies (Anthony 1977).

Even though Anthony called this 'the strongest bid for legitimate control that has ever been made' (1977: 240), he had his doubts as to whether it had yet convinced many British employees. At the time, absenteeism and disputes made life difficult for employers and workers were contemptuous of managers taking their own work so seriously and still more so of their invitation to employees to share their delusions. Outside the workplace, Anthony could see a reassertion of romantic individualism on the left but, for all that he could see young adults rejecting managerial careers, indeed treating their values with contempt,[8] there would be no romantic retreat from industrialism (Sayre and Löwy 2005). Work was fated to be the dominant value in our lives and even the trade unions, with their economism, were just as much 'pure apostles of the theology of work' (Anthony 1977: 274, 278). Young adults might express a preference for the professions over management but they did not realize that the professions were already being converted to the spiritual value of work and losing their grip on older ideas of the morality of service.

The work of Boltanski and Chiapello, first published in 1999 (see Chapter 1), showed how prescient Anthony's judgement was. They did not find the romantic individualism which managers translated into cognitive individualism in the works of Oscar Wilde but in the most radical demands heard on the streets of Paris in May 1968. The protesters' demands for authenticity and liberation coalesced into a romantic, or 'artistic', critique developed by libertarian and ultra-left groups along with 'self-management' currents in trade unions. Capitalism was long-practiced at heading off threats through incorporation and in

1968 it faced a crisis of authority in the factory as well as civil disorder on the streets. In response, the demands for expressive creativity, fluid identity, autonomy and self-development would be met by the corporation. Boltanski and Chiapello ([1999]2005) claimed that, in order to do this, the corporations engaged in wholesale restructuring which directly benefitted their profitability. This claim will be scrutinized in Chapter 14 but for now we can recognize the importance of 1968 as a source of ideas for cognitive individualism, while insisting that this was far from the first example of people management being inspired by romantics.[9]

CONCLUSION

Many authors reserve the concept of neoliberalism to describe the actions of governments, for example privatization, deregulation, stricter welfare and attacks on the trade unions. If we follow this practice, we will need to use another term (such as 'the new spirit of capitalism'?) to refer to the parallel processes occurring in markets and organizations that involve private companies as well as governments (Streeck 2014). For example, changes made within people management to safeguard equal opportunity included both a legal framework and a corporate response. Both were as necessary to neoliberalism as changes in trade union law, so I propose that it makes sense to refer to them in the same way.

We now have in place all the necessary pre-conditions of the neoliberal settlement which were required of education, labour markets and workplaces. The remaining steps towards the settlement were political, including the 1979 general election which brought a Conservative Party led by Margaret Thatcher to power in the UK and the 1981 presidential election which installed Ronald Reagan in the White House (Streeck 2014). These political steps were conditioned by voters' increasing confidence that the contribution individualism made to efficiency made unfettered capitalism the best guarantor of individualism for the whole population.

From the point of view of capital, gains to efficiency were probably much less significant than the gains in bargaining power which followed from the success of the strategy to undermine trade union power and disarm more informal elements of worker control over production (Streeck 2014). The number of employees who belonged to trade unions now began to decline dramatically (see Chapter 1) and would do so for the next three decades. Yet, the success of people management in replacing collective bargaining with myriad individual employment relationships also increased the expectations employees had of those relationships. Peter Anthony (1977) thought that raising employees' expectations that they would be given non-alienated labour would force employers into constant tinkering with the division of labour. In later chapters, we will consider whether, with or without such tinkering, the effects of disappointing those raised expectations have become increasingly obvious.

NOTES

1. The typology is from Fevre (1992) but was in use in employment law in the UK in the early 1980s. For applications, see Fevre (2003, 2011).
2. What Dobbin et al. (1994: 275) call 'a general expansion in the social construction of the individual'.
3. The 1995 Disability Discrimination Act departed from this principle because it was felt to be insufficient protection where people with disabilities were concerned.
4. It is for this Kantian reason that Anthony (1977: 287) said Morris was (unfairly) seen as 'an antecedent in the development of self-actualizing theory'.
5. In the process, the original professional morality of the personnel manager who served their employee clients (like a doctor or lawyer might) was totally submerged. They became HR specialists who 'identify themselves squarely with other managers in their devoted pursuit of efficiency, profit and survival' (Anthony 1977: 255).
6. And see Chapter 1, particularly the brief mention of Foucault's influence on these ideas (Bowring 2015).
7. And 'the rejection of these humane, warm, and loving approaches' was portrayed 'as deviant, criminal, or lunatic' (Anthony 1977: 257).
8. Anthony 1977: 298.
9. Or of capitalism learning from Romanticism (Campbell 1987).

11. The neoliberal settlement

This chapter will convey us from 1976 to the era of global neoliberal hegemony described in Chapter 1. Previous chapters have described a series of struggles that drew on two different types of individualism, lasted for more than two centuries and ended with a comprehensive victory of cognitive over sentimental individualism in the USA. Other countries eventually followed the American lead, even when they had very different histories of engagement with individualism. The election of Margaret Thatcher in 1979 is always mentioned in accounts of neo-liberalism but insufficient attention is usually paid to explaining how it came to pass that a leader like Thatcher had become electable in the first place. The answer to this conundrum can be found in the convergence between the UK and the USA, in the fields of work and education, by 1976. Understanding this convergence shows us why Thatcher's election was both a starting gun for the spread of neoliberalism around the world, and a template for later neoliberal victories.

Thatcher's election showed that British politics was now converging with the USA, just as the two countries had already converged in the fields of education and work. It is a mistake to imagine that the election of Ronald Reagan in 1981 showed that the UK was leading the USA into the neoliberal future. That Reagan and Thatcher were apparently of one mind simply served to disclose how much political convergence had already occurred. It should not detract us from the more important point that for decades the UK had – albeit for very different reasons for much of the time – made changes in education, labour markets and workplaces that made it more like the USA. Thatcher's victory was a sign of this convergence which would be repeated, sometimes in very similar ways, in other countries around the globe (Hall and Lamont 2013).

In order better to explain this, I will borrow the idea of a 'Minsky moment' from the theories of economist Herman Minsky. Such a moment is one where the participants in an inflating market decide that the game is up and they had better sell up or lose their shirts. This revelation for the insiders is inevitably followed by disaster for everyone else, but here the bankers and traders who have their moment of terrifying insight are replaced by ordinary citizens. I particularly have in mind the better-off working-class voters who switched from the Labour Party to Margaret Thatcher's Conservatives in 1979 (Särlvik and Crewe 1983). They switched because they had decided the political choices that they and their parents and grandparents had made had failed or, at least, were no longer relevant.

The great attraction of drawing the parallel with a Minsky moment is that it underlines how enormous and sudden the change was: a whole political project appeared to go from boom to bust in a startlingly short space of time (Somers and Block 2005; Streeck 2014). Indeed, so quick was the change that, for many years later, some of us continued to believe the project was still standing rather than, like a piece of scenery in a silent movie, taking a comically long time to fall. For those who did grasp the enormity of the change that had taken place, it seemed that Thatcher herself had managed something almost magical, a kind of reinvention of an economy and society.

This overstates Thatcher's political acumen since the key voters who would win her the election had already changed their minds and only awaited a politician who espoused their views. All the same, the change was breathtaking. In 1976 and 1977, the developments described in previous chapters as spreading individualism to the less powerful and privileged seemed to be taking maximum effect in the UK. According to one highly respected authority (Atkinson 2015), 1977 was the high point of British income equality and we saw in Chapter 1 that trade-union membership was approaching its all-time high. In neither case was there any sign that the marriage between individualism and equality had come to an end, yet within a couple of years it seemed that a century of reform had turned the dreams of Tom Paine into the prophecies of Herbert Spencer.

There were Labour governments in the four decades after this but none could be called socialist and none fundamentally disagreed with the idea that individualism was more important than equality, or the idea that collectivism might give you equality but not individualism. In this sense, Thatcher was quite right to call the New Labour party of Tony Blair her greatest achievement. The most helpful way to understand the new era that was dawning in the run-up to the 1979 election is as a neoliberal settlement still very much in place at the time of writing.

WHY PEOPLE VOTED FOR NEOLIBERALISM

The Conservatives trailed in the two UK polls taken in 1976 but led in 21 out of 22 polls running up to the election in May 1979, however this does not mean that everyone had their Minsky moment.[1] The Conservatives had only 44 per cent of the popular vote and many of those votes were cast by their traditional supporters. It was a relatively small number of working-class voters who had been prepared to give neoliberalism its start in British politics by earlier changes in education, labour markets and workplaces. Although some of them may have been first-time voters, I will refer to them as 'swing voters' in what follows.

It has often been suggested that the swing voters were more achievement-orientated than their parents but, as we know from previous chapters, this is only the most visible element of the cognitive individualism that had made such strides in education and people management. Working-class voters might now aspire to home ownership, consumer goods, foreign holidays and some sort of career progression for themselves and, perhaps, some limited social mobility for their children (Streeck 2014). However, they could only think their aspirations realistic because they believed that education and people management had been reformed over many decades. When enough people (but nothing like the majority) decided they now knew that schooling, labour markets and workplaces were set up in a way that would allow them, and their children, to follow individualist goals, they became potential supporters for a party that would found the neoliberal settlement.

The voters who switched to Margaret Thatcher's Conservatives were amongst those Britons who thought they knew that widespread comprehensive schooling had completed the construction of an education system in which individual potential and talent were encouraged and rewarded. They had some notion that education experts had worked to establish the best mechanisms for encouraging and recognizing individual achievement. Beyond the schools, they knew that modern labour markets and organizations were also meant to be dedicated to recognizing and rewarding talent. To this end, they thought employers drew on comparable expertise to that available in the education system. Some patronage and favouritism might still exist but, since they were so obviously not in an employer's interests, they would not last much longer. Modern employers were, it seemed to them, much more likely to think of their employees as valuable human capital than as blue-eyed boys (Streeck 2014).

If they were young enough to have been through fully comprehensive schooling, the swing voters of 1979 might have learned all of this at school, although rather more of them may have heard the message from their employers. Of course, many teachers (and perhaps some of the HR managers) may have had no intention whatsoever of preparing their charges to be supporters of neoliberalism. Indeed, teachers were being castigated for indoctrinating their pupils with left-wing notions by industrialists and Conservative politicians (Chitty 1989). Their class-rooms were a far cry from the incubators of employability and enterprise that they were to become but we have to remember the Minsky moment. The teachers may have been trying to persuade their pupils to challenge the class system but the swing voters were already convinced that class was an irrelevance (Beck 1992; Giddens 1991).

The left-wing teachers and HR managers who thought their job was to insulate employees from the worst ravage of capitalism were all of a piece with the egalitarian and highly unionized society of the mid-1970s. Margaret Thatcher gave the swing voters a chance to insist that the existing political culture had done all the good it could accomplish and had now become an obstacle, particularly to them and their families. They were receptive to her message that all of the conditions required for individualism were now in place and that it was time to dismantle the supports that had been erected during the long struggle to extend the benefits of individualism beyond a tiny elite. These included the high taxes and welfare benefits which supported income equality, as well as the central importance of trade unions in public life. All of this was becoming a threat to the practice of individualism by people like themselves, and the same could be said of the left-wing teachers who were no longer part of the ideological drive for a better life but rather a dangerous threat to it (see Chapter 10).

This change has frequently been understood as working-class voters ceasing to see themselves as working class – perhaps because they changed occupation or location – and changing their voting habits accordingly. This view tends to treat political allegiance on a par with deciding which sports team to support and does not take seriously the way voters understood the world around them and made sense of their own experiences (of education and work, for example). The point is not so much that those who voted for Thatcher's Conservatives ceased to think of themselves as working class but that they ceased to see class as relevant to their lives (Savage 2000). For our purposes, it is much more fruitful to see changes in identity as the product of changes in people's knowledge and understanding rather than the other way around (Särlvik and Crewe 1983). Certainly, labour market entrants in the 1970s knew that they could not access many of the traditional jobs in manufacturing and extraction which had employed their parents, but this did not mean they acquired the identities of more traditional Tory voters. It was rather their understanding of the world that they saw opening up for them as individualism became a reality that made them vote for Thatcher in 1979 (Fevre 2000b, 2003).

Swing voters might trust their understanding that individualism had become available to all because it was confirmed by expert educators, psychologists and human relations professionals, but that did not mean the voters shared this expertise or even wished to rely on it. They were more likely to rely on *common sense* (see Chapter 2) in which we make sense of the world by drawing on our immediate experience and the experiences of others. Common-sense knowledge of schooling, labour markets and workplaces convinced the swing voters that the great transformation of the UK into a society where individualism was available to all, was well advanced by 1979. However, common sense is not simply another word for observation, since it has accumulated its own body of knowledge just like any other form of cognition. Common sense is less refined, but it shares with the experts (indeed with all of social science) the idea that it makes sense to talk of something all humans share, by virtue of being human. In common sense (but not social science), it is easy enough to grasp what this something is with the concept of human nature which makes us behave as we do. We can access it by looking inside ourselves and confirm it by (unsystematically) observing what others do.

Common-sense knowledge of how people behaved in a commercial society had a history of many centuries, and some of the components of that knowledge which came to the fore in 1979 had been familiar to Adam Smith 200 years earlier (see Chapter 3). They included the conviction that human nature always tended towards selfishness, which could be expressed in laziness as well as a desire for riches. They also included the idea that it was the balance of these elements of human nature that created a world in which those who worked hard made their fortunes and those who chose not to strive could not be helped. In the nineteenth century, there had been a formidable challenge to these views from the sentimental individualist belief in the goodness of human nature. Sentimental individualism held that the distinction between achievers and non-achievers was an artefact of inequality rather than human nature: most people simply did not have the opportunity to better themselves. In the following two centuries of social and political development, much effort was devoted to giving everyone this opportunity.

At the end of this process, a crucial group of voters decided that what they could now see around them confirmed that the better part of the job was done and the effect of human nature on behaviour was as visible as it had ever been. Since opportunities were now tolerably equal, the rationale for sentimental individualism to inform politics or public policy was fast disappearing so the counterweight to those old common-sense convictions lost its purchase. The swing voters were now open to a politics that brought those convictions back into the driving seat: if those who needed help had now been helped, their continued failure to succeed was explained by human nature, particularly their laziness and obduracy. On the other hand, those who succeeded were the ones who preferred riches and esteem to taking their ease. Swing voters could see ample evidence for these propositions in their own daily experience as well as in the experiences of others (including those reported in the news media).

This kind of evidence is not usually sufficient to satisfy social scientists, although there would be some like Charles Murray (1996) whose ideas owed something to Herbert Spencer, who were content with it. Murray also made the link between the excesses of sentimental individualism and inequality when he argued that it was the excessive generosity of the welfare state that was responsible for the multiplication of the work-shy and feckless (Somers and Block 2005). The swing voters of 1979 were already primed to make this connection themselves. Common sense could find sufficient confirmation through non-expert experience and observation that individualism relied on equality of opportunity – facilitated by education and people management – but guaranteed unequal outcomes. The Conservative Party under Margaret Thatcher profited by articulating this view in the language that common sense used, making frequent references to the value of daily experience and unsystematic observation and to what everyone knew about human nature. This language became a long-standing feature of British politics although its genesis is often referred to in misogynistic terms. It is assumed that it was used because Thatcher was being presented as a housewife to enhance her appeal to a part of the electorate, but this rather misses the point.

In their 1979 manifesto, Thatcher's Conservatives told the voters they recognized that the people who deserved to benefit from individualism were being hampered by those who failed to recognize that the great individualist transformation had already been achieved. They would restore 'the health of our economic and social life, by controlling inflation and striking a fair balance between the rights and duties of the trade union movement [and] ... incentives so that hard work pays, success is rewarded and genuine new jobs are created in an expanding economy' (Conservative Party 1979: Part One). The manifesto told voters that the forces of collectivism were exhibiting exactly the sort of destructive partisanship of which Spencer had warned (Chapter 7). Just as Spencer had predicted, succouring these forces threatened to put civilization into reverse:

During the industrial strife of last winter, confidence, self-respect, common sense, and even our sense of common humanity were shaken. At times this society seemed on the brink of disintegration ... Some of the reasons for our difficulties today are complex and go back many years. Others are more simple and more recent. We do not lay all the blame on the Labour Party: but Labour have been in power for most of the last fifteen years and cannot escape the major responsibility ... They have made things worse in three ways. First, by practising the politics of envy and by actively discouraging the creation of wealth, they have set one group against another in an often bitter struggle to gain a larger share of a weak economy ... Second, by enlarging the role of the State and diminishing the role of the individual, they have crippled the enterprise and effort on which a prosperous country with improving social services depends ... Third, by heaping privilege without responsibility on the trade unions, Labour have given a minority of extremists the power to abuse individual liberties and to thwart Britain's chances of success. One result is that the trade union movement, which sprang from a deep and genuine fellow-feeling for the brotherhood of man, is today more distrusted and feared than ever before. (Conservative Party 1979: Part One)

The manifesto was an epitaph for the age of sentimental individualism and it drew on all the familiar Spencerean themes. Even though the class system was dead, the trade unions were intent on moulding politics in its image for their partisan ends and, of course, the state was bloated and parasitical. It had encouraged dependency which was the antithesis of individualism. The Conservatives would 'support family life, by helping people to become home-owners, raising the standards of their children's education, and concentrating welfare services on the effective support of the old, the sick, the disabled and those who are in real need' (Conservative Party 1979: Part One).[2] If poverty and shiftlessness persisted alongside affluence, then two centuries of experimenting with attempts at equality had finally proved that individualism and equality were not compatible. For the next 40 years, no British political party which contradicted this view could win power.

From the late 1970s, countries around the globe made the transition – at different rates of change (Hall and Lamont 2013) – from a politics in which governments and companies had to be pressed to extend individualism to every individual to a politics in which governments and companies themselves claimed to be the champions of individualism. In these new neoliberal settlements, governments argued (as Spencer had urged) that anything slowing down the process which was putting the fate of individualism in the hands of companies was retrogressive. The identification of individualism with the existential interests of capitalist organizations was of course bound up with the tendency to exaggerate the capabilities of cognitive individualism, and credit its ersatz moralities, as described in earlier chapters.

EDUCATION AND PEOPLE MANAGEMENT IN THE GLOBAL NEOLIBERAL SETTLEMENT

As neoliberal settlements were established in countries around the world, earlier settlements were consolidated (Barnes and Hall 2013; Boltanski and Chiapello [1999]2005). Governments reshaped public policy in support of the idea that individualism was only ever safe with a capitalist organization, or with an organization that could do a passable impression of behaving like one (Bozeman 2007; Streeck 2014). This drove their continued development of education systems, the reform of employment and the diffusion of 'new public management' throughout the public and third sectors. The countries that subsequently reached their own neo-liberal settlements did not experience these reforms in the same order or at the same pace (Hall and Lamont 2013; Streeck 2014), but there were sufficient similarities to give credence to the neoinstitutionalist view that the changes were the products of a worldwide culture (Meyer and Bromley 2013).

One particularly glaring example of the world system at work was the massive global expansion of education (Meyer and Bromley 2013), which rapidly acquired a distinctive neoliberal tone. Across the world, governments and companies joined together to promote the idea that the purpose of education was to foster an individualism which would be responsive to the ever-changing globalized division of labour. As I have pointed out in earlier chapters, this was a far cry from Adam Smith's vision of education as an antidote to the depredations of the division of labour. Tony Blair's insistence on 'education, education, education' in the UK was simply one sound-bite in a global campaign to persuade people that the expansion of education was the key to their chances of fulfilling their potential within the global division of labour (Brown et al. 2012).

We have already encountered ideas such as employability and the learning society but these and other similar ideas (like the knowledge economy) actually drew on the other key educational concept in global neoliberalism: human capital. In Adam Smith's usage, the parallel between investment in education and training and investment in physical capital was designed to persuade his readers that people approach education looking for a return on their money (see Chapter 3). It implied nothing about the relationship between education and productivity, and still less did it rely on the idea that people would have to carry on educating and training themselves to fit into a global division of labour. People would invest in education because they knew the market would reward them, but this could simply be a question of accessing the privilege congealed in some elite occupations like the law which had erected educational entry barriers to keep out those who could not afford to invest.

In neoliberal times, the concept of human capital was so transformed that it encapsulated both the idea that education was the universal route to individualism and the idea that individualism was something capitalism could not do without (Fevre 1992, 2003; Fevre et al. 1999). Not only did capitalist organizations (and all the other organizations which were now supposed to behave like them) promise that their most precious assets were human, but they also depended on those assets differentiating themselves to fit the roles the organizations had made available. In its neoliberal guise, human capital was a distillation of the existential commitment of capitalism to individualism. Everyone was exhorted to invest in their human capital because, unless they did, capitalism would not only be unable to deliver individualism to them but would also wither away for lack of nourishment. The idea of human capital showed that, when they differentiated themselves into the types of workers capitalism required, they were simply behaving as sensible investors rather than volunteering to save capitalism the cost of preparing its own workforce (Schofer and Meyer 2005).

We should not forget that this preparation entailed more than simply getting qualifications. Not only were people required to school themselves to make sure they could take advantage of the opportunities for individualism that capitalism provided, but they were also meant to tailor themselves to those opportunities as they evolved. If the theory of human capital was right, this process must begin in kindergarten and so the belief that a changing division of labour would always provide sufficient opportunities for self-determination spread to elementary education around the world. From very early on in their educational careers, pupils were encouraged to consciously shape their individuality in anticipation of the job they might have. When they first entered the labour market, they were already well prepared for an interview in which they would demonstrate that the job they wanted was a perfect fit with their personality and ambitions (Brown et al. 2012). They would also be required to demonstrate that they had acquired qualifications of course, and the worldwide phenomenon of educational expansion was proof of just how seriously governments learned to take their role as facilitators of individualism.

From the late 1970s, successive governments had accepted that it was their responsibility to encourage and facilitate citizens' investment in their human capital. National prosperity and even prestige and influence depended on how enthusiastically they did this compared to the citizens of other nations (Meyer and Bromley 2013). Countries could easily be compared with each other by using measures such as average years of schooling and the possession of various qualifications which were deemed to be roughly equivalent. Such measures were frequently used by the supra-national organizations which saw educational expansion as a panacea, including the OECD, the IMF and the World Bank (Meyer and Bromley 2013). They served as a log of the successful efforts made by other countries to catch up and surpass the USA (Schofer and Meyer 2005). For example, by 2014 the USA was still in the top five OECD countries for the proportion of 25–64 year olds with tertiary qualifications, but in the younger age groups the USA was slipping down the league table as more countries around the world expanded their education provision. In 2014, the USA was no longer in the top half-dozen OECD countries and even the UK had passed the USA in the percentage of 25–34 year olds with tertiary education. A year earlier, the proportion of British and American 15–19 year olds enrolled in education was the same at 81 per cent, slightly below the OECD average of 84 per cent (OECD 2015: 41, 316).

By this point, a global consensus had established that a much more reliable way to measure these differences in national human capital was a standardized testing regime – the Programme for International Student Assessment (PISA) run by the OECD. PISA's academic attainment tests confirmed that the likes of Korea, Taiwan, China, India and especially Singapore were outstripping the USA and most European countries, and this was not simply a matter of more years in schooling. Education in these Asian countries was not only as, or more, extensive as it was in the USA, but it was also more intensive. For a given year of schooling, their citizens appeared to be accumulating far more human capital than their counterparts in the USA. Country after country took up the idea that human capital was the key to national prosperity, influence and esteem, and this necessarily implied that they had put in place the conditions required for the acceptance of their own neoliberal settlement (Schofer and Meyer 2005).

Throughout the world, governments accepted that education was the universal route to individualism and that individualism was something capitalism could not do without (Meyer and Bromley 2013; Scott, Meyer and associates 1994; Thomas et al. 1987). Albeit that this did not always happen very quickly, they also followed the USA (and the UK) in putting in place the preconditions for a neoliberal settlement in labour markets and workplaces (Hall and Lamont 2013). One of the Thatcher governments' key strategies had been to paint the trade unions as obstacles to individualism. From the successful 1979 campaign onwards, strike action, particularly in the public sector, was presented as an infringement of the individual liberties of service users. After the election, the unions were also portrayed as infringing on the liberties of employees in a variety of ways. These included the union tactic of increasing the leverage of strike action by seeking the support of employees in other organizations, for example those supplying an employer whose workers were on strike. Another target was the 'closed shop' in which workers were given no choice but to enrol in a particular union if they wanted to work for a particular employer or industry. Then there was the manner in which the unions decided to take action without a process which preserved the individual's right of self-determination.

Public support was gathered, and union resistance weakened, in a series of set-piece battles in which unions in the public and private sector were manoeuvred into disputes which they could not win. Government involvement in these disputes varied from mere cheerleading on the employers' side to (well-concealed) close involvement in the initiation and conduct of disputes (e.g. Fevre 1989). In addition, successive neoliberal governments in the UK pursued a course of legislative reforms which were presented as means to the enhancement or preservation of the individual liberties of employees and service users. For example, at the time of writing a Conservative administration proposed to require at least half of a union's eligible members to take part in a ballot for a decision on industrial action to be valid. In addition, at least 40 per cent of eligible members would have to vote in favour of action if it were to take place in core public services (health and education, transport and fire services). By this point, successive governments had established a framework for the resolution of the problems which employees had once had to rely on the unions to solve (Bagguley 2013, Barmes 2015).

Between 1997 and 2007, New Labour governments were particularly active in the extension of rights meant to facilitate the self-determination of individual employees. Existing protections and rights of redress covering unfair dismissal, payments of wages and for redundancy, employment contracts and discrimination on certain equality grounds were extended in an ad hoc way. Individuals acquired additional rights in relation to working time, a national minimum wage, paid annual leave and work–life balance. As a member of the European Union, the UK was also required to extend anti-discrimination law to cover discrimination on grounds of sexual orientation, religion and belief. In equality matters, individual employees might rely on information, advice and, in some circumstances, advocacy from the various equality bodies established by government. Government helplines and the network of Citizens' Advice Bureaux were intended to provide the information employees would need to know if any other of their rights had been breached, and how they might seek redress (Fevre et al. 2009).

The general principle of the individual employment rights framework was that employees would, if at all possible, seek initial resolution through discussion with their employer, and seeking to have rights imposed through an employment tribunal was considered a last (and expensive) resort. The exceptions to the expectation that individuals would see to it that their rights were observed were low pay, health and safety and the rights of the most vulnerable workers. In these cases, the government established agencies which allowed it to play a direct role in enforcement (Fevre et al. 2009). The latter would obviously have been anathema to Herbert Spencer, although he might have welcomed the idea that employees would no longer take most of their problems to trade unions because they had their own more effective channels for individual enforcement and redress.

Instead of seeing neoliberalism 'as a blanket laid over the world', we should understand that its impact differed with the context of its arrival and that context was influenced by the 'creativity' of local political actors (Hall and Lamont 2013: 10; Streeck 2014). Some of those already engaged in extending individualism used neoliberalism as an opportunity to carry on their work. In the UK, and in many other European countries, people made use of neoliberal discourses and structures, particularly those couched in terms of rights and productive worth, in their own attempts to foster the self-determination of employees. Something similar sometimes happened at the company level where the human resource management literature faithfully documented the increasing individual-ization of employment relations at the initiative of employers long before an individualized rights framework was in place in the UK and elsewhere (e.g. Storey and Bacon 1993).

The reform of HRM practices to facilitate the growing recognition of individual workers was believed to undermine the trade unions (Deery and Mitchell 1999), but we will see (Chapter 12) that, when employees engaged with the processes employers established to encourage them to resolve their problems individually,[3] they often drew on collective resources. It is rarely pointed out that one of the defining policies of neoliberalism, new public management (NPM), was also very much concerned with the individualization of employment relations in that remaining bastion of unionism, the public sector (see Chapter 1).

However, it was often the professions and their associations, rather than the trade unions, which were portrayed as obstacles in the way of individual self-determination. It is a mistake to conceive of NPM as simply concerned to extend the principles of the market to the public sector, unless these principles include individualism. Thus, one justification for the extension of management by objectives within NPM (Bozeman 2007) was that it increased the opportunities for autonomy available to managers and administrators. As in other examples of cognitive individualism, their greater autonomy was presented as conducive to organizational efficiency. They would no longer be hide-bound by bureaucracy, vested interests or political interference but would be allowed the space to fail or succeed by their own efforts. To this end, they were vested with devolved budgets and greater powers, and measurable performance targets were facilitated by external auditing and the widespread introduction of measures which fed into league tables, allowing comparisons between organizations and even countries (Meyer and Bromley 2013).[4] From managers and administrators, these innovations were extended to public-sector professionals themselves, with some rather mixed effects (Fevre 2003, 2007).

At least in the initial stages, there were many members of the long-established professions who thought that making them subject to NPM diminished their autonomy, for example through the replacement of professional judgement with managerial considerations. For instance, to neoliberals clinical judgement was no longer superordinate because it implied the derogation of individual responsibility to a collective which might well preserve all sorts of inefficiencies in order to feather its own nest.[5] But to the professionals who had spent a lifetime acquiring the ability to make these judgements, the ersatz nature of managerial morality was often painfully obvious, for example where targets failed to improve, or actually damaged, the welfare of those who used public services (Fevre 2003).

In what remains of this book, we will consider the question of whether, in gaining individual rights instead of collective representation, employees really did improve their lot. It would be consistent with our earlier discussions of cognitive individualism if the delivery did not match the promises made by governments and employers (Streeck 2014). I emphasized throughout these discussions that it was the extravagant promises of cognitive individualism rather than its demonstrated effectiveness that undermined sentimental individualism. This might also apply to the individual employment rights framework (Bagguley 2013, Barmes 2015), including anti-discrimination legislation.

As noted in Chapter 10, the level of discrimination, for example in labour markets, is notoriously difficult to gauge, but particularly so where it is illegal. Discrimination has natural camouflage because the reasons for any hiring, promotion and firing decisions are often shrouded in mystery and, at the same time, claimed by the competing rationalities discussed in the previous chapter. When decision-makers must also avoid saying they were influenced by discrimination in favour of or against anyone, but most of all the affected employees, surveys of the experience of discrimination amongst employees are very poor guides to its prevalence. This also explains the huge discrepancies between levels of discrimination reported in surveys of employees and more ingenious attempts to measure it, including field tests with dummy job applications which typically suggest much higher levels (Fevre et al. 2011). Many citizens may actually be aware of this discrepancy in a general way: they may not know that they have suffered discrimination but the proportion of citizens who believe that employment discrimination is widespread remains high, for example across the EU countries (TNS 2012).

Cognitive individualism within people management prepared the ground for neoliberalism by persuading citizens that capitalism required the ever-greater extension of individualism just as people required air to breathe. This assumption was reiterated on every occasion that a 'business case' was made for 'equality and diversity' (Fevre 2003; Fevre et al. 2012). If benefits for business could not be identified, then any proposal in question would, by definition, fail to extend individualism, but employees were not always convinced by this tautology. In effect, they were sometimes suspicious that their employers' avowals of commitment to equality and diversity might stem from an ersatz morality. We can find evidence of this where insistence on the ubiquitous business case appeared to convince employees that their employers were only paying lip service to equality in order to achieve their own ends, for example the appearance of legal compliance (Fevre et al. 2012).[6] Data like the high level of continued general awareness of discrimination suggest that employees may suspect that cognitive individualism generates an ersatz morality in which appearances can be all that matter. Nevertheless, those who are aware of discrimination are often in the minority and the next chapter will show that, when it comes to their own experience, employees seem to be reassured by circumstantial evidence that their employer is complying with the law.

In the remaining chapters, we will find further evidence which sometimes casts doubt on the extent to which employees really are convinced they are benefitting from individualism. This doubt suggests that the tussle in people's minds between the expectations generated by sentimental individualism and what they are told has been achieved by cognitive individualism may not, after all, be quite at an end. For example, people tend to be more convinced that women are now getting more access to the benefits of individualism than members of other protected groups, particularly those defined by ethnic origin, disability and sexual orientation (TNS 2012). In regard to disability, special measures have been taken to address this deficit. For example, the Americans with Disabilities Act of 1990 put a large share of the duty to eliminate discrimination by way of 'reasonable adjustments' to the workplace on employers. We will return to this example (in Chapter 13) because the legislation was obviously a significant departure from the core principles of the individualized approach to employment rights. If anything, it was reminiscent of some of the ideals of the socialist romantics who wished to see work changed to accommodate individuals rather than the other way round.

Further evidence of resistance to the blandishments of cognitive individualism could be found in employees' scepticism about the extent to which government and corporate enthusiasm for notions of employ-ability and the entrepreneurial self really extended individualism (Fevre 2003). It may be, however, that this evidence is now out of date and simply an indication of temporary difficulties in a transitional phase in which employees were gradually won round by changes in education and people management after 1976–7. From this point, organizations began to adopt the ideas of Strategic Human Resource Management, one of the primary functions of which was to ensure that employees would never doubt that employability and the entrepreneurial self would extend their own opportunities for self-determination. The HR manager now sat on the company board and this showed how the company cared about meeting all the individual needs of employees as well as confirming how important investing in their (self-)development was to the company.

In Chapter 1, we learned that such developments meant that employers required more of their employees, but this version of the story failed to mention how this was presented to employees as a wonderful opportunity for them to live out their lives in the manner only once available to the elite. From now on, their employer would make it possible for them to exercise their autonomy in every imaginable way. Younger workers were particularly prone to acquiring strong expectations that this was exactly how work should be (Fevre et al. 2012; Streeck 2014). They did not want to exit an educational system fully attuned to cognitive individualism only to find they were treated as indistinguishable cannon fodder for companies once they got into work. They wanted their efforts and talents to matter and strategic HR assured them that they mattered very much.

THE CLASSLESS SOCIETY

The classless societies produced by each neoliberal settlement around the world did not resemble the society represented in the American ideology of agrarian capitalism. Rather, they resembled the later version of an American classless society which was more in tune with the theories of Spencer and in which John Dewey saw a betrayal of the promise of American egalitarianism. In this version, education, labour markets and workplaces were believed to have been constructed in a way that made them conducive to individualism. It was nevertheless recognized that inequality would not disappear and might even increase. Competition in education, labour markets and workplaces would allow individual differences in ability and attitude to count in a way that they would not have done when individual competition was blunted by trade unionism or an interventionist state (Barnes and Hall 2013). As we read in Chapter 1, '[t]he harder you shake the pack, the easier it will be for some cornflakes to get to the top'. This was both a form of legitimation and a call to those who wanted to succeed to do all they could to make sure they and their offspring kept ahead of the competition.

Americans had long since come to terms with the idea that those who did well in the competition would try to pass on their privileges to their progeny by giving them an advantage in education, labour markets and workplaces. In reasoning that Adam Smith would have understood, they thought nothing could be done to prevent this without damaging everyone's chances of succeeding. For themselves, they had the 'natural confidence which every man has, more or less, not only in his own abilities, but in his own good fortune' (see Chapter 6). This confidence underpinned the American Dream which told even the poorest that they could ruin their chances of riches by trying to stop the rich perpetuating privilege. If their confidence was misplaced, they would fail but then they would have nobody to blame but themselves.

The Dream was like a bizarre version of John Rawls' 'veil of ignorance' (Rawls 1971). The idea of the veil was that it would make the rich discount their present privilege when considering distributive justice, but the Dream made poor Americans discount their *under*-privilege. Behind their veil of ignorance, they felt they could overcome the odds without collective help in the form of trade unions, welfare or state interference to limit the freedoms of those who had more privileges. Earlier in this chapter, I suggested that those who switched their votes to Margaret Thatcher's Conservatives in the UK had more modest dreams of beating the odds, and perhaps this was no surprise given the history of the British class system. In the aftermath of the 2008 financial crisis, Americans tempered their expectations but the majority still held on to the American Dream (see Chapter 6). In the USA under Obama, just as in Thatcher's Britain, there was no serious challenge to the world view that decades of cognitive individualism had put in place. Expectations may have been modest but the existence of the classless society was not in doubt.

It is not the purpose of this book to demonstrate that most inequality in the world is a reflection of the operation of class systems, but it may be as well to recapitulate the reasons why many social scientists think this is the case. There have been legions of empirical studies of the way different classes operate in education systems. There have also been some studies of the way that different classes operate in labour markets and workplaces. Most of these studies suggested that levels of engagement with the competition in schools, labour markets and workplaces varied between social classes. In simple terms, the middle and upper classes were better at understanding and playing the game (Fevre 2003). Within education, for example, Adam Smith's description of investment in human capital as an elite strategy to preserve and enhance advantages still applied, though more widely (Ball 2003). To gain an edge, people paid for private tuition of one form or another, but they also might pay a premium for housing which gave access to better schooling.[7] In the USA, where poor children were now in the majority in public schools (Southern Education Foundation 2015), the magnet schools programme channelled public resources to the richest and made sure that those with privileges got off to a flying start without paying for private education. This further increased the inequalities between rich and poor and, particularly, between white Americans and African-Americans (Blanchett 2006; Haney et al. 2004; Kozol 1991, 2005; Leonardo 2007; Nichols et al. 2005; Orfield et al. 2004; Solomon et al. 2005). Similarly, social-scientific studies of labour markets demonstrated that access to social networks helped the middle and upper classes to hang on to their advantages.

In fact, common-sense understanding of the way that education, labour markets and workplaces functioned was not that far behind social science. Members of the American working class understood that making the world appear to be more meritocratic was bound to favour the middle classes because they were more competitively minded, for example during schooling (Lamont 2002). In the workplace, the achievement orientation of the CEO was not always mimicked in the lower reaches of the corporation, even though its supposed diffusion was accepted wisdom in neoliberal societies (see Chapter 10). This much and more – for example, the importance of social networks – could be accepted as part of common sense without leading people to scepticism about the classless society. To question its existence required theory as well as observation, and this was beyond the powers of more empirical social science as well as common sense.

The neoinstitutionalist theory encountered in previous chapters allows us to see the idea of a classless society as the creation of the class system itself (Meyer et al. 1987). For example, it reveals the involvement of middle classes in the (re)construction of individuals and societies in a way which reflected their class interests. Thus, we saw in the previous chapter how (middle-class) managers strove to put themselves in a position where they could claim they were hiring for efficiency and therefore embedding cognitive individualism in labour markets. Managers reproduced, and reinforced, their class position by doing their best to make the interdependence of capitalism and individualism seem the natural state of affairs. In turn, the hiring practices that were meant to facilitate this interdependence made a major contribution to the reproduction of the class system from one generation to the next.

At the end of his essay on individualism, John Dewey (1929/30) gave an example of a working man who had tried in vain to get someone to listen to his ideas about increasing productivity.[8] Dewey wanted to underline the inability of economic individualism to reward people for creativity and innovation, particularly if the class system was being put in question. Chapter 10 showed how class discrimination could be an effective solution to the thorny problem of selection. Since those who were better off were not recognized and rewarded because they were more efficient, the 'classless' society was characterized by systematic indirect discrimination aimed at the working class (Ashley et al. 2015; Fevre 2013). In a savage irony, capitalism's reputation as a bastion of individualism was bolstered by using class criteria to recruit.

We know (see above) how difficult all discrimination is to detect but class discrimination appears to be exceptional: people are generally blind to it because, instead of class, they see variations in worth and merit (Barnes and Hall 2013; Fevre 2013). This is most obvious in the case of non-educational criteria but it applies to educational qualifications as well (Ashley et al. 2015; Fevre 1992; Fleetwood 2006), and it is the product of all the work done to embed cognitive individualism in education and people management to make society appear classless. In the UK, for example, people think class has hardly any effect on the way people are treated in the workplace. The most popular reasons for unfair treatment recorded in research are individual psychological characteristics and relationships. Few people think employees are unfairly treated because they are members of protected groups, but less than 1 in 100 believe that class discrimination occurs in the UK (Fevre et al. 2009). To transform the UK from a society which all its members recognize as class-ridden to a society where class is virtually irrelevant has been one of the most remarkable achievements of neoliberalism.

CONCLUSION

The promises of cognitive individualism are becoming so extravagant that we cannot help but wonder if their non-fulfilment might eventually shake employees' faith in their authenticity in another, very different, version of a Minsky moment. Previous chapters raised this possibility of disappointed expectations and promised to ask how much employees had actually gained from cognitive individualism. It was also suggested that, even before policies and procedures were put to the test, employees might think that what their employers were offering sounded too much like paying lip-service to admirable individualist goals. Quantitative evidence of employees questioning the plausibility of the fulsome claims of cognitive individualism would give us some reason to consider the possibility that people are torn between expectations generated by sentimental individualism and what they are told can be achieved by cognitive individualism.

NOTES

1. Ipsos MORI archive (2013). The shift in the polls was well established before the 'Winter of Discontent' in which public services deteriorated with a series of public-sector strikes over the Labour government's attempt to cap pay rises. I am certainly not suggesting that neoliberal ideas capture all of social life, even in the longer term (Streeck 2014, and see the introduction to Hall and Lamont 2013).
2. Across the globe, citizens' support for state welfare proved more resistant to neoliberalism than their views on the relationship between effort, reward and worth (Barnes and Hall 2013) but further reductions in welfare never seemed to be very far down the political agenda.
3. As part of the broader individualization of all relations with employees described in earlier chapters.
4. PISA, discussed earlier, is one such comparative measure.
5. Just as Adam Smith had warned: see Chapter 3.
6. Meyer and Bromley (2013) extend this point beyond equality and diversity to other forms of compliance.
7. Walford and Jones (1986) described a middle-class complacency with the introduction of comprehensives which was grounded in the knowledge that comprehensives could be turned into something like the grammar schools if the middle classes clustered in the residential areas around their chosen comprehensive schools (also see Ball 2003; Power et al. 2003).

8. In 2011, 24% of British workplace managers agreed that unions help to find ways to improve workplace performance. There had been little change since 2004 (van Wanrooy et al. 2011, 2013).

12. The apotheosis of individualism at work

The previous chapter suggested that it was difficult for anyone who trusted capitalist companies, governments and supporting organizations to serve as the guardians of individualism to reach the conclusion that class might be a cause of inequality. This chapter will add some very reliable and robust statistical confirmation that such trust is widespread. The British research it summarizes was very expensive to undertake and comparable data for other countries are not widely available. Nevertheless, the research shows that, in one country at least, employees' faith in their employers' devotion to individualism is strong and cognitive individualism continues to make inroads in the workplace.

EMPLOYMENT RIGHTS

Chapter 10 described the UK's individualized employment rights framework as a keystone of neoliberalism. Trade union members are in a minority and mostly concentrated in the public sector and the majority of employees are apparently reliant on a host of employment rights covering recruitment and dismissal and a great deal in-between. Are they content to do without the help and protection of the trade unions? While managers would much rather deal directly with employees,[1] it is by no means certain that public opinion agrees with them. A 2013 British poll showed 8 out of 10 adults still thought trade unions were essential to protect workers' interests. Whereas in the years before and after the election of Margaret Thatcher's Conservatives in 1979 most believed the unions had too much power, in 2013 only a third did so (Ipsos MORI 2013).[2] The proportion of Americans who wanted the unions to have less influence was very similar to this in 2015. Although the size of the majority which approved unions in the USA fell during the twentieth century, approval only dipped below 50 per cent in 2008 and had recovered to the levels seen in the 1990s by 2015 when 6 out of 10 Americans said they approved of the unions (Saad 2015).

These opinion polls are inexpensive but use methodologies and sampling procedures which make them less reliable than a study like the 2008 British Fair Treatment at Work survey which used the best available methods to achieve representative and reliable results, building on an earlier, very large pilot survey (Grainger and Fitzner 2007).[3] The main survey recorded a high level of knowledge of, and satisfaction with, the individualized employment rights framework (all survey results in this chapter are from Fevre et al. 2009). The statistical details of the survey are readily available elsewhere and I will limit myself to more discursive explanation. So, in 2008 less than a quarter of employees felt poorly informed about their rights and this level was not much higher amongst more vulnerable workers like the very young or the low paid. The figures had improved since the pilot survey in 2005, suggesting that the New Labour government had been adept at spreading the message of cognitive individualism. We already know, however, that this was not just a job for government and people were more than twice as likely to feel well informed if they also thought their employer took their rights 'very seriously'. It is as well to pause to consider the wider significance of this.

Without any evidence to go on, we might assume that neoliberal individualism is atomized and competitive, and that workers have become fierce libertarians who are more than happy to rely on their own resources. At least so far as British workers are concerned, the empirical data tell us this is not true. Not only do they want a framework of employment rights to protect them, but they also want employers and others (see below) to help them access these rights. The workplace turns out to be not that different to the school in that people expect wraparound support from their institutions so that they can benefit from individualism.

We can now move on to look at some of the results of multivariate (MV) analyses designed to show us which variables really matter by looking at them all at the same time. A hypothetical example shows how useful this kind of analysis is. A study of the causes of type II diabetes might conclude that those who spend a lot of time watching TV are more likely to develop the disease. In MV analysis, we can look at this relationship along with many others and perhaps find that there is a much stronger relationship between the disease and diet and exercise (and also genetic factors). People who spend time watching TV may seem to have a higher risk but this is only because they are also more sedentary and have a more risky diet. The relationship with TV viewing disappears once we look at all the relevant factors together (Grontved and Hu 2011).[4]

MV analysis of the 2008 British Fair Treatment survey showed that managers were nearly twice as likely as everyone else to feel well informed about employment rights. This is hardly surprising since most managers would have some sort of role in making other employees feel the security of a wrap-around employment rights framework. Permanent employees were also more likely to feel well informed: this was not the kind of rugged individualism in which practical libertarians thrived without the security of a permanent attachment. Workers need a solid relationship with their employer to feel the support of the individualized framework of rights. More proof that believing employers cared about rights to employees' feelings of being well informed about rights came from a question about equal opportunities policies. If a worker knew their employer had such a policy, this served as a robust indicator of how confident they felt about their employer's commitment to individualism (see below). It also meant they were nearly twice as likely to feel well informed about their rights.

I mentioned above that it was not just governments and employers that could help workers feel that individualism was safe in their workplaces. The other prominent contributors to that feeling were the trade unions and, given that individualized employment rights are usually supposed to undermine the need for trade unions, this comes as some surprise (Bagguley 2013; Barnes and Hall 2013). In the Fair Treatment survey, workers employed in workplaces with trade union recognition were 40 per cent more likely to feel well, or very well, informed about their rights. This accords rather well with the opinion polls which suggest that unions are considered necessary to protect employment rights, however the majority of the workers in the survey did not work in places with recognized trade unions.[5]

Once again, we see the dangers of subscribing to the idea that individualism and collectivism are necessarily opposed: the collective resources of governments, companies and even trade unions help people believe in the reality of individualism. The Fair Treatment survey produced several proofs of this fact, such as in the answers to a question about where people would go if they needed more information about employment rights. The vast majority claimed to know where to find information on rights at work,[6] but they did not think they would ask a lawyer or do their own research. Half would go first to a workplace source, usually (line or HR) managers, and their next most important source of information was a trade union (and not necessarily one with a presence in the employee's own workplace). A sizeable minority of the people who went to trade union sources for information were not even union members (also see Barnes and Hall 2013).

Not only are collective resources required to provide the scaffolding for individual employment rights (Bagguley 2013), but the feeling of wrap-around support may not survive an encounter with a real-life problem. MV analysis of the Fair Treatment survey showed that employees who actually experienced problems were only about a third as likely to feel informed about their rights and this had nothing to do with any objective lack of knowledge on their part. This suggests that the usual default setting for workers is to assume individualism is safe in the workplace – for example, they know what their rights are – until this is put to the test. We can therefore expect those people who have been disappointed by the shortcomings of individualism in the workplace to be different to other employees. We can expect them to be less sure of cognitive individualism in the workplace, and more cynical about its claims.

This analysis implies what has already been hinted at: the bulk of employees may not actually know as much about employment rights as they claim to when they say how well informed they are. Such complacency would be another indicator of the high level of trust employees place in their employers and governments to safeguard individualism. The Fair Treatment survey asked about knowledge of specific rights, including some fictional ones included to test this very possibility – for example, the survey claimed that employers had a legal duty to seriously consider requests for flexible working for those who care for elderly relatives. Sizeable minorities thought the fictional rights existed, and expressed the same level of confidence in fictional rights and real ones. This suggests that much 'knowledge' of fictional and real rights had a common source in the assurance people felt that they lived in a society characterized by cognitive individualism. In such a society, it was perfectly plausible that the fictional rights existed. By the same token, then, knowledge of rights need have little to do with useful knowledge which workers can use to make sure their rights are observed.

Much of their knowledge of real rights was in fact very sketchy, unless respondents were likely to be personally affected. Moreover, they systematically exaggerated the value (coverage, benefits and level of enforcement) of the rights they knew about. It begins to look like there are more romantic individualists in the British workplace than the HR managers who are professionally committed to publicising their employer's ability to fulfil dreams and wishes. There are also romantics amongst the employees who remain credulous about the affinity between capitalism and individualism until evidence to the contrary stares them in the face. Not only are they prepared to believe in the existence of rights that do not exist, but they also look at many of their existing rights through rose-tinted spectacles.

There is no better proof of this than the fact that, in the Fair Treatment survey, 6 out of 10 workers thought they knew enough about their rights. This is the sort of cognitive individualist foundation that makes the neoliberal settlement seem impregnable, and it is important to understand the contribution that employers have made to it by encouraging their employees to see them as the guardians of individualism. Just over half of British employees said they did not need to know much about their rights at work because their employer acted reasonably. Amongst this group, 9 out of 10 said they knew enough about their rights, but things were different amongst the minority who said they would still need to know about their rights whether their employer acted reasonably or not. Fewer than 4 out of 10 of this group said they knew enough about their rights and, as we might expect, they were more likely to have actually experienced problems than the more complacent group.

EQUAL OPPORTUNITIES, SELF-DETERMINATION AND OTHER MEASURES OF ROMANTIC INDIVIDUALISM

The majority of British employees think there is a comprehensive framework of individual employment rights in place and that they can leave it to their employers to see that their rights are observed because they are reasonable. For all but those workers who actually get into difficulty and try to make the framework function for them, individualism is safe with capitalism. Something like 6 out of 10 employees hold attitudes to individual employment rights which make them potential supporters of a neoliberal consensus, but how firm is this figure? Its firmness seems to depend on the efforts of governments (like New Labour), employers *and trade unions* (Bagguley 2013). For example, if employers create, or fail to manage, problems in the workplace, the 60 per cent bedrock of neoliberalism will erode, as it will if employers give the impression that they are unreasonable. In order to illustrate this relationship, we now look at equal opportunities.

Everything we have learnt so far suggests that the apparent ubiquity of equal opportunities may be crucial to the appearance of cognitive individualism. For example, Chapter 11 explained that personal experience of unfair treatment and discrimination is rare and that few people think that their employer treats the groups protected by equality laws in this way. Earlier in this chapter, we saw the effect of an employer having an equal opportunities policy on workers' confidence in their employment rights. Of course, having an equal opportunities policy also made employees much less likely to think that there was unfair treatment or discrimination in their workplace, irrespective of any actual experience (or observation) of unfair treatment or discrimination they might have.[7] But these are only examples of the more general point that concrete evidence of an employer's commitment to cognitive individualism (such as an equal opportunities policy) helps employees to believe that individualism is safe with their employer.

We know that having a trade union in the workplace also helped in this regard – perhaps because this added to the collective resources available and was also perceived as a sign of an employer's reasonableness. However, actually being in a trade union does not make people predisposed to think they can rely on their employer to champion individualism. Several questions in the 2008 survey suggested that British trade union members remain deeply sceptical of their employers' claims to precedence in advancing cognitive individualism. Indeed, no other group is as consistently sceptical of the affinity between capitalism and individualism. They are at the opposite extreme to the romantics who are most likely to be swayed by their employers' claims and promises. This might be because they consume information from their unions and other sources which make them cynical, or because a predisposition to distrust employers leads them to join trade unions. Somewhere in between the sceptics and the romantics is a group of realists who appear to recognize limits to the amount of individualism employers can, and perhaps ought to, advance. These realists may not be sceptical about the general commitment of employers to individualism (as trade union members tend to be), but they are sceptical about specific aspects of the promises of cognitive individualism, in particular equal opportunities.

We saw some hints of this realism in Chapter 11 but the realists are also revealed in some data derived from hypothetical questions on hiring practices (Fevre et al. 2011)[8] asked in both the 2008 survey and the earlier pilot. The question employees were asked was this: 'In filling YOUR JOB, if several people had the same skills or experience to do the job, would your employer be inclined to favour any of the following?' Multiple responses were allowed, although in practice most people chose from a list of demographic characteristics which were meant to make them think about the possibility of discrimination against protected groups. The final option given after 'a man', 'a woman' and so on was 'the best person for the job'. It was always the last option that respondents were given but, in 2008, 9 out of 10 people said this was how their job would be filled.[9] Of course, multiple coding meant it was possible for people to choose the last option and also say their employer would prefer someone white or someone without a disability (for example). In fact, only 1 in 5 people thought their employer might favour a particular demographic with the most popular being a man.[10]

Respondents were also asked why they thought their employer might behave in this discriminatory way. Again, multiple coding was allowed but most respondents opted for only one answer. The most popular answer by far was the requirements of the job, although there was some support for fitting in with the current employees and also the preference of managers. No other response (including prejudice or discrimination) managed to reach double figures. Thus, realists certainly do not think capitalism's promise of individualism is hollow because it hides prejudice. Instead, they suspect that there are inbuilt organizational obstacles to individualism. They may not be as sceptical as the trade union members but they have some reason to discount the more extravagant claims their employers make to be able to champion individualism, at least through the promotion of equal opportunities.

It is noteworthy that, when they point to the discrimination caused by the requirements of the job, employees are indicating that the division of labour trumps individualism, indeed they appear to believe that the demands of the division of labour would lead their employers to break the law.[11] Experimental analysis of the 2005 pilot survey told us more about those who thought their employer would favour two or more population groups (Fevre et al. 2011). Unsurprisingly, there was some overlap between the realists and the trade union members but the realists also tended to have a higher social class[12] and to be male employees. In other words, the realists tended to be those who would have access to inside information about the way people management in their organization worked. This result was supported by further analysis of any employees who thought their employers might favour a particular demographic because of prejudice or discrimination. As well as two protected minorities,[13] this group was more likely to have managerial duties and so recruitment and promotion processes may not have been as opaque to managers as they were to other employees. It is unlikely that many managers with recruitment experience would ever join the group of sceptics since they benefit from the inequality that cognitive individualism validates.

We already know that those with employment problems tend to be less complacent about their employment rights and we might suspect that this pattern would carry over into equal opportunities. There certainly was an overlap between those who felt that their employers would not safeguard individualism in a hypothetical question and those who reported unfair treatment or discrimination that had happened to them, or which they had observed happening to someone else. The 2005 Fair Treatment pilot survey showed that, if they had experienced unfair treatment of themselves or others for almost any reason (not limited to breaches of equal opportunities), they were more likely to have a bad or very bad impression of their employer. They were also more likely to say that their employer would hire someone from a particular demographic group and more likely to see this as prejudice or discrimination.[14]

On the other hand, experiencing discrimination did not by any means shake everyone's faith in their employer's commitment to individualism. In the pilot survey, roughly half of those who reported personal experience of discrimination thought their employer would hire the best person for the job in the hypothetical question. The default assumption that individualism and organizational success went hand in hand was hard to dislodge, even when it came up against contradictory evidence in employees' own experience, at least of discrimination and unfair treatment. Does the same conclusion extend to other everyday experiences of individualism in the workplace?

The 2008 Fair Treatment survey included a supplementary questionnaire which was completed by a majority of the main sample (Prior et al. 2010).[15] The questions suggested that the 60 per cent agreement with the assumptions about individualism which supported neoliberalism was fairly solid. Around three-quarters agreed, or strongly agreed, that they had some say over the way they worked and got the respect they deserved from their colleagues. Over 60 per cent said they often or always have a choice in deciding how they did their work. Of course, from the point of view of some old professions, and perhaps many academics, this might not sound much like self-determination, but it is a noteworthy counter-weight to our impression of modern workplaces as very like assembly lines (Brown et al. 2012; Taylor and Bain 1999).

That individualism means different things in different parts of the division of labour was underlined by some other results. Thus, over half said they often or always decided when to take a break at work and had a say in their own work speed. Only a third said they often or always have a choice in deciding what to do at work, however. The supplementary questionnaire to the Fair Treatment survey also included some questions which were designed to get at people's experience of individualism in their workplace more directly. These questions were also asked in a slightly different way in another British survey a few months earlier. The British Workplace Behaviour Survey (BWBS) was not quite as well resourced but it was nevertheless the most representative and reliable survey of workplace ill-treatment conducted so far (Fevre et al. 2010, 2012; Prior et al. 2008).

A quarter of the respondents to the Fair Treatment survey disagreed or strongly disagreed with the suggestion that where they worked the needs of the organization always came before the needs of the people. When pairs of variables were compared in simple bivariate analysis, this result was strongly correlated with having had no experience of problems at work, unfair treatment, discrimination, sexual harassment, bullying and harassment. For example, 4 out of 10 of those with experience of unfair treatment strongly agreed that the needs of the organization always came first, as against 1 in 7 of those not reporting unfair treatment. These proportions were similar for the experience of bullying and harassment. As before, disappointments with personal experience of individualism in the workplace seem to disabuse people of their default assumptions about the security of individualism in the workplace.

When only a quarter of the Fair Treatment respondents disagreed or strongly disagreed with the suggestion that where they worked the needs of the organization always came before the needs of the people, this does not seem sufficiently solid bedrock for a neoliberal settlement. The BWBS asked the question in a slightly different way because it did not allow people a neutral option (neither agree nor disagree) and made them choose between yes and no. When pressed to come down on one side or the other, as swing voters must do in a first-past-the-post electoral system, those who might have been neutrals in the Fair Treatment survey tended to come down on the side of their employer. So, in the BWBS 6 out of 10 employees said the needs of the organization did not always come before the needs of the people. Once more, 6 out of 10 gave capitalist individualism the benefit of the doubt.

The BWBS also revealed more information about the remaining 4 out of 10 employees who could not be counted as romantic individualists. In bivariate analysis, they were much more likely to be trade union members, recent employees, members of some minorities and men. It is plausible that recent employees who have lost their jobs are as sceptical about capitalism's commitment to individualism as trade union members.[16] Similarly, some members of protected groups may have experienced problems at work which made them more sceptical, although there seems to be no obvious reason why men might be more sceptical than women.

As well as asking whether people were always secondary to organizational concerns, both surveys asked employees if they had to compromise their principles in the workplace. Again, the existence of the neutral option depressed the proportion of workers who were sure individualism was safe in their workplace. All the same, 45 per cent disagreed, or strongly disagreed, that they had to compromise their principles. Once more, this result was strongly correlated with all the experiences which make people sceptical about individualism at work. In bivariate analysis, compromising one's principles was correlated with a wide range of problems at work, including unfair treatment, discrimination, sexual harassment and bullying and harassment. For example, twice as many of those who had experienced bullying and harassment were likely to think they had to compromise their principles.

Dispensing with a neutral option in the BWBS has a similar effect as before, with 7 out of 10 employees saying they did not have to compromise their principles, making the underlying support for individualism in the workplace seem stronger than ever. In bivariate analysis, those people who were most likely to say they had to compromise their principles were trade union members, non-Whites, workers with a disability, men and the under-45s. As before, there are more plausible reasons for the appearance of trade union members and members of protected groups in the list.

The final question in the sequence of three questions simply asked people if, where they worked, people were treated as individuals. Perhaps because it addressed the question of individualism in the workplace so directly, 6 out of 10 respondents to the Fair Treatment survey agreed, even though they might have chosen a neutral option. Just as before, bivariate analysis revealed that those who did not think people were treated as individuals were much more likely to have experienced problems at work, including unfair treatment, discrimination, sexual harassment, bullying and harassment. Thus, employees who had experienced unfair treatment were twice as likely to feel they had not been treated as individuals; and those who had experienced bullying and harassment were more than three times as likely to say they had not been treated as individuals.

In the BWBS, where the neutral option was removed, even more workers were prepared to give their employer the benefit of the doubt: 8 out of 10 said they were treated as individuals. The estimate that a fifth of the workforce are determined sceptics is reasonable,[17] and what a tremendous accolade that is for all the work done in people management! Given the history of alienating, demeaning and dangerous work in capitalism, a 60 per cent approval rate is remarkable enough, but 80 per cent is spectacular proof of the extent of the social and political transformation that has been brought about with the neoliberal settlement. In bivariate analysis of the BWBS, those who were the least likely to say their employer treated people as individuals were temporary workers, people with a disability that affected them on a daily basis, recent employees, non-graduates, those not born in the UK, employees who were not managers, non-Christians and, of course, trade union members.

This tells us that, apart from the trade union sceptics, there are other groups of workers who are less likely to believe in the triumph of individualism in the workplace, possibly because they have actually seen it put it to the test, as in the case of recent employees who have found their employer's commitment to individualism did not save them from being thrown out of work. Those with a more serious disability, and workers who are non-UK/non-Christian, may also be more likely to find individualism wanting in their own experience of the labour market and the workplace. The other sceptics seem to be those who are more peripheral to the changes in people management intended to reassure people of the pre-eminence of individualism. They include temporary workers, non-graduates[18] and even those who have no managerial responsibilities. Because these findings are significant for the future of work and politics, we will return to them below. Workers with disabilities will be a central focus of Chapter 13 and those workers neglected by people management will be a central focus of Chapter 14.

To sum up this chapter so far, we have seen a similar pattern replicated in one survey measure after another of employees' expectations and experience of individualism at work. A majority of employees are romantic individualists who see little reason to doubt the claims of people management that the workplace is a safe haven for cognitive individualism. Further research is required but these employees almost certainly make up the pool of voters from which support for neoliberal policies has been drawn. Indeed, if there is, in reality, only 1 sceptic in every 5 employees, the prospects for parties and politicians seeking to win votes by opposing neoliberalism seem to be bleak indeed. As long as the numbers of trade union members and more peripheral workers do not grow, and many more workers do not find the promises of individualism fall down when they are put to the test, there seems little doubt that neoliberalism will dominate work and politics for the foreseeable future.

BULLYING, HARASSMENT AND ILL-TREATMENT IN THE WORKPLACE

Chapter 11 concluded by suggesting that the promises of cognitive individualism might be becoming so extravagant that there is a possibility that their non-fulfilment might eventually shake employees' faith in their authenticity. The previous section does not suggest that this is very likely but in this section we will be reminded once more of the lengths that employers have to go to keep up their reputation as the guardians of individualism. While employees may turn a blind eye to many breaches of the trust they place in employers, we know that the expectations placed on employers have tended to grow over the decades as the scope of individualism has expanded. This section will explore employers' responses in more detail before considering whether, at some point in the future, rather more people will become sceptical about their ability to deliver individualism than at present.

Chapter 10 cited policies on sexual harassment as one of the more recent indications of the expansion of individualism spotted by neo-institutionalists. Sexual harassment itself was hardly novel at this juncture (Segrave, 1994), but the neoinstitutionalists' point was that making it the object of initiatives in people management was both new and a good example of what the expansion of individualism meant. In the present chapter, we have already seen that employees who have experienced sexual harassment are very like those who have experienced problems with employment rights, or discrimination, in the way they respond to direct questions about the extent of individualism in the workplace.[19] Nevertheless, sexual harassment seems an especially difficult area for employers to be able to demonstrate their competence in embedding cognitive individualism. At first glance, this seems to be more a matter of managing interpersonal relations than organizational ones but, on the other hand, it is open to employers to build a case for the harm sexual harassment does to their business, just as with any other infringement of individualist principles. Similarly, although cognitive individualism claims to pursue such breaches on the basis of solid evidence, the potential for such evidence to be disputed may be no greater in allegations of sexual harassment than it is in allegations of discrimination, unfair treatment or many other breaches of employment rights.

The people-management response to the requirement to encompass freedom from sexual harassment within cognitive individualism has included legislation. For example, in the USA and the UK, sexual harassment has been included within wider legislation outlawing discrimination and harassment towards people on the grounds of their sex.[20] Protection against harassment was also extended to cover all the groups protected by legislation but some countries have extended legislation to cover bullying and harassment directed towards any person, whether they are in a protected category or not. This has necessarily happened outside the framework of anti-discrimination law, for example Sweden passed an Ordinance on Victimization at Work in 1993 and in 2002 France legislated on bullying and harassment in its Social Modernization Law (Guerrero 2004). In the USA, there are some relevant state laws and US federal employment law covers bullying under safety and health.[21] There is no separate protection from bullying and harassment in the UK, unless a breach of employment rights has occurred or the affected employee is covered by the Equality Act 2010.[22]

The reluctance of some jurisdictions to extend legal protections for individualism in the workplace to include bullying and harassment against any individual indicates that this is something of a step-change in the expansion of cognitive individualism. Since specific anti-bullying legislation necessarily applies to individuals rather than categories of employees – or collectives – it is a much sterner test of legislators' commitment to individualism than equal opportunities legislation. Not all jurisdictions appear to be prepared to take this step. The lack of a standardized legal response suggests that, however it is defined – for example, as 'mobbing' in Sweden or *harcèlement moral* in France – bullying is (for now) the apotheosis of individualism in the workplace (Barmes 2015).

As with sexual harassment, there is no special difficulty in constructing a rationale for the importance of bullying to organizational success (Belsky 2012; Berkovic 2010; Fowler 2012). Similarly, the difficulties of finding evidence of infraction when there is only the word of the 'victim' and the 'bully' to go on is no different to many other examples of cognitive individualism. Rather, legislating against bullying is especially significant because it comes closer to recognizing the sacredness of the individual (see Chapters 1, 2 and 10) than any of the other protections we have been considering. Like laws on employment rights, and unlike equality laws, it extends protection to individuals rather than groups, but it differs from many aspects of employment rights in that it is not fundamentally concerned with breach of contract. Instead, the focus of concern is (usually explicitly) the dignity of the individual (Elliott 2007).[23]

In countries with protections against bullying, it is very often employers who are charged with safeguarding the dignity of their employees.[24] One very obvious response to this has been the proliferation of dignity at work policies, for example in the UK (Fevre et al. 2012). Most observers of the British workplace in, say, 1976 would have thought such an idea was preposterous, so how did it come about that, in a few short decades, capitalism came to be so committed to workers' dignity? Earlier chapters explored the relationship between sentimental and cognitive individualism in the nineteenth century, particularly in the context of social movements such as anti-slavery and the Common Schools Movement. If there had been space to do so, we might have extended the account to cover twentieth-century movements including civil rights, feminism and global human rights (Elliott 2007; Mathias 2013). The case of workplace bullying and harassment (and 'mobbing' and *harcèlement moral* and other variations such as workplace violence and abuse) has been little different to these examples in that a social movement brought this possibility of extending individualism to public attention.

The social movement which drew attention to workplace bullying spanned many countries, although there were few genuinely international figures or bodies within it. It included campaigners who had experienced bullying at work, experts (particularly Scandinavian psychologists), trade unions and professional associations, journalists, politicians and policy-makers. There is no doubt that in many countries this movement had a great deal of public support and, as in other examples, the success of the social movement persuaded the state and other organizations to devise laws, regulations, ethical guidance and policies (like dignity at work policies) designed to turn the hopes of sentimental individualism into cognitive individualist practice (Fevre et al. 2012).

Despite the fact that there was, for the most part, little overlap between the different, national parts of the international social move-ment, the innovations in cognitive individualism which resulted from it have been remarkably similar (D'Cruz 2012; Einarsen et al. 2010). As neoinstitutionalists would predict, employers have adopted a remarkably similar array of policies and commitments which have indicated their rapid conversion to this new arena for cognitive individualism. This is not to say, however, that these innovations have been effective (Barmes 2015). Employees very often view them as superficial, and perhaps as designed to secure legal or regulatory compliance or, indeed, to enhance company reputations. Where they or their representatives have tried to use their employer's policies to stop bullying or gain redress, they have often found this actually exacerbates the problem (Fevre et al. 2012).

The ineffectiveness of employers' policies on dignity and bullying is also evident in respect of bullying and harassment from clients and customers (sometimes including sexual harassment). Employers adopting policies and practices which sacrifice their relationship with clients and customers in order to make good their promises to employees would surprise many observers.[25] Employers could argue that the price of some lost customers would be more than balanced by improvements in corporate image and reputation, of course. An ineffective policy on customer harassment serves this purpose without offending any cus-tomers at all and provides a useful example of the way in which employers can square the circle when their commitment to individualism conflicts with their commitment to organizational success.

For example, in order to safeguard the dignity of their employees many service providers, both public and private, have promised to follow a 'zero-tolerance policy' towards violence from clients. Quantitative research shows that such violence is surprisingly common (Jones et al. 2011). Moreover, qualitative research suggests that many employees do not expect their employers to pay anything more than lip-service to the idea of zero tolerance and, indeed, consider violence from customers to be an unavoidable part of their jobs. Contrary to most expectations, this would apply particularly to workers in health and social care rather than the police or emergency services (Jones et al. 2011).

At least at first glance, measuring violence at work is easier than measuring other forms of bullying and harassment (Jones et al. 2011). Measurement implies the definition and operationalization of concepts and here, just as in education and other aspects of people management discussed in earlier chapters, psychologists have played a key role (Frank and McEneaney 1999; Frank et al. 1995; also see Elliott 2007; Mathias 2013). Their important contribution to the social movement that brought bullying and harassment into the public sphere has already been noted. A major part of this contribution was the work of Scandinavian psychologists like Leymann on the operational definitions of bullying and harassment (Fevre et al. 2012). For example, the psychologists defined bullying as sustained aggression from an individual or group which is intended to cause harm or as an escalating series of 'systematic negative acts' in which a more powerful person victimizes a subordinate (Einarsen et al. 2010; Fevre et al. 2010, 2012).

Along with these definitions, psychologists proposed various causes of bullying, including the personality characteristics of 'bullies' and their 'victims', dysfunctional groups, autocratic or absent leadership, poor communications and insufficient employee participation. Other environmental factors included high workload, low job control, role ambiguity and job conflict. All of these might make bullying more likely because they increase the possibility of disagreement over what people should be doing and lessen their ability to defuse or avoid conflicts (Fevre et al. 2012). Other findings of psychological research include the association of bullying with work intensification in the form of increasing job demands and pressure of insufficient resources. In fact, many aspects of organizational change were reported to be highly correlated with bullying, including a change of manager and organizational restructuring. Once more, the explanation given by psychologists was that such changes risk setting in train the psychological processes that lead to bullying behaviour. For example, changes in work tasks and workplace composition lead to role conflicts and insecurity which lead to bad behaviour.

The academic literature on human resource management describes all of these features as characteristics of the modern, high-commitment workplace (Appelbaum, 2002; Boxall and Macky, 2014; Kalleberg et al. 2009; Ramsay et al. 2000). Indeed, closer examination of the psychological literature on workplace bullying reveals that much attention has been focused on just such workplaces. Chapter 10 described the way in which conditions in modern workplaces were presented as proofs that employers were expanding the sphere available for individualism in the workplace. The proportion of organizations adopting high-commitment practices has continued to grow in subsequent years (van Wanrooy et al. 2013). It now becomes clear that, when psychologists focused on the problems created for dignity at work in these organizations, they were, in effect, trying to find ways to expand cognitive individualism to answer questions raised by earlier innovations in cognitive individualism in which they were also involved. Thus, with encouragement from psychologists, workers were promised all manner of self-actualization and self-development. When these promises went unfulfilled, psychologists were on hand to conceptualize this as bullying and propose a wholly new arena for intervention designed to address this second-order problem.

As the psychologists carried on with their work, they were engaged in an iterative process of the kind the neoinstitutionalists like to describe, as employers (and others, including professional bodies and trade unions) made various attempts to find good-enough solutions to the problems they had been posed. This helps to explain the ubiquitous and isomorphic anti-bullying and harassment policies of UK organizations (Fevre et al. 2012). Not only have psychologists given employers guidance about what their dignity at work policies should contain, but they have also proposed preventative work in selection, training and leadership, and remedies which make use of a wide range of psychological techniques and metrics. In much of this psychology, it is assumed that all the other aspects of cognitive individualism discussed in earlier chapters are already in place.

Psychologists do not often research, or consult for, small family firms. Their more normal subjects (and collaborators) are larger modern organizations which are very often complex and technologically sophisticated: a health service rather than a farm or a deep-sea trawler.[26] As well as their public commitment to the value of self-actualizing employees, these organizations all have their professional HR systems, sophisticated equal opportunities provision, and so on. In general, the interventions proposed by psychologists suggest that bullying should be addressed with more of the same institutional responses (Einarsen et al. 2010; Fevre et al. 2012). The implication is that bullying is a problem of an unmodernized and unprofitable workplace, but in Chapter 13 we will discover that this is in fact a long way from the truth.

The data and analysis discussed in the next chapter do not suffer from the restrictions on our understanding which necessarily come with following the psychologists' definitions of the problem and its causes. For instance, rather than leaving the definition of bullying in the hands of psychologists, it draws on employees' ideas about what amounts to bullying and what they count as dignity at work.[27] With these conceptions, it becomes possible to consider threats to individualism which are rarely mentioned by psychologists and never addressed in policies on dignity at work. For example, the operationalization of sickness absence policies by management is revealed as a frequent cause of employees' complaints of bullying and affronts to their dignity.

CONCLUSION

Chapter 13 provides further quantitative evidence to suggest that the gap between the solutions provided by cognitive individualism and the expectations of sentimental individualism is rather greater in respect of dignity and bullying than it is for employment rights and equal opportunities. We can however conclude this chapter with some thoughts on the trade unions which were also heavily involved in the social movement that brought bullying and harassment to public attention. They were perhaps particularly prominent in the UK and they continue to play a key role in the institutional response. Indeed, responding to these problems has become the major preoccupation of union organizations at the workplace level, as explained by this trade union official at a logistics and communication company:

> The biggest arguments that we have, I have, or debates or call it what you wish, with management is around individuals and how they're feeling and how they're being treated, how they feel they're being treated or perceived. That's the biggest interaction I have with management. It's not about the big-ticket issues.[28]

Outside the workplace, in their regional and national organizations, the trade unions have developed their own resources designed to help workers and their representatives.[29] They have sometimes drawn on the help of psychologists but, off the record, unions have sometimes made their own diagnoses of the roots of bullying and harassment, for example blaming 'macho-' or 'old-fashioned' management (Fevre et al. 2012). In this view, a manager's determination to brook no opposition to the right to manage is interpreted as stubborn resistance to the processes of modernization which tend to be synonymous with high-commitment workplaces. In this rather roundabout way, the unions confirm the modernizing message of the psychologists. Far from pointing to the failures of people management to embed individualism in the workplace, trade union officials and other observers theorize that this mission has not gone far enough. In this way, bullying and harassment can be made to fit seamlessly into the story of modernized workplaces and markets giving ever more scope to individualism because this is in the economic interests of employers.

Back at the level of the individual workplace, the trade union mission to address bullying and harassment has created intense pressures on unpaid worker representatives in the UK.[30] Like the employment tribunals which employers and governments find so costly, the caseloads of the representatives mirror individualism in action. Each employee gets individual attention at the price of creating a heavy burden of gathering evidence and progressing their case. Here too is the paradox noted earlier in this chapter: when problems arise, employees find that relying on collective resources is often the only hope they have of making their employer live up to their promise of individualism at work.

NOTES

1. In 2011, 18% of British workplace managers were not in favour of union membership and 80% would rather consult directly with employees. There had been little change in these figures since 2004 (van Wanrooy et al. 2013).
2. Note that the proportion who thought the unions had too much power was lower in the mid-1990s.
3. For further details of methodology, see Prior et al. (2010).
4. This study had insufficient data to include dietary intake and physical inactivity which might explain the negative effects of TV viewing so did not report MV analysis.
5. Of course, the proportion of people who were actually in trade unions themselves was even lower at 28%, in line with the union density figure for the UK given in Figure 1.3 in Chapter 1.
6. Again, a New Labour government had presided over a large increase in this measure in just three years.
7. Indeed, we will shortly see that another British survey showed that unreasonable behaviour was significantly more likely in medium-sized workplaces which were part of large, sometimes well-known, modern organizations with professional human resource departments, equal opportunities policies and policies on dignity at work. Some may even have had collective bargaining agreements with trade unions. The appearance of greater rationality is evidently no guarantee of self-determination in practice.
8. The survey adapted a question used in EU surveys: 'In (OUR COUNTRY) when a company wants to hire someone and has the choice between two candidates with equal

skills or qualifications, which of the following criteria may, in your opinion, put one candidate at a disadvantage?' Multiple responses were permitted and there were many of these. In answers to this question for the whole of the EU between 2008 and 2013 (TNS 2008, 2012), the proportion of respondents identifying age as a disadvantage had gone up to 54% from 45% in 2008, but look, manner of dress and presentation were down to 45% from 50%; skin colour or ethnic origin were down a couple of points at 39% but there was little change for disability (40%) and candidate's general physical appearance (37%). Class was not included amongst the criteria but speech/accent (30%) and address (8%) were included in 2012. The results for the UK tended to be around the EU averages. As noted in Fevre et al. (2011), the differences between these EU results and the results of the Fair Treatment at Work survey may be largely because (a) the EU survey asked if a characteristic put a candidate at a disadvantage rather than asking how an employer decided in favour of a candidate, and (b) the EU survey did not allow the response 'best person for the job' (or none of the above – unless spontaneously uttered). This makes it of very limited use for measuring how people feel about individualism in the workplace.

9. Up from three-quarters in 2005. All of the figures for the pilot survey are taken from Grainger and Fitzner (2007).

10. 6% of all employees, the same as in 2005, followed by 4% each for a woman and a younger person. Only 2% in both cases thought their employer would favour a certain race or ethnic group or someone without a disability; 1% an older person and 1% someone of a certain sexual orientation; 0% said someone with a certain religious belief.

11. These are the criteria of acceptability much criticized by social scientists in the 1980s and supposedly outlawed by later equality legislation (Fevre 1992, 2003).

12. Class A as opposed to class E.

13. Gay, lesbian or bisexual and non-UK born.

14. Those who said they had personally experienced discrimination differed from those who reported unfair treatment of themselves or others only in that they were more likely to say their employer would favour a man.

15. A self-completion methodology is less satisfactory than face-to-face interviewing but there appeared to be no obvious causes for concern about the representativeness of the sub-sample. Just over 4000 people took part in the main survey and all but 400 of them accepted the self-completion questionnaire at the end of the interview; 60% of these people returned the questionnaire.

16. Gallie et al. (2013) report that the UK Skills Survey showed fear of unfair treatment (not just arbitrary dismissal but also discrimination and victimization) increased in 2000–2012 as people feared for their jobs with recession and austerity.

17. Also supported by other Fair Treatment survey results, e.g. 1 in 5 employees thought they might be victimized or treated unfairly because of raising a complaint.

18. Suggesting that those most likely to feel they had been treated as an individual during their education found this was also the case in the workplace and the labour market. Employees with higher degrees were even more likely to feel they were treated as individuals than graduates.

19. That there were statistically significant results for this kind of ill-treatment is something of a marvel. The numbers reporting sexual harassment in both surveys were very small and (therefore) for this variable to achieve significance suggests that the correlation between it and measures of individualism was particularly strong.

20. For example, the US Equal Employment Opportunity Commission enforces Federal laws prohibiting employment discrimination. These laws protect employees and job applicants from unfair treatment or harassment by managers, co-workers or others in the workplace in the case of these protected grounds: race, colour, religion, sex (including pregnancy), national origin, age (40 or older), disability or genetic information (www.eeoc.gov/employers/index.cfm).

21. Bullying and harassment are included in 'workplace violence' and covered by the employers' duty to provide a safe workplace (www.osha.gov/).

22. Though in practice employees have taken recourse to civil action and other kinds of legislation, including The Protection from Harassment Act 1997 intended to protect against stalking.
23. Indeed policymakers in the UK flirted with a Dignity at Work Act (Bolton 2007).
24. Even where there is no explicit dignity at work law, thus, in the UK, *Dawson v Chief Constable of Northumbria Police* was brought under The Protection from Harassment Act 1997. In light of this case, employers were held to be vicariously liable for linked acts of harassment caused by the acts of two or more employees.
25. Such as the researchers who have documented sexual harassment in hotels and hospitality, e.g. Kensbock et al. (2015).
26. For a rare exception, see Dutt (2015).
27. For further details, see Fevre et al. (2010).
28. Previously unpublished interview content from one of the case studies in Fevre et al. (2012).
29. Some of these publications have drawn on the work of this author and his colleagues.
30. See e.g. the UK's National Work-Stress Network (www.workstress.net/), Foster and Fosh (2010) and Foster (2015).

13. The hidden injuries of cognitive individualism

Chapter 1 mentioned research linking neoliberalism and depression, for example arguing that people's mental health suffered when they were made entirely responsible for their own fate. Neoliberal individualism, it was suggested, subjected people to chronic insecurity, not simply because they might lose their jobs but because they never knew whether they were doing well enough in them. More recently, Paul Verhaeghe (2014), a Belgian professor of clinical psychology and psychoanalysis, claimed that neoliberalism caused not only depression but also self-harm, eating disorders and personality disorders.

According to Verhaeghe, all of these illnesses could be caused by the ersatz moralities described in previous chapters of this book, especially the attachment of moral meanings to success and failure in the labour market and workplace. Within the workplace, performance was ascertained through intrusive systems of monitoring, measurement and comparison, which increased our anxieties and made us fearful of other people, both as judges of our performance and as our competitors. One consequence of this fear was an increase in workplace bullying as workers vented their frustrations on those in the workplace who were unable to stand up for themselves.[1] This was an example of a more general increase in childish behaviour as people became dependent on arbitrary, shifting and often trivial signs of their worth. As a classic American sociological study would have put it, they were 'other-directed' and unable to rely on their own moral sense (Riesman 1950).

The idea that neoliberalism involved a loss of personal autonomy was at the centre of Verhaeghe's account, just as it is a major concern of this book. He argued that the promise of individualism was often deceptive, falsely claiming to offer freedoms that we could only blame ourselves for not grasping. He took much success and failure in the neoliberal economy to be beyond the control of the individuals involved, but argued that they generally did not realize how little control they had and so habitually attributed their success and failure to their own actions. This was especially corrosive of the mental health of those who blamed themselves for their lack of success. These are persuasive ideas but they are of limited use in helping us to understand the current situation without the right kind of data.

Even the notion that mental illness has increased is not securely anchored in empirical evidence. Chapter 1 noted that Alain Ehrenberg's thesis about mental illness and neoliberalism took the increased presentation of symptoms, and levels of medication, as evidence of rising rates of depression (Ehrenberg 2009). Both trends might actually be the result of a higher public profile for mental illness, together with reduced stigma for its sufferers (Walker and Fincham 2011). They could also be the result of the medicalization of problems previously understood as aspects of character and disposition, or of innovations in clinical therapies including the availability of new drugs (Fee 2000). Indeed, all of these contributory causes could themselves be consequences of the expansion of the idea of individualism to include an expectation of mental health for everyone, beginning with adults and then expanding to include children (Meyer 1987). That so much effort has been devoted to explaining the benefits to employers of addressing mental health problems might indicate the same process of institutional response to the challenges posed by individualism already discussed in earlier chapters (Harder et al. 2014). Once again, employers, and particularly capitalist employers, are required to be guardians of individualism, particularly under neoliberalism.

Far from individualism causing mental illness in the way that Ehrenberg and Verhaeghe imply, mental illness would therefore owe its treatment, its profile and indeed its origins to individualism. The connection between mental illness and neoliberalism would then be a spurious one, caused by their separate relationships to the growth of individualism. If the evidence for a causal connection between neoliberalism and mental illness really is in such short supply, why are so many writers and commentators convinced of it? One possibility is that they are generalizing from their own experience as successful professionals.[2] A British academic, for example, would have no difficulty in validating their proposition about increased performance anxiety by drawing on their own experience and the experiences of their acquaintances. Academics and writers are not necessarily representative of other occupations, however. We might also need to be wary of generalizing the experiences of European writers who have been embroiled in local struggles to preserve employment rights (for example, employment protection and limitations on the intrusion of work into family life) which do not exist elsewhere. In such cases, a public intellectual might well make arguments against the intrusion of Anglo-Saxon neoliberalism, without too much regard for the detailed correspondence between their arguments and the evidence base.

Now there are a great deal of data from many different countries on workplace stress: is increasing stress the obvious proof of the impossible and damaging demands of individualism? Finding evidence of a long-term increase in workplace stress is not easy and, even if it could be established, such an increase might have other causes. Moreover, it is possible that, as with mental illness, individualism has been implicated in the increased attention given to stress rather than in the underlying phenomenon (Meyer and Bromley 2013; Wainwright and Calnan 2002).[3] The institutionalization of stress looks very like the kind of institutional responses to the expansion of individualism we have encountered so many times in recent chapters, for example considerable effort has been devoted to arguing that capitalism has a vested interest in reducing stress. Thus, bodies like the Health and Safety Executive and the Advisory, Conciliation and Arbitration Service in the UK, the National Institute for Occupational Safety and Health and the American Institute of Stress in the USA, and the International Labour Organization have presented the elimination of stress as an organizational imperative, citing working days lost to stress and associated mental illnesses and making estimates of the cost of lost productivity, income and medical treatment.

Other sources of the data needed to support the idea that neoliberal individualism causes mental illness might include international evidence of the relationship between social capital and mental health (Brown and Harris 1978) or the relationship between inequality and mental illness (Wilkinson et al. 2011). In the case of the former, it could be argued that the replacement of collective agreements by an individualized employment rights framework is tantamount to the loss of the social networks and rich associational life theorized as social capital. The fact that, when faced with problems at work, employees still seek out the support of trade unions could be adduced as supporting evidence (Bagguley 2013, Barmes 2015). Evidence that inequality is associated with mental illness (amongst other health problems) might be offered as support for the suggestion that the imposition of moral responsibility on the individual for their success or failure creates psychological and emotional problems.

A third source of evidence is worth considering at greater length. This is the research drawn from many different countries that has established the range of health effects, including mental illness, caused by bullying and harassment in the workplace. The sheer number of studies, and the robust nature of many of their findings, suggests that the links between bullying and harassment and depression, anxiety and other disorders, including post-traumatic stress disorder, are now accepted (Einarsen et al.

2010). What these studies have not established is that the ill-treatment which psychologists label as bullying and harassment has increased because of individualism. There are no robust time-series data on which we can establish an upward trend and, even if one could be established, the incidence of bullying recorded in representative studies of working populations with sound research methods is frequently in single figures (Fevre et al. 2010). Such low figures hardly suggest that bullying and harassment have made a major contribution to the ill health caused by neoliberal individualism.

Perhaps, as with stress, individualism has not caused bullying and harassment but simply drawn our attention to it and made its eradication the responsibility of the employer? Encouraged by the psychologists who have catalogued its ill-effects, including the loss of organizational efficiency occasioned by the psychological effects of bullying and harassment, employers have accepted bullying and harassment as their latest test in the effort to prove themselves as the guardians of individualism.[4] We might therefore conclude that Verhaeghe's (2014) analysis was too superficial when he posited an association between bullying and harassment and individualism caused by anxious employees taking out their frustrations on vulnerable colleagues.

I want to suggest that the connections between bullying and harassment, individualism and neoliberalism run much deeper than is usually assumed. I have argued throughout this book that the original stimulus to the apparently limitless expansion of individualism was sentimental sense-making. Sentimental beliefs about what human life could be like made the extension of self-determination possible, and cognitive individualism had the task of adapting institutions to make these beliefs a reality. Whether this cognitive individualism was in tune with the American ideology of the nineteenth century, twentieth-century British socialism or twenty-first century neoliberalism, it was prone to over-claim how much the institutions could offer. To avoid over-reach, institutions might endeavour to take care to reduce their aspirations of sentimental individualism to a scale that would be achievable.

Cognitive individualism's treatment of human dignity is a good example of this more restrained approach. If injuries to human dignity are defined as the kind of interpersonal behaviour which brings to mind a parallel with the behaviour of schoolchildren, organizations are excused the much more difficult job of attending to the injuries that they have directly caused. Bringing the concepts of workplace bullying and harassment into wide circulation has helped to reduce the concept of human dignity so that it can be addressed with the (weak) regulation of interpersonal relations, organizational policies and procedures and its achievement monitored and audited with employee surveys.

As we saw in the previous chapter, this need not prevent employers presenting their policies on bullying as designed to achieve the much greater aim of protecting dignity at work. Nevertheless, we can predict that what employers and psychologists recognize as bullying and harassment will fall far short of what people feel is an assault on their dignity (cf. Wainwright and Calnan 2002). Evidence for such a shortfall might lend support to the idea that one link between neoliberalism and mental health problems can be located in the disappointed expectations of employees. In this case, so far as they have (sole or contributory) workplace causes, depression, anxiety and other conditions are caused by not having enough individualism rather than too much.

This is not to say that these employees recognize their employers have been party to ramping up expectations and then failing to satisfy them. As we will see, it is entirely feasible that employees experience the disappointment of their expectations as the consequence of their own, personal failings. This might be particularly likely when employers are insistent that they have all the policies and procedures required to ensure dignity at work. Self-blame would be a further aggravating factor: employees are told to expect to keep their dignity at work, but when they suffer indignities they add shame and guilt to a situation that may already be conducive to emotional and psychological problems.

INSUFFICIENT INDIVIDUALISM

What, if any, is the evidence for the idea that neoliberalism creates new risks to mental health because it offers to satisfy ambitions for individualism that it cannot possibly fulfil? From the foregoing analysis, it is clear that data on bullying and harassment are ultimately of little help in investigating the idea of a link between mental illness and disappointed expectations of individualism. Largely by confining aspirations to improved interpersonal relations between rank-and-file employees, these concepts have served to put a limit on the expansion of individualism. By definition, they can tell us nothing of what the organizations have been unable to deliver. We require a different conceptualization of human dignity which does not reduce it to the subject matter of psychology. To make a start, we need a neutral concept like 'ill-treatment' that takes dignity out of the schoolyard and leaves behind the notion that injuries to dignity in the workplace necessarily take the form of interpersonal conflicts (Fevre et al. 2012). How are we to operationalize 'ill-treatment' in order to find out how common it is, and compare its frequency to that of bullying and harassment?

In fact, the psychologists who were researching workplace bullying made a major contribution towards solving this problem, albeit that this might not have been their intention. In order to identify the kinds of behaviour that occurred during bullying, they developed a questionnaire for counting the frequency of 'negative acts' in the workplace (Einarsen et al. 2010). In choosing these 'negative acts', they seemed to have been mainly thinking about just the kind of ill-treatment that would injure dignity and signal a failure to deliver on individualism.

Since they were chosen to indicate what bullying might entail, we would expect some overlap between the negative acts and bullying but we would also expect the measures of ill-treatment to be more common. In the pilot survey (with over a thousand employees) for the BWBS, respondents were asked the questions in the 'negative acts' questionnaire as well as one of the standard bullying questions. Most of the people who had experienced this ill-treatment did not think they had suffered bullying (Fevre et al. 2012). Research by psychologists had usually shown that less than half of those who experienced a negative act reported bullying (Fevre et al. 2010), but in the BWBS the overlap was even smaller. For only 2 of the 22 negative acts did more than 4 out of 10 think they had been bullied and in most cases the proportion was much smaller.

The BWBS pilot was followed up with 'cognitive testing' designed to refine the psychologists' questions about 'negative acts', in order to produce 21 questions which would be valid and reliable measures of ill-treatment in the workplace (Fevre et al. 2010). The data from the main BWBS were analysed using component factor analysis which distributed the 21 items into three types of ill-treatment (Fevre et al. 2012). The first type was labelled 'unreasonable treatment' and included these eight items: (1) someone withholding information which affects your performance, (2) pressure from someone else to do work below your level of competence, (3) having your views and opinions ignored, (4) someone continually checking up on you or your work when it is not necessary, (5) pressure from someone else not to claim something which by right you are entitled to, (6) being given an unmanageable workload or impossible deadlines, (7) your employer not following proper procedures and (8) being treated unfairly compared to others in your workplace.

The second type of ill-treatment produced by the factor analysis, termed 'incivility and disrespect', covered: (9) being humiliated or ridiculed in connection with your work, (10) gossip and rumours being spread about you or having allegations made against you, (11) being insulted or having offensive remarks made about you, (12) being treated in a disrespectful or rude way, (13) people excluding you from their group, (14) hints or signals from others that you should quit your job, (15) persistent criticism of your work or performance which is unfair, (16) teasing, mocking, sarcasm or jokes which go too far, (17) being shouted at or someone losing their temper with you, (18) intimidating behaviour from people at work and (19) feeling threatened in any way while at work.

The final type was 'violence', consisting of (20) actual physical violence at work and (21) injury in some way as a result of violence or aggression at work. The researchers were surprised to find that the incidence of violence (6 per cent) was comparable to the incidence of workplace bullying in more representative studies with good sampling and data collection methods. Nearly all of those who experienced violence in the workplace also experienced both of the other types of ill-treatment (Fevre et al. 2012). The others types were far more frequent than violence: half of the British workforce had some experience of unreasonable treatment and 2 out of every 5 workers had experienced incivility and disrespect. A total of one in three had experienced a combination of unreasonable treatment and incivility and disrespect. Within each of these types, many respondents experienced several different types of ill-treatment. Amongst those who experienced un-reasonable treatment (items 1–8), 1 in 4 had suffered three or more different kinds of unreasonable treatment, and 1 in 10 reported five or more kinds. Within the group which reported 'incivility or disrespect', 1 in 4 experienced three or more types of this behaviour and it was, once more, about 1 in 10 who reported five or more varieties of incivility or disrespect.

These data may allow us to measure the gap between what employees feel is an assault on their dignity and what the employers and the psychologists see as bullying and harassment. However, if we are going to use this data to investigate the connection between individualism and mental illness, we will need to establish that the gap really does refer to disappointed expectations. We will also need to establish that these wider measures of injured dignity have anything to do with mental illness. Finally, we will need to investigate whether these data shed any light on speculative explanations of the mechanisms involved in the relationship between neoliberalism, individualism and mental illness, including the possibly corrosive effects of ersatz morality and the role of performance anxiety and self-blame.

BROKEN PROMISES AND MENTAL HEALTH

Carefully reading the 21 items listed above suggests that many of them ought to be very effective indicators of employees' disappointments with individualism in the workplace. If employees take individualism seriously, they have a right to expect to have a workload they can manage and to be asked to do what they are good at with the information they need to perform well. But it is not just unreasonable treatment that indicates the broken promises of individualism since employees who are treated as individuals will not expect to suffer gratuitous incivility and disrespect. In both cases (and even more so when there is violence), these measures of ill-treatment suggest that employees' fate seems to be out of their hands. Without the autonomy promised by individualism, there is nothing they can do to make work rewarding or, perhaps, even bearable.

On face value, then, it would be hard to consider any of the 21 counts of ill-treatment as anything other than obstacles to self-determination and infringements on individualism. Moreover, many of these measures, and particularly those of unreasonable treatment, take us further from the psychologists' analogy with the behaviour of the schoolyard and closer to the specification of the organization's direct responsibility for injuries to dignity (Bolton 2007; Sayer 2007). Moving beyond a psychological view of injuries to individualism widens the area of normal organizational activities that are affected beyond the inter-personal relations of rank-and-file employees. It now covers many areas of organizational life that employers may be uncomfortable dealing with, or incapable of addressing, through cognitive individualism. This is well justified theoretically: instead of reducing the aspirations of sentimental individualism to objectives that can comfortably be encompassed with familiar organizational responses, they are presented as fundamental challenges to organizational claims to value individualism. Stating the organization's position on inappropriate joking is one thing, but making the connection between injuries to individualism and pay or performance management opens up whole new areas of organizational activity for consideration. In some cases, we may even find that the organizational monopoly over the division of labour is shown to be incompatible with individualism.

The BWBS showed that 1 in 2 British employees had experienced one or more injuries to individualism in the previous two years (and 1 in 5 had experienced frequent and multiple frustrations of individualism). At first glance, it seems difficult to imagine how the idea of employers as the guardians of individualism could survive but, thus far, we are relying on our own interpretation of the ill-treatment measures. Was it the case that employees saw these measures differently, perhaps in the limited terms of bullying and harassment which reduce injuries to individualism to transgressions that organizations can accommodate without undermining their employees' belief that individualism is the key to organizational success?

In the BWBS, about a quarter of those experiencing unreasonable treatment and/or incivility and disrespect had experience of three or more types of ill-treatment. This 'troubled minority' were asked follow-up questions about the most serious ill-treatment they had suffered, for example workplace violence (Fevre et al. 2012). These questions included the type of person responsible for the ill-treatment: were they a client or a customer, a subordinate, a peer or a manager? Most unreasonable treatment originated with managers and supervisors, and even in incivility and disrespect, where co-workers and customers or clients were more frequently blamed, managers and supervisors were the most important. Violence was the only type of ill-treatment for which managers and supervisors did not receive most of the blame.

These results suggest that employees were more likely to see ill-treatment in terms of organizational failure than interpersonal problems like bullying. To confirm this, we simply need to revisit the list of the different kinds of ill-treatment with the knowledge that each of them was more likely to originate with a manager or supervisor. If you were on the receiving end of each of these forms of ill-treatment, what might you conclude about your employer's commitment to dignity at work? What might you conclude about the way your employer was selecting, training and managing your manager? Might you conclude that your manager had been told that, whatever the rhetorical commitment made by the organization, dignity and respect were superfluous to organizational objectives (Foster and Scott 2015)?

The troubled minority were also given a list from which they could choose as many reasons for their ill-treatment as they thought appropriate. The two most popular reasons were the same for violence, incivility and disrespect and unreasonable treatment. In all three cases, the majority reported 'it's just the way things are at work' and around a half cited 'the attitude or personality of the other person'. The only other options that attracted more than one in ten responses were 'your position in the organization' and 'people's relationships at work'. Figure 13.1 summarizes the bivariate analyses of all causes of ill-treatment.

A brief review of the results for violence and injury will show how these results can inform our discussion. Roughly half of the employees who experienced violence and injury said it was a consequence of the 'attitude or personality of the other person' involved (all data from Fevre

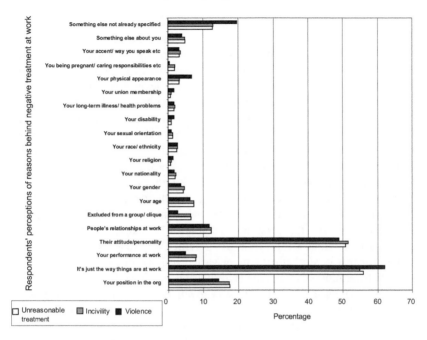

Figure 13.1   The causes of ill-treatment in the British Workplace Behaviour Survey

et al. 2012). We might imagine that this suggested they understood the causes of violence as lying well outside the direct responsibility of their employers and that a commitment to dignity at work, for example a 'zero-tolerance' approach to violence which promised the employer would prosecute all cases of violence against employees, was enough to preserve their reputation as guardians of individualism. Yet, two-thirds of those who had experienced violence and injury – including some of those who also blamed another person's attitude or personality – said this was 'just the way things are at work'.

It becomes easier to understand these results when we learn that many of the employees who experienced workplace violence were employed in personal service occupations where low-level violence from clients might be a frequent occurrence. As well as police officers, paramedics and firefighters, it was care assistants and nurses working in residential care settings or private households who reported that their experience of violence was just the way things were where they worked. While this might suggest a pattern of repeated, less serious assaults, it also suggested that zero-tolerance approaches which promised prosecution of any assault were so impracticable as to have fallen into disrepute.

The rhetorical commitment to zero-tolerance cost the employer nothing, whereas employees – and especially those who said it was their role that exposed them to violence – were aware that the risk of violence could only be reduced by significant change in the division of labour, including job redesign and higher staffing levels. In this case, there seemed to be strict limits on how much individualism they could expect of their employer. This conclusion was writ large in the 1 in 8 cases where employees agreed that a cause of the violence they had experienced was their 'position in the organization'. In other words, it really had not mattered who filled their role since they would have received the same treatment. Moreover, since it was the employer who created these positions they had indirect responsibility for their exposure to violence. It might be expected that if the ill-treatment measures were better understood in terms of interpersonal problems like bullying, this would be particularly obvious in the case of incivility and disrespect. In fact, the results for this type of ill-treatment varied little from the other two types.

As before, most respondents said that this was just the way things were in their workplace. Indeed, this was given as the more common reason than the attitude or personality of another person for most types of incivility and disrespect, with the exception of shouting, rudeness, intimidation and threats. It is quite salutary that exclusion by other employees and humiliation, gossip and teasing were all more likely to be traced back to the nature of the workplace, than to the interpersonal explanations that are usually associated with bullying. Exclusion and gossip were also associated with another minor reason for ill-treatment: relationships at work. This reason was cited more frequently for incivility and disrespect than it was for unreasonable treatment, nevertheless it hardly figured as a reason for insults and rudeness (Fevre et al. 2012).

The final evidence that the measures of ill-treatment are a valid and reliable way of measuring employees' perceptions of their employers' inability to deliver on their promises of individualism comes from MV analysis of all the factors that might be correlated with each measure. Excluding the two measures of violence and injury, the strongest correlations across all of the remaining measures were found to be with the three general questions on individualism described in Chapter 12: whether respondents thought that people always came second to the organization, whether they had to compromise their principles at work and whether their employer treated them as individuals. In Chapter 12, we used these questions to show how much consent and resistance might have been excited by the long process of rolling out cognitive individualism within organizations. Moreover, they are such a strong predictor of ill-treatment that they can also be used to represent important character-istics of workplaces that are hard to capture in a survey of employees.[5] However, here we use them to confirm that most measures of ill-treatment also record a broken promise of individualism.

Employees who thought people were not treated as individuals in their workplace were at the greatest risk of unreasonable treatment across the board. There were other strong predictors of unreasonable treatment – such as having less control over one's work or having a disability – but none were as strong as this direct measure of an employer's commitment to individualism. The other general question about not having to compro-mise your principles at work was just as significant a risk factor for unreasonable treatment as having less control and stronger than having a disability. Taken together, the three general questions about individualism were as good at predicting the risks of incivility and disrespect as they were for unreasonable treatment. At least two of the questions were a risk for every type of incivility and disrespect in the MV models for each of the 11 measures. Earlier in this chapter, we noted that Verhaeghe and others thought that forcing employees to compromise their principles in the neoliberal workplace might have a lot to do with work-related mental illness. We now know that compromising your principles is one of three general questions about individualism which were strongly correlated with the measures of ill-treatment, even when other variables were taken into account. However, we still require some less circumstantial evidence if we are to be convinced that injuries to individualism are implicated in mental illness.

ILL-TREATMENT AND MENTAL ILLNESS

The first data of interest are derived from the questions that respondents to the Fair Treatment survey were asked about the impact of seven of the 21 measures of ill-treatment. The seven were selected to represent unreasonable treatment, incivility and disrespect, and violence. They were: pressure from someone else to do work below your level of competence, your employer not following proper procedures, being given an unmanageable workload or impossible deadlines, being insulted or having offensive remarks made about you, being treated in a disrespectful or rude way, being humiliated or ridiculed in connection with your work, and actual physical violence at work (Fevre et al. 2013). Although the size of the effect was not as high as for the Fair Treatment question about bullying and harassment,[6] around 1 in 8 employees who had experienced one of these forms of ill-treatment suffered 'severe psychological effects'. In addition, at least 1 in 5 said they had suffered 'moderate psychological effects' for every 1 of the 7 measures bar the last one: actual violence.

This last, surprising result was the only case in which there was no statistically significant difference between the employees who had experienced ill-treatment and those who had not. In all of the other six types of ill-treatment, there was a clear statistical difference in the likelihood of both moderate and severe psychological effects. However, the fact that the result for violence did not achieve statistical significance is interesting when we remember that violence was the one area in which the three general questions about individualism were not strongly correlated with ill-treatment in MV analysis. Since the general questions about individualism were so strongly predictive of unreasonable treatment and incivility and respect, there is a suggestion here that ill-treatment is most likely to lead to psychological problems when it is most clearly and unambiguously an indicator of broken promises about individualism. This perhaps brings to mind an observation made by Fleischacker when commenting on a quote from Adam Smith (see Chapter 3):

> [E]ven where the material harm done is slight, an act of injustice suggests that the victim is somehow less worthy than the agent, and thereby constitutes an important symbolic harm. The anger that boils out of the passage indeed captures wonderfully how we feel when another person seems to imagine that we 'may be sacrificed at any time, to his conveniency or his humour'. (Fleischacker 2013: 488)

These reflections might give pause to anyone tempted to dismiss these results as simply confirming what we already know about the extent of the psychological harm associated with bullying and harassment. Between a third and a half of those experiencing these much more common forms of ill-treatment than bullying suffered moderate or severe psychological effects. If we take the most common type of ill-treatment – that of being given an impossible deadline or unmanageable workload – slightly more than 1 in 10 British workers experienced psychological harm from this one type of ill-treatment, perhaps four times as many workers as might suffer harm from bullying.

Other relevant data which come from further MV analysis of the BWBS showed impressive correlations between several types of ill-treatment and respondents' declarations that they had psychological or emotional problems (Fevre et al. 2012, 2013). We will, however, postpone detailed consideration of these data until later in the chapter and consider further data about work and the workplace instead. From what we have learnt so far, we would expect the most concerted efforts to persuade employees of employers' commitment to neoliberalism to take place in organizations which expect high levels of commitment from their employees. These are two sides of the same neoliberal coin: in return for safeguarding individualism and, indeed, because they safeguard individualism, organizations benefit from higher productivity.

The data on ill-treatment confirm what has sometimes been suggested in studies of workplace bullying, namely that some of the characteristics of high-commitment workplaces successfully predict ill-treatment even with statistical controls for other variables. In MV analysis of the BWBS, the predictors of ill-treatment included working at a fast pace and larger organizations. For example, feeling that the pace of work was too intense increased people's exposure to ill-treatment by 56 per cent. MV analysis also showed that it was those employees who would be most exposed to the expectations of high commitment who were more likely to report ill-treatment.

In MV analysis of the BWBS, permanent staff with managerial responsibilities were more likely to experience both unreasonable treatment and workplace violence. Better-paid employees were more likely to experience unreasonable treatment (Fevre et al. 2012). As Anthony (1977) noted 40 years ago, managers in particular have provided the model for high-commitment relations in the workplace.[7] They have therefore been amongst those most exposed to the disappointment of expectations, and we would expect them to report some of the ill-treatment that indicates broken promises, perhaps particularly unreasonable treatment. Once more, this underlines the departure from the expectations of Verhaeghe (2014) and many researchers of bullying[8] that it is mostly the weak and the vulnerable who are affected. This is perhaps much less the case for injuries to individualism than it is in bullying and harassment.

A further predictor of ill-treatment (most unreasonable treatment and several types of incivility and disrespect) was *reduced* control, and it was more strongly associated with unreasonable treatment, incivility and disrespect and violence than almost any other factor (Fevre et al. 2012). The key issue to note here is that the analysis also included a measure of *low* control which was not associated with any of the 21 measures of ill-treatment. It was the feeling of being deprived of autonomy, rather than never possessing it, that went with ill-treatment, and it is of course the former rather than the latter that we would associate with an affront to individualism and, particularly, with the disappointment of employees who had expected they were to have a more rewarding relationship with their work.

Some evidence of the effect of broken promises also came from MV analysis in which change in the nature of work and work intensification were shown to be risk factors for unreasonable treatment, although not for incivility and disrespect (Fevre et al. 2012). As with reduced control, employers who change the nature and pace of work put in jeopardy the work they have done to persuade their employees to see them as the guardians of individualism. Qualitative research confirms that a great deal of planning and operational attention is required to retain this reputation while also making significant changes to the nature and pace of work (Fevre et al. 2012). Without this effort, employees may begin to doubt that their individual contribution is valued and was perhaps ever valued. This need not imply, however, that they blame their employer.

The qualitative research undertaken in the companion case studies to the BWBS chronicled the stories of employees trying to respond to the pressures of high-commitment workplaces and pushing themselves to breaking point (Fevre et al. 2012; Foster and Scott 2015). They felt that their work had become unmanageable, their deadlines impossible, that what was happening to them was unfair and irrational, that there was a more reasonable way to achieve the organization's goals but that nobody was listening to them. If they resisted, they put themselves in line for personal attacks, especially from those senior staff who were passing on the pressures of the high-commitment workplace (Barmes 2015). Sometimes these managers told them they were not up to the job and should leave before things became even more unpleasant for them.

Some of the workers who chose to stay, or had nowhere else to go, blamed their managers (often in very bitter language) for what had happened to them (Fevre et al. 2012). They usually ascribed character faults to their managers which would explain why the managers were unable to uphold the organization's commitment to individualism. If there were colleagues who were obviously in the same position, this might lead to incivility and disrespect aimed at the managers, and even to what psychologists term 'upward bullying'.

If there were no colleagues to hold responsible, or it was implausible that the manager's character faults were to blame, employees who suffered ill-treatment could only conclude that their managers were pursuing the goals of the organization and that it was they, the employees, who were undermining these goals. They responded to the pressure and criticism by working harder and faster, and this often produced what their general practitioner or occupational health professional might eventually label as stress. With or without the label, employees in this position would often push themselves to the point at which they concluded that they were incapable of living up to the opportunities that they had been offered. Their employer was committed to individualism, certainly, but this had only exposed the employees' failings.

This qualitative research suggests that Verhaeghe (2014) and others are right to suggest that neoliberal individualism is implicated in the relationship between mental illness and the workplace. The cognitive individualism of the neoliberal workplace demands that the individual be judged according to the criteria the employer sets to measure their contribution. When employees fall short, there is no place to hide. Cognitive individualism puts all of the onus on the individuals' demonstration of their worth and it repeatedly demands new evidence of this (with every financial quarter, new project, new manager, new organizational initiative). Everything comes down to how you, on your own, handle the demands of work and this turns out to be an invitation to self-destruction.

In effect, the self-destruction of employees is the safety valve which allows neoliberalism to keep its promise of safeguarding individualism. If employees can respond to the demands that are placed on them, then the promise remains intact: their employer has simply given them an opportunity for self-development and to demonstrate flexibility and they have altered their habits and feelings about work accordingly. However, if they cannot respond – even if nobody could respond – the promise is preserved by blaming the employee rather than the employer. For this to work most effectively, the employee must accept the blame they are offered and in this way they are led into putting their own mental health at risk.

I have already noted that employees may sometimes support each other by sharing their uncomplimentary (and often reprehensible) views about the character of the person, usually a manager, they feel is failing to treat them as an individual. Given that roughly half of the British working population has some recent experience of injuries to individualism, this raises the question of why they do not turn from blaming their managers to identifying their private problems as a public issue. Yet, few of them are in a position to understand that there are so many other employees with whom to make common cause. This privilege is reserved for social researchers, worker representatives and those trade union members who read their trade union's literature. The rest of the workforce (a sizeable majority) have no way of knowing that there is a public issue at stake here and they only have their own families to tell them that it is not their fault and they are not on their own (Barmes 2015). Friends and family can confirm they are being badly treated, even bullied, but it is almost impossible for them to see this private problem as a public issue common not just to one organization but in the wider world of work (Fevre et al. 2012).

Despite what they might have assumed prior to suffering ill-treatment, employees cannot rid themselves of the feeling that they must be failing to meet the rational expectations of their employer, and this often produces an existential crisis that may lead to psychological and emotional problems. The risk of internalizing the problems created by organizations promising cognitive individualism they cannot deliver is common to everyone including managers. In MV analysis, managers were more likely to report unreasonable treatment (and violence), but we know from Chapter 12 that managers were also more likely to hold onto the idea that individualism was safe in their workplace. I also mentioned earlier in the chapter that employees with disabilities were more likely to experience ill-treatment and it is to detailed consideration of this group of employees that we now turn.

COGNITIVE INDIVIDUALISM AND DISABILITY

While not taking away from the way ill-treatment can trigger illnesses or make them worse, there is also a great deal of MV evidence from the BWBS to show that those who already had disabilities (including long-standing psychological conditions)[9] were more likely to suffer a variety of different forms of ill-treatment. Some of this treatment occurred in high-commitment organizations but the ill-treatment of employees with disabilities also illustrates some other ways in which employees pay for the broken promises of cognitive individualism. The British research discussed in this chapter shows that employing someone with a disability – especially certain disabilities (see below) – is a crucial test of an employer's ability to deliver on these promises and that, when they fail to deliver, the blame is invariably assigned to the employee (Fevre et al. 2012, 2013). Usually, this involves denying that the disability has anything to do with the individual's needs or capacities, and often this means that the employer will deny the employee has a disability at all.

Here, we are no longer always investigating the effect of change occasioned by the employer but rather the way the requirements of illness or impairment set tests for employers which they regularly fail. The test may be as simple as allowing an employee to keep a hospital appointment but, if the employer decides they cannot accommodate this, a similar situation is produced as when employees experience reduced control or work intensification. The promise to recognize people as individuals, to take seriously what they say and what their requirements are, is broken. In the BWBS and its associated qualitative case studies, employers were seen to fail these tests every day when they made decisions about sick leave, employees returning to work after sickness absence, the management of ongoing conditions, and 'reasonable adjustments' to work and the workplace required by UK legislation (Fevre et al. 2012; Foster and Scott 2015; also see Foster 2007). The Fair Treatment at Work survey also showed that employees with disabilities were twice as likely as other employees to experience a range of employment rights problems. In bivariate analysis, they were especially likely to report problems with sick leave or pay but also with holidays, rest breaks, number of hours or days worked, pay, contracts, complaints procedures, grievance procedures, health and safety, and retirement (Fevre et al. 2009).

The more common way of conceptualizing the idea of a broken promise in respect of employees with disabilities is provided by the social model of disability (Oliver 1983, 1990, 2003; also see Barnes and Mercer 2004). In the model, an impairment or a condition only becomes a handicap when society provides an environment (for example, the workplace) and structures social action (for example, work) in such a way that those with an impairment or a condition are put at a disadvantage (Fevre et al. 2013). The social construction of disability is one and the same as the failure of an employer to accommodate disability as one of the many requirements of treating employees as individuals.

Since most employees do not know the social model, they often blame themselves for their disadvantages (for example, their ill-treatment). This is especially likely in the case of mental illness where people may be less likely to recognize they are ill and even less likely to recognize they have a disability. In this connection, it is salutary to note that MV analysis of the BWBS shows that, of all the possible types of disability, it was a physical disability that was the more weakly associated with ill-treatment (Fevre et al. 2013).[10] That it was only significant for two of the 21 items, even at the lowest (90 per cent) level of significance, suggests that employers are better able to stick to their promises when their employees have an obvious physical disability like an impairment of sight, hearing or mobility. Of course, this only applies to those employers who hire such workers in the first place. Since their disabilities are so obvious, it makes them the easiest targets for discrimination at the recruitment stage and, in the UK at least, this discrimination contributes to an increasing gap in the employment rates of employees with and without disabilities (Fevre et al. 2013).

We now move on to consider other categories of employees where their disability would necessarily be less visible at recruitment and may not have been disclosed to employers. Because they are more likely to involve later-onset illnesses than physical disability, these same categories of disability are also more likely to be acquired after recruitment. A measure of the total impact of having a disability across the 21 multivariate models applied to the BWBS data set showed that for those with the obvious physical disabilities the likelihood of experiencing any ill-treatment at work was increased by 15 per cent. For those with a learning difficulty, psychological or emotional condition, the likelihood of experiencing any ill-treatment at work was increased by 177 per cent. For those with other health problems (including life-threatening conditions) like cancer, diabetes, hypertension, stroke, heart disease, pulmonary conditions, asthma and digestive or bowel disorders, the likelihood of ill-treatment was increased by 102 per cent.

MV analysis also allowed better specification of which categories of disability were associated with each kind of ill-treatment. Employees with psychological problems and learning difficulties were four times as likely to be treated unfairly, and employees with other health problems were seven times more likely to say they had been pressured not to claim something (perhaps sick leave or sick pay) to which they were entitled and three times more likely to say somebody was continually checking up on them. Those with other health problems and psychological conditions were three times more likely to say their employer had not followed proper procedures (Fevre et al. 2012).

It is certain that some of the association recorded in the BWBS between ill-treatment and psychological problems was further proof that ill-treatment had effects on employees' mental health. However, for reasons discussed elsewhere, these correlations also confirm that employees are more likely to suffer ill-treatment if they have a pre-existing psychological condition (Fevre et al. 2013). More fine-grained MV analysis of the BWBS tells us more about the way that different types of ill-treatment were associated with different categories of disability. Specifically, those in the psychological category were the most likely to experience nine types of ill-treatment, whereas those in the category of other health problems were the most likely to experience six types of ill-treatment (Fevre et al. 2013).

There was very little overlap between the types of ill-treatment associated with these two categories. Apart from being treated unfairly, and finding their employer not following proper procedures (one of the few types which was also associated with other health conditions), most ill-treatment of those in the psychological category took the form of incivility and disrespect. The ill-treatment of those with other health problems was more widely spread. While this might lend some support to the idea that some of the associations for the psychological category were the effects of ill-treatment on mental health,[11] the particular patterns of ill-treatment associated with the different categories could as well be a result of tailoring the ill-treatment to the disability or, rather, of the nuanced way in which disability is signalled in the workplace. For example, those in the category of psychological disabilities were much more likely to be subject to gossip and socially excluded.

In common with other employees, respondents with disabilities were more likely to blame managers for their ill-treatment: four in every nine said their managers were responsible followed by clients and customers (28 per cent) with co-workers a distant third (18 per cent).[12] They were also asked what they felt to be the root causes of this ill-treatment (Fevre et al. 2013). We might imagine that having a disability and experiencing persistent criticism, being shouted at, or even threats or violence at work, would lead to a conclusion that this ill-treatment was related to the impairment, but this was very unusual. Only 11 out of 284 respondents thought their impairment had anything to do with their ill-treatment and only 25 out of 284 felt that their ill-treatment was related to long-term illness or other health problems. Just like the majority of other types of workers, those with disabilities were most likely to give the reason for their ill-treatment as just the way things were at work, their position in the organization or their performance at work. Of course, this means that very few employees were recognizing their ill-treatment as discrimination which is not permitted under UK law (Fevre et al. 2012, 2013).

This is one more proof (see Chapter 11) of how ineffective the equality legislation delivered as part of the ambitious programme of cognitive individualism has proved itself. However, the whole story of the fate of workers with a disability, for example as captured in the social model, is proof of the general tendency of cognitive individualism to lead organizations to claim far more than they can ever deliver. People with disabilities offer employers the hardest test of their sincerity because they cannot be treated as the normal – meaning largely invariant – worker who employers have in mind when they make their promise to treat everyone they employ as an individual (Foster and Wass 2013). They can make good on this promise as long as those individuals do not actually behave like individuals. People with disabilities are the most likely to do this and they will always provide one of the key tests of how much individualism a society can claim to have achieved. They are the embodiment of the ideal of individualism which organizations cannot live up to and because of this they cannot escape punishment. Unfortunately, they are not alone: in MV analysis of the BWBS, being gay, lesbian or bisexual increased the overall risk of ill-treatment by 56 per cent.

LGB employees constitute another group whose existence puts the promises of individualism to the test. As with employees with less visible disabilities, it is hard for employers to screen them out with discriminatory recruitment practices,[13] yet their ill-treatment within the workplace amounts to discrimination. Moreover, as with employees with disabilities, LGB employees do not recognize that they suffer discrimination but find instead that their hopes about the freedoms that individualism ought to permit are unlikely to be borne out by their experience of the workplace (Einarsdottir et al. 2015a). They may be affected by this even where they have not disclosed their sexuality, indeed this may be why they do not disclose. Voluntary disclosure suggests a freedom they may not feel they have in the workplace, for example it implies that their idea of who they are as gay men or lesbian women will not collide with a stereotype (Einarsdottir et al. 2015b). However, like almost everyone else who suffers ill-treatment, LGBs rarely reach conclusions about the broken promises of individualism because, failing to see any obvious prejudice to resist, they resolve to adapt themselves to the situation. As with many employees with disabilities, they try hard to make themselves less like individuals to fit into a workplace that promised them something more (Einarsdottir et al. 2015a). In fact, it is a paper-thin individualism they are being offered – one that is highly gendered and one with concealed traps, many of which lead to ill-treatment (Einarsdottir et al. 2015b).

CONCLUSION

There is an alternative to employees taking on the burden of keeping cognitive individualism afloat by being less individual, making themselves ill or finding another job. They might choose to build a social movement which could turn their private problems into public issues. This movement would expose the broken promises and their attendant discriminations and, by demanding radical changes in work, and particularly the division of labour, would stimulate a new politics. The catalogue of ill-treatment shows us how high ambitions could be for individualism in the workplace, but how could such a social movement come about? From the previous two chapters, we know that, in Britain at least, it is only a minority that are sceptical about their employer's ability to deliver genuine individualism. However, we know from those chapters how important personal experience is to building scepticism. If this works for the experience of employment rights problems, unfair treatment and discrimination, sexual harassment, bullying and harassment, might it not also apply to ill-treatment in the workplace?

Trade unions provide one possible source of the leadership for such a movement but we have heard in previous chapters about the burdens they allow to accumulate on the worker representatives in workplaces which already have a union presence. The way in which the trade unions treat the worker representatives who deal with mounting caseloads of workers who have experienced ill-treatment gives little cause for confidence in their ability to assume leadership. We will return to these questions in the final chapter but first we need to deal with some other unexamined questions about the relationship between capitalism and individualism – questions that we have, up to this point, managed to keep at bay with the idea of neoliberalism.

NOTES

1. As suggested in some sociological studies (e.g. Hodson et al. 2006; Lopez et al. 2009; Roscigno et al. 2009a, 2009b).
2. For a similar argument on insecurity, see Fevre (2007).
3. Also see Furedi (2004), Ecclestone and Hayes (2009) and Warr (2007).
4. For example, American commentary on bullying and harassment now routinely identifies the associated costs to business, e.g. occasioned through absenteeism (e.g. Belsky 2012; Farrel 2002; Fowler 2012).
5. This gave rise to the 'troubled workplace' concept in Fevre et al. (2012).
6. The moderate and severe effects of bullying and harassment were higher than for any of the seven ill-treatment measures; 1 in 2 employees risked moderate or severe effects from bullying (Fevre et al. 2009).
7. Anthony (1977: 311–12) came very close to predicting that managers themselves would bear the brunt of the negative effects of such workplaces, including alienation and insecurity.
8. Such as Hodson, Lopez and Roscigno (Hodson et al. 2006; Lopez et al. 2009; Roscigno et al. 2009a, 2009b).
9. In their textbook, Harder et al. (2014) neglect to mention this and do not apply the social model of disability to mental illness in the workplace.
10. There was also little overlap with other categories of disability like mental illness.
11. This would be particularly likely for the correlation with violence in the workplace.
12. Bear in mind that these figures were derived from questions about the more serious incidences of ill-treatment.
13. There is no intersectionality problem here since LGB employees were no more likely to be disabled than others.

14. Insecurity, intensification and subordination

Organizations had once experienced individualism as an environmental factor, but in the twentieth century individualism became an essential component of their teleology. All organizations, not merely capitalist firms, were able to claim that it allowed them to fulfil their purpose of managing resources as efficiently as possible. This was, however, an inadequate description of the advantages that organizations saw in responding to individualism. They responded because '[t]o leave so valuable a resource as the self-activating individual unincorporated would be to irresponsibly neglect to manage a now rationalized uncertainty' (Scott and Meyer 1994a: 211).[1] This chapter explains that some of the uncertainty of the employment relationship was transferred to employees, while power transferred in the other direction: from individuals to organizations. This subordination was a major reason for the synchronicity between neoliberalism and increasing inequality.

'PRECARITY' AND INDIVIDUALISM

The dominant interpretation of the increased uncertainty associated with cognitive individualism is that it reduces job security. This thesis gathered support from the inception of the neoliberal settlement in the mid-1970s. The general claim that we were entering an age of insecurity featured in many of the works of the most popular social theorists of subsequent decades and the thesis took hold in Europe, and particularly France, before spreading to other countries (Fevre 2007). The strapline for the insecurity thesis was that nobody could, any longer, expect a job for life (e.g. Drucker 1995; Handy 1990). It implied that intervention from the state or a trade union was necessary to underwrite job security, and since such intervention was anathema to neoliberalism, employees at all levels were forced to rely on their own devices to fashion careers for themselves (Handy 1994). In practice, this meant that most must stitch together a succession of non-standard jobs in place of a proper career.

This form of insecurity should not be confused with other long-lived ideas about the threat of automation to jobs, or periodic concerns about job losses caused by the business cycle, since it was distinguished by the idea that insecurity was a feature of jobs rather than job losses. In some of the early portraits of the age of insecurity, attention was given to those who would thrive in the new age. They included the sports stars (and sometimes their managers) who would accumulate fortunes for themselves and their agents by moving from club to club. Other examples were the globe-trotting CEOs who profited from golden hellos and golden parachutes every time they changed job. There were others – independent content providers for broadcasters, freelance professionals of all types – who might be similarly blessed but these fortunate children of the age of insecurity disappeared in later accounts, for example Guy Standing's late classic of the genre.

Standing (2011) defined seven forms of labour security which were being dismantled: they ranged from health and safety regulations, protection against dismissal and representation, through training and barriers to skill dilution, to stable income and adequate opportunities. People who lacked these forms of security were being pushed down into a 'precariat' below the working class whose members were forced to survive on wages when other groups had further, and more reliable, sources of income. This process stretched income inequalities at the bottom of the distribution, but insecure workers were so desperate for the work that provided their only source of income that they were prepared to accept low pay and even no pay (in the case of internships which might lead to a job), and their desperation further exacerbated inequalities.

Those who were losing the seven forms of labour security were more likely to be in temporary or part-time work but also working for agencies and sub-contractors, as interns and even in dead-end situations like call-centre work which others might consider standard jobs. Call-centre workers fitted Standing's version of the thesis, unlike those who belonged in the traditional working class, because they stood naked before the market without an employer promising a career, or at least a job for life, and without trade union protection. While young workers, along with women and migrants, were said to be prominent in the 'precariat', Standing suspected that, around the world, more and more workers of all types would be pushed into the same position.

This is not at all what we would predict from the chapters in the second half of this book which described sustained efforts by organizations to present themselves as best able to deliver the promise of individualism. If they wished to present themselves as better able to do this than trade unions or governments, why would they increase the number of workers they treated as undifferentiated labour? Surely this would be to throw away all the work expended in people management to incorporate self-actualizing individuals? If the empirical evidence for the age of insecurity was as solid as many of its proponents claim, the thesis advanced in this book would be in tatters. It is not possible to hold the view that the neoliberal settlement in the most prosperous nations depends on a widespread promise of individualism and, at the same time, argue that job insecurity has burgeoned in those very countries.[2] However, neoinstitutionalist theory offered a compromise position of an emerging pattern in which insecurity might be concentrated in the less prosperous nations but would increase its presence in the more prosperous ones.

The compromise speculated that, as cognitive individualism developed, some parts of labour markets and workplaces in the more prosperous nations might be excluded from the promises of individualism that organizations made to their workers (Dobbin et al. 1994). This twin-track approach might arise if organizational resources were squeezed as growth slowed, but some neoinstitutionalists wondered why individualism which was not 'meaningful' should be particularly costly (Monahan et al. 1994: 270).[3] If organizations only acceded to individualism in order to increase control, or did not accede to individualism in any event but only appeared to, then there had to be other reasons for departing from it than scarce resources (Scott and Meyer 1994a). Individualism might give organizations 'justifications' as well as 'incentives' for roping off some jobs for workers who would be treated as undifferentiated labour. The idea of 'justifications' was more in tune with the underlying neoinstitutionalist approach. While remaining agnostic as to whether there was a clear economic case for or against insecurity, the 'economic climate' could make insecurity seem a legitimate reason for an organization to depart from its commitment to individualism (Scott and Meyer 1994a: 214; also see Fevre 1990, 2003).

In 2015 there was some evidence that justifications had been found to exclude some workers in prosperous countries from the promise that they would be treated as individuals, but insecurity remained far more common in the less prosperous nations. Bringing millions of people into a contractual relationship with employers was accomplished, as it had been many decades before in the more prosperous nations, by treating workers as undifferentiated labour rather than as individuals (Doogan 2009).[4] To equate the insecurity that most of these workers experienced with the condition of workers in the more prosperous countries is to dilute the concept so much that it loses analytical purchase.[5] To retain a meaningful notion of what insecurity entails (as in the International

Labour Organization concept of 'vulnerable employment') means recognizing that it has grown where the previous chapters in this book would predict: well away from those prosperous countries where organizations have had a real interest in responding to the contingency of widespread demand for the recognition of individuals.[6]

The historical record is not able to provide compelling evidence that jobs have become more insecure in the most prosperous nations. For one thing, the idea of increasing insecurity relies on an exaggeration of the amount of security enjoyed by earlier generations (Breman 2013; Fevre 2007; Strangleman 2007). The notion of a job for life would have seemed strange to most employees in the advanced industrial nations in the 1930s, or even in the booming 1950s, since workers usually change jobs more often when there are opportunities to move to a better position. Statistics which put average employment tenure for American workers at less than five years show how far off the mark the idea of a job for life has been, but they also show a gradual increase over time. For example, the amount of time British people stayed in a job during the last half of the twentieth century steadily lengthened (Doogan 2009; Fevre 2007; Green 2006; Gregg and Wadsworth 1999).

The proportion of the workforce in long-term employment in Europe and North America grew between 1983 and 2002, even as employment expanded and more attractive opportunities became available to incumbents as well as new entrants. In part, this pattern was caused by changes in occupational and industrial structure that meant that women in particular were more attached to their jobs. This is not to say that long-term employment did not fall in some sectors, particularly those less likely to employ women, like mining. However, the fastest growing sectors and occupations tended to be those in which employers were keenest to hang on to their employees (Doogan 2009). In both the UK and the USA, there was a further increase in job tenure in the first decade of the twenty-first century.[7] This is exactly what we would expect to see as the promise of individualism was extended to more and more workers.

Statistics for 'non-standard jobs' do not suggest an overall increase in job insecurity during the time that British and American organizations have been presenting themselves as the guardians of individualism. For example, the proportion of British jobs that employees thought were in some way temporary was at the same level (6 per cent) in August 2015 as in 1992 and the same proportion of these workers (35 per cent) would have preferred a permanent job.[8] There had certainly been some suggestion of long-term increases in some other types of non-standard job, but closer investigation of these patterns supports the neoinstitutionalist compromise position. For instance, the multiple factors that explained changes in different job categories[9] revealed the complex relationship between cognitive individualism and different types of employment.

Thus, part-time jobs were sometimes included in the 'non-standard jobs' that were said to have increased in the age of insecurity. They often made up the only category of job where it is possible to show a long-term increase, but whether this amounted to an increase in insecurity was another matter (Doogan 2009; Fevre 2007). Part-time work tended to grow where there was growth in the jobs which women were more likely to do, for example in health, education, social services and retailing. There was much debate about whether these jobs were part-time because employers created jobs which allowed workers, and particularly women, to engage with employment in the way that best suited their circumstances. Typically, these circumstances were defined by the unequal responsibility shouldered by women, rather than men, to care for dependents such as school-age children and elderly relatives. Other relevant circumstances included patterns of taxation and the cost and availability of private and public alternatives to this domestic care-giving. For example, patterns of part-time work were different where free or low-cost childcare was available (Wolf 2013).

The sociologist Miriam Glucksmann (2000, 2009) has argued that, in order to discern women's employment patterns, analysts need to understand the 'total social organization of labour', which includes both public and private welfare arrangements and the employment opportunities for workers, almost always women, who step in to provide care for dependent relatives. In the Scandinavian countries, for example, welfare states created many relatively well-paid jobs for women in health, education and social services, but this also created a much more segregated labour market than in the USA or the UK where dependent care was more mixed, including, for example, more informal arrangements (Wolf 2013). In both of these cases, the 'total social organization of labour' has been conditioned by cognitive individualism. States have responded in different ways to women's demands for autonomy and self-actualization, and employers have been required to take those different responses into account when making their own attempts to incorporate women (Doogan 2009).

Prior to the financial crisis and subsequent recession, there was no long-term upward trend in self-employment in the more prosperous countries (Fevre 2007). There was, however, a substantial increase in self-employment in the recession in the UK, although in the USA the numbers of non-agricultural (unincorporated) self-employed fell just as markedly between 2008 and 2014 (Bureau of Labor Statistics 2015: Chart 6). The UK was not alone in the EU in posting an increase, indeed two other countries saw self-employment increase at a faster rate. In 2014 the UK saw a 40-year peak and most of the rise in total employment since 2008 had been taken up by self-employment. There was a slight fall in self-employment in 2015 but one in eight workers in the UK remained self-employed. The increase since 2008 was largely a matter of fewer workers leaving self-employment rather than more workers joining. In line with this trend, a large part of the growth was amongst the over-50s and self-employment was growing fastest of all amongst the over-65s. Moreover, the average income from self-employment fell by a quarter in this time. Again, there were reasons to invoke the 'total social organization of labour' as self-employment trends were affected by patterns of taxation and welfare and particularly the perceived adequacy of pensions. One further indication of this was the change in the types of self-employed jobs people were taking. Construction and taxi-driving were still the most common but there had recently been an increase in management consultants (ONS 2015).

The final category of 'non-standard jobs' worth considering is those with 'zero-hours contracts' (ZHC) which give workers no guaranteed hours of work. After earlier uncertainties about the numbers, the UK's Labour Force survey for 2015 showed that about 2.5 per cent of people in employment had ZHC jobs. Compared to other employees, they were more likely to be women, young, part-time or in full-time education. About a third of them would have liked more hours though not necessarily in their current job. A survey of businesses counted twice as many ZHCs as employees had ZHC jobs for a number of reasons. Some ZHC jobs were omitted from the Labour Force survey because workers did not recognize they were in one, either because they did not understand the nature of their contract or did not remember they had one (for example, where they had not worked in the job for some time). ZHC jobs were also omitted if they were held in addition to a (full or part-time) standard job, and when workers held two or more ZHC jobs the Labour Force survey only counted one of them (ONS 2016).

There is no doubt that many workers with ZHC jobs were in a very precarious position and this may be particularly true of those with more than one job. Although we do not know how many of the jobs they held were ZHC, there is some evidence that workers with two or more jobs are in a particularly parlous state. For example, in 2014 they held 8.6 per cent of British jobs that paid less than a living wage (ONS 2014). In MV analysis of the Fair Treatment at Work survey, workers with more than one job did not know enough about employment rights, and they were one of the very few groups that was significantly more likely to experience unfair treatment or discrimination.[10]

Workers who do these jobs are close to undifferentiated labour, yet closer investigation reveals a more complicated relationship with cognitive individualism. While ZHC jobs were not believed to have increased because UK employers shifted from temporary workers to avoid the increased protection for temporaries under the Agency Workers Regulations introduced in 2011 (Overell 2013), they may well have increased as part of the growth in the student labour market (Doogan 2009). Chapters 8 and 11 explained the importance of expanded higher education to cognitive individualism and the growth in student jobs was a predictable result of the decision to fund this expansion by increasing student fees (Schofer and Meyer 2005; Scott, Meyer and associates 1994). Some ZHC jobs in retail and catering were tailored to accommodate students' need to earn income and not simply accumulate debt. A similar convoluted relationship between ZHC jobs and individualism can be found in the case of those workers providing domiciliary care for the elderly, and people with disabilities, who made up a significant proportion of those working in these jobs.[11]

Many of these workers were the epitome of precarity. They had none of the seven securities described by Standing, earned very little and spent their own time and money making themselves available to do the (unpredictable) hours they were paid for. Many of them had been transferred from local authority employment to the private sector, allowing the public sector to retain its reputation for employment security. It was, however, those private sector employers who provided care paid for by public funds that were responsible for many of the ZHC jobs. The deterioration of workers' conditions when their jobs were transferred to the private sector was a familiar story in British privatizations (Fevre 1986, 1989, 1990, 1991). Moreover, the inadequate level of public funding for care of this kind was recognized on all sides and this under-funding was the employers' justification for ZHC jobs. In addition, some of the care workers were employed directly by those in receipt of care as a result of policies designed to increase their autonomy (Spicker 2013). In this case, cognitive individualism for the care-receiver was achieved at the cost of treating the care-giver as undifferentiated labour (Gardiner and Hussein 2015).

To sum up, in none of these examples of non-standard work is there evidence that insecurity is making significant inroads into employment in more prosperous countries like the UK and the USA. There are some examples where cognitive individualism has been maintained for some workers but not for others, however here there have been particular 'justifications' and 'incentives', for example in the case of British privatizations. Indeed, the extent to which this twin-track solution to the problem of maintaining the reputation of organizations as the guardians of individualism has been adopted is probably much less than neo-institutionalists would have predicted two or three decades ago. There are exceptions to this, of course, and one of the most obvious of these was Japan.

In the last third of the twentieth century, Japan was held up as the example of an economy in which male workers could expect a job for life, but the proportion of employees in non-standard jobs grew to become substantial by the end of the century, perhaps as much as a third. This growth accompanied changes in employment regulation which increased protection for those in standard jobs, while decreasing protection of the growing, non-standard sector (Song 2012; Watanabe 2012, 2014). However, on closer inspection even this apparently straightforward twin-track approach turns out to be not quite so straightforward (Gottfried 2002; Shire 2002). The obvious justification for the growing insecurity of some employees was Japanese economic stagnation in the 1990s, but it could not have happened without changes in the Japanese political scene. Loss of union power in labour markets and in policy-making created an opportunity for the state to push on with neoliberal deregulation, though standard jobs were largely protected from deregulation (Watanabe 2012). Of course, Japan was not the only country to face economic problems or to embrace neoliberal deregulation. By comparing events in Italy and Japan, it is possible to see how the key to greater insecurity in Japan could be found in politics and particularly in the unions' loss of power and influence (Watanabe 2014).

This book has argued that cognitive individualism in education and employment was necessary to secure political support for neoliberalism. What we know of the limited evidence of increased insecurity in most prosperous countries suggests that political conditions are rarely conducive to the sort of developments which have occurred in Japan. Is this because increasing insecurity would put support for neoliberalism in doubt? The surveys we have been using up to now certainly suggest that security is part of the package people expect with individualism. For example, in bivariate analysis of the BWBS temporary workers were less likely to think their employer treated people as individuals (see Chapter 12). From this, we would assume that temporary workers would also be less confident that their employer would see their rights were observed. Indeed, in the Fair Treatment survey, those in a temporary job were less likely to feel well informed about their rights at work or to feel they knew enough about them (Fevre et al. 2009).[12]

Increased insecurity might put neoliberalism under political pressure. Even in the limited form it has taken so far, insecurity has occasioned some important political responses ranging from the regulation of temporary work by the EU, through campaigns over ZHC jobs in the UK, to very significant increases in support for parties opposed to neoliberalism in response to threats to long-term employment in public sector jobs in Greece and Spain (Streeck 2014). However, the best example of the way increasing insecurity can undermine support for neoliberalism is provided by migration (Barnes and Hall 2013).[13] Political conditions which allow migration – for example, the free movement of labour allowed within the EU – were an important achievement of neoliberalism which was jeopardized by the association between migration and job insecurity (Anderson 2010). For example, it was this association that fuelled support for the more extreme right-wing European political parties which expressed opposition to free movement of labour and some other political conditions which were dear to neoliberalism (e.g. Ford and Goodwin 2014).

While there may be no evidence that recruiting migrants increases job insecurity for other workers, this need not prevent people feeling insecure, especially where there are active press campaigns to persuade them that there is good reason to fear migration (Khosravnik 2009). The possibility of feelings of insecurity increasing where there has been no objective increase in insecurity has not been confined to people who fear the effects of migration. It has long been a perplexing issue for writers who have documented the lack of evidence for insecurity, that people nevertheless feel insecure (Doogan 2009; Fevre 2007). There are fairly recent British survey data which attest to these feelings (e.g. Burchell 2011; Gallie et al. 2014) – for example, the UK Workplace Employment Relations survey showed concerns about job security increasing between 2004 and 2011, and another nationally representative survey, the Skills survey, showed people's fears of losing their jobs lessened in the early 2000s but bounced back in the recession and, for the first time, were clearly worse in the public sector (Gallie et al. 2013, 2014; van Wanrooy et al. 2011, 2013). As with migration, some of these trends in feelings of insecurity may well have been influenced by what people heard and read, in this case commentaries on the end of jobs for life which, as we have just seen, lack empirical justification. However, they may also have been caused by some of the experiences of cognitive individualism described in Chapter 12. If struggling with the demands of cognitive individualism can cause employees to develop mental health problems, it is small wonder that the experience can make them feel insecure (Fevre 2003).

In this view, the idea of an end to the job for life is best understood as a reference to the way cognitive individualism requires that employees continually demonstrate their worth. They cannot rest on laurels earned in earlier years, thinking that their employer decided long ago that they were indispensable. In sentimental individualism, individual worth, once established, can be maintained in the beliefs that managers, for example, hold about an individual. In cognitive individualism, those beliefs are of no account (Strangleman 2012). What matter are the feedback from clients and customers, the weekly returns, next quarter's results, the annual appraisal and the performance action plan. Even if these tests are always safely negotiated, the insistence of cognitive individualism on a stream of evidence to prove that each individual is indeed worthy of his or her place is bound to be more unsettling. It does, however, have significant advantages for his or her employer.

WORK INTENSIFICATION AND INEQUALITY

Those workers who are obliged continually to demonstrate their worth are in an increasingly subordinate position (Streeck 2014). Chapter 1 described the concentration of power in organizations as people left the unions and collective bargaining was superseded. Cognitive individualism was an opportunity for a fundamental and long-lasting shift in the balance of power. Of course, this would not have happened if cognitive individualism had actually increased individual autonomy but, as earlier chapters have explained, individual employment rights, equal opportunity legislation and the rest of people management did not accomplish this (Barmes 2015). However, their failure was rarely evident unless cognitive individualism was actually put to the test, and not always then. It seemed that employees would simply trust their employer to look after them because they could see that it must be in the organization's interests to behave in the way the law suggested.

When things did go wrong, most employees' best hope of redress was to go cap in hand to a manager who, if they felt well disposed to the employee, had power they could exercise on their behalf. Fair Treatment data showed that large numbers of employees who were disappointed by the lack of individualism in work turned to their employer's human resource department, but this did not make a positive outcome more likely (Fevre et al. 2009). A positive outcome was much more likely when employees were able to utilize a personal relationship with a sympathetic manager.[14] One obvious difference between the human resource department and the manager was power: one might offer information on the operation of the framework of individual rights but the other could solve problems directly.

As we might expect, asking for the help of a trade union outside the workplace did not make a positive outcome more likely, however enlisting the help of a workplace union representative did. This was probably only rarely a matter of embedding an individual issue in collective bargaining,[15] but was effective because the union representative had influence over managers. We should bear in mind that most workers did not have a union representative in their workplace to provide such help. Employees gave up their trade unions on the promise of an individual employment rights framework which actually transferred power to their employers (Barmes 2015). If they could not rely on the good will of managers, it seemed their only hope of accessing influence under the new framework was to reinstate trade unions in the workplace.

In the Fair Treatment survey, the most common reasons people gave for contacting unions were to know about legal rights, for them to act on the respondent's behalf, to know about procedure or what to do next (Fevre et al. 2009). In addition, wanting justice or redress was a more likely reason to contact unions than other possible sources of help. Not all of those who asked for help were union members, but members were two and a half times more likely to take action to resolve problems. It was only at this point that many of them found out how little power they now had, even with the help of their unions. The most obvious example of this subordination was when employees pursued legal redress in an employment tribunal (something that happened in less than 1 per cent of the sample). In MV analysis, employees who used this route were 25 per cent *less* likely to solve their problems (Fevre et al. 2009). Of course, these problems would tend to be the more challenging ones but this only served to demonstrate how the individual employment rights framework failed to deal with more serious problems (Barmes 2015). In fact, most employees who took their employer to court did so because this was the last possible route to redress. If half of them felt the tribunal had helped, it was very often that they felt the justice of their cause had been recognized in law rather than because they had been able to make their employer recognize their rights in any meaningful way. In fact, 7 out of 10 left their employers.

All of this evidence of power transferred from employees to organizations begs the question of what employers use their employees' subordination to achieve. We already know, however, that British employees were more likely to complain about ill-treatment when they were employed in a high commitment workplace, and that most complaints of ill-treatment (made by every other British worker) were directly or indirectly related to work intensification. This latter point was confirmed by data on the impact of ill-treatment from the BWBS which can be interpreted as a measure of the extent to which employees would resist intensification if they had the power to do so.

It is highly significant that complaints about an unmanageable workload and/or impossible deadlines constituted the most common type of ill-treatment. Even controlling for their frequency, this type of ill-treatment remained the one that employees were likely to say had the greatest impact on them, much greater indeed than physical violence at work. The impact of violence was not a great deal different to other questions related to work intensification: having your opinions and views ignored; someone continually checking up on you or your work when it is not necessary; your employer not following proper procedures. The Fair Treatment survey also included selected questions about the impact of ill-treatment. Having an unmanageable workload and the employer not following proper procedures produced significant results for several aspects of impact. Around 1 in 10 employees who reported these problems said that they had a severe effect on their finances, physical health and relationships.

The BWBS and the Fair Treatment survey were large, representative surveys but the former was the first survey of its kind and the Fair Treatment pilot, undertaken a few years earlier, was not strictly comparable to the main survey. We must therefore turn to other large, representative surveys which have been repeated at regular intervals for evidence on work intensification *trends* in the UK. According to the Workplace Employment Relations survey, the proportion of employees saying their workload had increased rose between 2004 and 2011 (van Wanrooy et al. 2011, 2013). The Skills survey measured intensification in terms of hard work, high speed and tight deadlines and increases were recorded in all three measures between 2002 and 2011 (Felstead et al. 2013; Gallie et al. 2014). Two of the measures had been in place since 1992 and both had been rising since that time, peaking in the 1990s.

UK unemployment fell from 1993 until there was a small increase in 2006 (in advance of the larger increase from 2008), so these surveys had recorded something quite remarkable. Work intensification had occurred in increasingly tight labour markets in which we might expect workers to be able to use their increased bargaining power to resist intensification. One explanation for this apparent conundrum might be that, instead of taking advantage of buoyant demand by leaving employers who made work harder for employers who did not, employees stayed in order to benefit from the higher wages they were being offered in compensation. There is no support for this explanation in the BWBS or Fair Treatment survey, however. Workers who were being financially rewarded would be unlikely to see intensification as ill-treatment and, indeed, we also know that many of them suffered financially from intensification.

As we saw in Chapter 1, intensification is one way in which the transfer of power from workers to organizations could result in massively increased inequality (Streeck 2014). Transferring power from the individual to the organization allowed the latter to increase exploitation, thereby transferring income and wealth to a range of different actors: from the managers and CEOs who accomplished intensification to the more distant beneficiaries created by that other characteristic of neo-liberalism – financialization (Bone 2015; Brown 2015; Doogan 2009; Sayer 2015). Earlier chapters described the way managers exaggerated the extent to which they could select, train and manage for efficiency in order to cement their own power. They were rather more successful at using the power shift signalled by cognitive individualism to increase exploitation.

Earlier chapters also showed how crucial cognitive individualism was to creating and keeping privileged access to the more powerful positions in the division of labour and, indeed, to their very existence. For example, the idea that individual talents were recognized within people management justified enormous inequalities. We now have an additional reason for people with power to support cognitive individualism: it allows them, rather than the affected employees, to accrue the benefits of work intensification (Streeck 2014). It is no wonder that elites (old and new) have driven the adaption of organizations to cognitive individualism since they have personally benefitted from the transfer of power to organizations.

Throughout this book, I have insisted that goals set by sentimental individualism have often been egalitarian. Cognitive individualism is, by definition, evidence-based and if the existing state of affairs is unequal, cognitive individualism is quite likely to reject egalitarian goals as contrary to reason. Now we see how in the course of its application, particularly in people management, cognitive individualism has also been instrumental in increasing inequality and not simply reproducing it. In this way, the historic mission of individualism as the most potent force of modernity – spreading the opportunity for self-determination from tiny elites to the majority of the population of many developed countries – has been subverted.

Sentimental individualism diminished the power of elites like the Catholic hierarchy and the European aristocracy just as it gave more power to their subordinates. This very often had implications for the elites' ability to extract resources and create extreme inequalities of wealth. In the nineteenth and twentieth centuries, it was the capitalist class (sometimes in conjunction with administrative elites) which had the most to lose from individualism because it cost them political power and sometimes also power in the market and the workplace. In contrast to the 1990s, union power brought rising wages, and managers' rewards were not so very much greater than their employees'. This was still the situation in the UK on the eve of neoliberalism in 1975 when Britain reached its high tide of equality (Atkinson 2015).

From 1976 the elites fought back, very much as Spencer urged them to do a century before: clawing back the power that had to be conceded when popular gains were made in pursuit of individualism in the nineteenth and twentieth centuries. Streeck (2014) prefers to refer to the renewed ascendancy of the 'profit-dependent classes', but I take the term 'elites' to include both these and others who were less obviously dependent on profits, for example managers in the public sector, who gained power and resources through the same processes. The elites' most effective tools were governments and organizations, particularly the capitalist firm and its supporters in the administrative elites (Streeck 2014). Their tactics were to steal the clothes of sentimental individualism and promise to satisfy individualism themselves, at the same time discrediting social democratic governments (welfare states, nationalized industries) and organizations (civil society associations and especially trade unions) as the enemies of individualism.

Weakening institutions put in place over two centuries to advance individualism allowed elites to get on with restoring gross inequalities. This was not simply a matter of political strategy since, as economies changed, they were able to grab power which allowed them to do more than ensure the best-paying jobs went to their sons and daughters. The subordination of employees permitted a shift within wages to the higher-paid and from wages to non-earned income. We should however bear in mind that no elite, not even the capitalist elite, planned this strategy. It arose from a contingency which they did not engineer but struggled with for some considerable time before, finally, finding a way to turn it to their advantage. This way involved considerable deceit and subterfuge: in order to grab power and increase inequality, they had first to pretend they were giving it away, particularly in the market and the workplace.

CONCLUSION

This stealthy counter-revolution has been staggeringly effective in both the transfer of power and the increase in inequality consequent upon this transfer. Since, to credulous eyes, it allows the gains of the earlier revolution wrought by sentimental individualism to remain in place, we might think it one of the cleverest and most subtle counter-revolutions in history. It is certainly one of the most wide-ranging and effective, and who is to say it is completed? Will the majority simply be left with the husk of their formal democratic rights and negative freedoms (Brown 2015)? The future of work and politics looks to be increasingly a question of how far the power shift from the individual to the organization can go and whether anyone might successfully resist it. Those who drive it – mostly those who, one way or another, have most invested in capitalism, together with any others who are benefitting from rising inequality – may well continue to press home their advantage (Streeck 2014).

There is every reason for the elites to carry on *taking away* institutional support for individualism, making it less and less easy for people to exercise autonomy and self-development.[16] In 2015, the UK government was beginning to push for the dismantling of some of the apparatus mounted in order to support the extension of cognitive individualism in employment. Important parts of the framework of individual employment rights and equal opportunities were said to be no longer necessary because organizations were such capable guardians of individualism. What work will look like in the future largely depends on a politics in which the most important variable is how much individualism people feel is present in their societies. This does not however mean that the future of work and politics will be determined by calculations of self-interest. If voters were simply working out whether they would be better off with a mixed economy, or a unionized workplace, they might already have halted the counter-revolution (Streeck 2014). But neoliberalism has never been so unsubtle as to appeal to self-interest alone, and morality, or what masquerades as morality, has a huge part to play in the future of work and politics.[17]

NOTES

1. In contrast to writers like Boltanski and Chiapello ([1999]2005), the neoinstitutionalists did not imply that it was only capitalist organizations that, by nimble adjustment, were able to make an opportunity out of a crisis.
2. I agree with Doogan that anything that 'is new in contemporary capitalism can be inscribed under the banner of neoliberalism' (Doogan 2009: 211).
3. There is no space here to debate the continuity between this idea and the economists' theories of 'dual' and 'segmented' labour markets.
4. Insecurity in the more prosperous nations was more common in Spain, Mexico, Portugal, Turkey, Finland and Poland (Fevre 2007).

5. Rather than drawing on the extensive data resources of the International Labour Organization where he worked until 2006, Standing's arguments relied on examples provided by media coverage in few of the more advanced economies (also see Breman 2013).

6. As Breman (2013) pointed out, the 2013 *Global Employment Report* from the ILO found only 3% of those in 'vulnerable employment' in the developed countries (also see Spicker 2013).

7. According to the Bureau of Labor Statistics (2014), US median job tenure gradually increased from 2004 to 2014 for both men and women. The proportion of employed wage and salary workers aged 25 and over who had worked for at least ten years with their current employer also increased from 2004 to 2014, again for both men and women. In the UK, tenure was higher than the US figures for both men and women but the trends from 1994 to 2014 also reflect a continuation of the long-established upward trend, particularly for women (Gregg and Gardiner 2015).

8. UK Labour Force survey figures as of September 2015. Fevre (2007) described fluctuations in this measure over a slightly longer period. Flat numbers in the early 1980s were followed by slow growth between 1984 and 1988, and significant increases for men between 1991 and 1995 and for women between 1992 and 1995. This growth was short-lived and numbers declined from 1997 until 2006.

9. Including temporaries (Doogan 2009; Fevre 2007).

10. This was certainly not the case for temporary workers. In the BWBS it was actually permanent workers who were more likely to report ill-treatment (see Chapter 12).

11. In 2013, there were 150,000 domiciliary care workers on zero-hours contracts (Pennycook et al. 2013).

12. This was a result of MV analysis so it holds whether or not respondents had actually experienced problems at work.

13. Barnes and Hall (2013) also demonstrate a statistical correlation between broader inequality and hostility to immigration.

14. It goes without saying that favouritism and patronage are not conducive to individualism, however since cognitive individualism promises so much more than it can deliver, they become sensible supports for self-determination along with the help of worker representatives.

15. Perhaps because the problems were likely to involve work intensification issues which trade unions found it difficult to engage with, unless through collective bargaining over productivity. Aside from demanding increased wages or shorter hours, unions had a limited repertoire of responses to work intensification.

16. 'All capital still wants from people is that they give back to the market – perhaps not all at once, but certainly step by step and not too slowly either – the social and civil rights they fought for and won in historic struggles' (Streeck 2014: 159).

17. These are the grounds on which I can claim this book makes an original contribution. For example, the wholly admirable work of Streeck makes only the briefest mention of neoliberalism's moral victory (e.g. Streeck 2014: 160).

15. The future of work and politics

In a book which has so often insisted on the importance of contingency, the claim to foresight is problematic, but the analysis presented here allows us to see that some possibilities are more likely than others. The ways in which people understand their world have a big part to play in determining likely futures.[1] The most obvious way in which they might influence events is through political decisions in democratic countries. Even if we have reason to be sceptical about the degree of freedom people have to make these decisions, or change anything by them (Streeck 2014), misunderstanding individualism as self-interest blinds us to the possibilities that may arise in this way. As we saw in Chapter 1, friends and foes of neoliberalism identify a link between individualism and inequality. Most of them believe the essence of this link is that individualism encourages self-interest but this book suggests they are wrong. Any sensible discussion of likely futures depends, first of all, on rejecting the idea that what is wrong with individualism is self-interest.

SELF-INTEREST, MORALITY AND NEOLIBERALISM

To find a time when individualism could sensibly be defined as self-interest, we must go back much further than the dawning of the neoliberal age in 1976, to Edmund Burke and his *Thoughts and Details on Scarcity*, published almost exactly 200 years earlier. Like so many of his eighteenth-century peers, Burke was a devotee of old religion – an Anglican with Catholic leanings – who was sure that self-interested behaviour was moral because it was sanctioned by God. The theory this book has drawn on predicts that the decline of old religion which treated the social order as God's order would strip self-interest of its breastplate of righteousness[2] and make it much less attractive as a way of understanding the actions of oneself and others. Without this theory, we might argue that the decline of religion – any religion, since there would be no need for fine distinctions between 'old' and 'new' – would have the opposite effect. We could point to religious texts which inveigh against self-interested behaviour and argue that self-interest thrives well away from those parts of the world where people take religion seriously. We would conclude that history has proved J.S. Mill wrong and the freedom to make our own moral choices rather than follow God's plan has not pushed aside self-interest (see Chapter 1).

It is certainly possible to deny that reference to morality is required for people to pursue their own interests, for example to argue that self-interest is a part of human nature which requires no further sanction to express itself. For example, evolutionary psychology might claim that the individualism we now live by expresses our genetic programming to be self-interested (Fevre 2000a). In this view, the near two centuries of human history in which people – for example, the supporters of anti-slavery – did seem to behave in the way Mill had predicted were simply times when people identified self-interest in novel places. By using the conceptual legislation ridiculed by Hume (see Chapter 3), any behaviour can ultimately be revealed as self-interest. In this case, the decline of old religion simply required self-interest to be conceived in other ways, just as it was conceived in still other ways after 1976, but underneath the history nothing has changed: human beings are forever self-interested.

If we agree with Hume and reject reductionism, which would have us treat history as always superficial, we can attend to the contingencies that shattered the comfortable affinity between old religion and self-interest. They made self-interest vulnerable to moral attack on two fronts and weakened its appeal as a way of understanding the behaviour of oneself and others for many decades. The first battle-front was waged with Protestant religious individualism (Chapters 2–5). It often insisted on submission to iron discipline to curtail self-interest[3] and moral responsibility entailed not simply charitable giving but recognition that every other individual deserved just as much opportunity to obtain their own salvation.

The second front on which self-interest suffered assault was demarcated by a confrontation with sentimental individualism which had been stimulated – in dialectical fashion – by the eighteenth-century's own special product: a global economy of slavery (Baptist 2014; Blackburn 1989; Hancock 1997; Klein and Schwartz 1999; Pomeranz 2001; Solow and Engerman 2004; Williams 1944).[4] As so many British families knew, owning and trading in slaves was quite compatible with that moral self-interest sanctioned by old religion (Hall et al. 2014a, 2014b). Once they and others became less sure that God had made slavery moral, battle could be waged over the morality of practices which denied millions of other human beings access to the most basic requirements of individualism. Under Quaker influence, the evangelical William Wilberforce abandoned the old religion that sanctified the status quo but it was those who left God furthest behind – including many of those who, like Smith,

Paine and Owen, called themselves Deists – who were best able to make a new morality out of sentimental sense-making (see Chapters 2 and 3).[5]

The moralities launched by religious and sentimental individualism gave life to the anti-slavery movement in Britain and launched a string of human rights social movements that J.S. Mill and others would take as evidence of the moral defeat of self-interest. When religious individualism began to fail as faith waned further, sentimental individualism was increasingly required to carry on the fight, drawing strength from the Romantic Movement which rose up in response to industrialization (Gagnier 2010; Sayre and Löwy 2005).[6] Paine had originally thought that sentimental individualism would prosper under the conditions of a commercial society but, beginning with child labour, industrialization stimulated a wave of new sense-making from which people fashioned moral convictions which could fill the gaps left by retreating religious morality.[7]

The question of how we got from this point in British history to the post-1976 world of neoliberalism is perplexing. How was self-interest able to make such a miraculous reappearance after decades of Victorian moralizing and twentieth-century social-welfare consensus? There is certainly a great deal more history and contingency to take account of, and some of it will be reprised in the following section, but the simple answer is that there was no phoenix risen from the ashes. Eighteenth-century self-interest was not reborn in 1976.

In the nineteenth century, the intertwined strands of moral individualism – sentimental and religious – were so influential in social formation, particularly in the USA, that no ideology would have won democratic approval in the following century if it had been unable to present its moral individualist credentials. Far from returning to eighteenth-century self-interest, neoliberalism promised to do an even better job of attaining the goals of moral individualism and being faithful to its precepts (Streeck 2014). The essence of the sociological approach to understanding neoliberalism that has been taken in this book defines it as the era in which elites were once more able to regain the moral high-ground. They had lost advantage when ideologies of individualism undermined the justification for their privileges derived from self-interest sanctioned by old religion. Recognizing the ways in which those elites made peace with moral individualism is therefore crucially relevant to the search for foresight.

In the next section, I will summarize the reasons why I think neoliberalism can retain political legitimacy in the face of growing inequality as long as its promise of moral individualism still convinces enough people. Far from thriving away from those parts of the world where morality still matters, neoliberalism has persuaded millions of people around the globe that their lives are just as moral, perhaps even more moral, than lives lived by religious precepts. This is a departure from those critics of neoliberalism (who we met in Chapter 1) who assert that self-interest was foisted on people by elites which gained from us thinking of human beings in this way, for example by getting people to give up their adherence to collective action. These critics often drew on the ideas of Foucault to explain why people had acquired ways of making sense of the world which assured their own subjection (Brown 2015; cf. Bowring 2015). However, if we say that people may have, for example, voted for neoliberalism but did not mean to do so, then we have little hope of acquiring foresight. This is not to insist that votes for neo-liberalism are always freely cast or that neoliberalism necessarily relies on representative democracy to cash in on its promise to deliver moral individualism (Brown 2015; Streeck 2014). The absence of opposition (with or without meaningful democracy) may well suffice, but abstention and apathy and silent consent are also likely to follow from the acceptance that neoliberalism has assumed the mantle of moral individu-alism (see below).

CAPITALISM'S MORAL TURN

William Wilberforce's anti-slavery speech, discussed in Chapter 4, included several attempts to reassure men of business. While they ought to be convinced of the moral argument he was making, they should nevertheless be reassured that abolishing the slave trade would not harm their prosperity. By the point that Wilberforce made this speech, there was already a plan afoot to abolish the distinction between morality and self-interest altogether. In Chapter 3 we saw that, in the final years of the eighteenth century, utilitarianism began to popularize the idea that moral decisions were not to be derived from religious or sentimental beliefs but only from *knowledge* – in particular, knowledge of utility. This was the first attempt to make organizations, and especially the organs of public policy, fit for a world increasingly dominated by moral individualism. This first flush of cognitive individualism claimed it would make a better job of morality precisely because it was based in reason, indeed science, and not in partisan opinion, prejudice and superstition.

Of course, this cognitive individualism might not reach the same conclusions as sentimental or religious individualism about what was moral and what was not. Inequality might be moral if this was what an empirical investigation of people's utilities established. This early version of a morality based in cognitive individualism was successful – it influenced public policy as well as shaping social science – but it did not supplant the moral individualism developed from religion and particularly sentiment. Nevertheless, cognitive and moral individualism now came into closer and closer engagement. If the point of protest was to change the world, many of the goals of sentimental and religious individualism must necessarily be translated into the objectives of cognitive individualism if they were to be achieved (Gorz 1989; Habermas 1987; Simmel 1972; and see Chapter 8). Thus, the abolition of slavery required the legislation of 1807 and to be effective that legislation had to refer to matters of knowledge rather than belief. It notified those within its jurisdiction not that every human being was fundamentally equal but that the trade in slaves was now illegal. Enforcement entailed further knowledge such as the £100 fine which would be levied for every slave a ship's captain was found to carry when waylaid by a ship of the Royal Navy.

The legal and policy levers deployed by cognitive individualism could have unintended effects, for example the £100 fine on ships' captains proved an incentive to throw slaves overboard. The Royal Navy did not however rely on its sailors' wish to save their souls or salve their consciences. They were incentivized by head money for liberated slaves or a share in the bounty for captured ships which was higher if the slaves were still on board (Beeler 2006; Lloyd 1949). Slave traders responded to the British law by changing the flags of their ships to countries with which Britain had no treaty, thus placing the ships outside British jurisdiction. Britain passed more legislation allowing the seizure of neutral ships trading into French ports, but this exacerbated the deterioration in relations between Britain and America and contributed to the War of 1812. Worse still, attempts to stop the trade at source became an occasion for the expansion of British colonialism (Beeler 2006; Lewis-Jones 2011; Sherwood 2007).

Cognitive individualism was a messy business, for sure, so how did it ever contrive to take over the mantle of moral individualism? The key to this enigma was revealed in America in the decades after the war was concluded in 1815. The end of the war allowed further suppression of Native Americans and seizure of their lands. Both the extension of the frontier and the concurrent upsurge in nationalism were precursors for the development of the American ideology in the middle of the nineteenth century (Higham 1969). Later in the century, the ideology would serve as a bridge which allowed the mantle of moral individualism to cross over to cognitive individualism. In the course of the interaction between the American ideology and urbanization, industrialization and immigration, a new American cognitive individualism would develop which would prove as successful in shaping social organization as utilitarianism was in public policy.

The American ideology was inspired by a combination of nationalism and (millenarian) American Protestantism but the message of moral individualism also had to be given a sentimental slant as non-Protestants were to be absorbed within the nation. Just like Adam Smith, Tom Paine and Robert Owen, the nation-builders believed that nobody (or at least nobody white) was incapable of acquiring the good character, including virtues like prudence and hard work, which would bring them material prosperity. It was not only at Owen's utopian settlement in Indiana that education would play a key role in character formation. The American ideology of the middle of the nineteenth century was an example of shaping character according to the needs of a commercial society.

In hindsight, John Dewey (1929/30) insisted that the American ideology was a great deal more egalitarian than its successor, American cognitive individualism, which he called the new economic individualism. The society that the American ideology had helped to shape was one in which good character might be rewarded. It had the social, political and legal circumstances needed so that capacity and enterprise – not forgetting hard work, innovation and determination – would pay off as people built their farms and small businesses. These circumstances included the honesty, trustworthiness, civic virtue and social conscience which were also nurtured by the American ideology (and not just in school). By comparison with the ideologies of unequal and corrupt European societies, Dewey considered this egalitarian and republican moral individualism a success. Yet, it did not abolish American slavery or improve the conditions of Native Americans, and it flourished in a society which had yet to face the moral challenges which came with industrialization, urbanization and increasing inequality.

As Chapter 6 showed, the turning point in American history came when the agrarian republic spawned the industrial metropolis. Relatively late and sudden urbanization and industrial development, and further mass immigration, meant that, in a generation, the American ideology would begin to resemble the new economic individualism that Dewey could not abide. On this stepping stone to neoliberalism, the only necessary and sufficient expression of individualism was the pursuit of money. The 'pecuniary view' was fitted to a society in which inequality was increasing, and Dewey (1929/30) lamented the way in which 'capacity and enterprise' no longer mattered in the distribution of work and rewards. Success was its own justification, and, Dewey argued, the aspiration to see the beliefs about character reflected in the American nation (so different to the corrupt and unequal old world) gave way to an achieving society where individualism could only mean conforming to an aspiration to riches to incite the envy of others.

This was the point at which cognitive individualism could begin to aspire to take over the mantle of moral individualism from religion and sentiment. Rather than exposing the imperfections of the cognitive solutions (as in the aftermath of the abolition of the slave trade), the new economic individualism sought to conceal them. For example, the idea of character would eventually fall out of use (Sennett 1998). In its place, there would be 'merit' and, eventually, 'employability' and 'talent'. As the nomenclature changed, so did the moral implications of the idea. Where economic success had been a reward for virtue, it became simply a sign of the market's favour. To be sure, this favour could be presented as a reward for hard work and enterprise, but Dewey (1929/30) thought this attempt at moral justification was paper thin. The regard for good character had been replaced by a self-flagellating ersatz morality that was no longer confined to the elites but also extended to those who were very unlikely to succeed (Dobbin et al. 1994).

Dewey thought that the subversion of the American ideology ought to be interpreted as a denial of individualism, with a consequent loss of opportunities for autonomy and self-development. He could see that the American ideology lingered only in people's memories. They expressed a strong attachment to it, and claimed that it made their country more moral than others, but the USA could no longer claim to set an example to the rest of the world in its defence of equal opportunity, freedom (particularly of association and debate) and individuality (Dewey 1929/ 30; Monahan et al. 1994). It was the new economic individualism that was the root of the problem ('the pecuniary culture') and it caused not only inequality but also oppression, demoralization and confusion.[8]

As part of its incursion into moral individualism, cognitive individualism also put in place the conditions for employers – especially those large corporations – to become moral educators. Now they joined with the increasingly secular schools to do the work once done by churches and in social movements (anti-slavery, against child labour). It had taken nearly a century before employers began re-engineering the characters of their employees through training in the way that Robert Owen had first suggested. But now, as Chapter 10 explained, an initial, technical stage required 'disciplined and trainable employees', and might indeed involve reducing both autonomy and self-development. Later, there was the 'citizenship model' beginning in the USA during World War II and well established by the 1970s. Now training added new layers of ersatz morality, including 'proper organizational culture', in which employees must expect to be constrained 'by a general investment in civility' (Monahan et al. 1994: 257). By this point, the USA (and soon the UK) appeared to have extended the limitless faith it had long had in the efficacy of education to include training.

By 1976 American cognitive individualism had crossed the Atlantic. Most Americans and Britons understood that the most reliable source of self-worth and social recognition was to be found in the labour market and the workplace. They were learning to live with a new, masochistic and unforgiving moral individualism. Flogging themselves to acquire the merit which the labour market recognized might well be a hopeless task but it was, increasingly, the only way to behave morally (Sennett 2004). The workplace was now offered as the only safe home for their self-development and the expression of their personality (Hochschild 1997), but to act on this put them at constant risk of failing to live up to unforgiving judgements of their behaviour. The cognitive version of moral individualism was self-destructive and exacting precisely because it was founded in what was *known*. There was no arguing with an indifferent performance in education and rejection by employers. There was no arguing with repeated failures to achieve promotion or with the appraisals, performance improvement plans and metrics that your employer used to evidence their judgement. There was no arguing that past performance and service required recognition when work was intensified.

When moral individualism was cut adrift from sentiment and religion, the sphere for moral action shrank and moral individualism lost its capacity to inspire critique and reform. If success and failure in education, labour markets and workplaces was the only proof of moral worth, then morality would always be conservative, justifying the status quo no matter how unequal it became. Differences in income and wealth become self-justifying so that the CEOs deserved their higher salaries because they were highly paid (Chapters 6 and 14; Sayer 2015). Whereas sentimental and religious beliefs produced moral critiques of current social, political and economic arrangements, the idea that individualism was rooted in our knowledge of the human condition produced a distorted, or ersatz, morality.

The moral justification for inequality was an example of the way in which ersatz moral principles are raised from a body of knowledge. It was part of the familiar modern trend of rationalization which replaced belief with cognition (Bauman 1993; Fevre 2000a; Habermas 1987; Sorokin [1937/41]1957), but this book has shown that, for much of the last two centuries, there was a countervailing trend to establish sentiment alongside cognition in order to reinvigorate moral impulses, even while religious morality declined. There may be no popular, moral critique of capitalism, or of more general inequality and injustice, unless a similar sentimental belief system is constructed in the present century. Whether this might happen or not resolves into a question of whether people will grasp the inauthenticity of neoliberal morality. If they were to do this, they might conclude that beliefs rather than knowledge about individuals are a better guide to the further progress of individualism.

THE FUTURE OF WORK AND POLITICS

Far from being self-interested, people's adherence to the ersatz morality produced by neoliberalism is self-defeating and self-destructive. What we think the future might look like now becomes dependent on the extent to which we think people will come to realize they live in a society with precious little authentic individualism. To reach this point, they must also realize that they actually live in a world which is much closer to the one envisioned by Herbert Spencer than the one described by Adam Smith. Streeck (2014: 172) prefers to refer at this point to a 'Hayekian' rather than Spencerean world, but I find the parallel with Spencer more helpful still.[9] As we saw in Chapters 6 and 7, Spencer thought industrial society was incompatible with individualism since individuals could not make their own lives, never mind make the world (for example, extending individualism). Since individuals were of no account, except as the subjects of evolution, Spencer's view of how the world worked thoroughly undermines the claims of neoliberalism's ersatz morality. If people come to realize that this view is a good fit to their own societies, they will necessarily become sceptical of neoliberal ersatz morality.

According to Spencer, it was through encountering the harsh and unforgiving circumstances of industrial society, rather than through education and training, that character would eventually develop. All that was required was that people be self-interested, and evolution would fulfil its mission to improve humanity. What might those who have fared badly as inequality has increased gain for themselves by jettisoning the unforgiving and masochistic morality that currently persuades them not to act in their own interests (Fevre 2000a)? What freedoms might they gain by seeing that those who have done well by rising inequality act in their own interests (Bowring 2015)?[10]

Spencer did not think the characteristics that people demonstrated to acquire a role in the division of labour, and a place in an unequal society, had anything to do with the way that people might fulfil their potential when granted the freedom to do so by individualism. He would have thought that the idea that individualism was good for capitalist and other organizations, and vice versa, was nonsense. In contrast to military society, meritocracy entailed no competition since, in its wisdom, the market conducted a flawless process of selection in which everyone ended up where they would be most efficient (in state employment, the market did not rule so there was no selection for efficiency). There could be no self-development – with or without the help of organizations – making sure the interests of individuals and organizations were perfectly aligned. Instead, people were born with the capabilities required to fit them (eventually) into places in the division of labour. These capabilities differed according to whether people were more evolved or less evolved and these differences were obvious to everyone: they were the foundation of the class system.

To escape from this Spencerean world means removing the camouflage provided by an ersatz moral individualism which reveals the continued salience of class. Once we reject evolutionary explanations, we are free to consider that it might be class, rather than efficiency, that distributes people to places in an unequal society. For example, instead of meritocracy we can see discrimination by classes against other classes. This was apparent in the discussion of meritocracy in Chapter 8, for example in relation to educational achievement. Following Boudon's initial breakthrough, sociologists in the USA, and subsequently in the UK, established that the notion that education made people more efficient, as assumed by human capital theory, for example, should not be taken at face value. Chapter 3 showed how Adam Smith described privileged families investing in education for their offspring to give them access to good marriage partners and lucrative jobs. Smith did not imply that those who benefitted from the investment were any more efficient. He was describing the strategic perpetuation of class privilege in pursuit of well-understood self-interest and his analysis retains its validity (Streeck 2014).

At the level of political economy, human-capital theorists argued that more education must necessarily make countries more efficient but, as we saw in Chapter 11, neoinstitutionalist theory was sceptical about these claims. Instead, the expansion of universal education around the globe should be understood as a major component of moral camouflage for class-based discrimination and the perpetuation of class privilege. The fiction that individualism is in command in education obscures and legitimizes class subordination and the inequality it produces. The same thing happens in the labour market where, as we saw in Chapter 10, the market uses class characteristics to provide the criteria for selection, and in the workplace where it is not productivity but inequalities in power that determine the allocation of rewards.

Chapters 12 and 13 showed that, when we looked for evidence of individualism and efficiency in the workplace, we found a Spencerean world in which an individual was powerless to alter what was pre-ordained. This preordination did not refer to traits acquired through Lamarckian use inheritance being more, or less, efficient, but to the role of class in determining subordination. Put simply, senior managers had more chance of self-determination than others further down the organizational hierarchy. When we rejected the suggestion that whatever an organization decides must, by definition, be more efficient, we could see exactly how inefficient subordination could be in practice. Chapters 12 and 13 presented various proofs of how incapable organizations were of actually recognizing individuals (their worth and potential, never mind their needs) in a way that was consonant with advancing efficiency.

Behind the cover provided by moral individualism, organizations were benefitting from the opportunities for exploitation afforded by the increased subordination of their employees. Most obviously, they benefitted from the weakness and marginalization of the trade unions, so we understood, again, why weaker trade unions accompanied increased inequality. The point of a world which fits the theories of Herbert Spencer was not to develop the capacities of workers and distribute them where they could do most good, but to shift the balance of power between organizations and individuals to the detriment of the latter (Streeck 2014). This was particularly important in high-intensity and high-commitment workplaces where organizations were most determined that subordination should be complete and therefore intensification could proceed unhindered.

This intensification boosted inequality and in this, as in other ways, the fact of increased inequality confirmed the absence rather than the presence of individualism. Is there any evidence that the idea that individualism and equality can only now be had together might be catching on (Spicker 2013)? The theory used in this book suggests that increasing awareness would be needed if there was to be a significant challenge to the neoliberal settlement that presently supports increased inequality. It also suggests some possible future scenarios in which dissent from the political settlement might become significant, however I do not think any of them, separate or together, would necessarily lead to the demise of neoliberalism.

If members of the middle classes (for example, in the UK and the USA) were to become increasingly unhappy with the employment prospects of their children (Bukodi et al. 2015; Pew 2012, 2015), it would not be hard to imagine that some might lose faith in the efficacy of education. For example, graduates might conclude that, rather than blaming themselves for the limited benefits they had derived from education, education had been over-sold to everyone as an environment for self-development and the expression of the individual personality. This dissatisfaction would hardly address the growing gap between graduates and others, indeed it might be partly fuelled by a concern that the gap was narrowing (Brown et al. 2012). Another possibility might be the extension of disquiet about the highest salaries to scepticism about the justification of all income inequalities. However, the law can be made to punish those at the top who appear to be most self-interested, and least concerned with the justification of their rewards, so accommodating limited disquiet within the current political settlement (Masters and Binham 2012).

Concerns about the use of social networks, for example to access internships which lead to lucrative careers, suggest that some students and graduates (or their parents) are concerned about limitations on individualism in the labour market (Grice 2012). This is, however, a far cry from those graduates reaching an awareness that the labour market distinguishes in terms of class before individual characteristics. Raising such a suggestion in the USA, as Obama was alleged to have done in the course of his presidency (e.g. Duke 2015), invited the portrayal of a partisan attack on moral individualism. Although the American ideology has long since joined the walking dead, a scintilla of a hint that class might have something to do with inequality remains a kind of apostasy.

The limited likelihood of a future scenario in which people might begin to associate rising inequality with the absence of individualism is also evident from the example of women employees (Streeck 2014). The complaints of relatively well-paid women about the absence of gender equality near the top of the labour market may well become louder, but this need not signal increased scepticism about the degree of individualism that all women can access. We know from Chapters 10 and 11 how rare it is for anyone, including women, to think that discrimination occurs in recruitment or in the course of employment. The few who consider it possible are quite likely to be realists who think that employers discriminate for reasons of efficiency (because choosing recruits from particular groups is believed to be the way to find more efficient workers). It would take significantly increased awareness of the extent of discrimination, and incredulity about employers' claims to hire for efficiency (see Chapter 10), to get large numbers of women to the point of distrusting ersatz moral individualism. Without this increased awareness, the most vocal, and politically active, women will tend to limit their concerns to the glass ceiling and the difficulties of combining a successful career with parenthood. They will not be able to make common cause with women in the jobs at the bottom of the labour market, including some of the insecure jobs discussed in Chapter 14, if they remain persuaded that the income differentials between them are justified (Ehrenreich and Hochschild 2003).

As the work of Glucksmann (2000, 2009) suggested, some of the women who might be worried that they are not benefitting from individualism at the top of the labour market necessarily rely on the women at the bottom (especially migrants and working-class women) being badly paid. This applies not only to their own domestic workforce providing housekeeping and childcare services, but also to the army of badly-paid women working in education, health and social care. For example, we saw in Chapter 14 that raising the low pay of women providing care for the elderly and disabled in the UK would require a significant injection of tax-payers' money, including the taxes of higher-paid women. The example of Scandinavia, where there is even greater sex segregation in employment but much higher pay, reminds us that paying women in these sectors badly is ultimately a political choice (Fevre 2003, 2013; Wolf 2013). If more and more better-paid women in the UK and the USA were to begin to reverse this choice, it might suggest some increased awareness of the limitations of ersatz moral individualism.

A similar point applies to awareness of the causes of racial dis-advantage amongst minority populations. In the USA, for example, both the education and employment of African-Americans have provided textbook examples of the empty promise of individualism for well over a century.[11] As we saw in Chapter 5, slaves were almost wholly excluded from the nation-building phase of the American ideology. They were not, however, excluded from the new economic individualism which devel-oped after Reconstruction and which was gaining ground as the descend-ants of slaves were sucked into the industrial conurbations of the North along with other migrant groups (Franklin and Moss 2000). Everything that we have learned about the elaboration of American cognitive individualism would lead us to predict that once African-Americans were allowed into white schools and workplaces, they would be seen to fail (Ladson-Billings and Tate 1995; Taylor et al. 2009).

This prediction flows from the conclusion that education, labour markets and employment are unable to deliver individualism to anyone other than the members of some narrow elites. What we think of as individualism in each of these spheres is founded on institutionalized knowledge of the status quo. Thus, cognitive individualism asks us to observe the characteristics currently associated with failure and success and then to agree that these should be the characteristics used to give everyone the equal opportunity for self-determination and self-development. This ensures that inequality is validated and perpetuated. It is no wonder that a society built on class will use class criteria to determine success and failure and, in a society where slavery has made sure race and class coincide, it is entirely predictable that the criteria for success will systematically discriminate against the descendants of slaves (Blanchett 2006; Haney et al. 2004; Kozol 1991, 2005; Leonardo 2007; Nichols et al. 2005; Orfield et al. 2004; Solomon et al. 2005).

History left the USA with freed slaves and including them within cognitive individualism was necessary to the continuation of the nation-building project into the era of sudden and massive urbanization and industrialization. Their inclusion necessarily weakened Black separatism but gradually gave momentum to what became the Civil Rights Movement (Franklin and Moss 2000). The extension of equal opportunities in the 1960s and 1970s was in part a response to the demands of that movement but by 1976 the movement was in decline.[12] Just as the loss of momentum in British socialism created an opportunity for the neoliberal revolution, so also in the USA neoliberalism was able to assume the mantle of individualism and, eventually, take over the management of the extension of individualism to African-Americans. From this point onwards, the key factor affecting the relations between African-Americans and white Americans was the extent to which people were persuaded that individualism was safe in the hands of organizations because it guaranteed a perpetual source of increased efficiency and innovation.

The changes that followed political confirmation that people were persuaded that organizations were the guardians of individualism – for example, the shift towards ideas of human capital, employability and talent – all made racial disadvantage worse. This was the case with changes in education policy, for example the magnet schools and state-wide high-stakes testing regimes which followed the publication of the report *No Child Left Behind* (Leonardo 2007; Nichols et al. 2005; Orfield et al. 2004). Undertaken in the name of extending equal opportunity to access individualism in public schools, these changes nevertheless widened the gap in educational achievement between African-American children and other students. They also made sure African-American children received a smaller proportion of public resources, and helped to reinforce racism.

We saw in Chapter 7 on Spencer how, ever since the American ideology laid the foundations for the neoliberal settlement, the majority population could be reassured that it was *deservedly* benefitting from individualism simply by contrasting its situation with that of African-Americans. Even William Wilberforce had acknowledged the moral failings of slaves (see Chapter 4), and it was easy for the Americans of the agrarian republic to make the contrast with their own experience of moral individualism. As American cognitive individualism took hold, the failings of African-Americans were translated into the language of the new ersatz morality. Their evident failure to take advantage of the American Dream was proof of laziness or obduracy or, for those influenced by Spencer such as Herrnstein and Murray (1996, also Murray 1996), that evolution was in charge (Somers and Block 2005). The victories of the Civil Rights Movement enshrined equal opportunities in law but these victories were then turned against African-Americans as evidence of their failure to take advantage of the most level playing field in the world (Nozick 1974; Sowell 2015). Racism had now been modernized, for example it could claim that people of colour demanded more favourable treatment – such as through quotas and positive dis-crimination – simply because they were so evidently unable to take advantage of the opportunity for individual success that America had afforded them.

The racism that was present at every twist and turn of African-Americans' encounters with American cognitive individualism is one of the reasons why it was the USA, rather than the UK, that sowed the seeds for the neoliberal settlement which was then exported around the world. It is true that the American ideology was also a necessary foundation for American cognitive individualism but without slavery and its aftermath things might have been very different. No other group – not even other immigrants like the Hispanic migrants from South and Central America – has been as important to the perpetuation of the idea of the classless society in the USA as African-Americans. This is because the deep and persistent racism they have endured has made Americans blind to any evidence that the classless society is not what it seems. This stretches beyond justifications of white success and explanations of African-American failures to the underlying argument that inequality is not only compatible with individualism but produced by it. The American Dream and the idea that the USA leads the world in equal opportunities are kept alive by the subordination of African-Americans.

It seems from the foregoing that there is little chance of those who seem to have done a little better out of cognitive individualism deciding that the fate of those who have done less well shows how false the promise of individualism really has been. We know from previous chapters how difficult it would be for those who have done least well to mount the social movements that would lead people to question whether increasing inequality will always accompany individualism. This is not what happened with feminism or civil rights or, indeed, anti-slavery and many of those, like the low-paid workers employed in health and social care discussed in Chapter 14, who are best equipped to see the failures of individualism, have become effectively disenfranchised (Brown 2015; Streeck and Schäfer 2013). They were far less likely to have given their assent to the neoliberal settlement in the first place but its consolidation has demoralized them and forced them to abandon any attempt to improve their situation through collective action (Streeck 2014). More inequality means less political participation but the greater part of this decline took place amongst those whom neoliberalism need hardly bother to persuade.[13] If cracks are ever to appear in the political settlement, they will be the result of the actions of people who make common cause with those who are most disadvantaged by the settlement, just as the abolitionists made common cause with the slaves. This would require the generation of beliefs about human beings – social movements and their motive beliefs are mutually reinforcing – which cognitive individualism appears to rule out.

Cognitive individualism would have to be seen to fail in its own terms in order to open up the possibility of reinvigorated sentimental individualism. If cognitive individualism seems to have a firm grip on people's adherence to neoliberalism in respect of education and the labour market, including pay differentials, its hold is less certain in the day-to-day experience of life in the workplace. Chapters 12 and 13 explained that moving away from psychological concepts of bullying and harassment to a more sociological notion of ill-treatment revealed that half of the UK population had experienced some disappointment with the execution of cognitive individualism in the workplace in the previous two years.[14] In many of these cases, employees' complaints implied that individualism had failed even though it was obvious this would also damage efficiency or innovation.

It is possible to imagine that, from these small beginnings, people might begin to wonder if organizations really are as thoroughly committed to the extension of individualism in the workplace as they claim. If half the working population suspect that their individual efficiency is not factored into their treatment, they might eventually learn to question what the commitment to individualism serves to obscure. We remember from Chapter 13 that it was precisely in the high-commitment, high-performance companies – where we might think that individualism would be most important to efficiency and innovation – that more people could be found suspecting that the promise of individualism was a sham.

If individualism is seen to provide a camouflage for work intensification, employees might also be open to the idea that cognitive individualism has served to increase the power of capital through the neutralization of effective opposition from organized labour.

We know from earlier chapters that 1 in 5 employees already considers their own employer's commitment to individualism something of a sham. We know they are more likely to have found this out through experiencing ill-treatment and, perhaps, putting their employer's promises of individual treatment to the test when seeking remedies to problems at work. They are also more likely to be trade union members and it may be that the unions still contain some potential as vehicles for a wider social movement which could rebuild sentimental individualism. The early signs are not promising, however, since the unions appear to have become adept at helping employers to maintain their reputation as the guardians of individualism. In the UK, trade unions have, for example, learned to provide support when employers need to keep up the appearance that the individual employment rights framework can deliver when it is put to the test (see Chapter 12). They have long since acquired the habit of helping employers to manage for efficiency while neglecting the interests of their members.

Without social movements, beliefs cannot be disseminated but movements require beliefs to animate them in the first place. Whether or not trade unions play a role, any movement capable of rebuilding sentimental individualism would have to draw on a sentimental belief system which reaches beyond a critique of neoliberalism to offer an alternative vision of society. The sentimental fiction of Dickens, Kinsley and Harriet Beecher Stowe played an important role in the generation of Romantic beliefs which offered an alternative to the realities of British industrial capitalism and American slavery. Where might the contemporary equivalent of a core of beliefs capable of animating a new social movement be found? The data presented in Chapters 12 and 13 on ill-treatment, and organizational failures to treat employees as individuals, show that such beliefs will not be spontaneously generated from dissatisfaction with employers' broken promises. Similarly, the better enforcement of workers' rights will not provide the impetus for a new social movement, indeed it is not even certain that the one in five who is sceptical about their employer's commitment to individualism share their union leaders' dreams of extending workers' rights, for example rights of worker representation (Streeck 2014).

The revitalization of sentimental individualism requires more than renewed faith in the cognitive means to pursue it. The best example of what is really required is provided by the Disability Rights movement and its elaboration of the social model of disability. The Disability Rights movement has carried, and been carried by, the belief that, despite all the evidence to the contrary, people with disabilities are equal to those without. This core belief is productive of a morality which provides both a critique and an alternative vision of society. In employment, the social model of disability argues that it is not only the physical environment that prevents employees with disabilities from being treated equally. Other disabling factors include social relations in the workplace and the way that work is organized. In other words, like Owen and the Romantic socialists, and John Dewey, the Disability Rights movement teaches that equality requires control over the division of labour.

Struggles over disability rights can be seen as an example of the sort of politics that are required if positive freedoms are to be extended (Bowring 2015), however it is important to grasp that this politics originates in belief rather than knowledge and so is productive of sentimental rather than cognitive sense. The disability movement is motivated by beliefs about the equality of people with and without disabilities which accord with moral individualism (sentimental or religious). These beliefs override facts which suggest that people with disabilities are far from equal, for example the persistent disability employment gap (Baumberg et al. 2015). Not only does the sentimental belief in equality make plain the stigmatization of impairment but it also brings critical attention to the way cognitive individualism draws conclusions about a person's capacity from her current employment situation. When Oliver (1990) rightly described this process as the 'individual model' (as opposed to the social model), it was *cognitive* individualism that he was critiquing. A belief in the equality of people with and without disabilities is fundamentally at odds with the cognitive individualism which tells us that we can learn all we need to know of an individual by observing her current position.

The popularization of this belief and the moral principles that flow from it can be tracked through the adoption, around the world, of ideas which Robert Burgdorf brought to the American legislation designed to protect people with disabilities from discrimination. There is no doubt that the legislation has not been as effective as many had hoped (Burgdorf 2004). Indeed, it is doubtful whether the Americans with Disabilities Act (ADA) has resulted in an overall improvement in the employment situation of people with disabilities.[15] The Disability Rights movement remains a better example of a politics which can extend positive freedoms than, say, civil rights or feminism, but perhaps it is simply a matter of time before cognitive means are found which seem to satisfy its demands and drain the movement's energy? There is an alternative future for this politics but it would face opposition from inside the Disability Rights movement which has, quite rightly, grown wary of any attempt by the able-bodied to co-opt the movement to its own ends.

The movement has sometimes struggled to broaden its base because it has had a hard time persuading people with disabilities to adopt the social model and to consider that they might suffer ill-treatment or discrimination because of their disability (Fevre et al. 2013). This obstacle could be overcome, and wider mobilization achieved, by making a more explicit argument from sentimental individualism. An employee who suffers ill-treatment does not need to adhere to the social model to feel that she is not being treated as an individual, but of course this applies equally to employees with and without disabilities. Unpopular as it may be inside the movement, the best hope for mass mobilization may reside in the generalization of the movement's aims beyond the 1 in 5 who regularly identify themselves as having a disability, long-standing illness or impairment which limits their activity (Baumberg et al. 2015; US Census Bureau 2012).[16]

To be clear, I am not suggesting that the Disability Rights movement will grow because people without disabilities come to identify themselves as people with disabilities (although of course the proportion of people who will be affected by a disability during their lifetime is much higher than 1 in 5). I am suggesting, rather, that the Disability Rights movement could serve as the core of a much larger social movement able to challenge the neoliberal claim that capitalism is the best hope of individualism. Just as a belief in the equality of disabled people challenges the cognitive certainties of their current conditions, so a general belief in equality could challenge the explanations for the current situation of those who are not disabled but are in other ways deemed inadequate or 'perverse' (Somers and Block 2005).

Two centuries of the development of education, labour markets and people management mean that this could never be a case of turning the clock back to Paine's moral argument for equal opportunity to access the benefits of individualism. It would instead require a social vision beyond the inequalities apparently justified by differences in educational attainment and market rewards. A social movement of this type could challenge the ersatz morality of human capital and its defence of privilege, and develop a very different perspective on the morality of wage-setting.[17] Ultimately, such a movement would be able to generalize the lesson the Disability Rights movement teaches that without taking control over what is to be done and by whom it is not possible to challenge inequality. The division of labour is currently constructed in a way that disables people who have impairments, but it is also constructed in a way that guarantees general inequality and denies self-determination to the majority.

NOTES

1. I should emphasize once more that by 'people' I mean not only the members of elites but the majorities in the richer countries which have given their support to neoliberalism but have probably never heard the names of Hayek, Friedman, von Mises, Nozick or Dworkin (Brown 2015).
2. To borrow a phrase from Ephesians 6:14 also used by Laud Humphries (1970).
3. Thomas (1971) describes the way some Protestants could explain any amount of misfortune as the result of a failure to keep their self-interest in check.
4. This was not the mode of production which sowed the seeds of neoliberalism of course. Prosperity was far from widely spread in the slave economies which could not accommodate the extension of individualism beyond the slave-owning elite. This mode of production could never have developed the flexible capacities of later capitalism to adapt and absorb such innovations.
5. Deism attracted many notable campaigners against inequality, including Robert Burns: 'The coward slave-we pass him by ... . The Man's the gowd for a' that' (*For a' that*, 1795).
6. As we saw in Chapters 2 and 4, the parallel between slavery and the factory system was always on the lips of the Romantics and the sentimental individualist campaigners who were influenced by them.
7. Bernstein (2011) explained that, when it did arrive in the USA, the invention of the innocence of childhood – a potent first cause for sentimental sense-making – did not extend to African-American children.
8. Including an obsession with spending and complacency about going into debt.
9. Streeck might be in accord since his vision of the future of work and politics includes the replacement of 'national political discretion' by 'rational incentives (including negative ones such as fines) to fall in silently behind the destiny mapped out for them by the market' (Streeck 2014: 176; also see Brown 2015).
10. These may include many of the (1 in 5) realists who know how little individualism counts for in the workplace – see Chapter 12.
11. At least since it was pointed out by Du Bois (1903).
12. As signalled by the 1978 *Bakke v Regents of the University of California* decision against racial quotas.
13. Although of course it told them, as Spencer insisted it should, that they should behave like those who prospered (Brown 2015). This might be of no benefit to them but it did serve to buttress the ersatz morality of neoliberalism.
14. A non-psychological definition of the disappointments of individualism takes account of a much wider range of organizational activities than those which cognitive individualism can easily define and manage.
15. There is a great deal of evidence to suggest it did not (Acemoglu and Angrist 2001; Beegle and Stock 2003; Bell and Heitmueller 2009; DeLeire 2000; Hotchkiss 2004; Jolls 2004; Jolls and Prescott 2004; Kruse and Schur 2003; Schwochau and Blanck 2003).
16. There is some dispute about this estimate. In 2010, three UK surveys produced differences in prevalence rates within a range of 6–20%.
17. Perhaps adopting the ideas of organizations like the New Economics Foundation in the UK (www.neweconomics.org/).

Bibliography

Acemoglu, Daron and Joshua Angrist (2001), 'Consequence of employment protection? The case of the Americans with Disabilities Act', *Journal of Political Economy*, **19**, 915–50.

Anderson, Bridget (2010), 'Migration, immigration controls and the fashioning of precarious workers', *Work, Employment and Society*, **24**(2), 300–17.

Anthony, Peter D. (1977), *The Ideology of Work*, London: Tavistock.

Appelbaum, Eileen (2002), 'The impact of new forms of work organization on workers', in G. Murray, J. Balanger, A. Giles and P.A. Lapointe (eds), *Work Employment Relations in the High Performance Workplace*, London: Continuum, 120–48.

Ashley, Louise, Jo Duberley, Hilary Sommerlad and Dora Scholarios (2015), *A Qualitative Evaluation of Non-Educational Barriers to the Elite Professions*, London: Social Mobility and Child Poverty Commission.

Aspromourgos, Tony (2013), 'Adam Smith on labour and capital', in Christopher Berry, Maria Paganelli and Craig Smith (eds), *The Oxford Handbook of Adam Smith*, Oxford: Oxford University Press, 267–89.

Atkinson, Anthony (2015), *Inequality: What Can Be Done?* Cambridge, MA: Harvard University Press.

Bagguley, Paul (2013), 'Industrial citizenship: A re-conceptualisation and case study of the UK', *International Journal of Sociology and Social Policy*, **33**(5/6), 265–79.

Ball, Stephen J. (2003), *Class Strategies and the Education Market: The Middle Classes and Social Advantage*, London: RoutledgeFalmer.

Baptist, Edward E. (2014), *The Half Has Never Been Told: Slavery and the Making of American Capitalism*, New York: Basic Books.

Barmes, Lizzie (2015), *Bullying and Behavioural Conflict at Work: The Duality of Individual Rights*, Oxford: Oxford University Press.

Barnes, Colin and Geof Mercer (eds) (2004), *Implementing the Social Model of Disability: Theory and Research*, Leeds: The Disability Press.

Barnes, Lucy and Peter A. Hall (2013), 'Neoliberalism and social resilience in the developed democracies', in Peter A. Hall and Michèle Lamont (eds), *Social Resilience in the Neoliberal Era*, Cambridge: Cambridge University Press, 209–38.

Bauman, Zygmunt (1993), *Postmodern Ethics*, Oxford: Blackwell.

Baumberg, Ben, Melanie Jones and Victoria Wass (2015), 'Disability prevalence and disability-related employment gaps in the UK 1998–2012: Different trends in different surveys?', *Social Science and Medicine*, **141**, 72–81.

Beck, Ulrich (1992), *Risk Society: Towards a New Modernity*, London: Sage.

Beegle, Kathleen and Wendy Stock (2003), 'The labour market effects of disability discrimination laws', *Journal of Human Resources*, **38**, 806–59.

Beeler, Frank (2006), 'Maritime policing and the Pax Britannica: The Royal Navy's anti-slavery patrol in the Caribbean 1828–1848', *The Northern Mariner*, **16**(1), 1–20.

Bell, David and Axel Heitmueller (2009), 'The Disability Discrimination Act in the UK: Helping or hindering employment among the disabled?', *Journal of Health Economics*, **28**(2), 465–80.

Belsky, Gary (2012), 'Workplace bullying: The problem – and its costs – are worse than we thought', *Time (Business)*, 12 July, http://business.time.com/2012/07/12/workplacebullying-the-problem-and-its-costs-are-worse-than-we-thought/.

Berkovic, Nicola (2010), 'Workplace bullies cost $15bn each year', *The Australian*, 28 January, www.theaustralian.com.au/news/nation/work place-bullies-cost-15bn-each-year/story-e6frg6nf-1225824136075.

Bernstein, Robin (2011), *Racial Innocence: Performing American Childhood from Slavery to Civil Rights*, New York: New York University Press.

Berry, Christopher (2013), 'Adam Smith and early-modern thought', in Christopher Berry, Maria Paganelli and Craig Smith (eds), *The Oxford Handbook of Adam Smith*, Oxford: Oxford University Press, 77–104.

Beteille, André (1983), *The Idea of Natural Inequality and Other Essays*, Oxford: Oxford University Press.

Beteille, André (1986), 'Individualism and equality', *Current Anthropology*, **27**(2), 121–34.

Blackburn, Robin (1989), *The Overthrow of Colonial Slavery 1776–1848*, London: Verso.

Blake, Aaron (2014), 'The American dream is hurting', *Washington Post*, 14 September, www.washingtonpost.com/news/the-fix/wp/2014/09/24/the-american-dream-is-hurting/.

Blanchett, Wanda J. (2006), 'Disproportionate representation of African American students in special education: Acknowledging the role of white privilege and racism', *Educational Researcher*, **35**(6), 24–8.

Board of Education (1943), *White Paper: Educational Reconstruction*, London: Board of Education, www.educationengland.org.uk/documents/wp1943/educational-reconstruction.html.

Boltanski, Luc and Ève Chiapello ([1999]2005), *The New Spirit of Capitalism*, London: Verso.

Bolton, Sharon C. (ed.) (2007), *Dimensions of Dignity at Work*, London: Routledge.

Bone, John (2015), 'False economy: Financialization, crises and socioeconomic polarisation', *Sociology Compass*, **9**(10), 876–86.

Botting, Eileen Hunt (2014), 'Thomas Paine amidst the early feminists', in Ian Shapiro and Jane Calvert (eds), *The Selected Writings of Thomas Paine*, New Haven, CT: Yale University Press, 630–54.

Bourdieu, Pierre (1998), 'The essence of neoliberalism', *Le Monde Diplomatique* (trans. Jeremy Shapiro), http://mondediplo.com/1998/12/08Bourdieu.

Bowring, Finn (2015), 'Negative and positive freedom: Lessons from, and to, sociology', *Sociology*, **49**(1), 156–71.

Bowring, Finn and Ralph Fevre (2014), 'European sociologies and social theories of work', in Sokratis Koniordos and Alexandros Kyrtsis (eds), *Routledge Handbook of European Sociology*, London: Routledge, 143–57.

Boxall, Peter and Keith Macky (2014), 'High involvement work processes, work intensification and employee well-being', *Work, Employment and Society*, **28**, 963–84.

Boyd, Richard (2013), 'Adam Smith and civil society', in Christopher Berry, Maria Paganelli and Craig Smith (eds), *The Oxford Handbook of Adam Smith*, Oxford: Oxford University Press, 443–63.

Bozeman, Barry (2007), *Public Values and Public Interest: Counterbalancing Economic Individualism*, Washington, DC: Georgetown University Press.

Breman, Jan (2013), 'A bogus concept?', *New Left Review*, **84**, 130–8.

Brown, George W. and Tirril Harris (1978), *Social Origins of Depression: A Study of Psychiatric Disorder in Women*, New York: Free Press.

Brown, Phillip (1995), 'Cultural capital and social exclusion: Some observations on recent trends in education, employment and the labour market', *Work, Employment and Society*, **9**(1), 29–51

Brown, Phillip (2000), 'The globalisation of positional competition?', *Sociology*, **34**(4), 633–53.

Brown, Phillip, Hugh Lauder and David Ashton (2012), *The Global Auction: The Broken Promises of Education, Jobs, and Incomes*, New York and Oxford: Oxford University Press.

Brown, Wendy (2015), *Undoing the Demos: Neoliberalism's Stealth Revolution*, New York: Zone Books.

Bukodi, Erzsébet, John H. Goldthorpe, Lorraine Waller and Jouni Kuha (2015), 'The mobility problem in Britain: New findings from the analysis of birth cohort data', *British Journal of Sociology*, **66**(1), 93–117.

Burchell, Brendan (2011), 'A temporal comparison of the effects of unemployment and job insecurity on wellbeing', *Sociological Research Online*, **16**(1), 9, www.socresonline.org.uk/16/1/9.html.

Bureau of Labor Statistics (2014), *Employee Tenure in 2014*, Washington, DC: US Department of Labor, www.bls.gov/news.release/pdf/tenure.pdf.

Bureau of Labor Statistics (2015), *Charting the Labor Market: Data from the Current Population Survey*, Washington, DC: US Department of Labor, www.bls.gov/web/empsit/cps_charts.pdf.

Burgdorf, Robert (2004), *Righting the Americans with Disabilities Act*, Washington, DC: National Council on Disability.

Burke, Edmund ([1774]1999), 'Thoughts and details on scarcity', in *Select Works of Edmund Burke: A New Imprint of the Payne Edition, Vol. 4*, Indianapolis, IN: Liberty Fund.

Butler, R.A.B. (1945), Extract from a note from Butler to Dr Sophia Weitzman (ED 136/692), www.nationalarchives.gov.uk/wp-content/uploads/2014/02/ed-136-6921.jpg.

Callaghan, James (1976), 'A rational debate based on the facts', Speech at Ruskin College Oxford, www.educationengland.org.uk/documents/speeches/1976ruskin.html.

Campbell, Colin (1987), *The Romantic Ethic and the Spirit of Consumerism*, Oxford: Basil Blackwell.

Campbell, Tom (2013), 'Adam Smith: Methods, morals, and markets', in Christopher Berry, Maria Paganelli and Craig Smith (eds), *The Oxford Handbook of Adam Smith*, Oxford: Oxford University Press, 559–80.

Chitty, Clyde (1989), *Towards a New Education System: The Victory of the New Right*, Lewes: Falmer.

Cladis, Mark S. (1992a), 'Durkheim's individual in society: A sacred marriage?', *Journal of the History of Ideas*, **53**(1), 71–90.

Cladis, Mark S. (1992b), *A Communitarian Defense of Liberalism*, Stanford, CA: Stanford University Press.

Claeys, Gregory (1986), '"Individualism", "socialism", and "social science": Further notes on a process of conceptual formation, 1800–1850', *Journal of the History of Ideas*, **47**(1), 81–93.

Claeys, Gregory (1989), *Thomas Paine: Social and Political Thought*, Boston: Unwin Hyman.

Clery, Elizabeth, Lucy Lee and Sarah Kunz (2013), *Public Attitudes to Poverty and Welfare: 1983–2011 Analysis Using British Social Attitudes Data*, London: NatCen Social Research for Joseph Rowntree Foundation.

Conservative Party (1979), *Conservative General Election Manifesto 1979*, London: Thatcher Archive, www.margaretthatcher.org/document/110858.

Coutrot, Thomas (1998), *L'Entreprise Neo-liberale – nouvelle utopie capitaliste?*, Paris: Editions La Découverte.

Dardot, Pierre and Christian Laval (2014), *The New Way of the World: On Neoliberal Society*, London: Verso.

D'Cruz, Premilla (2012), *Workplace Bullying in India*, New Dehli: Routledge.

Deery, Stephen and Richard Mitchell (1999), 'The emergence of individualisation and union exclusion as an employment relations strategy', in Stephen Deery and Richard Mitchell (eds), *Employment Relations: Individualisation and Union Exclusion – an International Study*, Sydney: Federation Press, 1–17.

DeLeire, Thomas (2000), 'The wage and employment effects of the Americans with Disabilities Act', *Journal of Human Resources*, **35**, 693–715.

Department for Business, Innovation and Skills (2015a), *Trade Union Membership 2014: Statistical Bulletin*, BIS/15/300, London: Department for Business, Innovation and Skills.

Department for Business, Innovation and Skills (2015b), *Trade Union Membership 2014: Tables*, London: Department for Business, Innovation and Skills. https://www.gov.uk/government/statistics/trade-union-statistics-2014.

Dewey, John (1929/30), 'Individualism old and new', in Jo Ann Boydston (ed.), *John Dewey: The Later Works, 1925–1953. Vol. 5: 1929–1930*, Carbondale, IL: Southern Illinois University Press, 41–124.

Dobbin, Frank, John R. Sutton, John W. Meyer and W. Richard Scott (1994), 'Equal opportunity law and the construction of internal labor markets', in W. Richard Scott, John W. Meyer and Associates (eds), *Institutional Environments and Organizations: Structural Complexity and Individualism*, Thousand Oaks, CA: Sage, 272–300.

Dobbin, Frank and John R. Sutton (1998), 'The strength of the weak state: The rights revolution and the rise of human resources management divisions', *American Journal of Sociology*, **104**, 441–76.

Donnachie, Ian (2000), *Robert Owen: Owen of New Lanark and New Harmony*, East Linton: Tuckwell Press.

Doogan, Kevin (2009), *New Capitalism? The Transformation of Work*, Cambridge: Polity.

Dorling, Danny (2011), *Injustice: Why Social Inequality Persists*, Bristol: Policy Press.

Driver, Cecil (1946), *Tory Radical: The Life of Richard Oastler*, Oxford: Oxford University Press.

Drucker, Peter (1995), *Managing in a Time of Great Change*, New York: Truman Talley.

Du Bois, William Edward Burghardt (1903), *The Souls of Black Folk*, Chicago: A.C. McClurg.

Duke, Selwyn (2015), 'Obama plays class-warfare card – calls wealthy "society's lottery winners"', *New American*, 14 May, www.the newamerican.com/usnews/item/20876-obama-plays-class-warfare-card-calls-wealthy-society-s-lottery-winners.

Dumont, Louis (1977), *From Mandeville to Marx: The Genesis and Triumph of Economic Ideology*, Chicago: University of Chicago Press.

Dumont, Louis (1986), *Essays on Individualism: Modern Ideology in Anthropological Perspective*, Chicago: University of Chicago Press.

Durkheim, Emile ([1898]1969), 'Individualism and the intellectuals', reprinted in Stephen Lukes (1969), 'Durkheim's "Individualism and the Intellectuals"', *Political Studies*, **17**(1), 14–30.

Dutt, Manasi (2015), Indian Seafarers' Experiences of Ill-Treatment Onboard Ships, Cardiff University, PhD thesis, orca.cf.ac.uk/71472/2/Manasi%20Dutt%20Final%20Thesis%20ORCA.pdf.

Ecclestone, Kathryn and Dennis Hayes (2009), *The Dangerous Rise of Therapeutic Education*, London: Routledge.

Ehrenberg, Alain (2009), *The Weariness of the Self: Diagnosing the History of Depression in the Contemporary Age*, Montreal: McGill-Queen's University Press.

Ehrenreich, Barbara and Arlie Russell Hochschild (2003), *Global Woman: Nannies, Maids and Sex Workers in the New Economy*, London: Granta.

Einarsdottir, Anna, Helge Hoel and Duncan Lewis (2015a), '"It's nothing personal": Anti-homosexuality in the British workplace', *Sociology*, **49**(6), 1183–99.

Einarsdottir, Anna, Helge Hoel and Duncan Lewis (2015b), 'Fitting the bill? (Dis)embodied disclosure of sexual identities in the workplace', *Work, Employment and Society*, DOI: 10.1177/0950017014568136 [Online First].

Einarsen, Stale, Helge Hoel, Dieter Zapf and Cary Cooper (eds) (2010), *Bullying and Harassment in the Workplace: Developments in Theory, Research, and Practice*, London: CRC Press.

Elliott, Michael A. (2007), 'Human rights and the triumph of the individual in world culture', *Cultural Sociology*, **1**(3), 343–63.

Erickson, A.L. (2005), 'The marital economy in comparative perspective', in Maria Agren and A.L. Erickson (eds), *The Marital Economy in Scandinavia and Britain 1400–1900*, Aldershot: Ashgate, 3–20.

Farrel, Liz Urbanski (2002), 'Workplace bullying's high cost: $180M in lost time, productivity', *Orlando Business Journal*, 18 March.

Fee, Dwight (2000), *Pathology and the Postmodern: Mental Illness as Discourse and Experience*, London and Thousand Oaks, CA: Sage.

Felstead, Alan, Duncan Gallie, Francis Green and Hande Inanc (2013), *Work Intensification in Britain: First Findings from the Skills and Employment Survey, 2012*, London: Centre for Learning and Life Chances in Knowledge Economies and Societies, Institute of Education, www.cardiff.ac.uk/__data/assets/pdf_file/0006/118653/5.-Work-Intensification-in-Britain-mini-report.pdf.

Fevre, Ralph (1984), *Cheap Labour and Racial Discrimination*, Aldershot: Gower.

Fevre, Ralph (1985), 'Racism and cheap labour in UK wool textiles', in Howard Newby, Janet Bujra, Paul Littlewood, Gareth Rees and Teresa L. Rees (eds) *Restructuring Capital: Recession and Reorganisation in Industrial Society*, London: Macmillan, 7–20.

Fevre, Ralph (1986), 'Contract work in the recession', in Kate Purcell, Stephen Wood, Alan Waton and Sheila Allen (eds), *The Changing Experience of Employment*, London: Macmillan, 18–34.

Fevre, Ralph (1989), *Wales is Closed: The Quiet Privatisation of British Steel*, Nottingham: Spokesman.

Fevre, Ralph (1990), 'Sub/contracting and industrial development', in S. Kendrick, Pat Straw and David McCrone (eds), *Interpreting the Past, Understanding the Present*, Basingstoke: Macmillan, 196–216.

Fevre, Ralph (1991), 'The growth of alternatives to full-time and permanent employment in the United Kingdom', in Philip Brown and Richard Scase (eds), *Poor Work: Disadvantage and the Division of Labour*, Milton Keynes: Open University Press, 56–70.

Fevre, Ralph (1992), *The Sociology of Labour Markets*, Hemel Hempstead: Harvester Wheatsheaf.

Fevre, Ralph (2000a), *The Demoralization of Western Culture: Social Theory and the Dilemmas of Modern Living*, London and New York: Continuum.

Fevre, Ralph (2000b), 'Socialising social capital: Identity, the transition to work and economic development', in S. Baron, J. Field and T. Schuller (eds), *Social Capital: Critical Perspectives*, Oxford: Oxford University Press, 94–110.

Fevre, Ralph (2003), *The New Sociology of Economic Behaviour*, Thousand Oaks, CA and London: Sage.

Fevre, Ralph (2007), 'The power of nightmares: Flexibility, insecurity, social theory', *Work, Employment and Society*, **21**(3), 517–35.

Fevre, Ralph (2013), 'Social mobility, equity and the politics of recruitment', *Sociology Compass*, **6**(9), 740–50.

Fevre, Ralph, Heidi Grainger and Rioch Brewer (2011), 'Discrimination and unfair treatment in the workplace', *British Journal of Industrial Relations*, **49**(S2), s207–35.

Fevre, Ralph, Duncan Lewis, Amanda Robinson and Trevor Jones (2012), *Trouble at Work*, New York and London: Bloomsbury.

Fevre, Ralph, Theo Nichols, Gillian Prior and Ian Rutherford (2009), *Fair Treatment at Work Report: Findings from the 2008 Survey*, Employment Relations Research Series No. 103, London: Department of Business, Innovation and Skills.

Fevre, Ralph, Gareth Rees and Stephen Gorard (1999), 'Some sociological alternatives to human capital theory and their implications for research on post-compulsory education and training', *Journal of Education and Work*, **12**(2), 117–40.

Fevre, Ralph, Amanda Robinson, Duncan Lewis and Trevor Jones (2013), 'The ill–treatment of disabled employees in British workplaces', *Work, Employment and Society*, **27**(2), 296–315.

Fevre, Ralph, Amanda Robinson, Trevor Jones and Duncan Lewis (2008), *Work Fit for All: Disability, Health and the Experience of Negative Treatment in the British Workplace*, Insight Report No. 1, London: Equality and Human Rights Commission.

Fevre, Ralph, Amanda Robinson, Trevor Jones and Duncan Lewis (2010), 'Researching workplace bullying: The benefits of taking an integrated approach', *International Journal of Social Research Methodology*, **13**(1), 71–85.

Fielding, Steven (2008), *The Labour Governments 1964–70, Vol. 1: Labour and Cultural Change*, Manchester: Manchester University Press.

Fisher, Jonathan with Marine Blottiaux, Stéphane Daniel and Helena Oliveira (2013), 'The global financial crisis: The case for a stronger criminal response', *Law and Financial Markets Review*, **7**, 159–66.

Flam, Helena and Debra King (eds) (2005), *Emotions and Social Movements*, London: Routledge.

Fleetwood, Steve (2006), 'Re-thinking labour markets: A critical realist socioeconomic perspective', *Capital and Class*, **30**(2), 59–89.

Fleischacker, Samuel (2013), 'Adam Smith on equality', in Christopher Berry, Maria Paganelli and Craig Smith (eds), *The Oxford Handbook of Adam Smith*, Oxford: Oxford University Press, 485–500.

Foner, Eric (1989), *Reconstruction, America's Unfinished Revolution, 1863–1877*, New York: Harper & Row.

Ford, Robert and Matthew Goodwin (2014), *Revolt on the Right: Explaining Support for the Radical Right in Britain*, London: Routledge.

Foster, Deborah (2007), 'Legal obligation or personal lottery? Employee experiences of disability and the negotiation of adjustments in the public sector workplace', *Work, Employment and Society*, **21**(1), 6–84.

Foster, Deborah (2015), 'Devolution and disabled workers: The experiences of union equality representatives in Wales', *Industrial Relations Journal*, **46**(2), 153–68.

Foster, Deborah and Patricia Fosh (2010), 'Negotiating "difference": Representing disabled employees in the British workplace', *British Journal of Industrial Relations*, **48**(3), 560–82.

Foster, Deborah and Peter Scott (2015), 'Nobody's responsibility: The precarious position of disabled employees in the UK workplace', *Industrial Relations Journal*, **46**(4), 328–43.

Foster, Deborah and Victoria Wass (2013), 'Disability in the labour market: An exploration of concepts of the ideal worker and organisational fit that disadvantage employees with impairments', *Sociology*, **47**(4), 705–21.

Fowler, Janet (2012), 'Financial impacts of workplace bullying', 8 July, Investopedia, www.investopedia.com/financial-edge/0712/financial-impacts-of-workplace-bullying.aspx.

Francis, Mark (2007), *Herbert Spencer and the Invention of Modern Life*, Stocksfield: Acumen.

Frank, David J. and Elizabeth H. McEneaney (1999), 'The individualization of society and the liberalization of state policies on same-sex sexual relations, 1984–1995', *Social Forces*, **77**, 911–44.

Frank, David J., John W. Meyer and David Miyahara (1995), 'The individualist polity and the prevalence of professionalized psychology: A cross-national study', *American Sociological Review*, **60**, 360–77.

Franklin, John Hope and Alfred Moss (2000), *From Slavery to Freedom: A History of African-Americans*, New York: McGraw-Hill.

Fricke, Christopher (2013), 'Adam Smith: The sympathetic process', in Christopher Berry, Maria Paganelli and Craig Smith (eds), *The Oxford Handbook of Adam Smith*, Oxford: Oxford University Press, 177–200.

Freeman, Samuel (2010), 'Equality of resources, market luck, and the justification of adjusted market distributions', *Boston Law Review*, **90**, 921–48.

Furedi, Frank (2004), *Therapy Culture: Cultivating Vulnerability in an Uncertain Age*, London and New York: Routledge.

Gagnier, Regenia (2010), *Individualism, Decadence, and Globalization: On the Relationship of Part to Whole, 1859–1920*, Basingstoke: Palgrave Macmillan.

Gallie, Duncan, Alan Felstead, Francis Green and Hande Inanc (2013), *Fear at Work in Britain: First Findings from the Skills and Employment Survey 2012*, London: Centre for Learning and Life Chances in Knowledge Economies and Societies, Institute of Education, www.cardiff.ac.uk/__data/assets/pdf_file/0003/118641/4.-Fear-at-Work-Minireport.pdf.

Gallie, Duncan, Alan Felstead, Francis Green and Hande Inanc (2014), 'The quality of work in Britain over the economic crisis', *International Review of Sociology: Revue Internationale de Sociologie*, **24**(2), 207–24.

Gans, Herbert (1988), *Middle American Individualism: The Future of Liberal Democracy*, New York: Free Press.

Gardiner, Laura and Shereen Hussein (2015), *As If We Cared: The Costs and Benefits of a Living Wage for Social Care Workers*, London: Resolution Foundation.

Giddens, Anthony (1991), *Modernity and Self-identity*, Cambridge: Polity.

Gilbert, Jeremy (2013), *Common Ground: Democracy and Collectivity in an Age of Individualism*, London: Pluto Press.

Gillespie, Richard (1991), *Manufacturing Knowledge: A History of the Hawthorne Experiments*, Cambridge: Cambridge University Press.

Glucksmann, Miriam (2000), *Cottons and Casuals*, Durham: Sociology Press.

Glucksmann, Miriam (2009), 'Formations, connections and division of labour', *Sociology*, **43**(5), 878–95.

Goodwin, Jeff James Jasper and Francesca Poletta (eds) (2001), *Passionate Politics: Emotions and Social Movements*, Chicago: University of Chicago Press.

Gorz, Andre (1989), *Critique of Economic Reason*, London: Verso.

Gottfried, Heidi (2002), 'Comment: Stability and change: Typifying "atypical" employment in Japan', *ASIEN*, **84**, S31–33.

Grainger, Heidi and Grant Fitzner (2007), *The First Fair Treatment at Work Survey: Executive Summary – Updated*, Department for Business, Enterprise and Regulatory Reform (BERR), Employment Relations Research Series No. 63, www.berr.gov.uk/files/file38386.pdf.

Grampp, William D. (1965), *Economic Liberalism, Vol. 1: The Beginnings*, New York: Random House.

Green, Andy (1990), *Education and State Formation: The Rise of Education Systems in England, France and the USA*, London: Palgrave.

Green, Andy (1997), *Education, Globalisation and the Nation State*, Basingstoke: Macmillan.

Green, Francis (2006), *Demanding Work: The Paradox of Job Quality in an Affluent Economy*, Princeton, NJ: Princeton University Press.

Greg, R. (1835), Letter in the Annual Report of the Poor Law Commission, Appendix C, No. 5, https://archive.org/stream/annualreportofpo 01grea/annualreportofpo01grea_djvu.txt.

Gregg, Paul and Laura Gardiner (2015), *A Steady Job? The UK's Record on Labour Market Security and Stability since the Millennium*, London: Resolution Foundation.

Gregg, Paul and Jonathan Wadsworth (1999), 'Job tenure 1975–98', in Paul Gregg and Jonathan Wadsworth (eds), *The State of Working Britain*, Manchester: Manchester University Press.

Grenier, Paola and Karen Wright (2006), 'Social capital in Britain: Exploring the Hall paradox', *Policy Studies*, **27**(1), 27–53.

Grice, Andrew (2012), 'Clegg recruits big business to fight culture of unpaid interns', *The Independent*, 12 January, www.independent.co.uk/ news/uk/politics/clegg-recruits-big-business-to-fight-culture-of-unpaid-interns-6288349.html.

Griswold, Charles (1998), *Adam Smith and the Virtues of Enlightenment*, Cambridge: Cambridge University Press.

Grontved, A. and F.B. Hu (2011), 'Television viewing and risk of type 2 diabetes, cardiovascular disease, and all-cause mortality', *JAMA*, **305**, 2448–55.

Guerrero Maria Isabel S. (2004), 'The development of moral harassment (or mobbing) law in Sweden and France as a step towards EU legislation', *Boston College International & Comparative Law Review*, **27**(2), 477–500.

Habermas, Jurgen (1987), *Theory of Communicative Action, Vol. 2: Lifeworld and System – a Critique of Economic Reason*, Boston: Beacon Press.

Hall, Catherine, Keith McClelland, Nick Draper, Kate Donington and Rachel Lang (2014a), *Legacies of British Slave-Ownership, Colonial Slavery and the Formation of Victorian Britain*, Cambridge: Cambridge University Press.

Hall, Catherine, Nicholas Draper and Keith McClelland (eds) (2014b), *Emancipation and the Remaking of the British Imperial World*, Manchester: Manchester University Press.

Hall, Peter (1999), 'Social capital in Britain', *British Journal of Politics*, **29**, 417–61.

Hall, Peter (2002), 'Great Britain: The role of government and the distribution of social capital', in Robert Putnam (ed.), *Democracies in*

Flux: The Evolution of Social Capital in Contemporary Societies, Oxford: Oxford University Press, 21–57.

Hall, Peter A. and Michèle Lamont (eds) (2013), *Social Resilience in the Neoliberal Era*, Cambridge: Cambridge University Press.

Hancock, David (1997), *Citizens of the World: London Merchants and the Integration of the British Atlantic Community, 1735–1785*, Cambridge: Cambridge University Press.

Handy, Charles (1990), *The Age of Unreason*, Harvard, MA: Harvard Business School Press.

Handy, Charles (1994), *The Empty Raincoat*, London: Arrow.

Haney, Walt, George Madaus, Lisa Abrams, Anne Wheelock, Jing Miao and Ileana Gruia (2004), *The Education Pipeline in the United States, 1970–2000*, Chestnut Hill, MA: Center for the Study of Testing, Evaluation, and Educational Policy, Boston College.

Hanley, Ryan (2013), 'Adam Smith and virtue', in Christopher Berry, Maria Paganelli and Craig Smith (eds), *The Oxford Handbook of Adam Smith*, Oxford: Oxford University Press, 219–40.

Harder, Henry G., Shannon L. Wagner and Josh A. Rash (2014), *Mental Illness in the Workplace*, Aldershot: Gower.

Harkin, Maureen (2013), 'Adam Smith on women', in Christopher Berry, Maria Paganelli and Craig Smith (eds), *The Oxford Handbook of Adam Smith*, Oxford: Oxford University Press, 501–22.

Harvey, David (2005), *A Brief History of Neoliberalism*, Oxford: Oxford University Press.

Hayek, Friedrich (1948), *Individualism and Economic Order*, Chicago: University of Chicago Press.

Heath, Eugene (2013), 'Adam Smith and self interest', in Christopher Berry, Maria Paganelli and Craig Smith (eds), *The Oxford Handbook of Adam Smith*, Oxford: Oxford University Press, 241–66.

Herrnstein, Richard and Charles Murray (1996), *The Bell Curve: Intelligence and Class Structure in American Life*, New York: Free Press.

Higham, John (1969), *From Boundlessness to Consolidation: The Transformation of American Culture 1848–1860*, Ann Arbor, MI: William L. Clements Library.

Higham, John (1974), 'Hanging together: Divergent unities in American history', *Journal of American History*, **61**(1), 5–28.

Hindman, Hugh D. (2002), *Child Labor: An American History*, Armonk, NY: M.E. Sharpe.

Hipple, Steven (2004), 'Self-employment in the United States: An update', *Monthly Labor Review*, July, www.bls.gov/opub/mlr/2004/07/art2full.pdf.

Hipple, Steven (2010), 'Self-employment in the United States', *Monthly Labor Review*, September, www.bls.gov/opub/mlr/2010/09/art2full.pdf.

Hochschild, Adam (2005), *Bury the Chains: The British Struggle to Abolish Slavery*, London: Pan.

Hochschild, Arlie R. (1997), *The Time Bind: When Work Becomes Home and Home Becomes Work*, New York: Metropolitan Books.

Hodson, Randy, Vincent J. Roscigno and Steven H. Lopez (2006), 'Chaos and the abuse of power: Workplace bullying in organizational and interactional context', *Work and Occupations*, **33**(4), 382–416.

Hofstede, Geert (2001), *Culture's Consequences: Comparing Values, Behaviors, Institutions and Organizations across Nations*, Thousand Oaks, CA: Sage.

Honneth, Axel (2004), 'Organized self-realization: Some paradoxes of individualization', *European Journal of Social Theory*, **7**(4), 463–78.

Honneth, Axel (2012), *The I in We: Studies in the Theory of Recognition*, Cambridge: Polity.

Hotchkiss, Julie L. (2004), 'A closer look at the employment impact of the Americans with Disabilities Act', *Journal of Human Resources*, **39**, 887–911.

Humphries, Laud (1970), *Tearoom Trade: Impersonal Sex in Public Places*, New Brunswick, NJ: Aldine.

Hyndman, Henry M. (1884), *Socialism and Slavery*, London: The Modern Press.

Inglehart, Ronald F. and Christian Welzel (2005), *Modernization, Cultural Change, and Democracy: The Human Development Sequence*, New York: Cambridge University Press.

Ipsos MORI (2013), 'Trade unions are important but should not be so closely involved in the Labour Party', London: Ipsos MORI, www.ipsos-mori.com/researchpublications/researcharchive/3236/Trade-Unions-Poll.aspx.

Jackson, Brian and Dennis Marsden (1962), *Education and the Working Class*, London: Routledge.

Joas, Hans (2013), *The Sacredness of the Person: A New Genealogy of Human Rights*, Washington, DC: Georgetown University Press.

Johnson, Boris (2013), 'What would Maggie do today?', Speech at the Margaret Thatcher lecture, 28 November, London: Centre for Policy Studies.

Jolls, Christine (2004), 'Identifying the effects of the Americans with Disabilities Act using state-law variation: Preliminary evidence on educational participation effects', *American Economic Review*, **94**(2), 447–53.

Jolls, Christine and James J. Prescott (2004), 'Disaggregating employment protection: The case of disability discrimination', NBER Working Paper 10740.

Jones, T., A. Robinson, R. Fevre and D. Lewis (2011), 'Workplace assaults in Britain: Understanding the influence of individual and workplace characteristics', *British Journal of Criminology*, **51**(1): 159–78.

Kalleberg, Arne L., Torstein Nesheim and Karen M. Olsen (2009), 'Is participation good or bad for workers? Effects of autonomy, consultation and teamwork on stress among workers in Norway', *Acta Sociologica*, **52**, 99–116.

Katznelson, Ira and Margaret Weir (1985), *Schooling for All: Class, Race, and the Decline of the Democratic Ideal*, New York: Basic Books.

Kelly, Duncan (2013), 'Adam Smith and the limits of sympathy', in Christopher Berry, Maria Paganelli and Craig Smith (eds), *The Oxford Handbook of Adam Smith*, Oxford: Oxford University Press, 201–18.

Kensbock, Sandra, Janis Bailey, Gayle Jennings and Anoop Patiar (2015), 'Sexual harassment of women working as room attendants within 5-star hotels', *Gender, Work and Organization*, **22**(1), 36–50.

Khosravnik, Majid (2009), 'The representation of refugees, asylum seekers and immigrants in British newspapers during the Balkan Conflict (1999) and the British General Election (2005)', *Discourse and Society*, **20**(4), 477–98.

Klein, Herbert and Stuart Schwartz (1999), *The Atlantic Slave Trade*, Cambridge: Cambridge University Press.

Kozol, Jonathan (1991), *Savage Inequalities: Children in America's Schools*, New York: HarperCollins.

Kozol, Jonathan (2005), *The Shame of the Nation: The Restoration of Apartheid Schooling in America*, New York: Crown

Kruse, Douglas and Lisa Schur (2003), 'Employment of people with disabilities following the ADA', *Industrial Relations*, **42**, 31–64.

Ladson-Billings, Gloria and William F. Tate (1995), 'Toward a critical race theory of education', *Teachers College Record*, **97**(1), 47–68.

Lamont, Michèle (2002), *The Dignity of Working Men: Morality and the Boundaries of Race, Class, and Immigration*, Cambridge, MA: Russell Sage Foundation for Harvard University Press.

Le Goff, Jean-Pierre (1999), *La barbarie douce. La modernisation aveugle des entreprises et de l'école*, Paris: Editions La Découverte,

Le Goff, Jean-Pierre (2003), *Les illusions du management. Pour le retour du bons sens*, Paris: Editions La Découverte.

Leonardo, Zeus (2007), 'The war on schools: NCLB, nation creation and the educational construction of whiteness', *Race Ethnicity and Education*, **10**(3), 261–78.

Lewis-Jones, Huw (2011), *The Royal Navy and the Battle to End Slavery*, www.bbc.co.uk/history/british/abolition/royal_navy_article_01.shtml.

Lloyd, Christopher (1949), *The Navy and the Slave Trade: The Suppression of the African Slave Trade in the Nineteenth Century*, London: Frank Cass.

Lopez, Steven H., Randy Hodson and Vincent J. Roscigno (2009), 'Power, status, and abuse at work: General and sexual harassment compared', *Sociological Quarterly*, **50**, 3–27.

Lukes, Steven (1969), 'Durkheim's "Individualism and the Intellectuals"', *Political Studies*, **17**(1), 14–30.

Lukes, Stephen (1973), *Individualism*, Oxford: Basil Blackwell.

Macfarlane, Alan (1978), *The Origins of English Individualism*, Oxford: Basil Blackwell.

MacIntyre, Alasdair (1966), *A Short History of Ethics*, London: Routledge.

MacIntyre, Alasdair (1987), *After Virtue*, London: Duckworth.

Marx, Karl ([1867]1990), *Capital: Critique of Political Economy, Vol. 1*, Harmondsworth: Penguin.

Masters, Brooke and Caroline Binham (2012), 'UK looks to bridge regulatory divide with US', *Financial Times*, 5 February, www.ft.com/cms/s/0/40721b86-4ffb-11e1-a3ac-00144feabdc0.html#axzz3uIsROZmN.

Mathias, Matthew D. (2013), 'The sacralization of the individual: Human rights and the abolition of the death penalty', *American Journal of Sociology*, **118**(5), 1246–83.

McCoy, Drew (1980), *The Elusive Republic: Political Economy in Jeffersonian America*, Chapel Hill, NC: University of North Carolina Press.

McNamara, Peter (1998), *Political Economy and Statesmanship*, DeKalb, IL: Northern Illinois University Press.

Meyer, John W. (1987), 'Self and life course: institutionalization and its effects', in George M. Thomas, John W. Meyer, Francisco O. Ramirez and John Boli, *Institutional Structure: Constituting State, Society and the Individual*, Newbury Park, CA: Sage, 242–60.

Meyer, John W. and Patricia Bromley (2013), 'The worldwide expansion of "organization"', *Sociological Theory*, **31**(4), 366–89.

Meyer, John W., John Boli and George M. Thomas (1987), 'Ontology and rationalization in the Western cultural account', in George M. Thomas, John W. Meyer, Francisco O. Ramirez and John Boli (eds), *Institutional Structure: Constituting State, Society and the Individual*, Newbury Park, CA: Sage, 12–37.

Meyer, John W., David Tyack, Joane Nagel and Audri Gordon (1979), 'Public education as nation-building in America: Enrollments and bureaucratization in the American states, 1870–1930', *American Journal of Sociology*, **85**(3), 591–613.

Mill, John Stuart ([1859/63]2015), *On Liberty, Utilitarianism and Other Essays*, Mark Philp and Frederick Rosen (eds), Oxford: Oxford University Press.

Monahan, Susanne C., John W. Meyer and W. Richard Scott (1994), 'Employee training: The expansion of organizational citizenship', in W. Richard Scott and John W. Meyer and Associates (eds), *Institutional Environments and Organizations: Structural Complexity and Individualism*, Thousand Oaks, CA: Sage, 255–71.

Murray, Charles (1996), *Charles Murray and the Underclass*, in Ruth Lister (ed.), London: IEA Health and Welfare Unit.

Nardinelli, Clark (1980), 'Child labor and the factory acts', *Journal of Economic History*, **40**(4), 739–55.

Nichols, Sharon L., Gene V. Glass and David C. Berliner (2005), *High-stakes Testing and Student Achievement: Problems for the No Child Left Behind Act*, Tempe, AZ: Education Policy Research Unit.

Norris, Pippa and Ronald F. Inglehart (2009), *Cosmopolitan Communications: Cultural Diversity in a Globalized World*, New York: Cambridge University Press.

Nozick, Robert (1974), *Anarchy, State, and Utopia*, New York: Basic Books.

Nussbaum, Martha (2013), *Political Emotions: Why Love Matters for Justice*, Cambridge, MA: Harvard University Press.

Obama, Barack (2013), Remarks by the President on Economic Mobility, THEARC Washington, DC, 4 December, www.whitehouse.gov/the-press-office/2013/12/04/remarks-president-economic-mobility.

OECD (2014), *Factbook 2014: Economic, Environmental and Social Statistics*, Paris: OECD Publishing.

OECD (2015), *Education at a Glance 2015: OECD Indicators*, Paris: OECD Publishing, http://dx.doi.org/10.1787/eag-2015-en.

O'Hagan, Francis J. (2011), 'Robert Owen and education', in Noel Thompson and Chris Williams (eds), *Robert Owen and his Legacy*, Cardiff: University of Wales Press.

Oliver, Michael (1983), *Social Work with Disabled People*, Basingstoke: Macmillan.

Oliver, Michael (1990), *The Politics of Disablement*, Basingstoke: Macmillan.

Oliver, Michael (2003), 'Disability and dependency: A creation of industrial societies?', in J. Swain, V. Finklestein, S. French and M. Oliver (eds), *Disabling Barriers – Enabling Environments*, Milton Keynes: Open University Press.

ONS (2014), *Annual Survey of Hours and Earnings: Provisional Results*, www.ons.gov.uk/ons/dcp171778_385428.pdf.

ONS (2015), *Statistical Bulletin: UK Labour Market*, 14 October, www.ons.gov.uk/ons/dcp171778_417237.pdf.

ONS (2016), *Analysis of Employee Contracts that do not Guarantee a Minimum Number of Hours*, 9 March, https://www.ons.gov.uk/employmentandlabourmarket/peopleinwork/earningsandworkinghours/articles/contractsthatdonotguaranteeaminimumnumberofhours/march 2016.

Orfield, Gary, Daniel Losen, Johanna Wald and Christopher B. Swanson (2004), *Losing Our Future: How Minority Youth Are Being Left Behind by the Graduation Rate Crisis*, Cambridge, MA: The Civil Rights Project at Harvard University, http://files.eric.ed.gov/fulltext/ED489 177.pdf.

Overell, Stephen (2013), 'Job insecurity in the wake of a recession', ACAS *Employment Relations Comment*, London: ACAS, www.acas.org.uk/media/pdf/2/1/Job-insecurity-in-the-wake-of-a-recession.pdf.

Owen, Robert ([1813]1817), *A New View of Society*, London: Longman.

Owen, Robert ([1816]1959), 'Evidence to the Select Committee on the State of Children Employed in Manufactories, Parliamentary Papers, 1816, III', in A. Aspinall and E. Anthony Smith (eds), *English Historical Documents, XI, 1783–1832*, New York: Oxford University Press, 728–32.

Owen, Robert ([1817]1858), 'A Report to the Committee of the Association for the Relief of the Manufacturing and Labouring Poor', A Supplementary Appendix to Vol. 1, *The Life of Robert Owen Written by Himself*, London: Effingham Wilson.

Owen, Robert ([1833]1969), 'The address of Robert Owen denouncing the old system of the world, and announcing the commencement of the new', in Harold Silver (ed.), *Robert Owen on Education*, Cambridge: Cambridge University Press.

Owen, Robert ([1837]1969), 'The natural and rational classification of society', in Harold Silver (ed.), *Robert Owen on Education*, Cambridge: Cambridge University Press.

Pack, Spencer (2013), 'Adam Smith and Marx', in Christopher Berry, Maria Paganelli and Craig Smith (eds), *The Oxford Handbook of Adam Smith*, Oxford: Oxford University Press, 523–38.

Paganelli, Maria Pia (2013), 'Commercial relations: From Adam Smith to field experiments', in Christopher Berry, Maria Paganelli and Craig Smith (eds), *The Oxford Handbook of Adam Smith*, Oxford: Oxford University Press, 333–52.

Paine, Thomas ([1792]2014), *The Rights of Man*, reprinted in Ian Shapiro and Jane E. Calvert (eds), *Selected Writings of Thomas Paine*, New Haven, CT: Yale University Press.

Pennycook, Matthew, Giselle Cory and Vidhya Alakeson (2013), *A Matter of Time: The Rise of Zero-hours Contracts*, London: The Resolution Foundation.

Perelman, Michael (2005), *Manufacturing Discontent: The Trap of Individualism in Corporate Society*, London: Pluto Press.

Pew Research Centre (2015), *The American Middle Class is Losing Ground: No Longer the Majority and Falling Behind Financially*, 9 December, Washington, DC: Pew Research Centre, www.pewsocial trends.org/2015/12/09/the-american-middle-class-is-losing-ground/.

Pew Trust (2011), *Where Do We Stand in the Wake of the Great Recession? Economic Mobility and the American Dream*, Washington, DC: Pew Economic Mobility Project, www.pewtrusts.org/en/research-and-analysis/reports/2011/05/19/economic-mobility-and-the-american-dream-where-do-we-stand-in-the-wake-of-the-great-recession.

Pew Trust (2012), *Pursuing the American Dream: Economic Mobility across Generations*, Washington, DC: Pew Economic Mobility Project.

Piketty, Thomas (2014), *Capital in the Twenty First Century*. Harvard, MA: Harvard University Press.

Pomeranz, Ken (2001), *The Great Divergence: China, Europe and the Making of the Modern World Economy*, Princeton NJ: Princeton University Press.

Power, Sally, Tony Edwards and Valerie Wigfall (2003), *Education in the Middle Class*, Milton Keynes: Open University Press.

Prior, Gillian, Siân Llewellyn-Thomas and Luke Taylor (2008), *Workplace Behaviour Survey Technical Report*, JN 159977/174958, London: TNS Social.

Prior, Gillian, Luke Taylor, Siân Llewellyn-Thomas, Ralph Fevre and Theo Nichols (2010), *Fair Treatment at Work Survey 2008: Technical Report*, London: Department for Business, Innovation and Skills.

Prochaska, Frank (2006), *Christianity and Social Service in Modern Britain*, Cambridge: Cambridge University Press.

Putnam, Robert (ed.) (2004), *Democracies in Flux: The Evolution of Social Capital in Contemporary Society*, Oxford and New York: Oxford University Press.

Ramirez, Francisco (1999), 'Institutional analysis', in George M. Thomas, John W. Meyer, Francisco O. Ramirez and John Boli (eds), *Institutional Structure: Constituting State, Society and the Individual*, Newbury Park, CA: Sage, 316–28.

Ramsay, Harvey, Dora Scholarios and Bill Harley (2000), 'Employees and high performance work systems: Testing inside the black box', *British Journal of Industrial Relations*, **38**, 501–31.

Rasmussen, Dennis (2013), 'Adam Smith and Rousseau: Enlightenment and counter-enlightenment', in Christopher Berry, Maria Paganelli and

Craig Smith (eds), *The Oxford Handbook of Adam Smith*, Oxford: Oxford University Press, 54–76.

Rawls, John (1971), *A Theory of Justice*, Harvard, MA: Harvard University Press.

Read, Donald (1994), *The Age of Urban Democracy*, London: Routledge.

Riesman, David (1950), *The Lonely Crowd*, New Haven, CT: Yale University Press.

Roscigno, Vincent J., Randy Hodson and Steven Lopez (2009a), 'Workplace incivilities: The role of interest conflicts, social closure and organizational chaos', *Work, Employment and Society*, **23**(4), 727–73.

Roscigno, Vincent J., Steven Lopez and Randy Hodson (2009b), 'Supervisory bullying, status inequalities and organizational context', *Social Forces*, **87**(3), 1561–89.

Rose, Nikolas (1999), *Powers of Freedom*, Cambridge: Cambridge University Press.

Rosenfeld, Jake (2014), *What Unions No Longer Do*, Cambridge, MA: Harvard University Press.

Rubinson, Richard (1986), 'Class formation, politics, and institutions: Schooling in the United States', *American Journal of Sociology*, **92**(3), 519–48.

Saad, Lydia (2015), *Americans' Support for Labor Unions Continues to Recover*, Gallup Poll Social Series, Princeton, NJ: Gallup, www.gallup.com/poll/184622/americans-support-labor-unions-continues-recover.aspx.

Sandel, Michael (1998), *Democracy's Discontent: America in Search of a Public Philosophy*, Harvard, MA: Harvard University Press.

Sandel, Michael (2012), *What Money Can't Buy*, New York: Farrar, Straus and Giroux.

Särlvik, Bo and Ivor Crewe (1983), *Decade of Dealignment: The Conservative Victory of 1979 and Electoral Trends in the 1970s*, Cambridge: Cambridge University Press.

Savage, Mike (2000), *Class Analysis and Social Transformation*, Buckingham: Open University Press.

Sayer, Andrew (2007), 'Dignity at work: Broadening the agenda', *Organization*, **14**(4), 565–81.

Sayer, Andrew (2015), *Why We Can't Afford the Rich*, Bristol: Policy Press.

Sayre, Robert and Michael Löwy (2005), 'Romanticism and capitalism', in Michael Ferber (ed.), *A Companion to European Romanticism*, Oxford: Blackwell Publishing.

Schofer, Evan and John W. Meyer (2005), 'The worldwide expansion of higher education in the twentieth century', *American Sociological Review*, **70**(6), 898–920.

Schwochau, Susan and Peter D. Blanck (2003), 'Does the ADA disable the disabled? More comments', *Industrial Relations*, **42**(1), 67–77.

Scott, W. Richard and John W. Meyer (1994a), 'Institutional environments and the expansion of individuality within organizations', in W. Richard Scott and John W. Meyer (eds), *Institutional Environments and Organizations: Structural Complexity and Individualism*, Thousand Oaks, CA: Sage, 207–14.

Scott, W. Richard and John W. Meyer (1994b), 'The rise of training programs in firms and agencies', in W. Richard Scott and John W. Meyer and Associates (eds), *Institutional Environments and Organizations: Structural Complexity and Individualism*, Thousand Oaks, CA: Sage, 228–54.

Scott, W. Richard, John W. Meyer and associates (1994), *Institutional Environments and Organizations: Structural Complexity and Individualism*, Thousand Oaks, CA: Sage.

Segrave, Kerry (1994), *The Sexual Harassment of Women in the Workplace, 1600–1993*, Jefferson, NC: McFarland.

Sen, Amartya (2013), 'The contemporary relevance of Adam Smith', in Christopher Berry, Maria Paganelli and Craig Smith (eds), *The Oxford Handbook of Adam Smith*, Oxford: Oxford University Press, 581–92.

Sennett, Richard (1998), *The Corrosion of Character: The Personal Consequences of Work in the New Capitalism*, New York: W.W. Norton.

Sennett, Richard (2004), *Respect in a World of Inequality*, New York: W.W. Norton.

Sherwood, Marika (2007), *Britain, Slavery and the Trade in Enslaved Africans*, London: University of London Institute of Historical Research, www.history.ac.uk/ihr/Focus/Slavery/articles/sherwood.html.

Shire, Karen A. (2002), 'Stability and change in Japanese employment institutions: The case of temporary work', *ASIEN*, **84**, S21–30.

Siedentop, Larry (2014), *Inventing the Individual: The Origins of Western Liberalism*, London: Allen Lane.

Simmel, Georg (1972), *Georg Simmel on Individuality and Social Forms*, in Donald Levine (ed.), Chicago: University of Chicago Press.

Skocpol, Theda (1992), *Protecting Soldiers and Mothers: The Political Origins of Social Policy in the United States*, Cambridge, MA: The Belknap Press of Harvard University Press.

Skocpol, Theda (2004), 'Voice and inequality: the transformation of American civic democracy', *Perspectives on Politics*, **2**(1), 3–20.

Smith, Adam ([1759]1976), *The Theory of Moral Sentiments*, Oxford: Clarendon Press.

Smith, Adam ([1776]2005), *An Enquiry into the Nature and Causes of the Wealth of Nations*, Hazleton, PA: Electronic Classics Series Publications, www.discoverthenetworks.org/Articles/Wealth-Nations.pdf.

Smith, Craig (2013), 'Adam Smith and the New Right', in Christopher Berry, Maria Paganelli and Craig Smith (eds), *The Oxford Handbook of Adam Smith*, Oxford: Oxford University Press, 539–58.

Solomon, Patrick, John Portelli, Beverly-Jean Daniel and Arlene Campbell (2005), 'The discourse of denial: How white teacher candidates construct race, racism and "white privilege"', *Race, Ethnicity and Education*, **8**(2), 147–69.

Solow, Barbara and Stanley Engerman (eds) (2004), *British Capitalism and Caribbean Slavery: The Legacy of Eric Williams*, Cambridge: Cambridge University Press.

Somers, Margaret R. and Fred Block (2005), 'From poverty to perversity: Ideas, markets, and institutions over 200 years of welfare debate', *American Sociological Review*, **70**, 260–87.

Song, Jiyeoun (2012), 'The diverging political pathways of labor market reform in Japan and Korea', *Journal of East Asian Studies*, **12**, 161–91.

Sooben, Philip N. (1990), *The Origins of the Race Relations Act*, Research Paper in Ethnic Relations No. 12, University of Warwick: Centre for Research in Ethnic Relations.

Sorokin, Pitirim ([1937/41]1957), *Social and Cultural Dynamics*, Boston: Porter Sargent.

Southern Education Foundation (2015), *A New Majority: Low Income Students Now a Majority in the Nation's Public Schools*, Research Bulletin, Atlanta, GA: Southern Education Foundation, www.southern education.org/Our-Strategies/Research-and-Publications/New-Majority-Diverse-Majority-Report-Series/A-New-Majority-2015-Update-Low-Income-Students-Now.

Southey, Robert (1807), *Letters from England by Don Manuel Alvarez Espriella*, New York: D. Longworth.

Southey, Robert ([1819]1929), *Journal of a Tour in Scotland in 1819*, in C.H. Herford (ed.), London: John Murrary.

Sowell, Thomas (2015), *Wealth, Poverty and Politics: An International Perspective*, New York: Basic Books.

Spencer, Herbert (1864), *The Principles of Biology*, London: Williams and Norgate.

Spencer, Herbert (1865), *Social Statics*, New York: D. Appleton

Spencer, Herbert (1867), *First Principles*, 2nd edn, London: Williams and Norgate.

Spencer, Herbert ([1884]1960), *The Man versus the State*, Caldwell, ID: Caxton Printers.

Spencer, Herbert (1893), *The Principles of Ethics*, New York: D. Appleton.

Spencer, Herbert (1896), *The Study of Sociology*, New York: D. Appleton.

Spencer, Herbert (1898), *The Principles of Sociology*, New York: D. Appleton.

Spicker, Paul (2013), *Reclaiming Individualism: Perspectives on Public Policy*, Bristol: Policy Press.

Standing, Guy (2011), *The Precariat: The New Dangerous Class*, London and New York: Bloomsbury.

Standish, Alex (2009), 'America's "cash for grades" scandal', *Spiked*, 20 May, www.spiked-online.com/newsite/article/6739#.Vmk1aOKjKLU.

Stivers, Richard (2003), 'Ethical individualism and moral collectivism in America', *Humanitas*, **XVI**(1), 56–73.

Storey, John and Nicolas Bacon (1993), 'Individualism and collectivism: Into the 1990s', *International Journal of Human Resource Management*, **4**(3), 665–84.

Strangleman, Tim (2007), 'The nostalgia for permanence at work? The end of work and its commentators', *Sociological Review*, **55**(1), 81–103.

Strangleman, Tim (2012), 'Work identity in crisis? Rethinking the problem of attachment and loss at work', *Sociology*, **46**(3), 411–25.

Streeck, Wolfgang (2014), *Buying Time: The Delayed Crisis of Democratic Capitalism*, London: Verso.

Streeck, Wolfgang and Armin Schäfer (eds) (2013), *Politics in the Age of Austerity*, London: Polity.

TNS Opinion & Social Network (2008), *Discrimination in the European Union: Perceptions, Experiences and Attitudes*, Special Eurobarometer 296, Brussels: European Union.

TNS Opinion & Social (2012), *Discrimination in the EU in 2012*, Special Eurobarometer 393, Brussels: European Commission, Directorate-General Justice.

Tawney, Richard H. (1926), *Religion and the Rise of Capitalism*, London: J. Murray.

Taylor, Edward, David Gillborn and Gloria Ladson-Billings (eds) (2009), *Foundations of Critical Race Theory in Education*, New York: Routledge.

Taylor, Frederick Winslow (1919), *The Principles of Scientific Management*, New York and London: Harper and Brothers.

Taylor, Michael W. (1992), *Men versus the State: Herbert Spencer and Late Victorian Individualism*, Oxford: Oxford University Press.

Taylor, Phil and Peter Bain (1999), '"An assembly line in the head": Work and employee relations in the call centre', *Industrial Relations Journal*, **30**, 101–17.

Tegos, Spiros (2013), 'Adam Smith: Theorist of corruption', in Christopher Berry, Maria Paganelli and Craig Smith (eds), *The Oxford Handbook of Adam Smith*, Oxford: Oxford University Press, 353–71.

Thilly, Frank (1923), 'The individualism of John Stuart Mill', *The Philosophical Review*, **32**(1), 1–17.

Thomas, George M., John W. Meyer, Francisco O. Ramirez and John Boli (1987), *Institutional Structure: Constituting State, Society and the Individual*, Newbury Park, CA: Sage.

Thomas, Keith (1971), *Religion and the Decline of Magic*, London: Weidenfeld and Nicholson.

Tocqueville, Alexis de ([1840]2003), *Democracy in America*, London: Penguin Books.

Tuttle, Carolyn (2001), 'Child labor during the British industrial revolution', in Robert Whaples (ed.), *EH.Net Encyclopedia*, http://eh.net/encyclopedia/child-labor-during-the-british-industrial-revolution/.

Ure, Andrew (1835), *The Philosophy of Manufactures*, London: Charles Knight.

US Census Bureau (2012), *Americans with Disabilities 2010*, Washington, DC: US Census Bureau, www.census.gov/people/disability/.

van Wanrooy, Brigid, Helen Bewley, Alex Bryson, John Forth, Stephanie Freeth, Lucy Stokes and Stephen Wood (2011), *The 2011 Workplace Employment Relations Study: First Findings*, London: Department for Business, Innovation and Skills.

van Wanrooy, Brigid, Helen Bewley, Alex Bryson, John Forth, Stephanie Freeth, Lucy Stokes and Stephen Wood (2013), *Employment Relations in the Shadow of Recession: Findings from the 2011 Workplace Employment Relations Study*, London: Palgrave.

Verhaeghe, Paul (2014), *What About Me? The Struggle for Identity in a Market-Based Society*, London: Scribe Publications.

Wainwright David and Michael Calnan (2002), *Work Stress: The Making of a Modern Epidemic*, Buckingham: Open University Press.

Walford, Geoffrey and Stan Jones (1986), 'The Solihull Adventure: An attempt to reintroduce selective schooling', *Journal of Education Policy*, **1**(3), 239–53.

Walker, Carl and Ben Fincham (2011), *Work and the Mental Health Crisis in Britain*, Chichester: Wiley-Blackwell.

Ward, J.T. (ed.) (1970), *The Factory System, Vol. 2*, New York: Barnes & Noble.

Warr, Peter (2007), *Work, Happiness, and Unhappiness*, London: Routledge.

Watanabe, Hiroaki Richard (2012), 'Why and how did Japan finally change its ways? The politics of Japanese labor-market deregulation since the 1990s', *Japan Forum*, **24**(1), 23–50.

Watanabe, Hiroaki Richard (2014), *Labour Market Deregulation in Japan and Italy: Worker Protection under Neoliberal Globalisation*, London: Routledge.

Westergaard, John and Henrietta Resler (1975), *Class in a Capitalist Society: A Study of Contemporary Britain*, London: Heinemann.

White, Alan (2012), 'Why so many ex-soldiers end up in prison', *New Statesman*, 15 July.

Wilberforce, William (1791), Speech introducing the first parliamentary bill to abolish the slave trade on April 18th, Parliamentary Register, Vol. XXIX, http://parlipapers.chadwyck.co.uk/fullrec/fullrec.do?area= hcpp&id=pr_1780_1796.

Wilde, Oscar ([1891]1970), 'The soul of man under socialism', in Richard Ellman (ed.), *The Artist as Critic: Critical Writings of Oscar Wilde*, London: W.H. Allen.

Wilkinson, Richard G., Kate Pickett and Robert B. Reich (2011), *The Spirit Level: Why Greater Equality Makes Societies Stronger*, New York and London: Bloomsbury.

Williams, Eric (1944), *Capitalism and Slavery*, Chapel Hill, NC: University of North Carolina Press.

Willman, Paul, Alex Bryson and Rafael Gomez (2007), 'The long goodbye: New establishments and the fall of union voice in Britain', *International Journal of Human Resource Management*, **18**(7): 1318–34.

Wilson, Harold (1963), *Labour's Plan for Science*, Leader's speech to Labour Party Annual Conference, http://nottspolitics.org/wp-content/ uploads/2013/06/Labours-Plan-for-science.pdf.

Wolf, Alison (2013), *The XX Factor*, London: Profile Books.

Wuthnow, Robert (2004), *Saving America? Faith-Based Services and the Future of Civil Society*, Princeton, NJ: Princeton University Press.

Name index

Subject index